Praise for Robert Asahina's *Just Americans*:

"The book is an important—and readable—addition to the literature of a remarkable time and an extraordinary people."   —*The Rafu Shimpo*

"Throughout, in a smooth-reading storytelling style, Asahina reminds readers why the sacrifice of this most-awarded military unit was particularly poignant, and particularly unlikely."   —*The Honolulu Advertiser*

"Timely, thoughtful and meticulously researched. . . . Asahina re-creates the battles in impressively painstaking detail, making good use of battalion journals, diaries, self-published memoirs, and interviews with surviving veterans."   —*The New York Times Book Review*

"[*Just Americans*] more than does justice to the history of the 442d and the brave men who wore its patch and called it home. . . . I pray that the stories he tells become known far and wide, so that the 'mistakes' of our lamentable past may be less likely to be repeated."
          —Lucian K. Truscott IV, author of *Dress Gray* and *Heart of War*

"Many a survivor of that bitter 1944–45 winter of World War II will be happy to see the men of the 100th Battalion getting their bravery recognized. They became a legend among the Infantry units fighting in the Vosges Mountains."
          —Tony Hillerman (former member of C Company, 410th Infantry)

"It was with American enthusiasm and Japanese tenacity that Japanese-Americans overcame both persecution and resentment to fight most bravely on European battlefields in 1944–45, and Robert Asahina too needed both enthusiasm and tenacity to recover for history their doings and undoings. While adding to scholarship, the rich detail here masterfully presented makes for exciting reading. . . ."   —Edward N. Luttwak

ROBERT ASAHINA has been an editor at *Harper's, The New York Times Book Review, GEO,* and *The Public Interest;* a film critic for *The American Spectator* and the *New Leader;* and a theater critic for the *Hudson Review.* His articles and reviews have appeared in *Harper's, The Wall Street Journal, The Washington Post Book World,* the *Los Angeles Times Book Review, The New York Times Book Review, Art International, Yale Theater,* and other periodicals.

He has also been the editor in chief, deputy publisher, and senior vice president of Broadway Books, the president and publisher of the Adult Publishing Group of Golden Books Family Entertainment, a vice president and editorial director of Summit Books, and a vice president and senior editor of Simon & Schuster.

JUST AMERICANS

How Japanese Americans
Won a War at Home and Abroad

The Story of the 100th Battalion/442d
Regimental Combat Team in World War II

ROBERT ASAHINA

GOTHAM BOOKS

GOTHAM BOOKS
Published by Penguin Group (USA) Inc.
375 Hudson Street, New York, New York 10014, U.S.A.

Penguin Group (Canada), 90 Eglinton Avenue East, Suite 700, Toronto, Ontario M4P 2Y3,
Canada (a division of Pearson Penguin Canada Inc.); Penguin Books Ltd, 80 Strand, London WC2R 0RL,
England; Penguin Ireland, 25 St Stephen's Green, Dublin 2, Ireland (a division of Penguin Books Ltd);
Penguin Group (Australia), 250 Camberwell Road, Camberwell, Victoria 3124, Australia (a division
of Pearson Australia Group Pty Ltd); Penguin Books India Pvt Ltd, 11 Community Centre, Panchsheel
Park, New Delhi–110 017, India; Penguin Group (NZ), 67 Apollo Drive, Mairangi Bay, Auckland 1311,
New Zealand (a division of Pearson New Zealand Ltd); Penguin Books (South Africa) (Pty) Ltd,
24 Sturdee Avenue, Rosebank, Johannesburg 2196, South Africa

Penguin Books Ltd, Registered Offices: 80 Strand, London WC2R 0RL, England

Previously published as a Gotham Books hardcover edition, May 2006

First trade paperback printing, May 2007

1   3   5   7   9   10   8   6   4   2

Gotham Books and the skyscraper logo are trademarks of Penguin Group (USA) Inc.

The Library of Congress has catalogued the hardcover edition of this book as follows:
Asahina, Robert.
  Just Americans : how Japanese Americans won a war at home and abroad / Robert Asahina.
    p. cm.
  Includes bibliographical references and index.
  ISBN 1-592-40198-8 (hardcover)   ISBN 978-1-592-40300-4 (paperback)
  1. World War, 1939–1945–Japanese Americans. 2. Japanese American soldiers–
History–20th century. 3. World War, 1939–1945–Campaigns–Western Front. I. Title.
  D753.8.A83 2006
  940.54'210923956073—dc22   2005035926

Printed in the United States of America
Set in Janson Text with Clarendon BT
Designed by Sabrina Bowers • Maps by Virginia Norey

What constitutes an American? Not color nor race nor religion. Not the pedigree of his family nor the place of his birth. Not the coincidence of his citizenship. Not his social status nor his bank account. Not his trade nor his profession. An American is one who loves justice and believes in the dignity of man. An American is one who will fight for his freedom and that of his neighbor. An American is one who will sacrifice property, ease, and security in order that he and his children may retain the rights of free men. An American is one in whose heart is engraved the immortal second sentence of the Declaration of Independence.

Americans have always known how to fight for their rights and their way of life. Americans are not afraid to fight. They fight joyously in a just cause.

—HAROLD ICKES, "I AM AN AMERICAN DAY,"
CENTRAL PARK, NEW YORK CITY,
MAY 18, 1941[1]

America [is] a land where the question of our place in history is not answered for us. It's answered by us.

—BARACK OBAMA,
COMMENCEMENT ADDRESS,
KNOX COLLEGE, GALESBURG, ILLINOIS,
JUNE 4, 2005[2]

CONTENTS

GO FOR BROKE

★

442D REGIMENTAL COMBAT TEAM

★

100TH INFANTRY BATTALION

LIST OF ILLUSTRATIONS

PROLOGUE:
JAP ROAD

There is no doubt in my mind that every soldier of the 442d RCT consciously bore on his shoulders the reputation of all Japanese Americans.—GEN. MARK W. CLARK[1]

Beaumont, Texas, 2004

On July 19, 2004, a schoolteacher named Sandra Tanamachi patiently sat in a crowded room, awaiting the outcome of a Jefferson County commissioners meeting in Beaumont, Texas. Though she now lived in Lake Jackson, 50 miles south of Houston along the Gulf Coast, Tanamachi had traveled more than 140 miles northeast to join a crowd of around 150 people at the meeting. Nearly three hours would pass before the commissioners reached their decision on an issue that had pitted neighbor against neighbor in this small town on the outskirts of Port Arthur.[2]

But Tanamachi had been waiting much longer than anyone else in the room, or in the entire area. She had been locked in a dramatic struggle with the local officials for more than a dozen years.

Though she had never lived in Jefferson County until she was an adult, she could trace her family roots to Beaumont. Her paternal grandparents had moved there in 1921, when her father was seven years old. "On the day they arrived," she says, "my uncle Willie Tanamachi was born in the Hotel Deaux." Her father and uncles and aunts attended local schools in Jefferson County during the 1920s and 1930s, and her father played on the Beaumont High School football team.

So it was almost like a homecoming when Tanamachi relocated to Beaumont in the late 1980s. Her husband, a chemist, had been transferred

1

to a plant nearby, and she had landed a teaching job at Blanchette Elementary School. She went on to win recognition as a Southwestern Bell Teacher of the Year and along the way met "many wonderful people . . . good, decent, caring, and hardworking citizens" in Jefferson County.

Tanamachi was "proud to be a Texan"—and "equally proud of her Japanese heritage." She never thought the two would be in conflict. It was the last decade of the twentieth century, after all. Prejudice, though hardly eradicated in the United States, did not show its ugly face as often or as blatantly as it did in the past.

Or so she had thought until she saw the Winter Olympics on television in 1992. She had made a point of not only watching but also videotaping Kristi Yamaguchi in the figure-skating finals. After Yamaguchi's victorious performance, the network coverage gave way to local advertising. As Tanamachi absentmindedly listened, still celebrating the first Olympic gold medal ever won by a Japanese American, she was astonished to hear a commercial for a local catfish restaurant that ended in a jingle with the establishment's address: "Waaaaay down on Jap Road."

At first she couldn't believe what she had just heard. But there it was again on tape: "Jap Road."

For days afterward, Tanamachi couldn't shake those words out of her head. And then she began to notice them everywhere. On the way to school, she heard the jingle on her car radio. Going for groceries, she saw JAP ROAD in bold letters advertising the restaurant on a billboard, right along a main thoroughfare.

Finally she worked up the nerve to drive with her family to the other side of Jefferson County for a catfish dinner. There on a street sign were the words JAP ROAD, innocuously featured in familiar white sans serif type against a green background. From a design perspective, the letters were as blandly displayed as if they had spelled out "Main Street." But they might as well have read "Nigger Lane" or "Spic Alley" or "Kike Street." Her son, sickened at the sight, refused to get out of the car. Tanamachi and her family turned around and drove home.

But this was 1992, and American minority groups didn't have to suffer racial slurs in silence. Just a year earlier, the Texas House and Senate had approved a bill to change geographic names in the state that had offended African Americans and should have offended all Americans. Negro Tank in Cameron County had become Esteban Reservoir. Negrohead Lake in

Harris County was renamed Lake Henry Dyle. And so on across Texas.[3] But even "Negro" had been an improvement over the original word it had replaced in those place names: "Nigger." Surely "Jap" was equally offensive. In fact, in 1986 the 99th Congress of the United States had passed a concurrent resolution that "the term 'Jap' is racially derogatory and is offensive."[4]

So Tanamachi started a one-woman campaign to convince Jefferson County to change the name of Jap Road. At first she wrote an anonymous letter to the Houston chapter of the Japanese American Citizens League (JACL). "I was too scared to sign my name," she told *The Dallas Morning News* years later. Even though there are, remarkably enough, more than ten thousand Japanese Americans living in Texas—many of them, like the Tanamachi family, stretching back three and even four generations— she feared an adverse reaction in her small town. "It's not my way to make trouble for anyone," she said.[5]

It wasn't long, however, before Tanamachi wrote more letters—to the Jefferson County commissioners, to Texas state legislators, to Governor Ann Richards, to U.S. congressmen and senators from Texas, even to President Bill Clinton. And now she signed her name to all of them. Over the next year and a half the replies started coming in. Organizations such as the American Civil Liberties Union and the Anti-Defamation League pledged their support. But the official response was disappointing.

Governor Richards, hailed nationwide for her combative liberalism, wrote a stiff and perfunctory note: "Although I sympathize with your concerns, the state constitution prohibits my office from any involvement in this type of case." Tanamachi's letter to President Clinton was forwarded to the Civil Rights Division of the U.S. Department of Justice, which, in a cautiously worded response, did little more than "urge" Jefferson County to "consider changing these names which needlessly offend and are continuous reminders of a period of hysteria and racial bias we are all trying to overcome."

Of course, the U.S. Justice Department had even less jurisdiction over the routine administrative affairs of a Texas county than the governor had. But deference to states' rights and local control had always been a convenient excuse for inaction during the Jim Crow era. What Tanamachi was looking for was not a government official's carefully calibrated legalistic response but some political support—and some sense of moral responsibility and leadership.

Finally, in June 1993, she got permission to address a meeting of the Jefferson County commissioners. She had the floor virtually to herself. None of the local residents opposed to changing the road name showed up to speak out against her. But the majority of the commissioners were dead set against her. After all, their constituents were against her. It was not that they were racists, of course—far from it. The commissioners pointed out that Jap Road had originally been named in honor of a family named Mayumi who had lived in the area nearly a century ago. The residents of the road simply didn't want to be forced to change their mailing addresses, which many had used for years, some for decades.

Besides, there was the cost to the county of making new street signs, issuing new maps, changing directories. And what about the cost to the catfish restaurant, which had spent thousands of dollars over the years in advertising? Would it have to put up new billboards, print new menus, record a new jingle?

In the end, only one of the commissioners—the lone African American—voted in Tanamachi's favor. He had walked in her shoes, he said, and he knew offensive language when he heard it. But the other four commissioners prevailed. Jap Road would remain Jap Road.

Meanwhile, what she had been fearing came to pass. As her campaign went public, Tanamachi increasingly found herself on the firing line, alone—the target of ever-escalating threats from some of the "good, decent, caring, and hardworking citizens" among her colleagues and neighbors. Unsigned notes appeared in her in-box at Blanchette Elementary, telling her to "get a life" or "get over it," now that the decision had been made. She couldn't help wondering whether it was strangers who had such easy access to her school mail—or her fellow teachers. She also received threatening calls at work, and anonymous harassment kept her home phone ringing during the night. At a local school-supply store, clerks ignored her when she tried to buy classroom materials, so some friendly colleagues had to intervene. And, in a chilling echo of evil from an earlier era, night riders cruised past her house and shot up her mailbox. She dutifully filed a police report, but nothing came of it.

Still, Tanamachi had no intention of abandoning her fight. "I planned to work on it until the change was made," she says. "I hoped and prayed that it would be done in my lifetime."

★ ★ ★

What was driving Tanamachi was more than just outrage over a racial slur. Her sense of injustice had been heightened by a personal connection to a historic battle in World War II that should have put an end, once and for all, to the question of whether being a Japanese American was in conflict with being a Texan—or an American.

In recent years, that long-ago battle has been remembered, if at all, as merely a minor skirmish in a forgotten campaign that took place between D-day and the Battle of the Bulge, a footnote to the history of the war.[6] But six decades ago it was headline news.

At the end of October 1944, 211 men from four companies of the 141st ("Alamo") Regiment of the 36th ("Texas") Division were stranded without reinforcements or supplies for a week behind enemy lines in eastern France. It took four days of furious combat on the rugged slopes of the Vosges Mountains for the 442d Regimental Combat Team to break through to the isolated troops. In what became known as the Rescue of the Lost Battalion, the casualties the 442d suffered, including 42 deaths, exceeded the number of men rescued.

For their heroism in that mission, the governor of Texas had named the men of the 442d "honorary Texas citizens" in an official state proclamation.[7] And by displaying such bravery and sacrifice throughout Western Europe and Italy, the 442d had earned its reputation as the "most decorated unit in American military history for its size and length of service," according to Gen. George C. Marshall, Army chief of staff during World War II (and later secretary of state and Nobel Prize winner).[8]

In less than two years of World War II, the 442d "had participated in seven major campaigns in Italy and France, received seven Presidential Distinguished Unit Citations, and suffered 9,486 casualties," according to the Selective Service System, and was "awarded 18,143 individual decorations."[9] As Gen. Mark Clark, commander of the Fifth Army, to which the 442d was attached in Italy, pointed out, this was the record of a unit whose "original strength was about 3,500 men."[10]

But Tanamachi knew something else about the 442d that most Americans had forgotten, or had never known in the first place—that it was a racially segregated unit. The saviors of the "Texas" Battalion, the men who had sacrificed so much for their fellow Americans, were Japanese Americans, many of whom had volunteered from the "relocation camps" where their families had been incarcerated in the panic following Pearl Harbor.

During World War II, more than 22,500 Japanese Americans served in the Army of the United States.[11] Around 18,000 of them served in segregated units—in addition to the 442d, the 100th Battalion (Separate), formed out of Hawaiian troops after Pearl Harbor, which preceded the 442d in Italy and then joined the larger unit; and the 1399th Engineers Construction Battalion, which served in homeland defense of Hawaii. Most of the remaining Japanese American soldiers served with the Military Intelligence Service (MIS), attached as individuals or in small groups to separate units scattered across the Pacific and China-Burma-India theaters.*

Tanamachi was connected to the 442d not just by pride in her ethnic group's history but by her own family. Her uncles Willie, Walter, and Goro were 442d veterans. And her late uncle Saburo—like his brothers, a second-generation Texan as well as a second-generation (*Nisei*) Japanese American—had been one of those soldiers courageously struggling through the dark forests of the Vosges to rescue the Lost Battalion.

"The heroic exploits of the Japanese American soldier," according to General Clark, "should be an inspiration to all of what courage, loyalty, honesty, and devotion to America and its democratic ideals can achieve."[12]

★ ★ ★

---

*A very small number of Japanese American soldiers in World War II were integrated into regular units in various theaters of operation. By 1945, there were proportionately more Japanese Americans in the U.S. Army than in the general population of the United States, Hawaii, and Alaska; Japanese Americans as a group were overrepresented by more than 20 percent. Calculated from Dillon S. Myer, Director, "Nisei in Armed Forces," War Relocation Authority Administrative Notice No. 322, October 29, 1945, Archives II, RG 389; Historical Section, Army Ground Forces, *Ground Forces in the War Army: A Statistical Table*, 1946, Center of Military History; and U.S. Department of Commerce, Bureau of the Census, *Current Population Reports, Population of Counties by Decennial Census: 1900 to 1990*, and *Historical Statistics of the United States: Colonial Times to 1970*.

Washington, D.C., 2000

Four years after the Jefferson County commissioners originally ruled against Tanamachi, her husband was transferred again, and the family moved to Lake Jackson. It would be another seven years after that before her voice was heard again in Beaumont protesting the name of Jap Road. But in the meantime, the nation as a whole was acknowledging a debt to the Japanese American soldiers in World War II that had been forgotten in East Texas.

On June 21, 2000, in a crowded reception on the South Lawn of the White House, President Bill Clinton awarded the Congressional Medal of Honor to "some extraordinarily brave" soldiers who "never did receive the honors they clearly had earned" more than a half century earlier.[13]

In response to legislation introduced by Senator Daniel Akaka of Hawaii, the Department of Defense had reviewed the record of Asian American soldiers and determined that some of them had been unfairly denied the nation's highest military honor. Of the twenty-two belated recipients, twenty were Japanese Americans, all of whom had served with the 100th Battalion/442d Regimental Combat Team. (The two units had merged in mid-1944.) Along with the single Medal awarded immediately after the war, Japanese American soldiers won a total of twenty-one Congressional Medals of Honor, fifteen of them posthumously, for their valor in World War II.

Meanwhile, the highly decorated 36th "Texas" Division won seven fewer—a total of fourteen Medals of Honor. In fact, "during the war, only four army divisions earned more than ten Medals of Honor," and "now a single regiment [the 442d], one third the size of a division, would receive twice that number."[14]

Five of the twenty Japanese American Medal of Honor winners honored by President Clinton—including two surviving veterans, Barney Hajiro and George "Joe" Sakato—were recognized for their bravery in the Vosges Mountains during the end of October and the beginning of November 1944, three weeks that included the Rescue of the Lost Battalion.

It was a fateful period for Japanese Americans at home and abroad. In those same weeks, the Supreme Court was weighing the infamous *Korematsu* and *Endo* cases, which were to decide the legal fate of the more than 110,000 Japanese Americans who had been forcibly "relocated" from their homes on the West Coast to makeshift camps in the remote mountains, deserts, and swamps of the West, Southwest, and South. And, as election day, November 7, 1944, drew near, Interior Secretary Harold Ickes—whose department included the War Relocation Authority, in charge of the camps—had been urging President Franklin D. Roosevelt to shut them down before the Supreme Court ordered them closed.

But during those crucial days in the fall of 1944—while the men of the 442d were rescuing the Lost Battalion, after liberating the unknown villages of Bruyères, Belmont, and Biffontaine in the Vosges—many of their families and loved ones were still living behind barbed wire in unknown places such as Rohwer, Poston, and Tule Lake, "godforsaken spots in alien climes," as the historian Roger Daniels put it, where "no one had lived before and no one has lived since."[15]

"Rarely has a nation been so well served by a people it has so ill-treated," President Clinton declared. "They risked their lives, above and beyond the call of duty. And in so doing, they did more than defend America; in the face of painful prejudice, they helped to define America at its best."

One of the *Nisei* soldiers awarded the Congressional Medal of Honor by President Clinton was a sergeant who had earned a battlefield promotion to second lieutenant in October 1944. When he returned to the United States after the war—wearing his uniform and medals, a hook in place of the hand he had sacrificed to a German grenade—he tried to enter a barbershop outside San Francisco. But he was turned away with the words "You're a Jap and we don't cut Jap hair."[16] Instead of getting into a fight, Daniel Inouye went into politics. In 1959, he became the first U.S. congressman from the new state of Hawaii, and in 1962 he was elected U.S. senator, an office he holds to this day.

Later, in a ceremony at the Japanese American National Museum in Los Angeles, Senator Inouye characteristically described the 442d's heroism more modestly than President Clinton had. "We are not supermen," he said, referring to himself and the five other Medal of Honor winners seated behind him. "We are your neighbors."[17]

Or as Gen. Jacob L. Devers, commander of the 6th Army Group (to which the 36th "Texas" Division and the 442d belonged in the Vosges) said, the *Nisei* soldiers had "more than earned the right to be called just Americans, not Japanese Americans."[18]

* * *

Back in Lake Jackson, Sandra Tanamachi shared in the pride and excitement when George "Joe" Sakato, a longtime family friend, stood at attention before President Clinton and received his Congressional Medal of Honor. Tanamachi wanted nothing more and nothing less for Japanese Americans today than what the soldiers of the 442d thought they had won six decades ago—the right to be called "just Americans," and certainly not "Japs."

It would be another four years after the Medal of Honor ceremony before she could make her case again in Beaumont. But by 2004 the veterans of the Lost Battalion would help repay the debt that they, and the state of Texas, owed the 442d. And as these members of the "greatest generation" took on their final mission, the Rescue of the Lost Battalion—in that fateful fall of 1944—could finally be seen not only as a key episode in the fight to liberate France, but also as an important chapter in the struggle to free American citizens at home.

CITIZENS

ONE PUKA PUKA

The Mainland, Hawaii, and the 100th Battalion (Separate)

No combat unit in the army could exceed them in loyalty, hard work, courage, and sacrifice. . . . They were willing to take extra chances and do extra jobs in hopes that a grateful nation would maybe give their families, many of whom were in concentration camps formally known as "relocation centers," a few breaks that were long overdue. A lot of us who were in Italy used to scratch our heads and wonder how we would feel if we were wearing the uniform of a country that mistreated our families. . . . We marveled at those guys who didn't sulk but took a positive attitude about it and showed more character and guts per man than any ten of the rest of us.
—BILL MAULDIN[1]

Arkansas and Mississippi, 1942–1943

In early February 1943, a young American soldier got off a bus and approached a gate along U.S. Highway 165, a half mile north of the small town of Jerome, Arkansas. The barren landscape in front of him had been partly reclaimed from the Mississippi River Delta. But bayous and backwaters still extended swampy fingers into the surrounding flatlands, which were dotted with stumps where the dense forest had recently been razed.

Late afternoon was shading into early evening as he patiently waited for the Army guards at the gate to let him enter the compound lying beyond the barbed wire fence. Searchlights atop watchtowers around the perimeter of the camp suddenly clicked on, piercing the dim light and illuminating row after row of newly constructed barracks—an artificial community that had eerily risen out of the former swamplands. Armed sentries patrolled the dirt paths laid out in an orderly grid.[2]

The young soldier had traveled 120 miles from Little Rock. A recent graduate of Officer Candidate School at Fort Benning, Georgia, he was on his way to report for duty at Camp Shelby, Mississippi, 200 miles to the southeast, on the other side of the Delta from Jerome. With ten days to spare in his allotted travel time, he had decided to take a lengthy detour and visit some friends housed in the compound, a few hundred yards from where he stood.

But the sentries were "flabbergasted" by his appearance at the gate. It was not just that he was one of the first outsiders to visit this camp, which had been occupied for only a few months, since October 1942. What baffled the guards was the purpose of his visit. For behind the barbed wire at Jerome were not fellow soldiers but more than 8,000 Japanese American civilians, including babies and old folk.

In the months following Japan's surprise attack on Pearl Harbor on December 7, 1941, more than 110,000 Japanese Americans "had been removed from their homes" on the West Coast "by Army fiat," as the government itself belatedly acknowledged, and forcibly "relocated" to ten detention centers in remote areas of the United States—from Jerome in the Mississippi Delta to Tule Lake in the Cascade Mountains near the border of California and Oregon—where most of them would be confined for two and a half years. In these isolated camps, according to the government, they were "surrounded by troops and watchtowers. They had lost, temporarily at least, practically all freedom of movement and practically all opportunities of engaging in private employment and earning anything more than a subsistence livelihood."[3]

They had also lost their constitutional protections. Nearly two thirds of them were U.S. citizens by birth—known as *Nisei*, the second generation of Japanese Americans in the States—but they had been summarily stripped of their Fifth Amendment right to due process and denied the equal protection of the law. None of them had been convicted of, or even charged with, any offense that justified the government's destruction of the productive and law-abiding lives they had led before the war. More than a year after Pearl Harbor, the only crime they were guilty of was looking like the enemy.

Now the guards at the Jerome Relocation Center found themselves face to face with a soldier wearing an American uniform who also looked like the enemy, at least to the narrow vision of Caucasian eyes. But 2d Lt. Young Oak Kim was an American of Korean, not Japanese, ancestry. Torn between their instinctive reaction to his physical features and their well-trained response to the visible signs of his rank, the sentries "didn't know what to do," Kim recalls. "They told me to go to town. I said, 'No, that was the last bus. I can't go to town.'" So they made him wait while they busily conferred among themselves and consulted their superiors.

Finally, after "frantically making calls all over," they let Kim enter the camp. He had been standing outside in the winter evening for more than an hour.

★ ★ ★

Kim was in Arkansas to visit old friends who had been "relocated" from Los Angeles, where he grew up. His parents ran a small grocery store downtown, at Temple and Figueroa on Bunker Hill, and they were one of the few Korean families in the area. But several other immigrant communities were clustered together within a short distance of the Kims' store. The largest group in his neighborhood school, Central Junior High, was Mexican. From the east came kids from Chinatown, near Union Station. Next door was Little Italy, on Broadway. To the west, from Figueroa to Beaudry, was a Jewish neighborhood. And to the southeast, around First and Main, was Little Tokyo.

"I always had a sense that I didn't belong to any group," Kim remembers, "but that made it possible, I think, early in life to get along with everybody." It was not until he went to Belmont High School, "which was pretty much a Caucasian school," that Kim felt like a minority.[4]

After high school, Kim tried a year of community college, but dropped out when he saw friends who had gone to college working at fruit stands. "I figured, if that's all they got," he recalls, "then why go?" So he tried to enlist in the Army, "but they refused to let me join because I was Asian."* Then Kim's number came up in the prewar draft. "So I was accepted in the military, but I soon learned that they didn't take us because they wanted to—they took us because they had to."

---

*Kim's use of "Asian" is current as of the time of his oral history. The term used in the 1940s was "Oriental."

In basic training, Kim found to his surprise that he was an excellent soldier. Though he had never even held a gun before being inducted, he was the best marksman in his group. But when assignments were made after training ended, Kim was told he could be a cook, a clerk, or a mechanic—not an infantryman. When he asked why, his sergeant replied, "Wake up, wake up. You got the wrong shaped eyes. You got the wrong skin. Everything is wrong. You can't be a soldier. People like you aren't soldiers."

There must have been too many cooks and clerks, since Kim found himself assigned to further training as a mechanic. "It was a wonderful opportunity because I learned a lot," he says. He quickly rose to the rank of sergeant, in charge of dozens of half-tracks, trucks, and jeeps.

Then, on maneuvers in the desert during the summer of 1942, his company commander called him in and said, "Sign these papers." They were an application for Officer Candidate School (OCS), the intensive program that offered non-commissioned officers the chance to earn a second lieutenant's bars. With the rapid mobilization for war following Pearl Harbor, the Army urgently needed to fill the ranks of junior officers, and Kim's commander told him he had "too much brains and too much education" to be a sergeant.

In Infantry OCS at Fort Benning, the pressure was intense, with an attrition rate of about fifty percent. Kim "didn't see another Asian" while he was there. But once again, his native intelligence and aptitude helped him advance. After the graduation ceremony, however, while the rest of his class was assigned to other outfits, Kim received his bars but not his orders.

It was only after he complained that he was sent to join a new unit in training at Camp Shelby. And so began a journey that would take him a long way from Bunker Hill—from Arkansas to Mississippi, and then to Italy and France. And so, too, began the forging of a link, which would be tempered in combat, to a unique group of soldiers in the U.S. Army who would be his comrades and friends for decades to come.

★ ★ ★

When Kim finally got behind the barbed wire at Jerome, he felt he was on familiar ground. The "relocation center" was laid out much like the Army camps that had become his home, with more than six hundred buildings, including barracks, mess halls, and communal laundries and latrines. It had a military police compound, a row of warehouses, a fire station, a sewage treatment plant, and a hospital—all the elements of a self-contained Army base. As Kim had found out, entrances and exits were strictly controlled, and armed sentries patrolled the grounds and kept watch in towers around the periphery.

But Jerome—like the nine other "relocation centers" across the country (Rohwer, also in Arkansas; Poston, also known as Colorado River, and Gila River in Arizona; Granada, also known as Amache, in Colorado; Topaz, also known as Central Utah, in Utah; Minidoka in Idaho; Heart Mountain in Wyoming; and Tule Lake and Manzanar in California)—was actually a curious hybrid of military and civilian. In place of command headquarters, there were administration buildings for officials of the War Relocation Authority (WRA), the independent federal agency established almost a year earlier, on March 18, 1942, to run the camps—which had not even been built at that time. The Jerome center also included a sawmill, a hog farm, and more than six hundred acres of cultivated land for the residents to grow their own vegetables.

According to the WRA, the "relocation camps" had been designed not just to detain Americans of Japanese ancestry but to help them create "self-supporting and self-administered communities" that would "facilitate participation in the productive life of America both during and after the war."[5] Determining the balance between military and civilian—"detention or resettlement"—was the "crucial issue"[6] that had plagued the whole policy of "relocating" Japanese Americans from the very start.

On February 19, 1942, President Franklin D. Roosevelt had issued Executive Order 9066, which officially set into motion the "relocation." What was most remarkable about the order was what it did not say. It did not mention Japanese Americans, or any other ethnic group, by name. It did not appeal to "military necessity" as a justification for government action. It did not use the terms "detention," "resettlement," "relocation," "evacuation," or "internment."

In weirdly bland bureaucratic language, it simply authorized a solution to a jurisdictional issue that had not existed until it was defined by the order itself—the authority to prescribe war zones, not where armed conflict was actually taking place, but within the United States itself. Without imposing martial law, it gave the "Secretary of War, and the Military

Commanders whom he may from time to time designate" the following power:

> . . . to prescribe military areas in such places and of such extent as he or the appropriate Military Commander may determine, from which any or all persons may be excluded, and with respect to which, the right of any person to enter, remain in, or leave shall be subject to whatever restrictions the Secretary of War or the appropriate Military Commander may impose in his discretion. The Secretary of War is hereby authorized to provide for residents of any such area who are excluded therefrom, such transportation, food, shelter, and other accommodations as may be necessary, in the judgment of the Secretary of War or the said Military Commander, and until other arrangements are made, to accomplish the purpose of this order. The designation of military areas in any region or locality shall supersede designations of prohibited and restricted areas by the Attorney General under the Proclamations of December 7 and 8, 1941, and shall supersede the responsibility and authority of the Attorney General under the said Proclamations in respect of such prohibited and restricted areas.[7]

With a few strokes of his pen, Roosevelt had taken away the authority of the attorney general, Francis Biddle, to enforce and uphold the law within the United States and handed it over to the secretary of war, Henry Stimson, and "the Military Commanders whom he may from time to time designate." Put simply, the president had given the Army the power to wage war on American soil—against American citizens and the U.S. Constitution.

The War Department now had the authority to tell civilians where they could live and where they could not, and by implication what they could own and what they could not, which jobs they could hold and which they could not, whom they could associate with and whom they could not. Unhampered by due process or habeas corpus and unconstrained by the equal protection of the law, the Army could simply "exclude" anyone from any "prohibited and restricted areas" it chose to prescribe. It could summarily incarcerate any American, anywhere in the country.

But Executive Order 9066 was never meant to be applied as sweepingly as the language permitted. The whole policy, initiated with one of

Roosevelt's characteristic winks, had always been aimed at Japanese Americans on the West Coast. In the months between Pearl Harbor and the issuing of Executive Order 9066, no other American citizens of any other ethnic or racial group had been seriously targeted for any longer than a brief period spent exchanging memos.

The Army's Western Defense Command later explained why Japanese Americans were singled out:

> Because of the ties of race, the intense feeling of filial piety and the strong bonds of common tradition, culture and customs, this population presented a tightly-knit racial group. . . . It was impossible to establish the identity of the loyal and the disloyal with any degree of safety . . . an exact separation of the "sheep from the goats" was unfeasible.[8]

In other words, it was impossible to distinguish Japanese American citizens from Japanese citizens, Japanese American resident aliens from Japanese foreign nationals, loyal Japanese Americans from disloyal Japanese Americans—so they should all be "excluded," just to be on the safe side.*

But among the Army's General Staff in Washington, there had been considerable doubt concerning the necessity, or even the logic, of a full-scale "evacuation" from the West Coast. In early February 1942, Brig. Gen. Mark Clark, who would later play a large role in the lives of Japanese Americans, had rejected the "wisdom of such a mass exodus." The manpower and other resources required to "evacuate," house, feed, and guard 110,000 Japanese Americans—most of them for the next three years, and most of them American citizens—would "absorb like a sponge, many divisions."[9] Strictly on military grounds, and not out of any concern for civil liberties, Clark had sensibly warned the General Staff: "We must not permit our entire offensive effort to be sabotaged in an effort to protect all establishments from ground sabotage."[10]

In any event, the Justice Department, including the Federal Bureau of Investigation, not the army, had always exercised legal authority over

---

*During the past twenty-five years or so, revisionist writers on the fringes of the right have argued without much success that the revelations of MAGIC, the top-secret signals intelligence operation that intercepted and decoded Japanese diplomatic cables, justified the "exclusion" and "evacuation." For more on this claim, see the Appendix.

domestic affairs. The late chief justice William Rehnquist, commenting on the legal arguments the government advanced in support of its decision, pointed out:

> The submissions by the military showed no particular factual inquiry into the likelihood of espionage or sabotage by *Nisei* [American-born citizens of Japanese ancestry], only generalized conclusions that they were "different" from other Americans. But the military has no special expertise in this field, and it should have taken far more substantial findings to justify this sort of discrimination, even in wartime.[11]

And the Justice Department had already dealt with the problem Executive Order 9066 was supposedly addressing: "protection against espionage and against sabotage to national-defense material, national-defense premises, and national-defense utilities." In the immediate prewar period, through the attack on Pearl Harbor, and during the following two months, the Justice Department had already investigated, interrogated, and detained thousands of potential spies and saboteurs in the United States, including German, Italian, and Japanese foreign nationals and resident aliens, who were all interned under commonly accepted national and international laws and practices. Attorney General Biddle had already prescribed narrow areas from which all German, Italian, and Japanese foreign nationals and resident aliens were prohibited, such as the Embarcadero and Presidio in San Francisco and the airport in Los Angeles. All of these actions were consistent with the government's undisputed power to intern foreign nationals and enemy aliens.* To Attorney General Biddle and FBI Director J. Edgar Hoover, no further steps were necessary—and "no proved instances of sabotage or of espionage after Pearl Harbor among the west coast Japanese population were ever uncovered," according to the Army's own history.[12]

Biddle insisted that the Justice Department, which was supposed to have responsibility for enforcing federal laws in the United States, had "no power or authority"[13] to single out Japanese American citizens and "exclude" them from the West Coast. And if civilian authorities had no

---

*The U.S. government has the power to intern foreign nationals and enemy aliens—not citizens. Executive Order 9066 gave the Army vast powers over American citizens who happened to be of Japanese ancestry. See the Appendix for more details.

such power or authority, how could the military have it, in the absence of martial law? Even one of the Western Defense Command's most ardent proponents of "evacuating" Japanese Americans from the West Coast could only say that the plan "has the widest acceptance among the Congressional Delegations and other Pacific Coast officials," but that "no one has justified fully the sheer military necessity for such action."[14] As late as early February 1942, the consensus among both military and civilian officials was against any mass "relocation." To Stimson, who was a lawyer and understood the legal implications, the sweeping powers granted the Army by Executive Order 9066 threatened to tear "a tremendous hole in our Constitutional system."[15]

Nonetheless, on February 11, Roosevelt prevailed over the doubts of his advisors. Or rather the president washed his hands of the matter in what amounted to a stunning denial of responsibility. Presented by Stimson and his aide, John J. McCloy, with a series of options—ranging from a "lesser step such as the establishment of restricted areas around airplane plants and critical installations" all the way to "100 percent withdrawal" of Japanese Americans, citizens and noncitizens alike, from the West Coast—Roosevelt only authorized the "evacuation" but otherwise give the War Department carte blanche. He merely added, "Be as reasonable as you can."[16]

On February 20, 1942, the day after Roosevelt issued the order, Stimson authorized the commanding general of the Western Defense Command and Fourth Army, based in California, to "carry out the duties and responsibilities" imposed by the president. Specifically, Stimson classified "persons resident in the Western Defense Command" in five categories:

Class 1. Japanese Aliens

Class 2. American citizens of Japanese Lineage

Class 3. German Aliens

Class 4. Italian Aliens

Class 5. Any persons, whether citizens or aliens, who are suspected for any reason by you or your responsible subordinates, of being actually or potentially dangerous either as saboteurs, espionage agents, fifth-columnists or subversive persons.

Class 6. All other persons who are, or who may be within Western Defense Command.[17]

He then ordered the "exclusion of all persons in Classes 1, 2, 3, and 5" from wherever the commanding general designated "military areas." By addressing the Western Defense Command and putting "Japanese Aliens" and "American citizens of Japanese Lineage" in the highest categories, Stimson made it clear who the targets of Executive Order 9066 actually were. There were no analogous categories for "American citizens of German lineage" or "American citizens of Italian lineage." And unlike the immigrant generation from Germany or Italy, Japanese who had resided in the United States for decades had been barred from becoming American citizens by the Naturalization Act of 1870, the Supreme Court's decision in *Ozawa v. U.S.*, 260 U.S. 189 (1922), and the Immigration Act of 1924. That is, they were now damned for not being citizens, after never having been allowed to become citizens in the first place.

Executive Order 9066 and Stimson's memo gave enormous discretionary authority to a single man: Lt. Gen. John L. DeWitt, head of the Western Defense Command and Fourth Army, a career officer whose main achievement before Pearl Harbor had been serving as quartermaster general. During the debate over the "evacuation," DeWitt was notable mostly for changing his mind almost week to week. At different points he had completely opposed any "wholesale internment" and then favored measures that would have interned more German and Italian than Japanese aliens and resident aliens. Even more remarkable were his stunning non sequiturs, such as voicing "one of the principal arguments for evacuation": "The fact that nothing has happened so far is more or less . . . ominous."[18]

His chief tactical commander, Maj. Gen. Joseph W. Stilwell—who soon would far surpass his superior officer and rise to fame as commanding general of U.S. Army Forces in the China-Burma-India theater—regarded DeWitt as a "jackass."[19]

As head of III Corps, Stilwell was responsible for the coastal defenses from San Luis Obispo through Los Angeles to San Diego. He had the unenviable task of responding to the "wild, farcical and fantastic stuff" pouring out of DeWitt's headquarters. "The [Fourth] Army G-2 [intelligence staff] is just another amateur, like all the rest of the staff," Stilwell noted. "The higher the headquarters, the more important is calm. Nothing should go out unconfirmed. Nothing is ever as bad as it seems at first."

After Pearl Harbor, DeWitt's staff had been seriously considering a number of logistically ridiculous plans—including a mass evacuation of the entire city of Los Angeles (it was unclear where all the residents would go, or how they would get there, or what they would do for shelter and food)—based on a series of wild rumors. Fourth Army intelligence had reported the existence of a secret enemy airfield north of Palomar, where planes were concealed under alfalfa. It turned out to be an old field where the Ryan aviation company had parked some training craft. Other reports indicated that Japanese aircraft had approached San Francisco, but had turned back when the radio broadcasts they had been homing in on had been interrupted. "If turning off the radio broadcasts will win the war, there will be no objection from me," Stilwell noted sarcastically. "Common sense is thrown to the winds and any absurdity is believed."

In December, Stilwell shot down a proposal from a subordinate to "declare a war zone [in Los Angeles] east and west along Imperial Boulevard and north and south along Atlantic (three hundred square miles), combing the area for aliens, removing them and then preventing them from returning. How this was to be done he did not know." But little did Stilwell realize that, two months later, after he had left to command American troops in the China-Burma-India theater, this was exactly what his superior, DeWitt, was planning to do—and more.

This was the man who personally issued the orders—literally dozens of them—defining the "zones" on the West Coast from which Japanese American civilians were "excluded" and then forcing them to "evacuate" to temporary holding camps known as "assembly centers." But this was only the beginning, as DeWitt noted later:

> Essentially, military necessity required only that the Japanese population be removed from the coastal area and dispersed in the interior, where the danger of action in concert during any attempted enemy raids along the coast, or in advance thereof as preparation for a full scale attack, would be eliminated. That the evacuation program necessarily and ultimately developed into one of complete Federal supervision, was due primarily to the fact that the interior states would not accept an uncontrolled Japanese migration.[20]

In short, "exclusion" of Japanese Americans from the West Coast was not enough. After having instantly and arbitrarily turned 110,000 productive

Japanese Americans into homeless people, the military simply washed its hands of responsibility and passed on to civilian authorities the problem of finding a place for them to live, in areas where the local population did not want them in the first place. It was a slippery slope from the declaration of "military necessity" to the prescription of "military zones," then to the "exclusion" of only one group of citizens, then to their "evacuation" to makeshift "assembly camps," and finally to their transportation to "relocation camps," where—"necessarily and ultimately"—they would be "distributed" throughout the interior of the United States. And DeWitt, who had never concealed his personal prejudice against Japanese Americans, was just the man to slide down that slippery slope, bursting free of constitutional restraints—and of military logic.

But the skids had been greased by the highest authority. The military was just the instrument, and "military necessity" just the excuse, for what actually was a grotesque experiment in social engineering—as would become all too apparent within a few months, as the rationale of "military necessity" began to collapse. Stetson Conn, the author of the Army's official history, was "unable to find evidence that [Chief of Staff] General Marshall took any part in or was informed of developments in the planning of Japanese evacuation between 3 and 11 February," when the decision was made, and asserts that "the only responsible commander who backed the War Department's plan as a measure required by military necessity was the President himself, as Commander in Chief."[21]

DeWitt, evidently not a "responsible commander," could have unleashed such a swift and sweeping roundup of American citizens only on the president's behalf. Exercising power without responsibility, authority without leadership, Roosevelt had tried to keep his hands clean by passing the matter to the War Department in the first place, and by framing the whole policy not as "military necessity"—the very phrase absent from Executive Order 9066—but as a jurisdictional issue between the Justice and War Departments over the "prescribing" of "military areas."

★ ★ ★

At the time of Kim's visit, most of the "evacuees," as they were called, at Jerome and at nearby Rohwer, only twenty-seven miles to the north, were from the Los Angeles area. The very first Japanese Americans "evacuated" in the continental United States had been families on Terminal Island, in the port of Los Angeles. The island was the site of shipyards and an air-field, and the home of dockworkers and fishermen from a variety of eth-nic groups, including resident aliens as well as American citizens of Filipino, Portuguese, Italian, and Japanese ancestry.

Twenty-one-year-old Kikuko Nakao, who lived on Terminal Island with her mother, sister, and two brothers, had been working at a local can-nery to help support the family after her father, a fisherman, died. She re-members being "really scared" when she heard the news of Pearl Harbor. Two months later, the Navy assumed jurisdiction and ordered Japanese Americans—alone among the different ethnic groups—to "evacuate" Ter-minal Island, even though the United States was also at war with Italy. The Nakaos had two days to settle all their affairs and dispose of their property before the deadline of February 25, 1942. They had no place to go until some friends helped move them to a Japanese community center in nearby Norwalk. While they were leaving, strangers were waiting outside their apartment with trucks lined up to haul away whatever was left. These hu-man vultures made Kikuko's fifteen-year-old sister, Ikuko, "really mad."[22]

"Special police finally had to be stationed in the fishing village of Ter-minal Island, in Los Angeles Harbor, to protect families of interned aliens," the government later acknowledged:

> Junk and secondhand dealers were buying furnishings valued from $50 to $200 for $4 and $5 by telling panicky families that the government intended to seize their household belongings. Since no official state-ments were made in this period, victims were strongly inclined to be-lieve the rumors of the moment.[23]

The next stage in the "evacuation" was a brief period in which Japa-nese Americans were encouraged to move "voluntarily" from the West Coast. Some families were lucky enough to arrange for places to live in-land. B. Y. Kaneko, his wife, and three of their five children,[24] who had been living in the San Francisco Bay Area, moved in with family friends in Salt Lake City, Utah. But most Japanese Americans lacked the connec-tions and resources to uproot their families and dispose of property on such short notice. And the governors of neighboring states had quickly declared their unwillingness to accommodate large numbers of Japanese Americans voluntarily moving inland from the West Coast.

So the next stage of the "exclusion" was all but inevitable. On March 24, three days after the swift passage and signing of Public Law 503, which gave the Justice Department the power of criminal prosecution to enforce the "exclusion," the first forced "evacuation" took place from Bainbridge Island, Washington. Over the next few weeks, Japanese Americans throughout California and substantial parts of Oregon, Washington, and Arizona were ordered to leave behind their houses, businesses, farms, and personal property, apart from what they could carry in a suitcase, and proceed to fifteen temporary "assembly centers," where they would be detained under Army supervision while permanent "relocation centers" were being built.

In San Jose, a ten-year-old boy named Norman Mineta and his family boarded a train to an "assembly center" east of Los Angeles. Mineta was wearing his Cub Scout uniform. "Our parents wanted us to get integrated into American life as quickly as possible," he says today. "Scouting was one of those activities that they thought would do that."[25]

Seventeen-year-old Kiyoshi Fujimoto, nicknamed "Bones" because he was so thin, had been living and working with his family on a farm in Bell (now Bell Gardens), California, near Los Angeles. When the "evacuation" order came, "Bones" had to abandon his dog, Husky, and the Fujimotos had to put their household goods, horses, and farm equipment in the care of the people who took over their farm. (After the war, the government estimated that "in 1942, the evacuated people left behind them about $200,000,000 worth of real, personal, and commercial property. . . . Some lost everything they had; many lost most of what they had."*)

The Nakaos, who had been forced off Terminal Island, now had to leave the community shelter in Norwalk where they had been housed for only a few weeks. Their new home for the next five months was the same as the Minetas' and the Fujimotos': the Santa Anita Assembly Center, formerly (and subsequently) known as Santa Anita Park, where Seabiscuit

---

*The Wartime Handling of Evacuee Property, pp. 3, 108. The losses would be equivalent to about $6.4 billion in current dollars. Current dollars here and elsewhere are adjusted relative to per capita GDP (according to the Bureau of Economic Analysis, U.S. Department of Commerce). Other measures, such as the Consumer Price Index or the relative share of GDP, would show less or more constant dollars. Per capita GDP falls roughly in the middle range of adjusted constant dollars.

had won his last race just two years earlier. Horse stalls had been converted into temporary living quarters for the new inhabitants. Each stall, intended for a single family, had a lightbulb hanging overhead, and there was a water faucet for every two stalls. The communal showers and latrines were hundreds of yards away. Although the facilities had been cleaned and painted, there was no disguising the smell of the recent occupants. As summer arrived, the heat and stench became nearly unbearable.

"As much as we didn't think it was fair," Sachi Itaya, née Ito, remembers, "we didn't question it." She and her sister, Masako, and their parents "did just as we were told and disposed of all our possessions," as well as the family business, a bathhouse in Stockton, California. "Since we were allowed only a suitcase each, we only packed the necessary clothes and personal items." Then, along with their neighbors, they "went to camp"—the Stockton Assembly Center, located on the county fair grounds. "Everyone was helping each other, and everyone obeyed the orders," she recalls. Her senior year in high school had been disrupted, but she stayed in the "assembly center" long enough to graduate from the camp's makeshift school, at a ceremony held at the racetrack on the fair grounds.[26]

Over the next few months, the "evacuees" from the four West Coast states were transported from the "assembly centers" to the ten new camps inland that had been hastily constructed by the WRA. In his role as quartermaster general during the Depression, Lt. Gen. DeWitt had transported, sheltered, and outfitted the Civilian Conservation Corps (CCC). The Army's role in "relocating" Japanese Americans bore an eerie resemblance to the mobilization of the CCC, which had sent hundreds of thousands of unemployed men to camps in remote rural areas, where they had been engaged in building roads, reclaiming land, constructing bridges and dams, and other conservation efforts.[27]

Now, maintaining the same spirit of New Deal social engineering and public works, the "relocation camps" for Japanese Americans were placed on the sites of undeveloped federal reclamation projects (Tule Lake, Minidoka, and Heart Mountain), "on land meant for subsistence homesteads under the Farm Security Administration" (Rohwer and Jerome), and on Indian reservations (Poston and Gila River). True to the principles of federalism and localism, "unused land held by the City of Los Angeles for its water rights" became the site of Manzanar. Exemplifying cooperation between public and private sectors, the site for Topaz was assembled out of land that had been privately owned, county owned, and public domain. And honoring free enterprise, the WRA had bought privately held land for the site of Granada and for additional acreage at Rohwer. Since the locations were deliberately chosen for their remoteness, the instant communities formed by the WRA became some of the largest "cities" in the states where they were located.[28]

The "evacuees" destined for Rohwer and Jerome were among the last to leave the "exclusionary zone" on the West Coast. In September, after spending the summer in the sweltering horse stalls of the Santa Anita Assembly Center, Kikuko Nakao remembers being given less than a week's notice to prepare for a "destination unknown." Along with eight thousand other Japanese Americans from California, including the Fujimotos and Minetas from Santa Anita and the Itos from Stockton, the Nakao family traveled on trains, under armed guard with the window shades pulled down, for nearly a week.

When the "evacuees" arrived in what they were finally told was Arkansas, they entered a military-style compound surrounded by barbed wire and set amid thousands of acres of recovered swamplands. It was the Rohwer Relocation Center, very similar to what Young Oak Kim would see a few months later at Jerome, twenty-seven miles away. Most of the Nakao family would live here for the next two and a half years, as would Norman Mineta and his family, Masako Ito and her parents, and "Bones" Fujimoto's sister, mother, and father. But "Bones" himself, Sachi Ito, and Kikuko Nakao, in different ways but like many other Japanese Americans, would escape their confinement before the end of the war.

★ ★ ★

Kim stayed a few days at Jerome. His friends were living in "horrible conditions," with blankets strung up on clotheslines to separate families in the barracks. It was "like a cheap army camp," Kim remembers. He offered to sleep on the floor, but his friends scrambled all over the center to find him a cot. "I thought it was a terrible way to treat Americans," he says today. "They were just as much Americans as I was or anyone else was."

When his friends asked where he was going next, Kim remembers answering, "I'm going to the 100th Infantry Battalion. I think it's an all

Japanese American unit . . . they're supposed to be en route now from [Camp] McCoy [in Wisconsin] down to Shelby."

In fact, the 100th had already arrived in Mississippi. But when Kim reported for duty at Camp Shelby a few days later, the battalion had left for field maneuvers. So he spent the day getting briefed on the unit by Katsumi "Doc" Kometani, a dentist who was serving on the battalion commander's staff as an "unofficial father of the men," as Kim puts it.

From Kometani, Kim learned the 100th's peculiar history. When Japan had attacked Pearl Harbor, there were more than fourteen hundred Japanese American soldiers already serving in the 298th and 299th Infantry Regiments of the Hawaiian National Guard. Some of them had been inducted in the prewar draft. Others, like Masayuki "Spark" Matsunaga, had joined the ROTC at the University of Hawaii and earned a commission as a second lieutenant with the National Guard.

Although agitation for "evacuation" and "relocation" had succeeded on the West Coast of the mainland, similar pressure failed in Hawaii. With a population of more than 150,000, Japanese Americans were roughly thirty-seven percent of the total population of the islands, larger than any other racial or ethnic group, including whites. (On the mainland, Japanese Americans were less than one tenth of one percent of the nation's population.) Although most of them still inhabited an immigrant culture centered in the plantation camps run by the large sugar and pineapple growers, the Hawaiian Japanese Americans had, by sheer weight of numbers, a growing political presence and a vital role in the local economy.

Immediately after Pearl Harbor, the newly appointed military commander of the islands, Lt. Gen. Delos Emmons, had considered "evacuation" and "relocation" of Japanese Americans along the lines of the policy stateside. Hawaii was still a territory, not a state, much more subject to federal oversight even before the war. And because the islands were now under martial law, Emmons actually had much greater authority than his counterpart, DeWitt, had on the West Coast of the mainland.

But Emmons was a much calmer, more pragmatic, and more reasonable leader than DeWitt was. After reining in his initial impulse to "evacuate" Japanese Americans, Emmons took the time to listen to people who actually understood the threats of espionage and sabotage, and heeded the counsel of community leaders who knew the territory's Japanese Americans. Robert Shivers, the FBI's special agent in charge of the Honolulu office, had already concluded—as his boss, Hoover, had argued in Washington, D.C.—there was no reason to question the loyalty of most local American citizens of Japanese ancestry. Colonel Kendall Fielder, head of military intelligence in Hawaii, expressed the same kind of rational reservations that Brigadier General Clark had tried to voice on the mainland. There was no place in the islands to confine more than 150,000 Japanese Americans, and simply transporting them, housing them, and feeding them would divert resources and manpower that could be better employed actually fighting the Japanese enemy. Charles R. Hemenway, a prominent businessman (and later attorney general of the territory), helped establish local "morale committees," which facilitated cooperation between military and civilian and protected the interests of Japanese Americans (and all Hawaiians, since the territory was under martial law). And Hung Wai Ching, a prominent Chinese American, rallied business and civic leaders to convince Emmons not to act rashly against local Japanese Americans. They were clearly indispensable to the economy, not just as field hands but even as civilian workers in the defense industry, whether unloading ships in Pearl Harbor or maintaining Hickam Field, headquarters of the Army Air Force in Hawaii.

Put simply, Japanese Americans in Hawaii were much more integrated into the political, economic, and even military structure of the territory than were their counterparts on the mainland, who could be made to disappear without causing too much of a fuss. In Hawaii, Japanese Americans could not be "evacuated" or "relocated" without doing great damage to the sectors—business, government, military—in which they played such a significant role.

So it was not a legal or constitutional issue for Emmons, much less a strictly military question, but a pragmatic political decision. And it gave lie to the rationale of "military necessity"—the need to eliminate what DeWitt called "the danger of action in concert during any attempted enemy raids along the coast, or in advance thereof as preparation for a full scale attack"[29]—advanced in Washington, D.C., and California. If Japanese Americans had actually posed that danger anywhere, it would have been far greater in Hawaii, the American military command center and home of the fleet in the Pacific theater, than on the mainland, three thousand miles farther away from actual combat. Japan had already succeeded in a devastating attack on Hawaii, whereas the most it could accomplish against the continental United States was minor shelling from two submarines and a few bombs from a single plane—*after* the decision had already been made to "exclude" and "evacuate" Japanese Americans from the West Coast.*

Emmons, unlike DeWitt, was merely responsible enough to distinguish real threats from imaginary fears, he had the courage to resist political pressure, and he was rational enough to measure the real costs of "evacuation" against the fanciful benefits. Even though Hawaii was far more vulnerable than the continental United States, there was no "military necessity" to single out Japanese Americans as a group for "relocation" within the islands or to the mainland. Though martial law gave Emmons far more authority over everyone in Hawaii, not just Japanese Americans, he wielded it much more carefully than anyone on the mainland exercised the power of Executive Order 9066.

Still, though Emmons could find ways to evade, resist, and even defy pressure from Washington regarding Japanese American civilians, he was still part of the military chain of command. He could not refuse direct orders regarding Japanese Americans already in the Army. On May 28, 1942, Gen. George C. Marshall, Army chief of staff, ordered Emmons to reorganize Japanese American soldiers in the 298th and 299th Infantry Regiments into a provisional battalion.

"What a day that was," "Spark" Matsunaga later told *The Hawaii Herald*. "We were given orders to turn in all our arms and ammunition— those of us of Japanese ancestry. It was an emotional jerker for me to be forced into turning in my sidearms to my commanding officer after having stood ready to defend my country."[30] But Matsunaga and his fellow soldiers were mistaken in their outrage over the order to surrender their arms. They were not being accused or even suspected of disloyalty. They were merely being prepared for transport to the mainland.

The provisional battalion of Japanese Americans boarded the SS *Maui* and, a week later, steamed under the Golden Gate Bridge and docked in

---

*In his *Final Report: Japanese Evacuation from the West Coast* (Headquarters Western Defense Command and Fourth Army, 1942), DeWitt cited these minor incidents to support the "military necessity" of the "exclusion" and "evacuation"—even though the first of them took place a week after the decision to "evacuate"; the second, a month after Japanese Americans had already been "evacuated" from the area of the attack; and the third, another two months later.

Oakland. Upon arrival, they were redesignated the 100th Battalion (Separate) and shipped by train to Camp McCoy, Wisconsin.

In the "triangular" organization of the World War II Army, infantry battalions were composed of three rifle companies and a heavy weapons company. Three battalions made up an infantry regiment, and three regiments made up an infantry division. Battalions were "organic" components of regiments; they were not organized to function independently. And they were usually identified as 1st, 2d, and 3d, regardless of which uniquely numbered regiment they belonged to.

But the 100th was an overstrength battalion. Instead of four companies, it had six. Instead of the usual eight hundred or so soldiers, it had more than fourteen hundred.[31] And its designation by a unique number (usually reserved for regiments and higher units) and the word "separate" indicated its special status in the Army's tables of organization.

The 100th was the first and, at the time, only U.S. military unit made up of Japanese Americans (serving under officers who were predominantly Caucasian). There had been segregated units in earlier eras, such as the "colored troops" during the Civil War and their successors in the West, the "buffalo soldiers." And there were other segregated outfits during World War II, including the 92d Infantry Division for Negro (as they were called then) troops, the Philippine Scouts and the Philippine Army, and the 99th Battalion (Separate) for soldiers of Norwegian descent. But no other segregated unit was composed of soldiers whose parents had come from a country they were at war with—or whose own loyalty had been called into question.[32]

But the Japanese American soldiers found something to laugh about in their official designation as a "separate," or "orphan," unit. In Hawaii, the word *puka*, for "hole," could also refer to "zero" or "nothing." Footwear with a hole in it was called a "*puka* sock." A plan with problems had a "big *puka*." So the men of the 100th started referring to themselves as One Puka Puka—a battalion with holes in it, a big double nothing.

★ ★ ★

The day after Kim arrived, he met the commander of the 100th, Lt. Col. Farrant Turner. He took one look at Kim and said, "I'll have you transferred immediately." Kim remembers him saying, "Coming from the islands, I know that Koreans and Japanese don't always get along."

"You're wrong," Kim recalls responding. "They're Americans, I'm American, and we're going to fight for America." Later, Kim would learn that other officers had immediately asked for transfers when they discovered the 100th was a segregated Japanese American unit. But Kim's on-the-spot decision was both idealistic and pragmatic. He understood it was still a white man's Army. Serving with a "bastard" unit, as he called it, would give him opportunities he probably wouldn't have had elsewhere. "I realized right even then that if I wasn't with the 100th, I would be a PR officer or have some insignificant duty someplace else," Kim says, "because nobody was going to let me, as an Asian, command regular troops."[33]

But when Kim finally met his troops, his first thought was "God, what a motley-looking crew." "They all needed a haircut," he remembers, "most of them didn't have their shoes laced," and "they had their shirts out instead of inside their pants."

Of course, Kim realizes now, "they didn't think much of me either." He had three strikes against him from the outset—he was a mainlander, he was a *yobo* (Hawaiian slang for a Korean), and he was a "ninety-day wonder" (an OCS graduate). There wasn't much he could do about the first two, but he found he was due for an attitude adjustment regarding the third. "I was brainwashed," Kim admits about his OCS training. "I tried without much success to get them to get a haircut and do all the things I wanted" to maintain discipline. It wasn't until after the 100th entered combat that he "realized all that doctrine was BS," he concedes today. "What you look like and how you dress have nothing to do with how you're going to perform in combat."

Unknown to Kim, the enlisted men in the 100th had quickly come up with a nickname for their new junior officer—"GI [for 'government issue'] Kim." It was not meant as a compliment. But just as Kim's attitude would change, so would his men's.

Kim came to understand that one reason the men of the 100th were so lackadaisical was boredom. They had already been through basic training in Hawaii, a year before. They had been retrained at Camp McCoy six months earlier. And now they were going through training once again, at Camp Shelby. "Everyone was sick and tired of it," Kim recalls. "They won't admit it, but what they were doing was marching out in the morning, finding a comfortable place to have a lecture, and then falling asleep." After a few hours they would "eat lunch out there and then come back."

Kim began to see the Hawaiians' apparently easygoing ways masked fierce determination. "They were very, very intelligent," he recalls. "My platoon sergeant was a graduate of Texas Law School. You don't have law school graduates in the average outfit." Segregation had concentrated all the Japanese Americans across the spectrum into one battalion; in the rest of the Army, the best and brightest typically migrated to elite units (the Rangers, the Army Air Corps) or specialized units (engineers, field artillery). And the men of the 100th "were all in good physical condition," despite being smaller than the Army norm. Their average height was about five feet four inches.[34] Most of all, "they were strong willed," perhaps because of their relative maturity. Their average age was twenty-four, much older than the norm among infantry troops, which had lots of draftees as young as twenty (later, when the Selective Service regulations changed, as young as eighteen).

After overcoming his initial reaction, Kim states, "I never had doubts about their being good combat soldiers." To help prepare them for what he "thought real combat would be," Kim threw out the book and devised his own training plans. Rather than make the men relearn everything they already knew about marching in formation and shining their shoes, he took them in the field and "made every private act as a squad leader, every squad leader act as either the platoon guide or the platoon sergeant, and all the guys act occasionally as a platoon leader." He modified the machine guns used in training so they would fire live rounds. He "borrowed" small amounts of TNT for real explosions.

Most of all, he "taught them a procedure that later was accepted by the Army during the Korean War . . . movement and fire." Instead of emphasizing marksmanship from stationary positions, he stressed laying down overlapping fields of fire and constant, aggressive maneuver. On his own Kim was devising a doctrine of firepower that, independently, Brig. Gen. S. L. A. Marshall, the influential military historian,* would

---

*Marshall, who would play an important role in the formation of the 442d Regimental Combat Team, was one of the best-known and most controversial military historians of the twentieth century. After serving on the General Staff at the beginning of the war, he was assigned to the newly formed Army Historical Section, where he pioneered the writing of official combat histories based on "after-action interviews" conducted as soon as possible following an engagement. After the war, he was promoted to brigadier general and became a best-selling author of books such as *Pork Chop Hill*.

later make famous in his classic—and controversial—work, *Men Against Fire.*[35] "The men didn't appreciate it then," Kim remembers, "but the moment we hit combat, they realized, 'Hey, this is what we're supposed to really do.'"[36]

Most of the men in the 100th were draftees from the prewar induction, but they were as eager as volunteers to prove their patriotism, and they resented the idea of being kept out of combat. "We were all very, very much aware of the disadvantage of being Asian," Kim recalls.

They said for the Japanese Americans in Hawaii—'cause they were talking Hawaii; they were all from Hawaii—they had to do good. They had to succeed. They couldn't fail.

"None of us could say," Kim admits, "that we're going to be the greatest . . . that would just be hot air."

But we knew that we had to be as good as any other Caucasian outfit. . . . And we knew that we had to shed blood. That was the price we're going to pay. And we all had to be prepared to pay that price.

To Kim's surprise, the men of the 100th Battalion (Separate) took their ideas about being Japanese American as seriously as they did their training for real combat. In fact, they grasped that the two were related, and talked endlessly about how they would transform Hawaii when they returned as veterans from the war. They would then have the political base and the moral authority to move their people out of the plantations and into the seats of power.

His most famous book, *Men Against Fire*, published in 1947, is also his most controversial. Almost all of the criticism of his work, and of his reputation, has focused on a single issue: how Marshall supported his shocking assertion that the "ratio of fire"—the percentage of men in combat who actually used their weapons against the enemy—was only twenty-five percent or lower, "even for well-trained and campaign-seasoned troops." Over the years, questions have been raised about the breadth and depth of the interviews Marshall conducted to back up such an alarming claim. Many critics have concluded he either made up the number or, at best, generalized wildly from a very limited sample. Of course, Marshall has as many defenders as critics, and the debate has taken on a life of its own in periodicals and books. See endnote 35 for more detail.

"True, we played cards, we did all kinds of things," Kim remembers, but "the serious bull session" started when "it was too dark to play cards." The group of interlocutors included Kim, Matsunaga, another commissioned officer named Sakae Takahashi, and as many as fifteen or twenty others, but it was "never less than ten or twelve."

> We talked about forming a different political party, breaking the stronghold of the Big Five [the interlocking Caucasian firms that had dominated business, agriculture, and politics in the islands for decades], and changing the political dynamics in Hawaii.

"Every once in a while," Kim remembers, since he was neither from Hawaii nor a Japanese American, "someone would say, 'Well, how come you're in this?'"

> I said, "You're going to do it for the Japanese Americans, but in the end you're going to do it for all Asians . . . and that's why I'm here." I said, "I look like you. No one can tell the difference, and so when it gets done, it's going to be for everybody."[37]

"I'm against segregation," Kim insists. But "in hindsight, I'm happy the 100th was a segregated unit. Because then if it did well, we'd get credit." In the months that followed, Kim and the 100th would earn all the credit they got—and more.

2

KOTONK V. BUDDHAHEAD

Volunteers, the Cadre, and
the 442d Regimental Combat Team

The tactical unity of men working together in combat will be in the ratio of their knowledge and sympathetic understanding of each other. . . . When a soldier is unknown to the men who are around him he has relatively little reason to fear losing the one thing that he is likely to value more highly than life—his reputation as a man among other men.—S. L. A. MARSHALL[1]

Hawaii, the "Relocation Camps," and Mississippi, April 1943–July 1943

Barney Hajiro wanted to join the 100th Battalion (Separate) as soon as he heard about it. Working long hours as a member of the 1399th Engineers Construction Battalion in Oahu, he spent most of the year after Pearl Harbor fortifying artillery emplacements, laying barbed wire, reinforcing concrete, repairing roads and bridges, even building Kahuku airfield for the Flying Fortresses that would eventually play a key role in the defeat of Japan. But he wanted to fight with a gun, not a shovel.

On the mainland, supposedly to prevent sabotage and espionage, Japanese Americans had been "relocated" far from the factories and naval and air bases in the "military zone" of the West Coast. Meanwhile, in Hawaii, three thousand miles closer to an actual combat zone, where sabotage and espionage were much greater threats, it was Japanese Americans who were responsible for building and maintaining the islands' defenses.

Although their work had strategic importance, Hajiro and his fellow engineers—all Japanese Americans—were not permitted to bear arms in defense of their country. When he heard "the 100th had rifle training," he "felt proud" and wanted to join the battalion. But the 100th was not open to new recruits. So Hajiro picked up his tools and went back to grueling manual labor on Oahu, imagining a distant war and a faraway country. He had never seen "America," and when he later learned the 100th was in training on the mainland, he thought to himself, "I'd like to see that place."[2]

★ ★ ★

When Hajiro was growing up on a plantation in Pu'unene, on the island of Maui, even Honolulu seemed impossibly remote. His parents worked ten-hour days for a dollar a day. As a boy, Hajiro competed on his junior high school's track team and dreamed of running away from Maui and finding work in Honolulu. "I wanted to get ahead," he says simply. But he had to quit school after the eighth grade and work in the sugar-cane fields to help his parents support the other eight children in the family.

It was not until he was in his early twenties that he was finally able to board a cattle boat and cross the ocean to the neighboring island of Oahu. At first, Hajiro could find only temporary employment in Honolulu as a dishwasher and cannery worker. Then he landed a higher-paying job as a stevedore. But on December 7, 1941, when he saw Japanese Zeros flying overhead, and then smoke from the *Arizona* burning in the distance, he realized the life he knew was over. Now white people would "think we're the enemy."

In February 1942, in the last draft that would include Japanese Americans for another two years, Hajiro was inducted into the 1399th Engineers. But it would be more than a year before he would be handed a weapon.

Daniel Inouye, then a senior at McKinley High School in Honolulu, also recalled seeing Japanese planes overhead, and then the "dirty gray smoke of a great fire billowed up over Pearl and obscured the mountains and the horizon." He remembered he "looked up into the sky and called out, 'You dirty Japs!'" "Filled with grief and shame," as he recalled in his autobiography, Inouye "carried the full and bitter burden shared by every one of the 158,000 Japanese Americans in Hawaii":

Not only had our country been wantonly attacked, but our loyalty was certain to be called into question, for it took no great effort of imagination to see the hatred of many Americans for the enemy turned on us, who looked so much like him. And no matter how hard we worked to defeat him, there would always be those who would look at us and think—and some would say it aloud—"Dirty Jap."[3]

Whatever else they were, Japanese Americans did not think of themselves as Japs, though they felt free to use the term for the real Japanese enemy. In the Territory of Hawaii, Japanese Americans felt what Inouye felt: "We had *all* been attacked." The United States, not Japan, was their country. And it was not a patriotic abstraction that had been bombed, it was their physical homeland.

When "Remember Pearl Harbor" became a rallying cry, it meant something very different on the islands than it did on the mainland. In Hawaii, Japanese Americans themselves invoked the memory of the sneak attack as something they had suffered directly. In the States, nativist agitators turned the slogan not just against Japanese but also against Japanese Americans.

★ ★ ★

Long before Pearl Harbor, Imperial Japan had been promoting its vision of a "Greater East Asia Co-Prosperity Sphere" as an economic, political, and military bulwark in the Pacific against what it saw as the racist and hegemonic designs of the West. And during the prewar decades, Japan's worst image of the United States had been repeatedly reinforced by nativist alarms about the "yellow peril" in the American popular press, by the Naturalization Act of 1870, which denied citizenship to Japanese aliens already living in the United States, by the rapid passage of laws prohibiting resident aliens from owning land on the West Coast, by the Gentlemen's Agreement of 1907 and the exclusionary Immigration Act of 1924, which closed the borders to Japanese immigrants, and by the rabble rousing and political pressure of groups such as the American Legion, the Oriental Exclusion League of California, the Native Sons of the Golden West, and the Grange, along with their allies among the trade unions, including the American Federation of Labor and the Teamsters. After Pearl Harbor, the "relocation" had only fueled the fire of Japanese propaganda that the United States was waging a racist war.

Partly in an effort to refute charges of racism, by late spring of 1942, different arms of the U.S. government—surprisingly, the military in particular—had already begun ameliorating or even reversing the effects of Executive Order 9066. The value of the 100th Battalion (Separate), and of loyal Japanese Americans generally, in rebutting enemy propaganda was slowly becoming clear to the government.

In any event, American military successes in the Pacific had already started to weaken the whole rationale of "military necessity." In April, Col. James Doolittle had led the first air raid on Tokyo, making the Japanese leaders suddenly aware of their small island nation's vulnerability. In early June, almost six months to the day after Pearl Harbor, the American aircraft carrier fleet had decisively defeated the Japanese in the Battle of Midway—and, as a result, according to the historian John Keegan, "the whole course of the war in the Pacific had been reversed." The Japanese Navy and Air Force would no longer have the ability to strike long distance, virtually eliminating Japan's threat of invading Hawaii, much less the continental United States, and dramatically lessening the fear of sabotage or espionage. Although it would be a long, bloody war in the Pacific, Japan was "now condemned," as Keegan puts it, "to the defensive."[4]

Later in June, the Military Intelligence Service (MIS) began recruiting Japanese Americans who could speak Japanese—while DeWitt's Fourth Army was still holding their families in the "assembly camps"—to serve as translators, interpreters, interrogators, analysts, and propagandists in the Pacific Theater. Many of them would serve under Lt. Gen. "Vinegar Joe" Stilwell, American commander in the China-Burma-India theater and previously DeWitt's subordinate at the Presidio, who had disparaged his commander's panicky response to Pearl Harbor.

Far from being monolithic, authorities at all levels—federal, state, and local—were split among competing interests. As the harvest season approached and the defense industry ramped up, the governors of western and mountain states, who had at first strongly resisted the "relocation" of Japanese Americans in their jurisdictions, now suddenly reversed themselves, recognizing a willing pool of workers to fill jobs in agriculture and manufacturing vacated by men called to duty. As early as the summer of 1942, some Japanese Americans secured seasonal "leave" from "assembly centers" to work on farms. Shiro Kashino, who had been "evacuated" in March from Seattle to the Puyallup Assembly Center in Washington, got permission to work in the sugar beet fields of Idaho before he was even "relocated" to the Minidoka center. And no sooner had he arrived in Minidoka than the Army would offer him another opportunity to leave the camps.

Public and private demand for Japanese Americans to serve both military and civilian needs, in addition to the victories in the Pacific, had thus begun to undermine the logic of the "evacuation" almost as soon as "relocation" had begun. If the whole point of "excluding" Japanese Americans from the West Coast had been doubts about their loyalty, why were they suddenly trustworthy enough to work in vital sectors such as agriculture or in defense industries, not to mention military intelligence?

Of course, Japanese Americans were no more or less loyal after "evacuation," or after Midway, than before. What had changed in the six short months following Pearl Harbor was the willingness of various civilian and military officials and agencies, and private individuals and businesses, to treat Americans of Japanese ancestry as the citizens they were and always had been, rather than as virtual prisoners of war in their own country.

All along, WRA administrators had been releasing individuals for a variety of reasons that had nothing to do with "military necessity" or the absence of it. Sachi Ito, who had been "relocated" to Rohwer with her sister and parents from Stockton, married a young soldier named Sam Itaya, whom she had known in high school. He was stationed in San Antonio, and the newlyweds were free to move there in late 1942. Kikuko Nakao, who had been sent to Rohwer with her mother, sister, and two brothers from Terminal Island, met a farmer from Texas named Jerry Tanamachi through mutual friends. After five days of courtship, she agreed to marry him. She got permission to go to the nearby town of McGehee, Arkansas, to buy a wedding dress, and the couple was married at Rohwer by the center's preacher. There was a brief celebration with cookies and punch, and then the newlyweds went to live in Texas, where the bride was welcomed by the groom's family, including one of Jerry Tanamachi's brothers, Saburo.[5]

Episodes like this highlighted the absurdity of "relocating" Japanese Americans to camps in the same areas where other Japanese Americans had been living, and continued to live, without restriction. B. Y. Kaneko and his family, who had "voluntarily relocated" from the Bay Area, found themselves a life of freedom in Salt Lake City, while his in-laws and their children, the Tokunagas, were confined in the Gila River Relocation Center in the Arizona desert.

But the federal policy of "exclusion," which had been set in motion by the evasive bureaucratic language of Executive Order 9066, called for a bureaucratic response to undo it, even partially and gradually. The government was in no better or worse position now than it ever had been to determine the loyalty of individual Japanese Americans. But by the fall of 1942, when most Japanese Americans were just settling into the "relocation centers," the WRA was already trying to fashion a "leave clearance" policy that would justify releasing "evacuees" for both temporary and permanent jobs and housing everywhere across the country except the "exclusionary zones" in California, Oregon, Washington, and Arizona.

At the same time, the War Department was reconsidering its general restrictions against Japanese Americans in the military. In the spring of 1942, the Selective Service System, at Stimson's prompting, had peremptorily changed the draft status of Japanese American men from I-A, the highest category of eligibility for service, to IV-C, a category meant for "enemy aliens" who were "not acceptable to the armed forces because of nationality or ancestry."[6] This simple bureaucratic sleight of hand effectively turned draft-age American males of Japanese ancestry into noncitizens—or "nonaliens," in the Kafkaesque language of the Selective Service System. But the recruitment by the MIS of Japanese Americans contradicted this policy. So the Army, like the WRA, was also forced to reverse itself and come up with some way to justify letting go the very people it had incarcerated, in order for them to serve like any other Americans.

Eventually, by the end of 1942, the Army and the WRA had decided to undertake a joint "leave clearance" procedure requiring all adult Japanese Americans in the centers to fill out a formal document ("Statement of United States Citizen of Japanese Ancestry," DSS Form 304A) that came to be known as the "loyalty questionnaire."[7] But even though it was well intentioned, it would strike many Japanese not as an opportunity to prove their loyalty but as a bureaucratic insult added to the vast injuries they had already suffered.

★ ★ ★

Around the same time, Franklin D. Roosevelt presented a new "opportunity" to Japanese Americans. On February 1, 1943, almost a year after he had signed Executive Order 9066, the president authorized the formation of a regimental combat team to be made up of Japanese American volunteers:

> The proposal to organize a combat team consisting of loyal American citizens of Japanese descent has my full approval. . . . This is a natural and logical step toward the restitution of the Selective Service procedures which . . . were disrupted by the evacuation [i.e., the reclassification of Japanese American men from I-A to IV-C]. No loyal citizen should be denied the democratic right to exercise the responsibilities of his citizenship, regardless of ancestry. The principle on which this country was founded and by which it has always been governed is that Americanism is a matter of the mind and the heart; Americanism is not, and never was, a matter of race or ancestry.[8]

With these words, the 442d Regimental Combat Team was born. The president had gone partway toward giving back what he had personally ordered taken from Americans of Japanese ancestry. But rather than restoring the rights of due process and habeas corpus that all other citizens had, he offered Japanese American men only the responsibility that all other draft-age men had—to serve, and possibly die for, their country in time of war. With breathtaking piety, the very same president who had signed Executive Order 9066 now claimed "Americanism is not, and never was, a matter of ancestry." But there was still the issue of deciding just who qualified as "loyal American citizens"—and how that would be determined.

Later, when the 442d had distinguished itself in combat, it became one of those successes with many fathers. The idea seems to have originated with Col. Moses Pettigrew, of the Intelligence Branch (G-2) of the General Staff. Elmer Davis, director of the Office of War Information, endorsed the idea, along with his associate, Milton Eisenhower, who had been the first director of the WRA. The Japanese American Citizens League (JACL), the only lobbying group for Japanese Americans that had a national presence, took credit for applying political pressure. John J. McCloy, assistant secretary of war, was often honored after the war for promoting the unit within the Roosevelt administration—even while he was being damned for working conscientiously, even zealously, with De-Witt to manage the "evacuation."[9]

In its "final report" after the war, the WRA offered a revealing anecdote about the formation of the 442d:

> While the Director of WRA [Dillon S. Myer] was at the Gila River center in the fall of 1942 during the period of language school recruitment [for the MIS], he overheard one *Nisei* telling another that "nobody but a damned *Kibei* can get into this man's army."[10]

This was yet another example of the absurdity of the "military necessity" argument. *Kibei*—Japanese Americans who were U.S. citizens because they had been born in America, but who had been educated in Japan before returning to the States—were being recruited by the MIS because of their proficiency in Japanese and their experience living in Japan.* But those were precisely the same attributes that DeWitt, McCloy, and many others had regarded as raising doubts about their loyalty, on the grounds that it was impossible to tell the "sheep from the goats."[11]

The WRA report continued:

> Upon returning to Washington, the Director repeated this story to the Assistant Secretary of War [McCloy] and used it to illustrate the point that large numbers of *Nisei* who most earnestly wanted to demonstrate their loyalty to the United States were being somewhat arbitrarily denied the opportunity to do so. The Assistant Secretary, plainly impressed and generally sympathetic with the idea of *Nisei* service, promised to redouble his efforts to achieve some kind of change in the War Department's policy.
>
> The plan which the Assistant Secretary eventually devised and which was outlined to the Director and two of his staff members at the Sunday morning meeting in mid-January of 1943 was only a partial achievement of the goal which the Director had been seeking. But it

---

*Most *Nisei* spoke very poor Japanese, or none at all. Even the *Kibei* recruited by the MIS had to take intensive courses in Japanese before they were fluent enough to act as translators, interrogators, analysts, and propagandists.

was definitely a step in the right direction. It was based on the premise that Americans of Japanese ancestry should have at least the opportunity of volunteering for military service and that their accomplishments could be most effectively spotlighted and brought to the attention of the American public if they served in an all-*Nisei* unit.[12]

The WRA at least acknowledged that giving Japanese Americans the "opportunity" to die for their country was also a chance for public relations that "effectively spotlighted" their loyalty.

But a very different version of the birth of the 442d came from S. L. A. Marshall, at that time a major serving on the General Staff in Washington:

> The army, not the White House nor any group of civilian reformers, set about to repair the constitutional hurt to all our people through the enforced evacuation of Japanese Americans from the Pacific Coast. It was General George C. Marshall's own idea and was bucked to the office of Assistant Secretary John McCloy for implementation, but McCloy did nothing about it.
>
> The problem as a whole was dropped in my lap simply because my director had volunteered to General Marshall that I could write the program, including policy, and even the palaver that the field teams would put to the people at the War Relocation Centers. That entailed drafting the scheme for recruiting the 442d Combat Team of *Nisei*, putting through the General Staff the inducements we would offer the colonists [as those forced to live in the "relocation centers" were called] for their cooperation (such as post-war citizenship for the *Issei* [the older generation of Japanese immigrants, who had been denied American citizenship]), writing the White House message on the new departure, and circularizing the national press to win their active support.[13]

S. L. A. Marshall had been a junior infantry officer at the end of World War I and had a long career as a newspaperman before returning to uniform in World War II. Though he was not always the most reliable of sources, his account rings true because he was willing, alone among those involved in the plan, to acknowledge that it was "in a very real sense an absurdity." What he recognized was that offering Japanese Americans the "opportunity" to volunteer while at the same time trying to determine their loyalty in the coercive environment of the "relocation centers" was "a highly complex and multifaceted General Staff undertaking in a highly sensitive and volatile area":

> If it failed, there could be irreparable damage to the national honor and tradition. . . . The War Relocation Authority, Army Intelligence, and the provost marshal general were supposed to take it from there, either acting together, or with one of them assuming central direction. At the final conference, I found that each was sidestepping and ducking final responsibility out of sheer gutlessness. I volunteered to take charge of the field operation. . . . I expected heavy trouble at the camps.[14]

And that is precisely what he found.

★ ★ ★

The "leave clearance" form the Army and the WRA designed required the signature of all adult "evacuees" in the "relocation centers." Presented by military and civilian officials at mass meetings throughout the ten camps in February 1943, the form contained two questions that would tear apart the Japanese American community:

> 27. Are you willing to serve in the armed forces of the United States on combat duty, wherever ordered?

> 28. Will you swear unqualified allegiance to the United States of America and faithfully defend the United States from any or all attack by foreign or domestic forces, and foreswear any form of allegiance or obedience to the Japanese emperor, to any other foreign government, power or organization?[15]

These questions struck most Japanese Americans as both unreasonable and insulting. The only rational way to answer #27 would have been "Yes, if my constitutional rights are restored." But responses with qualifications were initially treated as negative answers. And #28 asked Japanese Americans who were already citizens to renounce an allegiance to a foreign power they had never had in the first place.

The latter question also placed the *Issei*—the first immigrant generation, who were the mothers and fathers of draft-age children—in an impossible bind. They had lived in the United States for decades. Most of them had arrived before the Gentlemen's Agreement of 1907 had curtailed immigration from Japan, and virtually all of them had been in residence since before 1924, when the Immigration Act had shut off the flow completely. But the naturalization laws had also kept them—unlike the immigrant generation from, say, Germany or Italy—from becoming citizens, so the *Issei* had lived as "resident aliens" for decades. Now they were being asked to renounce their loyalty to Japan, without any change in their status in the United States. As Marshall recognized, they would have to choose statelessness in order to prove their loyalty to a country that would not grant them citizenship.

This in turn put their children—American citizens by birth, even though they were now bizarrely referred to as "nonaliens"—in the position of choosing loyalty to their country, which had discriminated against them, over loyalty to their own families. Draft-age men wondered what would happen to their parents if they went into the Army. "The only thing I really recall thinking was 'Boy, I wonder what my parents would do in camp if I was—if I didn't come back,' " says Kim Muromoto, who was in Tule Lake with his family.[16] How could a government that would not even recognize the rights of its Japanese American citizens be trusted to care for resident aliens, who had been denied citizenship for decades?

Finally, because the format of the questionnaire and its presentation in the camps was so clumsy and bureaucratic, confusion spread about just what the consequences were of answering the questions. In early mass meetings, both sexes were given the same form, raising fears that Japanese American women, unlike any other American women, were eligible for the draft. Men of the *Issei* generation—most of them in their fifties and sixties*—also had to answer the same question about their willingness to serve in the military, even though they were well beyond draft age. And presenting the loyalty questionnaire at the same time as the formation of

---

*According to the WRA, the median age of the *Issei* generation was fifty-one, while the median age of the *Nisei* generation was eighteen and a half. Because of the restrictive "Gentlemen's Agreement," most *Issei* men had come to the United States before 1907 (though *Issei* women, usually much younger, often followed at later dates, primarily as mail-order brides or through arranged marriages), and practically all of them had come before the Immigration Act of 1924. This meant the *Issei* had been in the United States at least eighteen years, but most likely thirty-five years or more, by the time of the "registration." See Section V of War Relocation Authority, *The Evacuated People: A Quantitative Description.*

the 442d was announced led many draft-age men to believe a "yes" answer to question #27 would immediately commit them to volunteering.

S. L. A. Marshall, who traveled with different teams to several of the "relocation centers," immediately understood the foolishness of believing such a poorly conceived, badly worded, and ineptly administered questionnaire could determine the loyalty of Japanese Americans. He warned:

> The records made during the registration period will bear some witness as to the loyalty record of these people as a whole, but they are not fully to be relied upon because many of them tend to use the questionnaire as a document for their own advantage rather than to make an honest personal declaration. That is to say that they tended to ask themselves: "How shall I answer these questions in such [a] way to give myself the line of main chance?" and make their answers accordingly.[17]

Marshall also cautioned that many in the camps "construed the combat team idea as a form of segregation . . . as a stigma rather than as a chance to do something to better their position in the post-war world." Rumors spread that the segregated unit would be used as a suicide squad.

The whole "registration" process quickly degenerated into a series of confrontations—between "evacuees" and the WRA and Army representatives, and increasingly between those who answered "yes/yes" to questions #27 and #28, and those who answered "no/no." Some Japanese Americans threatened violence against other "evacuees" who complied with the "registration." There were sit-down strikes, angry demonstrations, and even a small-scale riot at Manzanar.

Intended as an "opportunity" for Japanese Americans to join in the war effort, the questionnaire instead struck many in the camps as exactly what it was—a demand that Japanese Americans, unlike any other American citizens, affirm their loyalty at gunpoint. It was obvious to everyone that answering a questionnaire added nothing to the government's ability to tell the "sheep from the goats."*

---

*Morris Opler, a WRA "social science analyst" at Manzanar and the brother of Marvin Opler, who had the same position at Tule Lake, stated succinctly that "a complex situation cannot be properly described by a word of limited meaning, such as 'loyal' or 'disloyal' . . . the problems of Manzanar are not to be settled with an adding machine." "Second Special Report on Registration," April 3, 1943, Archives II, RG 389.

In fact, the whole enterprise threatened to make the rationale for the "relocation" look ridiculous, even to its supporters. "I think that everybody is agreed—at least everybody here [in Washington] is agreed—that you can't keep them [Japanese Americans] in pens forever," McCloy told DeWitt. But DeWitt believed the "registration" was "a sign of weakness and an admission of an original mistake. Otherwise—we wouldn't have evacuated these people at all if we could determine their loyalty."[18] DeWitt continued to insist that "there are no persons of Japanese ancestry of 'unquestioned loyalty' to this country."[19]

Agreeing emphatically, Lt. Col. Karl Bendetsen, one of DeWitt's aides and a prime mover behind the "exclusion" and "evacuation," unwittingly revealed the twisted logic of the Western Defense Command:

> The issue is that the War Department is undertaking to determine their loyalty and to be responsible for that determination. It is going to be a little hard for the War Department to explain why when they were in Assembly Centers, under control, satisfying all the then requirements, that if it is possible to determine loyalty, they didn't do it then. And save 80 million dollars worth of Relocation Centers that were built. That's the fundamental point.[20]

In other words, a loyalty test in 1943 would not discover anything that could not have been determined in 1942, shortly after Pearl Harbor—before $80 million (more than $2.5 billion in current dollars, per capita GDP) had been wasted on the "relocation." Bendetsen thought he was raising an objection to the "registration" by pointing out how difficult it would be for the War Department to explain the "fundamental point"; what he actually was doing was exposing the whole sham of "military necessity." Mark Clark (by this time a lieutenant general), who had opposed the "evacuation" precisely because it squandered resources "in an effort to protect all establishments from ground sabotage,"[21] could not have expressed the absurdity of "military necessity" any better than Bendetsen did.

★ ★ ★

After nearly five thousand Japanese Americans answered "no/no" to the two questions, the WRA and the Army instituted a new policy of "segregation." The Army rounded up all the "no/nos," as they came to be called, from the nine other camps and transported them to Tule Lake, which it took control of after clearing the center of most of the "evacuees" who were not "no/nos." Tule Lake would become the only one of the "relocation centers" run by the Army instead of the WRA. Along with the "no/nos" at Tule Lake were aliens paroled from Department of Justice Internment Camps, persons denied "leave clearance" at other centers, and family members who voluntarily accompanied the "segregees" to Tule Lake, even though they would otherwise not have been segregated.[22]

More than 5,500 Japanese Americans—almost all of them "segregees" at Tule Lake—eventually tried to renounce their citizenship.* Some were cynically trying to avoid the draft. Others were attempting to calculate whether they might be better off in the event of a Japanese victory. But as Marshall had predicted, most of them were not actually expressing disloyalty but protesting the whole "registration" process—and the proof was that most of them later repudiated their repatriation requests. Perhaps the government actually expected, absurdly, that if there had been any disloyal Japanese Americans, they would willingly identify themselves on a questionnaire rather than simply lying, which would have been the obvious course of action for real spies or saboteurs. But rather than discovering disloyalty, the "registration" process actually encouraged it—or at least expressions of it.

Marshall recalled one exchange he had with a "hard-boiled" young man who had initially refused to "register."

> I said: "All right, then let's put the cards on the table. You haven't registered. What's on your mind?" His reply was this: "Major, have you ever received so many kicks that you made up your mind that you wouldn't take any more? Do you know what it means to feel that your country is doing everything it can to crush your pride? Do you know what it means

---

*Public Law 405 of the 78th Congress, which President Roosevelt signed on July 1, 1944, amended the Nationality Code of the United States and established a formal process for renouncing citizenship "whenever the United States shall be in a state of war and the Attorney General shall approve such renunciation as not contrary to the interests of national defense." By April 18, 1946, the attorney general had approved renunciation requests made by 5,589 citizens in War Relocation centers, 5,461 of whom resided at Tule Lake; 1,133 of the "renunciants" eventually went to Japan. See War Relocation Authority, *The Evacuated People*, Section XI.

to get to the point where you simply can't take it?" I answered him this way: "Yes, I know what it means, and if I were in your place I would probably feel the same way. You are not going to get any more kicks if I can help it. I feel that your heart is in the right place and that you understand what you are doing and it is not our intention to cause any trouble for boys like you. So you can return to the center, and as far as I'm concerned, you don't have to register at all." He got up with a surprised look on his face and thanked me. I didn't expect to see him again, but one half hour later he was in the registration hall and was volunteering for the United States Army.[23]

The Army and the WRA had originally expected three thousand volunteers for the 442d from the "relocation centers." But answering "yes/yes" was one thing, actually volunteering for combat duty was something else altogether. After the debacle of the "registration," less than half of the quota—only 1,208 men—enlisted stateside. In many cases they had braved the opposition, vocal and physical, of their peers, as well as the disapproval of their parents.[24]

"There were friends fighting against friends, there were brothers fighting against brothers, and it was terrible," says Tom Kawaguchi, who enlisted from Topaz. "And people asked, 'Why do you want to volunteer?' I just said, 'I don't understand what the argument is. Our country is being attacked and I want to defend it. It's that simple.' They looked at me and said, 'You must have holes in your head.' "[25]

"A lot of the parents had lost everything they had worked fifty years for," said Shiro Kashino, who had already experienced freedom from the camps as a seasonal agricultural worker, "and here their sons were going to volunteer for the country that had disowned them." But Kashino, who had "no ties with Japan,"[26] especially since both of his parents had died before the war, felt he "had to do something, even though our home was a concentration camp, because it would be terrible to live our lives like that."[27] He volunteered from Minidoka because "we had to prove ourselves as Americans . . . so we could get back to a normal life again."[28] He was one of 308 recruits from Minidoka, by far the greatest number from any of the ten "relocation centers." "This was my country," he felt strongly. "I was an American."

Rudy Tokiwa, who was confined at the Poston Relocation Center with his family, also remembers asking his friends, "Do we want to live like this for the rest of our lives?" He urged them to volunteer, "not for the United States government" but "for the Japanese American people."[29] He was one of four volunteers from his "block" at Poston, and one of 236 volunteers from the center, the second highest total among the camps.

At Rohwer, Takashi "Tak" Senzaki went to the community recreation hall to meet with Army recruiters. "There weren't too many people at that meeting," he remembers—only about two dozen potential volunteers. But Senzaki was going to sign up anyway. When he got home, he broke the news to his parents. Senzaki remembers his mother was "sad," but didn't say anything. But his father said, "This is your country, so you do what you think is right. Whatever you do, don't bring shame to the family name." Only forty men volunteered from Rohwer, the lowest number from any of the "relocation centers," and only forty-two, the second lowest number, from nearby Jerome, where Young Oak Kim visited.* Joe Nishimoto, whose family had been "relocated" from Fresno to Jerome, volunteered from Marion, Ohio, where he had subsequently gone to live with his in-laws. He and his brother-in-law, Sam Ishida, entered the service together. They would eventually fight side by side, in not only the same platoon but the same squad.

Many volunteers instinctively understood the coercion behind the government's call for volunteers who had no other freedom of choice. It was "like rubbing salt into wounds," according to Ernest Uno, who nonetheless enlisted from the Amache Relocation Center. "President Roosevelt's announcement to allow AJAs [Americans of Japanese ancestry] to volunteer was hypocritical."[30] Don Matsuda, who was at Heart Mountain, says he volunteered because he "felt that was the only way we could keep from getting kicked out and sent to Japan." He adds, "You know, nobody ever talks and says that kind of thing. When you're young, you just like to

---

*The number of volunteers from each of the ten "relocation centers" is from War Relocation Authority, *Semi-Annual Report*, January 1–June 30, 1943:

Central Utah (Topaz): 116	Jerome: 42
Colorado River (Poston): 236	Manzanar: 100
Gila River: 101	Minidoka: 308
Granada (Amache): 152	Rohwer: 40
Heart Mountain: 54	Tule Lake: 59

kid around. So we never said anything about why we volunteered."[31] Shiro Takeshita, another volunteer from Poston, recalls the "blinding dust storms and unbearable heat" of the Arizona desert. "In retrospect, it wasn't so difficult to volunteer from this insufferable situation."[32]

But Frank Seto, a boxer who had turned professional before the war, actually had found it difficult. He remembers a lengthy and frustrating series of attempts to volunteer:

> Before the war, I volunteered for the army. When they found out that I had a perforated eardrum, they rejected me. When the war started, I volunteered again, but they wouldn't take me because they classified me 4C, which was classified as an enemy alien. Later in 1942 when I was in Glasgow, Montana, topping sugar beets, my foreman informed me that they were forming the 442d. So I volunteered again at camp in Jerome, Arkansas, where they finally let me in and sent me to Camp Shelby, Mississippi.[33]

Five of the six brothers in the Masaoka family wound up in the 442d. One had been drafted before the war, three had enlisted from their homes outside of the "exclusionary zone," where they had been spared "relocation," and another had volunteered from the Manzanar Relocation Center. One of the brothers, Mike Masaoka, a leader of the JACL, spoke for all of them in defining what he called the "Japanese American Creed":

> Because I believe in America, and I trust she believes in me, and because I have received innumerable benefits from her, I pledge myself to do honor to her at all times and in all places; to support her Constitution; to obey her laws; to respect her flag; to defend her against all enemies, foreign or domestic; to actively assume my duties and obligations as a citizen, cheerfully and without any reservations whatsoever, in the hope that I may become a better American in a greater America.[34]

Even at the time, the hyperpatriotic language embarrassed or offended many Japanese Americans, especially since Masaoka and the JACL—whose membership, as the organization's name made clear, excluded the *Issei* generation, who were not citizens—had played a role in the "evacuation" and "relocation" that struck some as having crossed the line from cooperation to collaboration.* And the sentiments expressed in "the Japanese American Creed" did not begin to express the varied and complex reasons and motives young men (and a few women, who entered the Women's Army Corps) had for volunteering.

Yet Masaoka had identified the key issue: "duties and obligations as a citizen." It was grossly unfair, but even though the government had taken away their rights and privileges, the responsibilities of citizenship still remained for Japanese Americans, even in the camps.[†]

---

*This remains a contentious and divisive issue among Japanese Americans. Before the National Japanese American Memorial to Patriotism was dedicated in Washington, D.C., on November 9, 2000, many veterans fought to have Masaoka's name and the excerpt from his "Japanese American Creed" removed from the inscription. See http://javoice.com/intro.html and the "Lim Report" (http://javoice.com/limreport/LimTOC.htm) prepared for the national JACL.

[†]In Italy during 1945, the 442d would be attached to the 92d Infantry Division, the segregated descendent of the "colored troops" whom the abolitionist and former slave Frederick Douglass helped recruit for the Union Army during the Civil War. Among both blacks and whites, there had been resistance to the formation of "colored troops," but Douglass forcefully argued in favor of them:

> From East to West, from North to South, the sky is written all over, "NOW OR NEVER." Liberty won by white men would lose half its luster. "Who would be free themselves must strike the blow." "Better even die free, than to live slaves."
> I urge you to fly to arms, and smite with death the power that would bury the government and your liberty in the same hopeless grave.
> The case is before you. This is our golden opportunity.

After a meeting with Abraham Lincoln, Douglass described the president's candid analysis of the role of "colored troops":

> He began by saying that the employment of colored troops at all was a great gain to the colored people; that the measure could not have been successfully adopted at the beginning of the war; that the wisdom of making colored men soldiers was still doubted; that their enlistment was a serious offense to popular prejudice; that they had larger motives for being soldiers than white men; that they ought to be willing to enter the service upon any conditions. . . .
> I left in the full belief that the true course to the black man's freedom and citizenship was over the battle-field.

Lincoln's frank characterization of principle, prudence, and self-interest for "colored troops" could have applied equally well to Japanese Americans after Pearl Harbor. From *Life and Times of Frederick Douglass*, pp. 346, 353–4.

★ ★ ★

There were far more volunteers from Hawaii, where Japanese Americans had not been "relocated" or forced to "register" at gunpoint. Although the War Department had set a quota of fifteen hundred volunteers from the islands, more than ten thousand Japanese Americans—including Barney Hajiro and Daniel Inouye, who had both seen Japanese planes overhead and then black smoke rising from Pearl Harbor—answered the call to enlist when the formation of the 442d was announced. Like Hajiro, most Japanese Americans in Hawaii were poor, coming from the sugar and pineapple plantations, but "they got pride." When the 442d was announced, Hajiro continues, "If you don't go, you lose face."[35]

Isamu "Mike" Tsuji was a freshman at the University of Hawaii when the call for volunteers went out in the islands. "I was following the news and was beginning to feel that I should be doing something other than attending school," he recalls. "The U.S. was in trouble. If it lost the war, Japanese Americans in particular would be especially vulnerable."[36]

In Honolulu, four of the seven Kuroda brothers—Robert, Ronald, Wallace, and Joe—volunteered. Though Robert was a qualified electrician, he had been turned down when he tried to find work at Pearl Harbor. Since he was underage, he had to get his parents' permission to enter the service. Then, as his brother Joe told the *Honolulu Star-Bulletin* six decades later:

> Dad wouldn't sign, saying Robert already had a brother ready to enter combat. Robert turned to mother for help, and when mother asked, "Why do you want to go so badly?" Robert answered, "Because when I return from the war, Pearl Harbor Navy will have to hire me. I am an American."[37]

When the Hawaiian volunteers finally assembled on March 28, 1943, they were hailed by a crowd of fifteen thousand spectators at an official ceremony at Iolani Palace, formerly the seat of the Territorial Legislature but now the headquarters of the military government. "A delegation led by the civilian governor and others, including many who had worked toward the formation of the 442d, wished us well and 'Godspeed,'" Tsuji remembers, "Flower leis, the traditional Hawaiian farewell symbol, were distributed to all by young ladies in hula attire."

A week later, when the SS *Lurline*, a prewar luxury liner, steamed out of Honolulu Harbor, transporting the recruits to the mainland, a crowd estimated at more than ten thousand wished them *aloha*. "Very few of us, if any, had ever left the islands," says Tsuji, "so the idea of 'going to the mainland' was exciting, a great adventure, a journey into the unknown." The War Department had nearly doubled the quota from Hawaii after the disappointing turnout from the mainland. But so many men had volunteered that Daniel Inouye had barely made the cut. There were 2,686 enlistees on board the *Lurline*; he was officially number 2,685.

During the voyage across the Pacific to Oakland, spirits were high. As part of their send-off, many of the recruits had received going-away presents, "which in the Japanese community in Hawaii always translated into cash in envelopes," recalls Tsuji—usually substantial sums made up of numerous small donations from family members and friends. So nonstop craps and card games kept the troops entertained. But some of the men had less fun than others did. Barney Hajiro says he was a lousy gambler. "I always lose," he recalls, "never win in my life."[38]

Meanwhile, in the "relocation centers" on the mainland, the send-offs were more modest. Mickey Akiyama was the first of a hundred volunteers from Manzanar, and his "coworkers at the Manzanar garment factory took up a collection from their meager earnings," supplemented by contributions from his neighbors on the "block."[39] But some of the volunteers from the camps departed with no ceremony at all—sometimes alone, in the middle of the night, to avoid harassment from the "no/nos." Tak Senzaki left Rohwer, where there had been the lowest number of volunteers, at six in the morning, "all by myself." At the train station in McGehee, the clerk gave him a memorable initiation into the ways of the Jim Crow South: "You see that sign over there that says 'white'? Whenever you do anything, go to the one that says 'white.' "[40]

At Tule Lake, a 442d volunteer had found a separate table reserved for him in the communal mess hall. There was a bone lying there, and he was greeted with a Japanese curse: "Dogs eat here."[41]

★ ★ ★

In April 1943, three months after he had traveled with Army teams during the "registration" process and just as the volunteers for the 442d from Hawaii were sailing to the mainland, S. L. A. Marshall, now a colonel, reported to the General Staff on "an investigation" he had undertaken of "the situation at Camp Shelby, Mississippi."[42] The Army was concerned about racial conflict at the camp and in the neighboring town of Hattiesburg. White and black troops had clashed at other training centers in the South. And military personnel from the North, both white and black, were often unaccustomed to dealing with the constraints of Jim Crow.

The appearance of the 100th Battalion (Separate) more than two months earlier—just before Young Oak Kim had reported for duty—had introduced a new element into the racial mix at Camp Shelby. Marshall praised the men of the battalion for their exemplary behavior. They had "won for all Japanese Americans the friendly regard of a majority in the community and within the camp." He also cited "a better than average discipline and state of contentment in the Negro troops within this command and a friendly interest on their part in the Japanese Americans as another minority group."

But he also warned of local "house owners refusing to rent to Japanese," "Caucasian girls declining to dance with Japanese American soldiers at the USO," and "uncouth treatment of the Japanese Americans by some of the local M.P.s [military policemen]." Though the men of the 100th, and later the 442d, were eventually "extended the same hospitality as any white soldier" at the USO, Marshall continued, housing remained "extremely scarce in the Hattiesburg area, and it is to be expected that the white population will prefer not to rent to Japanese families."

Most of all, Marshall, a former newspaperman, criticized the Army's "faulty public relations strategy whereby all news of the Japanese troops is bottled by the War Department, thus surrounding them with an air of mystery and creating the suspicion that they are not to be trusted and that the unit has a sinister character." A local newspaper editor had pleaded with the authorities "to be allowed to say that this fine organization was at Camp Shelby" but was "turned down flat in spite of the fact that the town's people were seeing the American Japanese on the streets every evening."[43]

★ ★ ★

Despite Marshall's investigation, the Army was unprepared for one source of conflict—the different experiences and expectations of the Hawaiian and the mainland Japanese Americans.

The Hawaiians came to Camp Shelby buoyed by a shared sense of purpose and commitment. Most of them had grown up in plantation communities that were segregated by ethnic and national origin—Japanese, Chinese, Portuguese, Filipino—and thus reinforced strong group identities.* By contrast, although some mainland Japanese Americans lived in "Japan Towns" in large cities on the West Coast, just as many had grown up in isolated rural communities. "The difference was that we were the minority in the States," says Manabi Hirasaki, a volunteer from Grand Junction, Colorado, "and they were the majority in Hawaii."[44]

The Japanese Americans from the islands also dressed, spoke, and acted very differently from their stateside counterparts. When he first met the men of the 100th Battalion (Separate), Young Oak Kim had noted:

> These were not Japanese Americans in the true sense, and they were not
> Asians as I knew them on the mainland. They were Asians who wanted
> to be Hawaiians. They exhibited all the traits of a Polynesian culture
> rather than an Asian culture.

They had a "wonderful spirit," Kim recalls. They were generous, gregarious, and fiercely loyal to their "bruddahs." And they actually did wear brightly colored floral patterned shirts, untucked. They really did play ukuleles and go barefoot, just as they always had gone on the plantations.[45] (Having to wear boots "was the biggest problem" for the Hawaiians, says Don Seki, a volunteer from Oahu.[46])

When a Hawaiian Japanese American walked into a bar in Hattiesburg, he would buy all his buddies a round of beers. He couldn't understand why a mainlander would be off in a corner, nursing a drink by himself. What the Hawaiians didn't understand was that the mainlander had probably come from a "relocation center" where he had been making fourteen dollars a month. Now he was saving most of his Army pay, twenty-one dollars a month for a private, to send back to his parents in the camps.

The Hawaiian Japanese Americans, by contrast, had left Hawaii with large bankrolls. And some of them had turned their stakes into small

---

*This was the same kind of ethnic identification found in the separate turfs—physical and otherwise—of Irish Americans and Italian Americans who were neighbors in the Bronx. Their primary group allegiance was to their "own kind" in America, not to distant relatives across the ocean.

fortunes. Inouye ran a craps game and "cleaned up." "I was averaging $1,500 a month," he recalled, at a time when that was forty percent more than the annual per capita personal income of a civilian.[47] In fact, the Hawaiians were spending so much money on gambling, liquor, and entertainment that news of their profligacy in Mississippi reached as far away as Honolulu and Washington, D.C. Higher-ups in the WRA and the Army, as well as the Japanese community in Hawaii, discreetly urged the commanders of the 442d to rein in their troops for their own good.[48]

But the recruits thought little and understood less about their cultural, sociological, and economic differences. All the Hawaiians knew was that the mainlanders were cheap, aloof, and, to their way of thinking, affected. "Hawaii guys make lots of trouble and drink beer," Hajiro says today. They were "happy-go-lucky" and liked "getting drunk and playing ukulele." To Hajiro and his buddies, mainlanders were "boy scouts."

For their part, the mainlanders thought the Hawaiians were clannish, ill-mannered, and uneducated. And they literally could not understand the soldiers from the islands. Almost all of the Hawaiians spoke rapid-fire pidgin—the common parlance of the plantation camps, a mixture of English, Japanese, Chinese, Portuguese, Filipino, and Hawaiian.* To mainlanders' ears, it sounded like gibberish. "Ass why" meant "that's the reason." "Funny kine" meant "strange." "Cool head main ting" meant "no big deal." "S'koshi" meant "a little bit." "No talk stink" meant "don't speak ill of someone behind his back."[49]

And "when the Hawaiians came over, everybody had a nickname," recalls Christopher Keegan, recently assigned to the 442d as a "ninety-day wonder" in command of a heavy weapons company. "Some guys called another guy 'Papoose.' Who the hell was 'Papoose'? Who was 'Big Boy'? Or 'Short Stuff'?" The Hawaiians seemed to have lots of "weird names that didn't fit the guys. The guy called 'Big Boy' wasn't big."[50]

---

*In linguistics, a pidgin is a simplified speech enabling communication among groups with different languages (as opposed to a creole, which evolves out of a pidgin and becomes the native speech of a group). As strange as it sounded to mainland ears at the time (and still sounds today), pidgin was actually a sign of "Americanization," an indication that Japanese Americans in Hawaii were moving beyond their parents' Japanese (which was still typically used at home and within the first-generation immigrant community). Today's speakers of what is still called pidgin in Hawaii are, according to linguists, actually employing a creole.

To the Hawaiians, however, the mainlanders' standard English made them sound like *haoles*—white people, like Keegan. They sounded as if they were putting on airs. "They talk good English," Hajiro remembers, and the only people he and most of his fellow Hawaiians knew who spoke that way were their white plantation bosses. George Oiye, who had volunteered from his home state of Montana, where his family was the only Japanese American family for hundreds of miles, remembers being singled out for ridicule by the Hawaiians for the way he talked. They called him "Whitey."*

But Oiye and the rest of the mainlanders quickly mastered one phrase of pidgin. "Like beef?" was an invitation to fight. Brawls frequently broke out between the two groups, and the mainlanders found out the hard way that taking on one Hawaiian meant taking on all of his friends too. One night, a mainlander named Yuki Minaga "said or did something that offended the Hawaii guys," recalls Susumu Ito, whose sisters and parents were in the Rohwer Relocation Center. "After lights went out, curfew time, the Hawaii men sneaked in quietly" and started pummeling Minaga as he lay in his bunk. "I had to do something," Ito remembers thinking, "so I got up and tried to yank the fellow off who was beating Minaga. Then they started beating me up. We got bruised up pretty bad."[51] Recognizing that they needed to watch one another's back, the three mainlanders—Ito, Minaga, and Oiye—started a friendship that would sustain them through the darkest nights ahead.

The Hawaiians soon made up a name for their adversaries—*kotonks*, after the sound of coconuts splitting open. It was also the sound of mainlanders' heads hitting the ground. The mainlanders were just as quick to call the islanders "Buddhaheads"—not just a religious reference but a play on the word *buta*, Japanese for "pig."

★ ★ ★

But the roots of their conflict were military as well as cultural. "There was a lot of animosity," says Ito, "for good reason." Some of the Hawaiians

---

*The conflict between the two groups of Japanese Americans at Camp Shelby may remind contemporary readers of the division among African Americans between "acting white" and "keeping it real." But for all their disparagement of mainlanders as "white," Japanese Americans from Hawaii were about as authentically Japanese as contemporary "gangstas" are genuinely African.

had been through ROTC at the University of Hawaii and expected to command companies. Others "thought they were going to be the sergeants and noncoms," says Keegan. But "the skeleton force was already there, all we had to do was fit the pieces in."[52] Before any of the volunteers had arrived, either from the mainland or Hawaii, the cadre of officers and noncoms for the 442d had been filled by soldiers already in the service stateside, such as Keegan, who became commander of M Company, a heavy weapons company.

Many of the noncoms in the cadre were Japanese Americans who had already been in the Army on the mainland before Pearl Harbor. Unlike Japanese Americans in Hawaii, who had been concentrated in the 298th and 299th Infantry Regiments of the Hawaiian National Guard before the 100th Battalion was formed, Japanese Americans stateside had been integrated as individuals throughout the service. Now many of them had been transferred from their units and sent to Camp Shelby. One of them was Jack Wakamatsu, who had been drafted in 1940 and had served in the Seventh Army at Fort Ord, California, under "Vinegar Joe" Stilwell. Wakatmatsu's family was in Manzanar. His family's farm in Venice had been left in the care of a Caucasian business associate, who promised to use the profits from sharecroppers on the land to cover expenses and pay taxes.

Another was Sus Ito, who had also been drafted in 1940. Growing up in Stockton, he had always felt like a "second-class citizen." When he had tried to find work as an auto mechanic after attending trade school, the union denied him membership. In the Army after Pearl Harbor, he was not permitted to carry a gun at Fort Sill, Oklahoma. "They could have hired a bunch of civilians" to do the "totally nonmilitary" work he was assigned. "I hated it," he remembers thinking. "The war's going on—what are we doing sitting here?" When he heard about the 100th, he says, "I wished I was with them."[53]

Then, in early 1943, "the scuttlebutt was that we were going to Mississippi," Ito remembers, "but we didn't know why we were going there." Because of his mechanical background, Ito wound up as a sergeant in charge of trucks in the service company of the 522d Field Artillery Battalion, a support unit of the 442d Regimental Combat Team. But all he could think was "Here I am fixing trucks again—this isn't going to be like being in the war."

Although their mother was "very proud" he was in the Army, Ito was the family's only son. So she warned him, "Don't volunteer for anything. If necessary, go to jail." But Ito had an "overpowering urge to see what the war was really like." So without telling his parents, he volunteered to serve as a forward observer for the 522d, right on the front line alongside the riflemen, calling in artillery fire. "I had always thought I would probably not get killed," Ito says simply. "I didn't think my number was up."

"At the time, I had no thoughts about trying to prove myself," he says today, "but in the end it turned out to be that." While at Camp Shelby, Ito would travel from Mississippi to see his parents and sisters in Rohwer. Though he was in uniform, as Young Oak Kim had been when visiting nearby Jerome, Ito had to show his pass to gain entrance. And once past the armed guards at the gate, he was struck by the "stark and unforgiving" scene before him—the barbed wire, the watchtowers, the dirt roads, and the black tar-paper barracks.

"To see how they lived there was shocking," Ito remembers. "What my mother wrote to me really didn't convey what it looked like." His father, mother, and two sisters lived in a single room with a potbellied stove. "We put up sheets to divide the room into living and sleeping quarters," his sister Sachi remembers.[54] Ito was "depressed" to see "families lining up in mess halls to eat. Even more degrading was the common bathroom facilities with no walls between them."

But "it was always a very special occasion" when he came to visit, his sister recalls. "Our mother would always have a royal welcome for him." "For the most part, they had accepted this as their fate," Ito remembers. "As unjust as it was then and seemed to them to be, it was a consequence of the time." To Ito, the Japanese Americans in the camps "made the most of the limited situation. Being bitter about it wasn't going to resolve the issue." Ito was determined he "wasn't going to be a victim."

★ ★ ★

Some of the tensions between the *kotonks* and the Buddhaheads began to abate after Col. Charles W. Pence, a World War I veteran who was now the commander of the 442d, arranged for groups of soldiers to visit Rohwer and Jerome. (Later, groups of civilians from the "relocation centers" would also visit Camp Shelby.) Each of the companies sent ten men, all from the islands—"just by coincidence," Daniel Inouye says, with the hindsight of sixty years. "So here we are with our ukuleles and guitars," Inouye recalls, "singing all the way from Mississippi to Arkansas."[55]

They were "so funny," remembers Ikuko Nakao, who had been "relocated" from Terminal Island to Rohwer and whose sister, Kikuko, had left to marry Jerry Tanamachi. Some of the Buddhaheads performed a hula for the young women in the camp. But though the Hawaiians seemed exotic to their hosts, the "relocation center" was even more of a surprise to the Buddhaheads. Expecting nothing but a dinner, a dance, and a good time, the Hawaiians were even more unprepared than Ito had been for what they saw.

Their hosts at Rohwer had set aside extra rations and invited the soldiers to stay with families in the barracks. But "we said no," Inouye remembers. "We tried our best to be happy," and instead slept in the trucks from Camp Shelby, in the mess halls, even outdoors.

On the way home, "the mood on the trucks was different. No one sang. There was no conversation, not a word, just quiet," Inouye remembers.

> It was all mind boggling. . . . The thing that went through my mind constantly was: "I wonder what I would have done. Would I have volunteered?" We [Hawaiians] volunteered from a community that was generous. We weren't herded away. But these guys were herded into camps like this, and they volunteered.

The 442d "was not formed when we volunteered, nor when we arrived in Camp Shelby," Inouye declares. "It was formed after this visit. We were blood brothers."[56]

It was an experience that helped unite the otherwise divided *Nisei*. Robert Katayama, who had volunteered out of Farrington High School in Honolulu, was one of the Hawaiians who visited the Jerome Relocation Center. They "passed the word around" after they got back, he recalls. "I think that brought about a better understanding between the two groups."[57] "It opened their eyes," Ito says, to see the living conditions at the center. "I was pissed off for the relocation guys," Barney Hajiro remembers. "In Hawaii we don't have that stuff."[58]

"The cadre and the Hawaiians meshed together," says Keegan. "The team that really became famous was being built because of that."[59] The men's understanding of the fate they shared not just with their fellow soldiers but with everyone in the "relocation centers" helped give birth to the spirit of loyalty and self-sacrifice that military historians call "unit cohesion."

What the Army had to create in other troops—the willingness to die for the man in the foxhole next to you—already stretched through the fabric of relationships among the Japanese American soldiers. "I liked the idea of a segregated unit because it would feel more like home," says Manabi Hirasaki. "I felt as though I could depend on my friends more."[60] Some, like the Masaokas, were literally brothers. Many more were cousins or distant relatives, or, in the numerically small immigrant community, neighbors or acquaintances. "I knew all the fellows from San Francisco and from the Bay Area," recalls Tom Kawaguchi, who volunteered from Topaz. "We kind of felt like brothers. We really looked after each other. There was an unspoken trust between us that was evident constantly." All were highly motivated to demonstrate their loyalty. "We had a chance as a unit to prove something," Kashino said. "Individually, I don't think we could have made a name for ourselves."[61]

By concentrating Japanese Americans in the 100th and 442d, the Army had unwittingly created what amounted to elite fighting units. Most of them volunteers, older and better educated than the average troops (with even the most highly qualified serving as riflemen because they had been barred from transferring to specialized units), and highly motivated, the *Nisei* soldiers were more like the newly formed Rangers, modeled after the British Commandos, than like ordinary infantry outfits. "I knew we had something special when we finished cadre training," Keegan says, "because these people were so devoted to what they did."[62]

* * *

Still, although the *kotonks* and Buddhaheads had a common country of origin, what they actually shared was not any particular quality of being Japanese American, much less Japanese, but the experience—shared by most American-born children of immigrants—of being torn between loyalty to their elders and rejection of their immigrant ways. Japanese Americans were more like the younger DiMaggios or Greenbergs than they were like their own distant cousins or aunts or uncles or grandparents in Japan. "I felt that this was my country," says Kawaguchi. "I didn't know any other country."[63]

Like teenagers and young adults everywhere, the *Nisei* took their cultural cues—along with their language, whether mainland American English or pidgin—from their peers, not from their parents, the *Issei*. So much so, in fact, that the Buddhaheads in particular found laughable the idea that their loyalty was to Japan, not America. "How can we be spies for them when we can't even speak Japanese?" Stanley Akita remembers thinking. "They wouldn't understand our pidgin anyway—nobody does."[64]

The younger generation played baseball, chased members of the opposite sex, tinkered with cars, listened to big band music on the radio, played hooky from school.* Although the Western Defense Command asserted without evidence that Japanese Americans were "a tightly-knit, unassimilated racial group,"[65] the distinguished sociologists Robert Park and Herbert Miller had concluded years earlier that Japanese Americans were "capable of transforming their lives and practices more rapidly than any other immigrant group." The *Issei*, they noted, "are not citizens, but their children are and they wish them to be. They are anxious to break up their own colonies, to engage in all sorts of occupations, to acquire American manners, and to get education—all with the motive of adapting themselves to this country."[66]

---

*Like many immigrant groups, the first generation of Japanese Americans tried to pass on the culture of their native land to the younger generation. Just as Jewish immigrants from Eastern Europe sent their children to yeshivas, many *Issei* parents sent their children to Japanese language schools and courses of instruction with Shinto priests. But all the veterans I interviewed regarded their schooling in Japanese language, religion, and culture as a burden they endured for their parents' sake. (And significant numbers of both generations had already converted to Christianity.) To a man, they said they would rather have been playing baseball or doing anything else besides studying what they saw as their parents' culture. Although the number of students in Japanese language and religious schools was regarded as evidence that Japanese Americans were not "assimilating," in fact it was most likely evidence of the opposite—an attempt by the *Issei* to preserve a culture they saw as disappearing among their children. In its volume *Wartime Exile*, pp. 47–49, the WRA cited scholars who agreed that the accusation that Japanese language schools "foster anti-American ideas" was "without basis," and that the effort to "impart a knowledge" of the language was a "relative failure."

When Daniel Inouye disagreed with one of his Shinto instructors, he was "half-dragged, half-carried" to the door by the teacher, who threw him "with full force into the schoolyard," calling him "a faithless dog." Inouye's parents allowed him to drop out of Japanese school—and as a result, he says, "for the first time, I suppose, I knew what it was to feel like an American." (*Journey to Washington*, p. 38.)

But decades of restrictive immigration policies, alien land laws, organized opposition from unions and civic organizations, a hostile press, nativist harassment, and the war had made even more arduous the typical—and typically difficult—process of economic, then cultural, and finally political integration followed by all Americans, ever since the days of the first settlers.

"I was not specifically conscious that I was Japanese," recalls Ted Tsukiyama, who grew up in Honolulu. In school, he had studied the Constitution, memorized the Gettysburg Address, and even played John Alden in a school play—getting into the spirit of someone whose "ancestors came over on the *Mayflower*." Tsukiyama had "Japanese eyes, an American heart." As he puts it, "I'm not a Japanese living in America. I'm an American who happened to be of Japanese ancestry." But Pearl Harbor made him realize that white people thought, "You're not one of us—we can't trust you." It was a "tremendous shock."[67]

For the men of the 442d, many of whom were under twenty-one and therefore too young to vote, volunteering was their first, and would be their most significant, political act. It expressed something more basic than ethnic or cultural identity or patriotism. It declared not what made them different from other Americans but what they had in common with them. At a time when their citizenship was in question, volunteering for the Army was their affirmation of citizenship and their acceptance of its responsibilities. Whatever their individual motives and reasons might have been, collectively their actions spoke louder than their words. Before they became recognized as heroes, as they would be, the men of the 442d acted as citizens first, even though their government did not fully acknowledge them as such—and even though they often had to overcome the opposition of their parents and peers.*

---

*The political scientist Eliot Cohen correctly points out that "in the liberal state, a man is a citizen prior to military service, not because of it." (*Citizens and Soldiers: The Dilemmas of Military Service*, p. 123.) But citizenship, which had been denied the *Issei* generation for decades, was also effectively taken away from the *Nisei* generation by Executive Order 9066. This had the effect of reversing the priority and making their citizenship depend on military service. The coerciveness of the "registration" consisted precisely in demanding loyalty of people who could not become citizens (the *Issei*) and of people (the *Nisei*) who had to offer themselves up to the military, as no other citizens had to, before their full citizenship was acknowledged by their own government.

"There was democracy going on right in [the 'relocation'] camp, in spite of the enclosure," says Kawaguchi. "A 'no/no' answer was all part of the democratic process . . . somebody else had his choice and I had my choice."[68] The vast majority of Japanese Americans were acting like good citizens simply by obeying the law and acceding to government control of their lives, just or unjust, whether it was martial law in Hawaii or the "evacuation" and "relocation" on the mainland. A small minority, regardless of how tainted their motives were, exercised one right that had not been taken away from them: the right of free speech, of protesting what they regarded as unfair treatment. And the smallest minority stepped forward and assumed the ultimate duty of citizenship: serving their country and risking their lives in war.

Even though it had been the Army that had "evacuated" the Japanese Americans from the West Coast, it was also the Army that had provided them with the opportunity to affirm their citizenship. In a letter to Hirasaki's father, Colonel Pence wrote:

> To you I extend my congratulations. By your sacrifice you have enabled him to enlist voluntarily, and become a symbol of the loyalty and patriotism of our Japanese American population. Without compulsion or persuasion he made the brave and manly choice to fight for the American way of life. He freely chose to exercise the responsibilities of his citizenship.
>
> I am sure that you are proud of the soldier you have given us. With him, and others like him, we shall make a glorious record for the Japanese Americans in our country.[69]

To the *Nisei* soldiers, dealing with Caucasian officers "who looked at them as no different from any other," says Tsuji, "was a never-to-be-forgotten experience." It was "an experience that would make considerable impressions on them, not only in combat, but also later in life," Tsuji states. "They were learning what it was like to be treated as 'equals.' "[70]

During training, Lt. Col. James M. Hanley, commander of the 2d Battalion of the 442d, overheard a reporter ask one of the Buddhaheads, "What has impressed you the most about your training here?"

> "They are trying to teach us to stay alive," came the answer without hesitation.

Although the reporter might have been surprised by the reply he did not pursue the matter further in my hearing. I thought a great deal about that remark. Why should he be surprised we were trying to teach him to stay alive on the battlefield? Why should that be the most important thing he learned?

Later, Hanley spoke to enlisted men, officers, and the 2d Battalion chaplain, Hiro Higuchi.

I found that many Japanese families in Hawaii, particularly those in rural areas in the outlying islands, lived in a more homogenous society which held to the "old ways," philosophy, and mores. In Japan the family was expected to "give a son" for the emperor, and he was not necessarily expected to return. So when the young man understood that we, the officers and instructors, expected him to survive, he was surprised.[71]

The men of the 442d were truly becoming citizen soldiers, in their understanding that combat would test not just their military strength but their civic commitment—as well as their country's responsibility to them.*

★ ★ ★

In May 1943, Assistant Secretary of War McCloy, a prime mover behind both the "evacuation" the previous year and the formation of the 442d, candidly admitted "there no longer existed any military necessity for the continued exclusion of all Japanese from the evacuated zone."[72] But there was no decision to end the "exclusion" and allow Japanese Americans to return to the West Coast. Most of the "evacuees" would remain in the "relocation camps" for another year and a half or more.

In June, while the 442d was beginning its training, the 100th Battalion (Separate) returned to Camp Shelby after two months of maneuvers in

---

*According to the sociologist Morris Janowitz, in institutions such as the American Army, "conscripts and civilian reservists are defined as citizens rather than 'mere' subjects. Citizenship focuses on the balance of individual rights versus the prerogatives of the state and its leaders." In other words, it is not just what individuals do for the state, but what the state does for individuals. (Janowitz, "Military Institutions and Citizenship in Western Societies," in *Military Conflict*.)

Louisiana. A month later, on July 20, the battalion received its colors and readied itself for battle. The Army heraldic section had proposed an emblem with a red dagger and the motto "Be of Good Cheer." Both of these had struck the men of the 100th as ridiculous. After some back and forth, the emblem was changed to a shield featuring the helmet worn by Hawaiian chieftains and the traditional *ape* leaf used to ward off evil spirits. The motto, which the men of the 100th had surely earned because of the surprise attack on their homeland, was "Remember Pearl Harbor."

Over the following year, the 442d would earn its own colors. The quartermaster general had originally submitted a design showing "a red and white bomb-burst behind a yellow gauntleted arm holding a sword white and red."[73] Until the officers of the 442d vigorously protested, it apparently had not occurred to the Army how the symbolism could have been misconstrued as the yellow-skinned arm of a Japanese soldier brandishing a bloody weapon against the backdrop of the attack on Pearl Harbor. McCloy asked Colonel Pence to come up with a new design.

The emblem finally approved would be a hand holding the torch of liberty against a blue crest surrounded by red and white stripes. And the motto of the 442d would be "Go for Broke," pidgin gambling slang for "shoot the works."*

---

*Fred Ryoso Hamaishi remembers "all first sergeants being asked to submit possible mottos for the 442d." Though "many submitted mottos in Latin," Hamaishi suggested "Go for Broke." "This phrase reminded me of one my parents always used whenever older brothers started fighting, *makete katsu*, 'win in losing.'" (Hamaishi, oral history in *And Then There Were Eight*, p. 150.)

3

"WHAT WE'RE FIGHTING FOR"

Draftees and Replacements

The well-publicized bravery, dedication, and brilliant achievements of the 442d Regimental Combat Team aroused the admiration of the American public at the time and brought home the fact that Japanese Americans, too, were loyal citizens and could and would fight for our country at least as well as any others. . . . It is not too much to say that within the space of a few months this small military unit convinced most Americans of their individual merit as citizens.—GEN. MARK W. CLARK[1]

Mississippi, Florida, Italy, and the "Relocation Camps," January–August 1944

When the formation of the 442d was first announced in early 1943, George "Joe" Sakato was living in Glendale, Arizona. He had moved there from Colton, California, in San Bernardino County, where his family ran a butcher shop and fruit stand.[2]

While he was growing up, everyone called him "Joe." But when he was old enough to understand, he learned his father had thought the name was spelled "Geo," which he had seen in newspapers. He gave that spelling for his son's birth certificate, where it was treated as an abbreviation for "George." So "George" it was, but only for official purposes.

During the brief period of "voluntary evacuation" in early 1942, the Sakatos had moved their family from California to Arizona, where relatives of their older daughter's husband lived. They had packed whatever they could fit into a truck belonging to a fruit and vegetable contractor who had offered to help them move. Though they had just bought a new meat cooler for eight hundred dollars, the pressure of leaving on such short notice forced the family to sell it to predatory buyers for only five hundred dollars—and, as Sakato puts it, "they had to throw in the rest of the store as well."

In Glendale, northwest of Phoenix, they had settled south of the railroad tracks. According to the War Department's arbitrary mapping of the "exclusionary zone" in Arizona, Japanese Americans living on one side of the tracks had to be "evacuated" and "relocated" to the Poston center in the Colorado River Valley, more than 150 miles away, while those on the other side could continue to live and work where they were.

During a brief stint as a farmhand in Arizona, Sakato had lost twenty-five pounds, so he decided he should look for another job. He was working in a grocery store when he first heard about the 442d. Taking it as a sign that the military in general would be open to Japanese Americans, Sakato volunteered for the Army Air Force. "I always wanted to be a pilot," he says. He had fond memories of going to an airfield in San Bernardino County, where a World War I veteran would fly local kids around the countryside in an old Curtiss JN-4D "Jenny" biplane. Sakato would sell newspapers and deliver *The Saturday Evening Post* for weeks until he had saved a dollar to pay for a flight.

But the Army had segregated Japanese Americans in the 442d precisely because they were still unwelcome elsewhere in the military. So Sakato returned to the grocery store. It would be another year before he entered the service.

★ ★ ★

By the summer of 1944, the question of Japanese Americans' loyalty should have been answered once and for all. Japanese Americans such as Ted Tsukiyama, who had "Japanese eyes, an American heart," had entered the Military Intelligence Service, some of them as early as the summer of 1942, and had been distinguishing themselves in the China-Burma-India theater, under Lt. Gen. "Vinegar Joe" Stilwell, and in the Pacific theater. The registration in the "relocation centers," including the divisive loyalty questions, was a year and a half in the past, and the "no/no" boys had been "segregated" at Tule Lake. And during the preceding two years, more than thirty thousand Japanese American civilians who had qualified for temporary or permanent "leave clearance" had left the camps for the Army or for jobs and for new places to live, everywhere around the country except for the "exclusionary zones" in California, Oregon, Washington, and Arizona.*

Meanwhile, the volunteers for the 442d from the mainland and from Hawaii had finished a year in training at Camp Shelby. "They couldn't wait to go" to war and follow in the footsteps of the 100th, Christopher Keegan remembers. "Everybody in the regiment was following what they were doing in Italy. Some of them had brothers and cousins in the 100th. They got a firsthand accounting of what combat was like."[3] Attached to the 36th "Texas" Division, the 442d had followed the 100th to Italy in May 1944. And the two factions within the 442d were joining together as well. Before the troops left the States, the Buddhaheads who had attacked Yuki Minaga and Sus Ito in the barracks at Camp Shelby were identified. But the two *kotonks* decided the chief harm had been to their pride. The mainlanders and the Hawaiians shook hands and agreed to "take it out on the Germans."

Since January 1944, Japanese Americans had also been drafted from the "relocation centers," mostly without incident, from the rest of the mainland, and from Hawaii, and were now in training at Fort Blanding, Florida, and at Camp Shelby. And other Japanese American soldiers who had already been serving individually in nonsegregated Army units were assembling as replacement troops for the 100th and 442d.

★ ★ ★

Most important of all, the 100th Battalion (Separate) had been performing heroically in combat in Italy for the preceding nine months. The battalion had left for Oran, North Africa, on August 21, 1943. A month later it had joined the 34th "Red Bull" Division, part of the American Fifth Army under Lt. Gen. Mark Clark, formerly of the General Staff, who had

---

*As of the beginning of 1944, 20,682 "leaves" had been granted, and the number steadily increased throughout the year. See Capt. Clarence R. Herbert, Chief, Japanese-American Branch, memo to Col. Alton C. Miller, January 10, 1944, Archives II, RG 389. By August, the number had reached more than 30,000. As of that date, the "number of Japanese already relocated by the War Relocation Authority" was 28,503. There had been 1,208 volunteers for the Army a year and a half earlier, and draftees had started leaving the camps in early 1944. See Maj. Gen. C. H. Bonesteel, memo to Chief of Staff, War Department, August 8, 1944, Archives II, RG 499.

argued against the "relocation" of Japanese Americans from the West Coast.

For the next year, Clark was the battalion's most enthusiastic sponsor. Taking a personal interest from the moment the 100th entered combat, Clark had cabled Gen. Dwight D. Eisenhower that the "efficiency" of the battalion was "very good" in its initial encounter with the enemy. The men displayed a "quick reaction to hostile opposition." He noted the troops had "employed all available weapons unhesitatingly.... Personnel well be-haved and accepted with friendliness and confidence by all ranks." Most tellingly, Clark remarked, "Hospitalization from sickness practically nil as men prefer to remain with command. Morale high."[4]

This was the just the first, and the least, of the praise the men of the 100th earned during the Italian campaign, from the fall of 1943 through the summer of 1944. Right after Thanksgiving, on November 29, the bat-talion ran into a fierce firefight on Hill 841, near Cerasuolo. A heavily armed contingent of Germans attacked the left flank of B Company, where a platoon including Sgt. Allan M. Ohata and Pvt. Mikio Hasemoto made a heroic stand. The two men killed twenty of the charging Germans, with Hasemoto emptying four magazines of his BAR (Browning Auto-matic Rifle) before it was damaged by enemy fire. Disregarding his own safety, Ohata ran fifteen yards to cover Hasemoto's dash to pick up an-other BAR. They then continued firing until Hasemoto's newly retrieved weapon jammed. Dodging a machine-gun barrage, Hasemoto picked up an M1 and, with Ohata, took out another ten Germans. Hasemoto and Ohata held their ground against yet another assault, shooting seven more enemy soldiers. The two then charged against the remaining Germans and captured three prisoners.

In an A Company offensive on Hill 841 during the same day, Pvt. Shizuya Hayashi made a one-man attack "in the face of grenade, rifle, and machine gun fire," according to a citation issued later.[5] "Firing his auto-matic rifle from the hip, he charged and overtook an enemy machine-gun position, killing seven men in the nest and two more as they fled." After a German 88 opened up on his platoon, Hayashi returned fire and single-handedly killed nine Germans, took four prisoners, and forced the re-maining troops to retreat.

The next day, Hasemoto and Ohata continued to hold their ground "with grim determination," as a later citation put it.[6] But enemy fire killed

Hasemoto while they were repelling yet another attack. It would be nearly six decades before the heroism of Hasemoto, Ohata, and Hayashi was properly acknowledged.*

In the grim winter and spring that followed, the 100th Battalion (Separate) went on to prove its worth in some of the bloodiest battles of the war, including Cassino and Anzio. It was "one of the most valuable units in the Fifth Army," according to Clark. "These Nisei troops seemed to be very conscious of the fact that they had an opportunity to prove the loyalty of many thousands of Americans of Japanese ancestry and they willingly paid a high price to achieve that goal."[7] Clark was "proud to have them in the Fifth Army."

Clark had singled out Young Oak Kim for praise as an "able and hard-boiled" warrior.[8] Kim and his campfire buddy from Camp Shelby, Sakae Takahashi, captain of B Company, had emerged as natural leaders, inspiring their troops with their intelligence and daring. The men of the 100th had not called their Korean American officer "GI Kim" for many months. Now he was "Samurai Kim," and they could always spot him in combat. In winter and summer, through mortar barrages and machine-gun fire, he wore just a knit cap on his head. He reasoned that the silhouette of his helmet was an invitation to snipers—that it was better not to get shot at in the first place than to hope your helmet would stop a bullet.

By early 1944, casualties had reduced the 100th by more than half, earning it the nickname of "the Purple Heart Battalion." In late January, Clark warned his superiors that "additional losses . . . have reduced this unit to 663 enlisted effectives. Further losses in this unit without replacements will render it ineffective as a combat Infantry Battalion."[9] By April 1944, replacements for the 100th had started arriving from Camp Shelby, drawn from the 1st Battalion of the 442d Regiment. The two units of Japanese Americans were slowly becoming one. As the men of the 100th had realized since their campfire sessions in Mississippi, they were "guinea pigs," fighting not just for themselves or for Hawaii but for all Japanese Americans—and all Americans.

---

*The three earned Distinguished Service Crosses at the time and won upgraded Congressional Medals of Honor (Hasemoto and Ohata, posthumously) in June 2000.

In May, at Anzio, Kim—by then a captain—and Pfc. Irving Akahoshi went on one of the most daring raids of the Italian campaign. Leaving the 100th's command post around midnight, they crawled slowly but steadily through hundreds of yards of shrub, pausing only when they heard German patrols nearby. By morning they were near an enemy outpost. Bellying their way through knee-high grass, they silently overpowered two enemy soldiers and, in broad daylight, forced them to crawl back with them across the same expanse they had covered in the dark. By afternoon, they had delivered their prisoners for interrogation. Clark personally decorated Akahoshi and Kim with Distinguished Service Crosses, the Army's second highest award.* Their breathtaking raid added to the intelligence gathering that helped make possible the breakout from the Anzio beachhead a few weeks later. And the 100th spearheaded Clark's drive on Rome at the beginning of June.

On D-day, June 6, 1944, the Allied invasion of France put Germany on the defensive for the first time in Western Europe. Japan had already been retreating in the Pacific for two years. There was now no possibility of a Japanese invasion of the mainland, and espionage and sabotage by Japanese Americans had never materialized after Pearl Harbor, even in Hawaii, where the threat had been greater. With the war turned decisively in the Allies' favor, the whole raison d'être for the "exclusion" and "evacuation" of Japanese Americans from the West Coast—and for their "relocation" to, and confinement in, camps—had disappeared.

★ ★ ★

On April 13, 1944, Harold Ickes, secretary of the interior, whose department had recently absorbed the War Relocation Authority, issued a stirring statement regarding the fate of Japanese Americans on the mainland and "the character and reputation of our own democracy":

> All of the Japanese Americans who were evacuated from the West Coast have undergone and are undergoing a most intensive investigation. Those concerning whom there is any basis whatever for a suspicion of disloyalty have been sent to internment camps or are being segregated at Tule Lake. This segregation process is virtually complete, and the

---

*The Distinguished Service Cross required the approval of an Army or theater commander such as Clark. The Congressional Medal of Honor required the approval of the secretary of war.

thousands of Japanese Americans who remain at the other centers are, by all reasonable tests, loyal American citizens or law-abiding aliens. They are entitled to be treated as such. Those who do not believe in according these people the rights and privileges to which they are entitled under our laws do not believe in the Constitution of the United States.

All of us recognize that, in time of war, we are subject to orders and restraints which would be intolerable in time of peace. All of us— regardless of race or religion—are subject to the overriding demands of military necessity in time of war. No one who is loyal to the United States objects to this. But when military necessity does not require it, no one of us who is an American citizen or a loyal alien can be deprived of his rights under the law. I believe that the only justifiable reason for confinement of a citizen in a democratic nation is the evidence that the individual might endanger the wartime security of the nation.[10]

And a month later, on May 17, Secretary of War Henry L. Stimson noted in his diary, "No more reason to keep loyal Japanese in camp." The next day, he wrote that "G.C.M. [Chief of Staff Gen. George C. Marshall] thinks Japanese should be released. . . . Point to great fighting record of Japanese unit [the 100th Battalion (Separate)]."[11]

But on June 12, 1944, Franklin D. Roosevelt sent a memo to Ickes and Edward R. Stettinius Jr., acting secretary of state, which exposed the president as someone who, by Ickes's own description, did "not believe in the Constitution of the United States." Although it was less than a week after D-day, Roosevelt had other things on his mind than the success of the most important offensive of the war. While Allied troops were still struggling to break out from the beachheads in Normandy, the commander in chief was worried about slowing down the progress of noncombatants at home.

"The more I think of this problem of suddenly ending the orders excluding Japanese Americans from the West Coast," the president wrote, "the more I think it would be a mistake to do anything drastic or sudden":

As I said at Cabinet, I think the whole problem, for the sake of internal quiet, should be handled gradually, i.e., I am thinking of two methods:

(a) Seeing, with great discretion, how many Japanese families would be acceptable to public opinion in definite localities on the West Coast.
(b) Seeking to extend greatly the distribution of other families in many parts

of the United States. I have been talking to a number of people from the
Coast and they are all in agreement that the Coast would be willing to receive back a portion of the Japanese who were formerly there—nothing
sudden and not in too great quantities at any one time.

Also, in talking to people from the Middle West, the East and the South, I
am sure that there would be no bitterness if they were distributed—one or
two families to each county as a start. Dissemination and distribution con-
stitute a great method of avoiding public outcry.

Why not proceed seriously along the above line—for a while at least?[12]

This memo revealed the president at his worst—wheedling instead of
leading. Instead of exercising authority to solve a problem he had created
in the first place by issuing Executive Order 9066 and delegating power to
the military over the fate of Japanese Americans, he was trying to coax his
cabinet into going along with him "for the sake of internal quiet." Rather
than taking a public stand against nativist agitators, he wanted to solicit
"public opinion" to determine what would be "acceptable." Instead of
shaping policy through political give-and-take and relying on the judgment of government officials he had appointed, he was appealing to the
authority of unnamed "people from the Coast" and "from the Middle
West, the East, and the South." Rather than seeking to do what was right,
he was chiefly interested in "discretion" and "avoiding public outcry."

"To undo a mistake is always harder than not to create one originally,
but we seldom have the foresight," Roosevelt's wife, Eleanor, had written
nine months earlier. But the president and the first lady still clung to the
fantastic notion that the way to handle the "problem" of Japanese Americans was through "dissemination and distribution" of families, one at a
time, in separate counties throughout the hinterlands. The "relocation" of
Japanese Americans was just a variation on parts of the National Industrial
Recovery Act of 1933, which meant "to provide for aiding the redistribution [sic] of the overbalance of population in industrial centers"—i.e.,
moving people out of the cities to rural areas.[13] Though the Supreme
Court had declared the NIRA unconstitutional two years later, the idea of
social engineering through "redistribution" of people had never died in
the mind of New Dealers.

"We should never have allowed any groups to settle as groups where
they created a little German or Japanese or Scandinavian island and did not
melt into our general community pattern," Eleanor Roosevelt asserted.[14]
This sentiment showed how little the original motive for the "relocation"

had to do with "military necessity" and how much it was the result of New Deal social policy taken to a maniacal extreme—with a racial twist. And, perhaps most shockingly of all, the "mistake" the first lady referred to was not the "evacuation" and "relocation" of Japanese Americans, but the government's having "allowed" them to live and work and own property where they chose, just like any other Americans.

For decades, Italian Americans had been living in "Little Italys" in New York City and San Francisco, and for two and a half years, the United States had been at war against fascist Italy, but the president did not argue for their "dissemination and distribution." For decades, a section of New York City's Upper East Side had been known as "Germantown," and before Pearl Harbor, the German American Bund had mobilized tens of thousands in public—and sometimes violent—demonstrations supporting Hitler. The FBI had broken up an active ring of German spies in Manhattan, and German saboteurs had even landed by U-boat at Amagansett, New York, and Ponte Vedra Beach, Florida, carrying hundreds of thousands of dollars in cash as well as TNT and other material for bombs.[15] And in the six months after Pearl Harbor, German submarines off the East and Gulf Coasts of the United States "managed to sink some 185 ships, totaling about 965,000 gross tons."[16] German attacks on the East and Gulf Coast were not just threats, they were actually taking place. Yet there was no "relocation" of German American citizens on the East Coast or anywhere else in the States, and no government program to break up the "little German . . . island" on the island of Manhattan, much less the numerous localities actually named Germantown across the country. Of course there had been no "relocation" of Scandinavian Americans.

And like many of the spurious rationales for the "relocation," the claim that Japanese Americans on the mainland had "settled as groups" in a "little . . . island"—and therefore required "dissemination and distribution"—was simply false. Before Pearl Harbor, almost half (forty-five percent) of the Japanese Americans on the West Coast were farmers, and a substantial portion of the remainder (another eighteen percent) were involved in agricultural businesses (trucking, wholesaling, and retailing through fruit and vegetable stands). "Nearly two-thirds of the total working force was directly dependent on agriculture," according to the WRA. "A considerable proportion of the remainder was in a service relationship to farmers and produce handlers."[17] This is hardly the picture of a group in a "little island" or ethnic enclave.

In fact, it was their dispersal, not their concentration "as groups," that caused problems for Japanese Americans. As the government would belatedly conclude after the war:

> The primary virtues of the Japanese farmers—willingness to take infinite pains, to work with great diligence to bring low value land to production, to live soberly and with frugality—became the faults which caused alarm; because the *Issei* farmer was a part of a visible minority, his ability to compete could be attacked by political as well as economic means.[18]

Though they "operated only 3.9 percent of all farms in the state [of California] and harvested but 2.7 percent of all cropland harvested," just prior to "evacuation" Japanese Americans were producing:

Ninety percent or more: snap beans for marketing; celery, spring and summer; peppers; strawberries.

Fifty to ninety percent: Artichokes; snap beans for canning; cauliflower; celery, fall and winter; cucumbers; fall peas; spinach; tomatoes.

Twenty-five to fifty percent: Asparagus; cabbage; cantaloupes; carrots; lettuce; onions; watermelons.

In other words, they were a "competitive threat"—"the fact that competition was within a narrow range of products, and successful within that range, may account for the severity of the prejudice against the Japanese in agriculture."[19] It was precisely because they were often visibly isolated in rural communities, not because they were concentrated in "Japan towns," that Japanese Americans could be dealt with "by political . . . means."

But having authorized the military to rip them from the homes and farms and businesses and communities they had spent decades establishing, Roosevelt now thought Japanese Americans should be "distributed" in areas across the United States where they had no jobs, no property, no friends, and no family awaiting them—because an impersonal administrative state surely knew what was best for them, whom they should associate with, what jobs they should hold, where they should live. But as bad as "evacuation" and "relocation" had been in the name of "military necessity," the idea of forced "dissemination and distribution" was almost surreal in its bland paternalism and authoritarianism. And the only "bitterness" Roosevelt feared—or seemed capable of imagining—was not that of Japanese Americans, whose suffering had been caused by Executive Order 9066, but of people in communities where "one or two families" of Japanese Americans might be "distributed." With "military necessity" all but abandoned as a rationale, all that remained were faith in the naked power of social engineering and cynical calculation of political interest.

The very next day after Roosevelt's memo, Assistant Secretary of War John J. McCloy expanded on the president's ideas in a phone conversation with Maj. Gen. Delos Emmons, formerly the military commander in Hawaii, who had succeeded Lieutenant General DeWitt as head of the Western Defense Command:

> I just came from the President a little while ago—keep this to yourself—he put thumbs down on this scheme [to end or to modify the "exclusion" of Japanese Americans from the West Coast]. He wants to reinvigorate the distribution in the rest of the country and it is all right, he said, to introduce some very gradually as a relaxation of the general program into California but to do it on a very gradual basis and nothing like the scheme that we have in mind.

Then McCloy got to the heart of the matter:

> He [the president] was surrounded at that moment by his political advisors and they were harping hard that this would stir up the boys in California and California, I guess, is an important state. . . . He won't let us go ahead on any such large scale reintroductions [of Japanese Americans to the West Coast].[20]

The constitutional rights of Japanese Americans and the challenges looming ahead for the Supreme Court in the *Korematsu* and *Endo* cases—not to mention simple human decency—were irrelevant. McCloy even disregarded his own words from a year and a half earlier, when he had told

DeWitt, "You can't keep them [Japanese Americans] in pens forever."[21] In the end, it was just political calculation.

It was an election year, and Roosevelt was seeking an unprecedented fourth term. The lives of actual Japanese Americans—who, unlike any other citizens, had been forced to "register" and swear their loyalty— mattered less to the president than the abstract fear of a "stir" that might be caused by their release among "the boys in California," where the "competitive threat" of Japanese American farmers had been the greatest. The president's liberal supporters, who should have been horrified at such pandering to reactionary sentiment, could turn a blind eye only because Japanese Americans on the mainland were numerically insignificant and politically impotent. Lacking powerful patrons or even the rudimentary mechanisms of political influence, they had been forced to surrender their lives and become wards, if not prisoners, of the newly emergent welfare state.

During the summer, the Western Defense Command had yet another new head, Maj. Gen. C. H. Bonesteel. On August 8, he wrote a memo to Gen. George C. Marshall, Army chief of staff, arguing for an end to the "exclusion" of Japanese from the West Coast. "When the exclusion was originally ordered," Bonesteel stated, "the situation was very different from that which exists at the present time."* He began by describing the situation immediately following Pearl Harbor:

Two years ago, an attack on the West Coast was a definite probability. Even an invasion on a large scale had to be considered as a possibility. At that time the eviction of all persons of Japanese ancestry was thoroughly justified on the ground that there was every reason to believe

---

*Quotes in this section are from Maj. Gen. C. H. Bonesteel's memo to Chief of Staff, War Department, Washington, D.C., regarding "Exclusion of persons of Japanese Ancestry from Military Areas of the Western Defense Command," August 8, 1944, Archives II, RG 499. Throughout, Bonesteel referred to Japanese Americans as "Japanese," the same term he used for the people of Japan. He was, of course, not alone in making this mistake, which Roosevelt often made. The failure to distinguish among people of a foreign country, immigrants from that country who had been resident aliens in the United States for decades but had been barred from citizenship, and their children, who were American citizens, exemplified precisely the confusion and prejudice behind Executive Order 9066.

that among the Japanese population on the West Coast there were a large number of persons who might commit acts of sabotage and espionage and who might greatly assist Japanese military and naval units in connection with an attack or invasion. The lack of knowledge of the attitudes of individual Japanese and the utter impossibility of determining which ones could be classed as loyal made the mass exclusion an appropriate and proper step in the defense of the West Coast.

Of course, Bonesteel's account contradicted two and a half years of government policies. Far from being an "utter impossibility," the loyalty of individual Japanese Americans had been determined over and over again, since as early as the summer of 1942—more than two years earlier than Bonesteel's memo—when students and seasonal agricultural workers were first granted "leave" from the "assembly camps." During the same period, the MIS had also begun recruiting Japanese Americans from the "assembly camps," even before construction of the permanent "relocation centers" was complete. And of course the official "leave clearance" procedure, including the controversial "loyalty questionnaire," and recruiting for the 442d had begun in early 1943, a year and a half before Bonesteel's memo.

So it is hard to avoid the conclusion that Bonesteel was simply parroting the party line as a way of emphasizing the obvious changes in the military situation:

Today many of the conditions which motivated the decisions of two years ago no longer exist. In my opinion, a major invasion or an attack on a relatively large scale upon the Pacific Coast is not within the capabilities of the enemy, either at present or in the predictable future. . . . It is hard to conceive of any possible action on the part of the Japanese military and naval forces, and that of Japanese in the United States, which can seriously change the final outcome of the war.

The War Department had even gone so far as to reclassify the West Coast in Defense Category A, Bonesteel noted, "which assumes that the Pacific coastal frontier 'will probably be free from attack but for which a limited defense should be maintained against possible but improbable isolated raids.'"

"I am convinced," Bonesteel concluded emphatically, "that there no longer exists adequate military or legal reason justifying the continuance of the mass exclusion of Japanese from the prohibited areas of the Western Defense Command."

And, unlike the president, Bonesteel did not engage in any wishful thinking about the post-"relocation" desires and plans of Japanese Americans on the mainland. "It is my opinion, and that of many who are familiar with the attitude of the Japanese," he wrote, "that the majority of those now in relocation centers will not be willing to go to any place other than the area of their original homes." Bonesteel was also clear-eyed about the "large numbers of Americans in the West Coast states who are definitely opposed to the return of the Japanese." He warned, "We cannot overlook the fact that there will be considerable unrest, disturbances, and some physical violence when the Japanese are returned." But he also noted the "considerable number of important groups that feel strongly that the Japanese who are citizens are entitled to their rights as such. They stand ready to do everything possible to assist the returning Japanese."

In conclusion, Bonesteel argued for a system that should have been in place from the beginning: centralized intelligence sharing among the FBI, WRA, War Department, Army and Navy intelligence, and the Western Defense Command, and case-by-case reviews of "only persons who as individuals are considered to be dangerous to the military security." Beyond that, he simply recommended "approval of the decision that mass exclusion of persons of Japanese ancestry is no longer justified by the military situation."

Bonesteel's reasonable memo should have been all the more compelling because it was written strictly from a military perspective, coolly appraising the pros and cons of a policy that obviously no longer corresponded, if it ever had, to reality. Since the rationale for the "evacuation" and "relocation" had always been presented as "military necessity," it was not too much for Bonesteel to expect that his careful analysis of a "difficult and sensitive problem" from a military perspective would carry at least as much weight as the exaggerated, irresponsible, and simply false contentions of his predecessor DeWitt, two and a half years earlier. But Bonesteel's sensible recommendation would be ignored for another three months.

★ ★ ★

While Roosevelt was worrying about adverse reaction following a "drastic or sudden" change in policy, the War Relocation Authority understood that public opinion could be led as well as followed. In his April release, Ickes had emphatically stated:

> The major emphasis in War Relocation Authority operations is now on restoring the people of all WRA centers except Tule Lake as rapidly as possible to private life.[22]

Beyond merely taking the side of Japanese Americans, Ickes understood both the moral demands of leadership, as Roosevelt did not, at least on this issue, and the political value of good publicity. Under Ickes's aegis, the WRA issued a pamphlet, "What We're Fighting For," which featured "statements by United States Servicemen about Americans of Japanese Descent."[23] It was a shrewdly compiled collection of correspondence testifying to the loyalty and heroism of Japanese Americans in all theaters of the war.

In a letter to the editor of the *Lamar (Colorado) Daily News*, James Corning, an Army lieutenant, skewered nativist illogic by asking, "Why don't our American racists demand the internment of all Japanese Americans in uniform? . . . And why don't they apply the same rule to all Americans of German descent which would include General Eisenhower and [Wendell] Willkie?"

A serviceman whose name was withheld wrote:

> As a U.S. Marine, I am not in the habit of begging anyone for anything, but there is one thing I will beg for. I beg my fellow citizens to give the loyal Japanese Americans their God-given right to life, liberty, and pursuit of happiness that, I sincerely hope, is guaranteed by our Constitution.
>
> I landed on Guadalcanal in August 1942, and have as much dislike for Japanese militarism as anyone, but please, let's give these fellows a chance. How about it, Americans?

Time magazine published a letter from 2d Lt. E. D. Chasse on February 14, 1944: "I just came from Italy where I was assigned to the Japanese

100th Battalion. I never in my life saw any more of a true American than they are."

And another veteran of the Italian campaign, Lt. Marshall Haines, wrote a letter to Vernon McCann of the *Auburn (California) Journal*, which was reproduced in part in the *Pacific Citizen* on September 9, 1944:

> See where there is a lot of controversy about the Japanese returning to California. Also that proper respect has not been shown the Japanese American soldier. Things like that sure go against the grain with me.
>
> We had been sitting and living in foxholes at Anzio some 63 days. Then the big push out and the capture of Rome. They [the Japanese American infantrymen] wiped out the last heavy German resistance we met some 12 miles north of Rome and then it was practically a walk into the city.
>
> I know that all of the combat men here in Italy think the world of the Japanese American soldiers. Their record is so outstanding that they have recently been awarded a Presidential citation.
>
> They have never failed to take an objective since I have been fighting with them. They have shown as much bravery as the American doughboy, and in some cases more.

The War Department joined in the WRA's propaganda campaign. "Spark" Matsunaga, one of the members of the 100th's campfire bull sessions at Camp Shelby, had been knocked out of combat by a land mine in Italy. Transferred back to the States, he was assigned to work with the WRA and deliver speeches highlighting the achievements of Japanese Americans in the Army. Before hundreds of gatherings across the country, he told military and civilian audiences that Japanese Americans were fighting "because they had to prove that they were worthy to be called American." And he made explicit the sacrifices of the *Issei* generation, the older Japanese Americans in the camps who could not even claim citizenship:

> In the Heart Mountain relocation camp in Wyoming there is a mother who has given six sons to the service and whose seventh son has volunteered and is ready to be called up. Yet she can never become one of us.[24]

And there would be no family exemptions, no "saving Private Ryan" for her, or for the parents of the five Masaoka brothers, or the four

Kuroda brothers, or for any other Japanese Americans who had more than one son fighting not just in the same combat zone but in the same unit—the 442d.

* * *

When Japanese Americans were finally subjected to the draft in early 1944, the number of inductions nationwide had already begun to decline. Between 1940 and the end of 1943, more than seven million American men had been inducted into the Armed Forces. The total for 1944 would be around 1.6 million, roughly half the number of each of the preceding two years.[25] From the standpoint of manpower procurement planners in the War Department, victory was already on the horizon. Gen. George C. Marshall, chief of staff, was making his famous "ninety-division gamble" that the number of ground troops forecast in the spring of 1944 would be adequate to win the war. It was a wager he would come perilously close to losing.[26]

By the time the draft reached into the "relocation centers," the government's effort to measure the loyalty of Japanese Americans by their willingness to join the Army made even less sense than it ever had. The original volunteers for the 442d from the camps in 1943 had sometimes chosen to serve their country against the wishes of their parents and the pressure of their peers. They had stepped forward under extreme duress. At some level, they knew that being forced to prove their loyalty made a mockery of the very notion of loyalty. If it is demanded, not earned, it is fealty, the tribute due a lord, not loyalty as properly understood in a liberal democracy. Yet somehow the volunteers for the 442d had refused to let the coercion they faced rob them of their dignity of choice. They were expressing allegiance to a higher understanding of what it meant to be an American, and a citizen, than their own government's debased notion of loyalty.

The draftees from the camps in 1944 had to make a very different choice, in a changed environment. Presented with an induction notice, Japanese Americans—in the camps, elsewhere on the mainland, or in Hawaii—were little different from other Americans. They could answer it, or they could evade or resist it and face the legal consequences. But their choices were no more, or less, coerced by government than anyone else's choices were. When the notice from the Selective Service System arrived, it didn't matter if you were inside a "relocation center" or outside,

Japanese American or Caucasian American. Uncle Sam wanted you, and you had to respond.

Still, answering a draft call and thereby assuming the ultimate burden of citizenship—risking life in the defense of country—were every bit as honorable as volunteering was.* The majority of American soldiers in World War II were draftees, after all, as were most of the original members of the 100th Battalion (Separate) and most of the cadre of the 442d.† And once in uniform and in combat, draftees faced the same bullets as volunteers faced. But now the loyalty of Japanese Americans would not take the form of coerced answers to badly worded questions on confusing forms drafted by inept bureaucrats. It would be measured under fire by their fellow soldiers battling a common enemy.

★ ★ ★

When Sakato was drafted in March 1944, he was ordered to report to Fort Douglas, Utah.[27] Even then, he still dreamed of "going to flying school in

---

*The sociologist Morris Janowitz writes:

> [A]t each point in the definition and redefinition of citizenship, the impact of military institutions must be taken into account. Citizenship in Western nation-states is not only a result of industrialism and urbanism and the associated socio-political movements. In fact, the thrust of my analysis is embodied in the formulation of Friedrich Engels: Contrary to appearance compulsory military service surpasses general franchise as a democratic agency. ["Military Institutions and Citizenship in Western Societies," in *Military Conflict*, p. 71.]

The political scientist Samuel P. Huntington has argued that "liberalism does not understand and is hostile to military institutions and the military function." (*The Soldier and the State: The Theory and Politics of Civil-Military Relations*, p. 144.) But as Eliot Cohen has noted, philosophers of liberalism have actually favored conscription, for egalitarian reasons. According to Alexis de Tocqueville, "The government may do almost whatever it pleases, provided it appeals to the whole community at once; it is the unequal distribution of the weight, not the weight itself, that commonly occasions resistance." And to Thomas Jefferson, "the necessity of obliging every citizen to be a soldier . . . was the case with the Greeks and Romans and must be that of every free state." Cohen quotes Tocqueville and Jefferson in *Citizens and Soldiers: The Dilemmas of Military Service*, which advances a critique of the all-volunteer army that, as of the time of this writing, seems eerily prescient.

†Two-thirds of all servicemen in World War II were drafted, according to Director of Selective Service, *Selective Service and Victory*, p. 154.

Texas or Arizona." Instead he wound up in Fort Blanding, Florida, west of Jacksonville. "Was I disappointed," he says. The training grounds, at the peak of the war, covered more than 150,000 acres near the St. John's River, and as Sakato remembers, the swampy area was filled with chiggers, water moccasins, coral snakes, and crocodiles.

One of Sakato's most vivid memories of basic training was his performance on the rifle range. The first time he fired his M1 at the bull's-eye a hundred yards away, all he saw was "Maggie's drawers," the spotter's signal that he had missed the target completely. "It took some time before I was able to hit close to the bull's-eye," Sakato recalls. The lesson he took away from the rifle range, which he would remember in combat more than six months later, was not what his instructors would have wished. Marksmanship was fine for snipers, Sakato would conclude, but fighting at close quarters demanded a different kind of firepower.

At Fort Blanding, Sakato met Saburo Tanamachi, one of the four brothers of Jerry Tanamachi, the Texas farmer who had met his wife, Kikuko Nakao, at the Rohwer Relocation Center. Saburo Tanamachi had been drafted from San Benito, Texas, but he had grown up in Beaumont, where he graduated from elementary and junior high school, and Brownsville, where he finished high school. (Three other Tanamachi brothers would also serve in the military.) Saburo was "very studious," according to his brother Willie, "and focused on what he wanted to do."[28] Tanamachi and Sakato would become fast friends in the short time they served together in the 442d.[29]

Other soldiers had followed a very different route from Sakato's and Tanamachi's to Fort Blanding. A year after Pearl Harbor there were more than three thousand Japanese Americans on the mainland already serving in the Army before the 442d was formed.[30] Among them was Shig Doi, who had grown up on his family's eighty-five-acre farm in Auburn, northeast of Sacramento in Placer County, California. Although alien land laws prevented Japanese immigrants from owning real property in the state, their children were American citizens by virtue of *jus soli*. So many Japanese American families did what the Dois had done—they purchased land in their adult children's names.

For Doi, growing up in Placer County meant learning to deal with bigotry from even before his first day at school. " 'Why, you dirty Jap . . . ,' " he recalls, "those were fighting words." By high school, he says, "even the teachers" showed the same "hostility and prejudice." So the local Japanese Americans kept to themselves.[31]

In 1942, Doi was drafted in the brief period after Pearl Harbor but before the War Department had issued its discriminatory policy against Japanese Americans, and before his parents were sent to the Amache Relocation Center in Colorado. "In Placer County the lawyers' sons got deferred," Doi recalls, "but us peons got sent." He did his basic training at Camp Grant, in Illinois, where he worked as a dental technician through early 1944. While he was there, "my first sergeant asked me once why I never went home on furlough," Doi remembers. "I said to him, 'Where would I go? I have no home.'"

Then he was transferred to Fort Blanding. "Later on we found out why we were there," Doi says. "The 442d and the 100th were fighting in Italy. They needed replacements, so they scrounged the whole United States Army, and whoever had a Japanese surname ended up in Alabama or in Camp Blanding for combat training." There, along with new inductees like Sakato and Tanamachi and hundreds of others bound for the 442d, Doi underwent training all over again. But he found it useful, because it included instruction in all kinds of weapons. Since they were meant to be replacements, they had to be able to step into various positions in different platoons—rifle, mortar, machine gun. Doi learned to handle a BAR, a heavy but powerful weapon that a single man could fire from the shoulder like an M1. But unlike the standard government-issue rifle, it fired a rapid burst of bullets with a single pull on the trigger.

When he got a twenty-one-day furlough from Fort Blanding, Doi finally decided to visit his parents in Amache. But he wound up spending only "two or three days," he recalls, "because it was so depressing." The day he was leaving, his mother wanted to fix him something to eat, but she couldn't, because "there wasn't anything."

On the train ride back to Fort Blanding, "one Caucasian guy asked me, 'What kind of camp is that? What kind of army camp is that?'" Doi remembers. "And, Jesus, I just couldn't tell him what the hell it was. So I kept my mouth shut."

* * *

After basic training, Sakato, Tanamachi, Doi, and their cohorts went to Camp Shelby for further training. There, another contingent of mainlanders ran into Hawaiian Japanese Americans for the first time. Repeating the pattern from a year earlier, "the group from the States was always getting into fights with the Hawaiians," Sakato recalls. The mainlanders "could not understand the pidgin English the Hawaiians were using," and "the Hawaiians wanted to know who in the stateside did not want to fight in the war"—word of the "no/no" boys had reached the islands. So once again the *kotonks* fought with the Buddhaheads, but "after you fought with them," Sakato recalls, "they became the best of buddies."

Sakato also remembers a run-in with white soldiers at Camp Shelby who called the 442d replacements "dirty Japs." After a few beers, "the fight was on," he recalls, turning into a "big brawl" that spilled over into the nearby town of Hattiesburg, Mississippi. After the melee was broken up, the camp commander called each battalion onto the parade ground to remind them, as Sakato puts it, "why we were there"—to fight the enemy, not each other.

After less than a month at Shelby, the replacements were shipped to Camp Kilmer, New Jersey, where they were given a three-day pass. With his friends Saburo Tanamachi, John Tanaka, and Sho Tabata, Sakato took the train to Manhattan, where they booked a room in a famous hotel. "It cost us a lot of money," Sakato says, "but we could say that we stayed at the Waldorf Astoria."

But that was their last taste of freedom before shipping abroad. From Camp Kilmer, the next stop was Newport News, Virginia, where ships were waiting to take them to the combat zone overseas. "We had to walk up a gangplank with our full field pack and big duffel bag filled to the brim" and carrying a rifle, Sakato recalls. "That was tough for me. I was a tiny runt compared to the other guys."

★ ★ ★

Still other soldiers had followed even more circuitous routes to join the 442d as replacements. Though the Army had accepted him as a volunteer one month after Pearl Harbor, Al Takahashi had been shuttled around for the next two years—from Fort McArthur in San Pedro, California, to Camp Roberts in Paso Robles, from Fort Leonard Wood, Kansas, to Fort Cooke, Nebraska. "They absolutely didn't know what to do with us [Japanese Americans]," he recalls. He had a pilot's license, but the Army Air Corps would not accept his application. "I was turned down cold when they saw my face," he says.[32] Instead, he was assigned as an officer's orderly, shining shoes and keeping stoves stocked with wood, as a supply clerk, typing requisitions and laundry lists, and as a mechanic, even though his unit was not motorized.

"I was disgusted," he said. "I joined to fight. I wanted to get into the Air Corps, and look what I'm doing." His family had been in the Poston Relocation Center for almost two years when Takahashi finally got the opportunity to carry a gun. After combat training at Fort McClellan, Alabama, he boarded a transport ship for Italy in the summer of 1944. "To me it was an adventure," he remembers. "I'm going into battle." And he says, "I was happy because I was going into an outfit that was really something"—the 100th Battalion.

★ ★ ★

While Sakato, Tanamachi, and Doi were finishing their training, still more Japanese Americans followed them to Camp Shelby. One of them was Sgt. Willie Tanamachi, Saburo Tanamachi's brother, who had already been in the Army for almost four years. At Shelby, he joined battalion headquarters in the cadre training new recruits, many of whom had been inducted straight out of the "relocation camps." And as training progressed through the late fall of 1944, he found time to visit Rohwer, where his sister-in-law Kikuko's mother and sister were still confined.

Another Rohwer resident, "Bones" Fujimoto, who had been forced to leave his pet dog behind when his family was "relocated" from California, had been drafted after the school year ended. He had turned eighteen in March 1944, while he was still a student at the high school in the camp. When he had registered for the draft, he was designated IV-C, for "enemy alien." Just before taking the physical, he had spent a couple of months in the hospital of the "relocation center," suffering from pleurisy, "probably caused by the cold winter days and nights."

A month later his classification was changed to I-A, and he was inducted. But unlike Tak Senzaki, who had left Rohwer by himself at 6:00 A.M. a year earlier, Fujimoto was not alone. More than forty of his friends and acquaintances from the center were called up at the same time. When Fujimoto broke the news to his parents, their reaction was "*Shikataganai*," a Japanese word signifying resignation—"It can't be helped."

Later, at Fort Blanding, Fujimoto would learn that the group just before his—including Doi, Sakato, and Saburo Tanamachi—had fought in a battle in the Vosges Mountains in eastern France that would make the 442d famous. One of the soldiers there on the front line would write a letter to his former company commander back home. "Train them good," he would warn, "they're going to need it."[33]

SOLDIERS

The Southern France Campaign
★
August–September 1944

London

GERMANY

Arnhém

Antwerp

BELGIUM

Cologne

Dieppe

Ardennes

LUX.

Frankfurt

Rheims

Moselle R.

Metz

Strasbourg

Caen

Paris

St. Dié

Épinal

Bruyères

45th

36th

Dijon

3d

45th

Bourg

36th

Geneva

SWITZERLAND

Lyon

3d

F R A N C E

Rhône R.

Grenoble

ITALY

Montélimar

36th

Gap

3d

Durance R.

36th

Nice

Avignon

45th

Cannes

Aix

Marseilles

Toulon

36th Division
[VI Corps]

45th Division
[VI Corps]

3d Division
[VI Corps]

Mediterranean Sea

Rambervillers

St.-Dié

Grandvillers

Belmont

Bruyères

Biffontaine

Épinal

Lépanges

La Houssière

Les Poulières

Moselle R.

Area of detail

Adapted from Texas Military Forces Museum, *The Story of the 36th Infantry Division*; Center of Military History, *Southern France*; and Jeffrey J. Clarke and Robert Ross Smith, *Riviera to the Rhine*.

4

DRAGOON

The 36th "Texas" Division and the Race up the Rhône

The best invasion I ever attended was that of southern France.
—BILL MAULDIN[1]

The Côte d'Azur and the Rhône Valley, August–October 1944

The last thing 2d Lt. Marty Higgins remembered before hitting the ground and tasting dirt was a whack on his butt.[2] It was mid-August 1944, shortly after the invasion of southern France, and the platoon Higgins led was on point as the Allied forces rapidly swept toward the Rhône River from their original beachhead southwest of Cannes. An outbreak of sniper fire had suddenly pinned down his entire unit, A Company of the 141st ("Alamo") Regiment of the 36th ("Texas") Division. Now it was up to Higgins and his men to break through the bottleneck.

After regaining his feet, Higgins and his platoon regrouped and flushed out the Germans, who swiftly surrendered in the face of superior numbers. Enraged and perhaps a little humiliated by his ignominious dive for cover, Higgins almost shot the captured snipers on the spot. "My platoon sergeant, thank God, restrained me," he recalls with relief sixty years later. When he calmed down, Higgins dusted himself off and checked for wounds. He found a sniper's bullet had neatly pierced his back pocket, scarred a notebook he had stuffed there, and then exited without even nicking him. All he had felt was the impact.

Though he was to fight for four more months in France, this would be the first and only time Higgins came close to losing his head in combat. It was also just the first of many close calls—which he would survive, he was certain, thanks to his wife's prayers back home, to his conscientiously saying the Rosary and making the Stations of the Cross, and to a strong dose of the luck of the Irish.

Up to and even including that episode, the invasion of southern France had gone more smoothly than Higgins or anyone else in the American Army had dared to hope. It would be another two months before the 442d Regimental Combat Team rejoined the 36th Division in the Vosges Mountains, 350 miles to the north, near the Swiss-German border. But in the meantime, the whole campaign—from the "second D-day" on the Côte d'Azur on August 15, 1944, to the arrival of the Allies in the Vosges in October—would cover more ground and capture more prisoners in less time than any other Allied operation up to that point, including the far better known invasion of Normandy in June. It was to become the most successful, but least known, American campaign of the entire war.

★　★　★

Higgins had arrived at the "Texas" Division following a circuitous route that began in New Jersey. After graduating in 1939 with a bachelor of science degree in economics from St. Peter's College in his hometown of Jersey City, he had joined the National Guard and wound up in the 101st Cavalry Regiment, which he regarded as a plum assignment—because he wanted to ride horses. He had been introduced to the sport by his sister, and he was "looking forward to riding every day and getting paid for it."

One month short of being discharged in January 1942, Higgins found himself, after December 7, 1941, stuck in uniform for the duration of the war. But like Young Oak Kim, he was recruited for Officer Candidate School when the need for junior officers increased dramatically during the massive mobilization after Pearl Harbor. In November 1942 Higgins earned his commission and subsequently joined the 10th Cavalry Regiment of the 2d Cavalry Division, "the last horse outfit in the Army," he recalls fondly. The only mounted troops active in Europe during World War I, the 2d Cavalry Division had been reactivated in early 1943.[3]

The 10th Cavalry was a historic unit that had first been activated at Fort Leavenworth, Kansas, on July 28, 1866. Back then it was made up of "buffalo soldiers"—black volunteers who had been former slaves or Union Army veterans (some of whom had answered Frederick Douglass's call for recruits). More than seventy-five years later, it was still a "colored" unit—though, like the 442d, with white officers.

Higgins's service with the 10th Cavalry was "probably the finest year" of his life. The unit was stationed at Camp Lockett, California, which the Army had constructed—under Lt. Gen. John L. DeWitt's direction—in the Campo Valley, sixty miles southeast of San Diego. The "buffalo soldiers" were on patrol along the Mexican border, guarding the San Diego & Arizona Eastern railroad, Morena and Barrett Dams, and electric transformers and relay stations.[4] "We rode six days a week, including a review on Saturdays, [and] spent Sundays jumping or playing polo," he remembers. "We had a ball, a lot of laughs, and [were] excused from duty if it interfered with the game." Although he didn't know it at the time, the fun and games amounted to an education in tactics that would help him later in combat. And it wasn't just the polo that made it such a memorable year. "I completed my life of bliss by getting married," he says, to Marjorie Jewkes, "the finest gal I had ever met."

In the spring of 1944, after a year of training, the 2d Cavalry Division was shipped off to Oran, North Africa. Higgins was, by his own admission, "naïve" enough to believe that he would go into combat with his "buffalo soldiers"—on horseback. But he quickly learned the unit was due to be deactivated, and not just because cavalry was obsolete in modern warfare. "The U.S. Army didn't seem too keen on putting black troops into combat," Higgins says. The 1st Cavalry Division had already been serving as infantry in the Pacific theater, but the "buffalo soldiers" were being reorganized into service and engineer units—even though Higgins thought that the ratio of men under his command who were "fighting material" was "excellent." "I questioned the government policy at that time," he states emphatically, "and still do to this day."

Offered a chance to be the executive officer of a noncombat unit, Higgins declined. "The vast majority of junior grade officers wanted to get into combat," he recalls, and "staying with the troops we arrived with was a detour from fighting." So he chose to leave his beloved cavalry behind, though vowing never to remove from his uniform the crossed sabers pin signifying mounted troops.

In June 1944, Higgins was assigned to the 36th Division in Italy as a replacement officer. He remembers meeting his new battalion commander, Lt. Col. James G. Balluff, who welcomed him and then "got right to the issue: 'Lieutenant, I know you do not have to wear crossed rifles on your collar, but the infantrymen you command will probably think more of you if you embrace their service.'" So Higgins changed his insignia and became a rifle platoon leader in the unit he would be identified with for the rest of his life.

★ ★ ★

When Higgins joined the 36th, it was already in training for the "second D-day" in France two months later. But for all the successes it would achieve, which later seemed like a foregone conclusion, the invasion of southern France had been in danger of never happening in the first place.

To Allied war planners at the highest level, southern France was at first regarded as a sideshow on the western front. The Americans, led by Gen. George C. Marshall, Army chief of staff, had always favored a plan that was eventually code-named OVERLORD—an invasion from England across the Channel, culminating in a frontal assault on Germany through the low-lands of Belgium and Holland. (After it took place, this cross-channel invasion would be remembered forever by its launch date, D-day, although there were countless D-days throughout the war.) Marshall and the Joint Chiefs of Staff were skeptical of almost any American involvement in the Mediterranean. It was only over their objections that President Roosevelt had agreed with British prime minister Winston Churchill to involve the United States in the invasions of North Africa, in 1942, and Sicily, in 1943.

Since then, the British and Americans had continued to wage the grueling—and by most people today, forgotten—campaign on the Italian peninsula. The British favored continuing to exploit the hard-earned gains in the Mediterranean rather than risking a full-scale invasion and opening a "second front" in Western Europe. And their strategic perspective did have some justification. As it wore on, the Italian campaign would tie up two of the toughest and most experienced German armies—the Tenth and Fourteenth, under the theater commander, *Generalfeldmarschall* Albert Kesselring—for almost two years, manpower that would otherwise have been turned against the Russians on the eastern front or eventually against the British and Americans on the western. Deposing Benito Mussolini in September 1943 was politically significant and removed Italy from the trio of Axis powers. And Mediterranean bases had provided stepping-stones to the Balkans, where resources valuable to the Germans, such as the Ploesti oil fields in Romania, believed to be supplying sixty percent of Germany's crude oil, were laid bare to Allied air strikes.[5]

But their opposition to an invasion of Western Europe through France also revealed the British war planners as prisoners of their own history. They were fearful of refighting the last war, when the failed invasion of Turkey at Gallipoli in 1915 came to haunt a whole generation of the military, particularly the architect of the failed plan, the first lord of the Admiralty—Churchill. And the power of the British Empire had always been exercised through its Navy. A "blue water" strategy, as opposed to a continental orientation involving massive commitments of troops, furthered British colonial interests in the eastern Mediterranean, which centered on the Suez Canal, guaranteeing access to India and Singapore (both still parts of the empire then).

Perhaps most of all, Churchill was convinced that the heart of Germany could be reached by penetrating the "soft underbelly" of Eastern Europe. American planners did not regard this as a sound strategy, but Churchill's vision was as much political as it was military. The prime minister was looking beyond the war to the peace that would follow. As the Russians advanced on Germany, he could clearly see that the Eastern European countries liberated from Nazi control would remain under the heel of Communism after the war.

The differences between the British and American strategies came to a head in the Cairo and Tehran Conferences in November and December 1943. By this time, planning for OVERLORD had been under way for months, though the British still favored increasing efforts in Italy and the eastern Mediterranean. But at Tehran, the Russians unexpectedly threw their support behind an invasion of southern France, by this time codenamed ANVIL, to support OVERLORD in the north. Joseph Stalin was as concerned about Churchill's postwar intentions in the Balkans as the prime minister was about his. But the Soviet leader also recognized that ANVIL could provide both tactical and logistical assistance to OVERLORD without depleting the Italian front, where manpower and matériel were too limited in any event to permit a full commitment to a Balkan strategy. And Stalin keenly felt that only a "second front" launched by invading France could relieve the pressure on the USSR, which had borne the overwhelming cost—in matériel, territory, and lives, both military and civilian—of fighting the Germans for two and a half long years.

But matters were still not settled. Just a month or two later, in early 1944, ANVIL risked being canceled altogether. The stalemate at Anzio, where the Allied forces would be stuck on the beachhead for four months, "consumed resources that planners had already earmarked for ANVIL,"[6] according to the Army's official history. Long-range weather forecasts, tides, and the changing cover of darkness during the cycles of the moon made the beginning of June the last feasible period for a cross-channel invasion in the north during the late spring of 1944. If a landing in the south could not be organized in time, or if the Italian campaign suffered too much from the diversion of resources, ANVIL would be left on the drawing board.

But the Allied breakout from Anzio in May suddenly freed the men and matériel for ANVIL. The original idea had been to launch OVERLORD and ANVIL simultaneously, with the hammer of the primary invasion in the north of France striking the anvil of a secondary landing in the south. With D-day now only a month away, it would be impossible to coordinate the two landings. But General Dwight D. Eisenhower, supreme commander of the Allied Expeditionary Forces, who was responsible for carrying out OVERLORD, realized that ANVIL could still aid the main Allied thrust, even if it were launched two months later, by protecting the right flank of the advancing armies in the north and by opening another supply route from the Mediterranean port city of Marseille up the Rhône.

Still, Churchill made one last plea to Roosevelt to follow a Balkan strategy instead. With Lt. Gen. Mark Clark's Fifth Army knocking on the gates of Rome at the beginning of June, just before D-day in Normandy, Churchill suggested that an assault on the Po River Valley, north of Rome, could take the Allies to the Ljubljana Gap in Slovenia and beyond, all the way to Germany. Diverting even minor resources—not to mention the three American divisions slotted for ANVIL—from Italy to southern France, Churchill argued, would be throwing away a chance to strike hard and deep at the German heartland.[7]

But this time Roosevelt heeded Marshall, the Joint Chiefs, and Eisenhower. For better or worse, the president did not share Churchill's bleak vision of postwar Eastern Europe—or perhaps he thought that OVERLORD was too important to risk for a chancier strategy in the Balkans. In the end, Roosevelt stood firmly behind ANVIL as a necessary complement to OVERLORD, and Churchill finally relented. Two months after the Allied invasion of Normandy, the "second D-day" would take place on the Côte d'Azur.

* * *

ANVIL was in the hands of some of the most battle-hardened personnel in the entire American Army. In fact, because they were drawn from the Mediterranean theater, where they had been on the ground for a year and a half, both troops and commanders in ANVIL had more combat experience than their counterparts in OVERLORD had. "The officers and men of both the American corps and its three divisions probably constituted one of the most experienced teams in the Allied camp, in contrast to the many green American divisions that went ashore at Normandy," according to the Army itself. "Most were veterans of the North African, Sicilian, and Italian campaigns who had long been accustomed to working with one another."[8]

Overall responsibility for ANVIL belonged to Lt. Gen. Jacob L. Devers, who had succeeded Eisenhower as commander of the American Army in the Mediterranean. Devers exercised authority in four areas. He was Deputy Supreme Allied Commander, Mediterranean Theater; Commanding General, NATOUSA (North African Theater of Operations, U.S. Army); Commander, Advanced Detachment AFHQ (Allied Force Headquarters); and Commanding General of the 6th Army Group, which, after the invasion of southern France, included the American Seventh Army and the First French Army.

Leading the Seventh Army was Lt. Gen. Alexander Patch, a senior officer who had seen action from nearly the beginning of the ground war. At Guadalcanal in 1942, Patch had led the Americal Division, officially described as "the first United States Army unit to conduct an offensive operation against the enemy in any theater."* According to Army historians, Patch was "a professional soldier's general who was more at home with his own staff and troops than with outsiders and less concerned with the prerogatives of command than with getting the job done."[9]

---

*The Army Almanac, first edition, p. 572. American troops, including the Army, had been on the defensive in the Philippines and elsewhere in the Pacific theater following Pearl Harbor. The Navy and the Marines were on the offensive before the Army was in the Pacific.

An American field army at this stage of the war typically consisted of two or three corps, but the Seventh had only one: VI Corps, led by Maj. Gen. Lucian K. Truscott Jr., one of the most seasoned and aggressive combat leaders in the U.S. military—and perhaps the most underrated general of World War II.* Like Marty Higgins, Truscott had been trained as a cavalry officer. He had served on Eisenhower's staff and as a deputy to Gen. George C. Patton, with whom he shared a love of horses and polo. He had also been a founder of the Rangers, the special American unit modeled after the British Commandos; an observer at the abortive raid on Dieppe; a brigade commander in the invasion of North Africa; the commander of the 3d Division in Sicily, where he distinguished himself as "arguably the best American division commander in the war"; and the leader of VI Corps in the breakout from the Anzio beachhead.[10]

For the invasion of southern France, VI Corps would include the 3d ("Rock of the Marne"), 45th ("Thunderbird"), and 36th (nicknamed "Texas" because it had originally been a National Guard unit in Texas and Oklahoma that had been activated after Pearl Harbor) Divisions.

---

*Roger J. Spiller, the George C. Marshall Professor of Military History at the U.S. Army Command and General Staff College, wrote in *American Heritage*, Volume 53, Number 5 (October 2002):

> Lucian Truscott was arguably the best American division commander in the war, and for him it was a long war indeed, stretching from Morocco and Tunisia through Sicily to mainland Italy—two amphibious assaults there, at Salerno and at Anzio—and to southern France, where he took VI Corps up the Rhône Valley. He took over the Fifth Army in Italy late in 1944 and finished the war with a campaign against desperate German resistance in the Po Valley. Not one of his campaigns could have been called easy; his troops fought their way over some of the worst terrain and against some of the most determined enemy the European theater had to offer. Truscott was raised as a cavalry officer. He had wit and dash and a talent to lead, a fine mind, and a ready pen. After the war he wrote one of the best memoirs by any American fighting general, *Command Missions*. But in a miscarriage of history, he has disappeared from the view of all but the most serious students of the war.

There is far less secondary source material available on Truscott, Patch, and Devers than on most of the Allied commanders who were their peers in other theaters of World War II. Though Truscott wrote his memoirs, Patch and Devers did not, and of the three, only Patch has been the subject of a full-length biography. (There is a brief, 122-page biography of Devers; see the sources.) The relative neglect of Truscott, Patch, and Devers is a serious lapse among scholars of World War II.

Each had an authorized strength of more than fourteen thousand soldiers. The 3d, which Truscott had led from February 1943 through February 1944, would be the only American division that, by the end of the war, had fought the Germans on all of the western fronts. It first saw action in North Africa in November 1942, capturing half of French Morocco. In July 1943, it landed on Sicily, where it fought at Palermo and captured Messina. In September 1943, it hit the beaches at Salerno and suffered, at the Volturno River and Cassino, some of the bloodiest battles of the Italian campaign. Then the 3d battled fierce German counterattacks at Anzio for four months before the breakout from the beachhead.

During most of this period, the 36th and 45th soldiered alongside the 3d as part of Clark's Fifth Army. The 45th saw action at the Volturno River and the mountains north of Cassino, while the 36th fought at the Rapido River and Cassino.* Both divisions were at Anzio, and the 36th went on to enter Rome on June 5, the day before D-day in Normandy.

Going into the invasion of southern France, the commander of the 3d Division was Maj. Gen. John "Iron Mike" O'Daniel, who had served as Truscott's deputy and then succeeded him when Truscott took over VI Corps. The 45th was headed by Maj. Gen. William W. Eagles, who had also served under Truscott. The only question mark among the senior officers was Maj. Gen. John E. Dahlquist, commander of the 36th Division, who would soon play an outsized role in the history of the 442d.

Unlike his counterparts in the 3d and 45th, Dahlquist had never led troops in combat before ANVIL. This was not unusual for a senior American officer who had risen through the ranks during the two decades of peace between the wars—even Eisenhower had never been a battlefield commander. Dahlquist had briefly served as a junior officer with the Allied occupation forces in Germany after World War I, and had then held a variety of service and training positions, where he had impressed his superiors with his diligence and mastery of logistical details. He had earned praise for writing a manual on the operation of machine guns and for reorganizing the Army's post office. One of his strong suits was personnel

---

*The 36th Division did not share the 442d's fondness for Mark Clark. In testimony before the Military Affairs Committee of the U.S. Senate after the war, veterans of the "Texas" division held him personally responsible for the heavy losses suffered in the abortive crossings of the Rapido River in January 1944.

management. Dahlquist had earned his first general officer's star stateside. His rise through the ranks had been unspectacular but steady, a testament to his devotion to the military at a time when it was not an esteemed career choice. He was certainly well qualified to serve on Eisenhower's staff in a clandestine military liaison mission to prewar England, where he first heard the news of Pearl Harbor.

Now Dahlquist had "the difficult task," as the official campaign history put it, "of turning around the 36th Division's reputation as a 'hard luck' division, one that had suffered heavy casualties at San Pietro in December 1943 as well as during the Rapido River crossing one month later." On top of that, before Higgins joined the 141st in June, the regiment had "gone through a number of commanders in Italy and appeared to be the black sheep of the division."[11] And this problem of continuity of command would plague the 141st from southern France through the Vosges Mountains, where its fate and that of the 442d would intersect in tragic, and heroic, circumstances.

★ ★ ★

On July 27, Lt. Gen. Mark Clark awarded a Distinguished Unit Citation to the 100th Battalion (Separate) for its decisive role a month earlier in the Battle of Belvedere, north of Rome. In their first major action since landing in Italy, the 2d and 3d Battalions of the 442d had been stopped by SS troops commanding the high ground overlooking the coastal highway. Hastily called out of reserve, "with insufficient time for a proper physical reconnaissance but with a determined desire to fulfill its important mission," according to the citation, the 100th "quickly formulated its plan and launched the operation"[12]—a three-pronged attack that closed off the town of Belvedere and caught the Germans by surprise from behind. Fighting at times without artillery support, and facing "murderous fire from all types of weapons and tanks," the 100th stubbornly and methodically destroyed the SS battalion, killing 178, wounding 20, capturing 73, and driving the remainder out of Belvedere.

"We respected the 100th," recalls Pvt. Barney Hajiro, who had seen black smoke rising from Pearl Harbor. "They were in combat and we were just trainees. They saved us."[13] By this time, Hajiro had earned a reputation as a "goof-off," which he acknowledged, and a troublemaker, which he feels to this day was unwarranted. He had already been court-martialed once, after a fistfight stateside with a noncom, who Hajiro says refused to give him his rations. And no sooner had the 442d landed in Italy than Hajiro was court-martialed a second time, once again for fighting. He had come to the rescue of a fellow GI who was being beaten up by Italian civilians. But the soldier he was trying to help had fled before the Military Police arrived, so Hajiro wound up taking the fall.

After the court-martial, his commander said that since he wanted to fight so much, he would be transferred to a rifle company. Hajiro had originally been a runner in M Company, a heavy weapons unit. Now he found himself in I Company, carrying a BAR, an automatic weapon he knew nothing about. In the short period before the 442d left for France, Hajiro had a lot of catching up to do. He and his friend Pfc. Takeyasu Onaga, the assistant BAR man, worked "day and night" to master the weapon.*

Although his new commander in I Company, 1st Lt. Sadaichi Kubota, was skeptical about taking on someone with a reputation as a troublemaker, Hajiro pleaded with him for another chance—a third chance. He promised he would "never fight again." "I keep my nose clean," he told Kubota. "I don't make trouble." Most of all, Kubota remembers Hajiro saying, "I'm not a bad guy."[14] Combat in Italy had scared him for the first time in his life. Though he had been eager to carry a gun back in Honolulu, when he saw dead bodies in Italy, all Hajiro could think was "I want to go home to Hawaii."

The 100th and 442d had entered a rest camp at Vada when Clark presented the Distinguished Unit Citation. There they learned the two

---

*For a fictional account of what carrying a BAR means, see Richard Yates, "The B.A.R. Man," in *Eleven Kinds of Loneliness*:

> "Try walkin' twenty miles on an empty stomach with that B.A.R. and a full ammo belt on your back, and then lay down in some swamp with the water up over your ass, and you're pinned down by machine-gun and mortar fire and your squad leader starts yellin', 'Get that B.A.R. up!' and you gotta cover the withdrawal of the whole platoon or the whole damn company. Try it sometime, Mac—*you'll* find out whatcha gotta have. . . ."
>
> The short soldier looked him over. "That figures," he said. "You got the build for a B.A.R. man. That old B.A.R.'s a heavy son of a bitch."
>
> "You're right," Fallon said. "It's heavy, but, I wanna tellya, it's a damn sweet weapon in combat. . . ."

Japanese American units would be formally combined. The 442d had arrived in Italy with only two battalions, the 2d and 3d, instead of the normal three. Most of the men in what had been the 1st battalion at Camp
Shelby had already been absorbed as replacements by the 100th, while
the remainder had stayed behind to train the next wave of recruits. So
the 100th Battalion was "separate" no longer; it became the 1st battalion
of the 442d Regiment. But in honor of its pioneering role, by personal
order of Gen. Marshall, chief of staff, it kept its designation as the
100th, an exception to the customary numbering of organic battalions in
a regiment.[15]

By this time, Clark had learned that, in addition to losing the three divisions of VI Corps to ANVIL, he would be giving up the 442d as well. In
a last-minute plea, he urged General Marshall to reconsider:

> The 100th Battalion has done a magnificent job, and we are very proud
> of it. I consider it most unfortunate that present ANVIL plans call for
> its removal from Fifth Army early in September. This battalion has be-
> come an integral part of the 34th Division, and a strong feeling of mu-
> tual respect and admiration has been established between it and the rest
> of the division. . . . I can understand why the 442d Infantry regiment
> should probably be taken from us. However, I do feel that the 100th
> Battalion should remain with the division, even though it is actually a
> part of the 442d Regiment. . . . I trust that you will forgive me if I con-
> tinue to hope that the southern France operation will be so successful
> that it may not be necessary to take the 100th Battalion after all.

Ever since his days on the General Staff in Washington, Clark had
continued to push for a reasoned view of Japanese Americans in combat as
well as at home. Now he was arguing that the *Nisei* troops should be truly
integrated into the Army, if not man by man, at least battalion by battalion, rather than segregated in a single regiment.

> I trust that the publicity for the 100th Battalion and the 442d Infantry
> has been satisfactory to you. . . . I was sorry to see the War Department
> organize the Japanese American battalions into a regiment. It seems to
> me that we would get a much greater propaganda effect if they could be
> employed as separate battalions in as many theaters as possible.[16]

But his plea fell on deaf ears. The entire 442d Regimental Combat Team, including its new battalion, the 100th, would join the southern France campaign as a "bastard" or "orphan" unit, attached to Dahlquist's 36th "Texas" Division.

★ ★ ★

Shortly before the "second D-day," the code name ANVIL had been changed to DRAGOON because of fears that security had been compromised. This was a propitious sign for former cavalrymen like Truscott and Higgins, since the word "dragoon" originally referred to armed soldiers on horseback. The opportunistic and freewheeling style of the cavalry, which Truscott and Higgins had mastered on the polo field and which Truscott had put into action under Patton in Sicily, was well suited to the invasion of southern France. From the moment the troops hit the beaches, rapid maneuver—rather than the massive assault that characterized the Normandy landing two months earlier—was the order of the day for the commanders and troops of VI Corps.

On August 15, 1944, the "second D-day," the 36th was to attack the northern end of the beachhead, near Saint-Raphaël on the Fréjus Gulf, just southwest of Cannes. Truscott had put his "least experienced unit"[17] there to defend the flank of the two more veteran units to the south. It would be the second amphibious operation for the 36th, the third for the 45th, and the fourth for the 3d Division.

The "Texas" Division was scheduled to land at 0800. Watching the action from the headquarters ship *Catoctin*, Truscott was astonished when "the whole flotilla of landing craft halted just a few thousand yards from the beach. What was wrong?" While he watched "helplessly," he noted in his memoirs, "to our profound astonishment the whole flotilla turned about and headed to sea again. [Vice Admiral Henry K.] Hewitt, Patch, and I were furious."[18]

Truscott learned that the naval commander in charge of the landing, Rear Admiral Spencer S. Lewis, had—without consulting Dahlquist— diverted the flotilla after failing to breach underwater obstacles in the Fréjus Gulf. After the delay, the 36th executed a previously determined alternate plan a short distance away, and Truscott noted grimly that "Dahlquist's landings otherwise had gone off satisfactorily and the opposition had not been heavy."

Later, Truscott discovered that Dahlquist had actually "sent a message to Admiral Lewis congratulating him for his prompt action in changing the plan of landing." "I made known to Dahlquist," Truscott wrote later, "my complete displeasure with this procedure. It was in fact almost the only flaw in an otherwise perfect landing." The clearing of the beach took an additional day, and Truscott was convinced the subsequent delay in seizing the airfields near Fréjus cost VI Corps air support in the drive toward the Rhône.*

"Except for the otherwise astounding success of the assault," Truscott wrote, the delay in the 36th's landing "might have had even graver consequences." It was the first, but not the last, time Truscott would entertain doubts about Dahlquist's judgment under fire.

★ ★ ★

Although the 100th and 442d remained in Italy in August, one unit of the Combat Team joined the invasion of southern France. The 442d's Antitank Company was chosen to land by glider and secure the roads leading from the Mediterranean shore. S/Sgt. Frank Seto, the boxer who had been turned down repeatedly as a volunteer until he had been able to enlist from the Jerome Relocation Center, remembers "praying" when the C-47 transport plane that had been hauling his glider cut it loose for the final descent to the beach.

Seto had been lying on a jeep secured by ropes and a cable inside the glider. When it landed, one of the wings "hit a tree and hurled us right into the side of a hill," Seto recalled nearly sixty years later.[19] The ropes tying down the jeep snapped, but the cable held. "If that broke, it would have killed both the pilots in the front," according to Seto. "The motor in the Jeep even went through the radiator."

---

*The authors of the Army's official campaign history, *Riviera to the Rhine* (pp. 123–24), dispute Truscott's assessment, since "it is doubtful that engineers could have begun work on the airfields near Fréjus before the 17th, when surveys actually began." Although conceding that the "entire matter is academic," the authors conclude: "Truscott's postwar contentions may signify little more than his frustrations with some aspects of the campaign that followed," among which the failure to stop the German retreat at Montélimar a week and half later surely ranked near or at the top. What the delay at the beachhead and the missed opportunity at Montélimar had in common, of course, was Dahlquist.

When he heard moaning from the cockpit, Seto went forward with his first-aid kit. "Hollering for medics," he found a wounded officer who had "cut his face up real bad." Seto "wiped him off with bandages." Both of the pilots had broken legs. "The radio operator was all right," Seto recalls, "but he was knocked a little cuckoo."

After paratroopers who had landed ahead of them connected with the glider troops, Seto and the rest of the antitank company set up roadblocks near the beachhead. "But it turned out the Germans didn't attack that day," Seto remembers.

In fact, enemy opposition was light throughout the "second D-day." And during the next two days, the three American divisions "penetrated farther and more easily than planners had thought possible," according to the Army's official history, controlling the "vital Toulon–St. Raphael corridor, making it nearly impossible for German ground forces to launch a significant attack on the Allied beachline."[20] VI Corps had captured 2,300 prisoners and suffered only 95 killed and 385 wounded during the landing. The historian Samuel Eliot Morison called DRAGOON/ANVIL "an example of an almost perfect amphibious operation from the point of view of training, timing, Army–Navy–Air Force cooperation, performance, and results."[21]

As the 3d and 45th Divisions rapidly approached Aix-en-Provence, Patch and Truscott saw an opportunity for the 36th to drive north and encircle any Germans withdrawing from Provence. It was a plan that called for exactly the kind of skills learned on the polo fields. All the "laughs" Higgins had enjoyed in training with the 2d Cavalry "influenced my actions in combat," Higgins says. "I used Cavalry tactics in fighting the Germans, a culmination of all the experience I had to that point."

"We were attempting to set the stage for a classic—a 'Cannae'—in which we would encircle the enemy against an impassable barrier or obstacle and destroy him," Truscott wrote later. The plan was to force a German retreat up the Rhône, the main north-south artery in southern and central France. About ninety miles from the coast, just beyond Montélimar, the river valley narrowed at the Cruas Gorge, with "barely room between the foot of the precipitous ridge and the east bank of the Rhône for the highway and railroad."[22]

It was here that Truscott planned to spring his trap. Montélimar, famous for its nougat and chocolate, is a storied medieval town on a hilltop, with a Romanesque citadel, Château des Adhémar, overlooking the Rhône. The steep cliffs just east of the river command the whole valley. "If the fortunes of war permitted us to seize this terrain," Truscott wrote, "we could block the retreat of enemy forces to the north along the east bank of the Rhône." The danger, however, was as clear as the opportunity: "If the enemy gained this terrain, we would be confronted by an enormously strong position which would be difficult to turn, and which the enemy could hold long enough to make good his escape." With his three divisions in VI Corps, Truscott saw a chance to destroy or capture twice as many Germans. Air reconnaissance and intelligence had suggested that at least three full German divisions, parts of four or five others, and other miscellaneous troops were still amassed south of Montélimar.

Speed was the critical consideration. But Higgins and his men were puzzled by the movement of their unit. "One of our assignments," Higgins remembers, "was to clear a hill, to prevent the enemy from establishing OPs, Observation Posts, and report Jerry activity. We encountered very few enemy soldiers; we were ahead of their withdrawal [up the Rhône]; we remained there overnight." But the following day, "we were pulled off the hill. Then we were sent up again for the second time."[23]

At 2045 on August 20, Truscott sent an urgent message to Brig. Gen. Fred W. Butler, assistant commander of VI Corps, who was leading a special armored task force designed for rapid advance movement: "You will move at first light 21 August with all possible speed to Montélimar. Block enemy routes of withdrawal up the Rhône valley in that vicinity. 36th Division follows you."[24]

Butler reached Montélimar in the late afternoon and tried to capture the town, but was driven back. Worse, "he had overlooked the vital importance of the high ground just north of Montélimar," Truscott noted, "particularly the long ridge just to the east of and parallel to Highway 7 between Montélimar and Courcourde," which the Germans had seized instead, forcing Butler's unit into a defensive position.

Two days later, Dahlquist and the 36th arrived, but they, too, were repelled. Truscott was disappointed by their performance. "There were mistakes," he wrote later, "as I pointed out to Butler and Dahlquist, but it was water under the bridge." What was important now was to seize the ridge and gain control of the high ground over the Cruas Gorge.

The next day, Truscott learned, to his "profound dismay," that Higgins's unit, the 141st Regiment, and VI Corps artillery, which both should have made contact with Butler's task force, were actually off-line. Truscott was concerned enough to visit 36th Division headquarters in person, but Dahlquist was absent. His chief of staff told Truscott that Dahlquist had delayed sending the 141st and artillery until he could confirm that the Germans were not moving in strength into the area, as he had been informed earlier. But Truscott knew that the reports of enemy movement were "inaccurate and exaggerated." In fact, some four thousand Germans had just surrendered to the 143d Regiment, another unit of the 36th Division, in order not to give themselves up to partisan irregulars advancing with the American and French armies—a "very brave group," according to Higgins, which "completely lacked discipline, combat training, and fear."[25] After four years of occupying France, the Germans were not about to trust their fate to these French partisans.

Truscott was "angry" at Dahlquist's lack of progress. Though he did not feel he could "tell Dahlquist how to deploy his command for battle," Truscott "thought he should have some guidance, as this was his first division command in battle." So he left a strongly worded note at 36th Division headquarters for Dahlquist, ordering him to advance on Montélimar immediately "with the bulk of his division":

> I visited your Command Post this morning and, as your Chief of Staff has probably informed you, was considerably upset because my original instructions covered in subsequent messages had not been carried out. Apparently I failed to make your mission clear to you. The primary mission of the 36th Division is to block the Rhône Valley in the Gap immediately north of the Montélimar. For this purpose you must be prepared to employ the bulk of your Division.[26]

At this point, the Germans were still continuing to retreat to the north of Montélimar. Truscott was "most unhappy." "In spite of assurances" from Dahlquist, the "block on Highway 7 was not effective." The planned trap could not be sprung because of Dahlquist's failure to act quickly and aggressively. In fact, far from being trapped, the Germans had launched a counterattack eastward, though Butler and his task force had stopped them in their tracks.

On August 25, Truscott once again visited Dahlquist's command post. This time he was even more shockingly blunt in his confrontation:

> John, I have come here with the full intention of relieving you of your command. You have reported to me that you held the high ground north of Montélimar and that you had blocked Highway 7. You have not done so. You have failed to carry out my orders. You have just five minutes in which to convince me that you are not at fault.

It was almost unheard of for an Army corps leader to relieve one of his division commanders, a two-star general, in the middle of a major engagement. In his defense, Dahlquist insisted "he had done as well as could be expected." Reports sent to him had indicated his troops were already occupying the high ground above the Rhône, he claimed. It had not been until a day later that he learned they were on a different hill, just to the east of the cliffs overlooking the river. Then the Germans had counterattacked and cut his supply route from the south. But now Dahlquist said he had four artillery battalions in place to rain fire down on Highway 7.

Patch joined Truscott and Dahlquist near the end of their encounter. Perhaps it was the senior general's intercession, or maybe Truscott found Dahlquist's account an adequate explanation rather than simply an excuse.* Whatever the case, though Truscott "did not fully concur" with Dahlquist, he ultimately "decided against relieving him."

Heavy fighting continued over the next few days. On the twenty-seventh, Col. John W. Harmony, commander of the 141st Regiment, Higgins's unit, was wounded. Lieutenant Colonel James H. Critchfield, who had led the 2d Battalion of the 141st, stepped into his role and had to spend "the better part of the day trying to extricate two of his attacking infantry companies that had been surrounded."[27] Two days later, Col. Clyde E. Steele took over the regiment. But even he would stay in command for barely a month.

---

*The authors of *Riviera to the Rhine* suggest that some of Dahlquist's failures at Montélimar were less his fault than a consequence of the 36th Division's already outrunning its sources of supply: ". . . by dark on 19 August the gasoline supply situation had become critical." (p. 206) "[O]perating on a logistical shoestring, the so-called hard-luck 36th Division had at least given a beating to almost every retreating German division, forcing them to run a gauntlet they would not quickly forget." (p. 169)

As the German forces withdrew up the Rhône, Higgins and his unit advanced to "a ringside seat to one of the most spectacular events of the war."[28] A German Panzer outfit entered a gorge below, and from the high ground he "watched them attack another unit in a classic battle pattern." It was almost like being on field maneuvers and observing a full-scale war game from above. But the Germans were beyond the range of the light weapons of an infantry company, and there were no forward observers with Higgins's company to direct artillery fire on the enemy below.

Watching the Germans as they retreated, Higgins thought about what it really would be like to shoot fish in a barrel. The sheer violence and destruction of the engagement were paradoxically highlighted because it took place in "one of the most beautiful areas in the whole world." "I knew it at the time," Higgins now recalls, "but could not appreciate the view, considering the circumstances."

★ ★ ★

Despite Dahlquist's lapses, the Battle of Montélimar was a partial success. The Americans had suffered 1,575 casualties, including 187 KIA (killed in action), 1,023 WIA (wounded in action), and 365 MIA (missing in action)—less than five percent of the troops committed, "although the concentration of casualties in a few infantry battalions of the 141st and 143d regiments," according to the official history, "attests to the bitterness of some of the fighting and the length of the conflict."

But German losses were "considerably higher." During the last ten days of August, 5,800 Germans became POW (prisoners of war) and about 600 were KIA, 1,500 WIA, and 2,160 MIA in the chaotic retreat from Provence—about twenty percent of the German strength in the area.[29]

Truscott had a more qualitative impression of the Battle of Montélimar. In his memoirs, he cited the "after action report" of VI Corps:

> Division artillery, using direct and tank fire, ranged up and down the highway delivering a steady stream of fire on the completely disorganized, bumper to bumper column of vehicles which included armor and horsedrawn guns and equipment. 36th Division artillery continued to hammer away at the motionless enemy vehicles which continued to jam up bumper to bumper along Highway 7. . . .

And in his own direct prose, Truscott continued:

> From Montélimar north to Loriol, road and railroad were lined with tanks, trucks, guns, and vehicles of every description. Hundreds of railway cars loaded with guns and equipment, including no less than seven of the long range railway guns like the "Anzio Express" which had tormented us so much at Anzio. Hundreds of dead horses and dead bodies littered the plain south of Loriol. Engineers cleared the roads with bulldozers before our own transport could use them. And the sight and smell of this section is an experience I have no wish to repeat.
>
> I know of no place where more damage was inflicted upon troops in the field.

Yet significant elements of the German XIX Army had eluded Truscott's trap at Montélimar. They would meet the Americans again in less than two months in the Vosges Mountains, where VI Corps would confront tactical challenges unimagined in the rapid-maneuver warfare of southern France.

Still, "even if Montélimar had not been a perfect battle," Truscott would conclude, "we could still view the record with some degree of satisfaction." Summing up the successes of DRAGOON/ANVIL near the end of August, he concluded:

> In fourteen days, at a cost of 1,331 killed and wounded, the VI Corps had encircled Toulon and Marseille, almost destroyed the German XIX Army east of the Rhône, captured 23,000 prisoners, and was more than a hundred miles north of the beaches with elements still another hundred miles farther on.[30]

But Dahlquist, who had regarded Montélimar as "a great opportunity," had by his own account "fumbled it badly."[31] The rapidly shifting circumstances on the polo field had taught Higgins, as they had Truscott, that the "most significant quality of leadership" on the battlefield was "decisiveness." Indecision threatened the faith of the men whose lives depended on their leaders' judgment.

Dahlquist would not have another "great opportunity" for decisiveness during the next six weeks, as the 36th Division and the rest of VI Corps raced up the Rhône in pursuit of, more than in combat with, the Germans. His next opportunity, in the Vosges, would subject not only his own troops but also the 442d to a very different and much harsher test of his leadership.

ORDER OF BATTLE
IN THE VOSGES MOUNTAINS, OCTOBER 1944

Supreme Headquarters Allied Expeditionary Forces (SHAEF)
Gen. Dwight D. Eisenhower

6th Army Group Southern Group of Armies
Lt. Gen. Jacob L. Devers

Seventh Army
Lt. Gen. Alexander Patch

VI Corps
Maj. Gen. Lucian K. Truscott, Jr.
Maj. Gen. E. H. Brooks (Oct. 25)

36th Division ("Texas")
Maj. Gen. John E. Dahlquist

442d Regimental Combat Team ("Go for Broke")
Col. Charles W. Pence
Lt. Col. Virgil R. Miller (Oct. 29)

HEADQUARTERS COMPANY

ANTITANK COMPANY

CANNON COMPANY

MEDICAL DETACHMENT
T/5 James K. Okubo

SERVICE COMPANY

232D ENGINEERS

206TH ARMY BAND

522D FIELD ARTILLERY BATTALION
Lt. Col. Baya Harrison, Jr.

HEADQUARTERS BATTERY

A BATTERY

B BATTERY

C BATTERY
2d Lt. Sus Ito
S/Sgt. George Oiye
T/4 Yuki Minaga

SERVICE BATTERY

MEDICAL DETACHMENT

100TH ("PURPLE HEART") BATTALION
Lt. Col. Gordon Singles
Capt. Young Oak Kim

HEADQUARTERS COMPANY

A COMPANY

B COMPANY
Capt. Sakae Takahashi
T/Sgt. Al Takahashi

C COMPANY

D COMPANY

2D BATTALION
Lt. Col. James M. Hanley

HEADQUARTERS COMPANY

E COMPANY
2d Lt. Daniel Inouye
Pvt. George "Joe" Sakato
Pvt. Saburo Tanamachi

F COMPANY
1st Sgt. Jack Wakamatsu

G COMPANY
Pfc. Joe Nishimoto

H COMPANY
Capt. Christopher Keegan
S/Sgt. Robert Kuroda

3D BATTALION
Lt. Col. Alfred Pursall

HEADQUARTERS COMPANY

I COMPANY
T/Sgt. Shig Doi
T/Sgt. Takashi Senzaki
S/Sgt. Shiro Kashino
Pvt. Barney Hajiro

K COMPANY

L COMPANY

M COMPANY

21st Army Group	12th Army Group
Northern Group of Armies	Central Group of Armies
Field Marshal Bernard Montgomery	Lt. Gen. Omar N. Bradley

French First Army
Gen. Jean de Lattre de Tassigny

XV Corps
Maj. Gen. Wade H. Haislip

3d Infantry Division	45th Infantry Division
("Rock of the Marne")	("Thunderbird")
Maj. Gen. John E. O'Daniel	Maj. Gen. William W. Eagles

141st Regiment	142d Regiment	143d Regiment
("Alamo")	Col. George E. Lynch	Col. Paul D. Adams
Col. Carl E. Lundquist (Oct. 7)		
Col. Charles H. Owens (Oct. 28)		

1ST ("LOST") BATTALION	2D BATTALION	3D BATTALION	131ST F. A. BATTALION	132D F. A. BATTALION
Lt. Col. William Bird	Lt. Col. James H. Critchfield	Maj. Walter Bruyere III	2d Lt. Erwin Blonder	

HEADQUARTERS COMPANY
Capt. Bill Hawkins

133RD F. A. BATTALION

A COMPANY
1st Lt. Marty Higgins
T/Sgt. Ed Guy

155TH F. A. BATTALION

B COMPANY
1st Lt. Harry Huberth

111TH COMBAT ENGINEER BATTALION

C COMPANY
1st Lt. Joe Kimble

111TH MEDICAL BATTALION

D COMPANY
1st Lt. Gordon Nelson
S/Sgt. Jack Wilson
Cpl. Gene Airheart

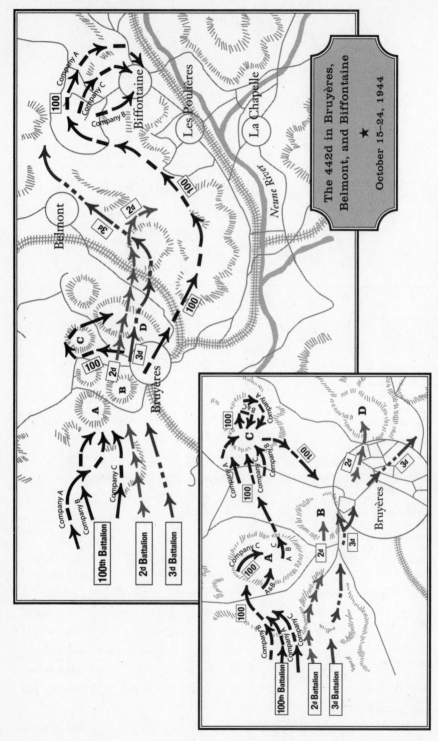

The 442d in Bruyères, Belmont, and Biffontaine

October 15–24, 1944

Adapted from MTOUSA, *442nd Combat Team*, and Pierre Moulin, *U.S. Samurais in Bruyères.*

5

DOGFACES

The Liberation of Bruyères

*Rocks are better than mud because you can curl yourself around the
big rocks, even if you wake up with sore bruises where the little rocks
dug into you. When you wake up in the mud your cigarettes are all
wet and you have an ache in your joints and a rattle in your chest.*
—BILL MAULDIN[1]

The Vosges Mountains, Eastern France,
September–October 1944

On the morning of October 15, 1944, Pvt. George "Joe" Sakato was sitting under a tree next to Pvt. Yohei Sagami, another rifleman in E Company of the 442d Regiment. The 1st and 2d platoons of E Company had
already advanced a couple hundred yards ahead, in the direction of
Bruyères, and the 3d platoon, Sakato's unit, was awaiting orders. It was
cold and damp, and daylight was just beginning to penetrate the mist. Artillery played a muted overture in the distance.

Everyone was "all nervous and on edge."[2] To relieve the tension,
Sakato—the "tiny runt" who had struggled up the gangplank under his
field pack, en route to Italy—jumped to his feet, put two fingers under his
nose, raised his right hand in a stiff-armed salute, and shouted "*Sieg heil*—
in case we lose!" He thought his crude imitation of Adolf Hitler would
raise a few laughs and settle everyone down. Instead, it provoked a chewing out from the lieutenant who led his platoon, who "didn't think it was
funny," Sakato remembers. Judging from his last name, Sakato says, "He
must have been of German descent."

Suddenly the sound of artillery became louder. Sakato heard himself

yell, "Incoming!" And the next thing he knew, he was lying ten feet away
from the tree he had just been leaning against. He checked himself for
wounds, then looked back and saw Sagami lying motionless on the
ground. A stream of blood as thick as a pencil was spurting from a wound
at the base of his neck. Sakato "tried to stop the blood from coming out,"
but realized he would "have to choke him to stop it." He "hollered for the
medics," who "gave him some plasma, but he died on the way down the
hill."

Sakato and his fellow riflemen anxiously looked around for their lieutenant to issue orders, but he had disappeared into the gray dawn. "He ran
down the hill back to headquarters," Sakato remembers, or "so the captain
said on the radio. So T/Sgt. Tsuneo Takemoto took over the platoon."
Sakato "ached all over" from the blast that had thrown him through the
air, and he later noticed a cut he had missed on his wrist from a shell fragment. But he moved forward with his platoon into the early-morning
fog—and whatever lay beyond.

It was the first day of the Battle of Bruyères. It was also the first day of
combat for Sakato, who had arrived as a replacement only a month or so
before. And for the 442d it was the beginning of the campaign in the Vosges Mountains, the first day of a long journey into the nightmare of combat in the black woods of eastern France.

★ ★ ★

The vivid images of World War II that have endured through the decades include Joe Rosenthal's photograph of the raising of the American
flag on Iwo Jima and Robert Capa's shots of the landing on Omaha Beach
on D-day. Yet for the soldiers on the front lines, perhaps the most widespread and recognizable images of the war as they experienced it were
not photographs but drawings—the cartoons by Bill Mauldin that appeared regularly in *Stars and Stripes* and in papers across the United
States.

Mauldin's genius was in illustrating both the horror of combat—
expressed in the black comedy of mundane indignities suffered by ordinary foot soldiers—and the camaraderie born of shared misery and fear.
The lousy food, the petty regulations that made little sense in training and
no sense whatsoever when bullets were whizzing overhead, the ridiculous
behavior of rear echelon officers out of their element, the outsized longing

for the simple pleasure of a shower or a cup of hot coffee—all of these and more were the subject of Mauldin's stark pen-and-ink sketches. His goal was to "make something out of the humorous situations which come up even when you don't think life could be any more miserable."[3] Without showing any blood and gore, he effectively chronicled their toll on the human spirit, as well as the resilience of enlisted men in the face of almost unimaginable devastation. To Mauldin, they were "men who are able to fight a ruthless war against ruthless enemies, and still grin at themselves," though "it doesn't seem funny at all sometimes when you stop and think it over."

His greatest creations were two mournful-faced soldiers named Willie and Joe, representative GIs ("government issues") in the infantry, "the group in the army which gives more and gets less than anybody else," according to Mauldin. "They don't get fancy pay, they know their food is the worst in the army because you can't whip up lemon pies or even hot soup at the front, and they know how much of a burden they bear." In panel after panel, week in and week out, Mauldin showed Willie and Joe in one sodden foxhole after another—unshaven, bedraggled, exhausted. "Those guys," Mauldin wrote, "really know what real weariness of body, brain, and soul can be."

Willie and Joe were constantly griping—the infantryman's prerogative—about their miserable circumstances. And it was the darkness of their humor in the shadow of even blacker circumstances that expressed their constant struggle to retain even the smallest shred of humanity—such as a dry pair of socks—during the inhumane state of war. Mauldin took great pains to reveal, beneath their complaints, their "nobility and dignity," which "come from the way they live unselfishly and risk their lives to help each other." They exemplified the foot soldiers "who have really gone through hell"—the "few hundred thousand who have lived through misery, suffering, and death for endless 168-hour weeks . . . despite their bitching and griping and goldbricking and mortal fear, they are facing cold steel and screaming lead and hard enemies, and they are advancing and beating the hell out of the opposition."

Mauldin was careful not to identify Willie and Joe by unit or, for the most part, campaign, because all soldiers "are convinced that their division is the best and the only division . . . you'd have to mention six other outfits if you talked of one." The absurd situations Willie and Joe found themselves in were instantly recognizable to GIs everywhere—from Europe to the Pacific. But Mauldin based his two characters on real men he saw every day in his own outfit—the 45th Division, part of VI Corps. And the real-life versions of Willie and Joe were fighting alongside the 100th Battalion and 442d Regimental Combat Team in Italy and France. (In fact, Mauldin himself would battle on behalf of 442d veterans when they returned home to face prejudice after the war.)

Caked in mud as they usually were, Willie and Joe were often almost indistinguishable from each other—and were intentionally drawn that way. Mauldin knew firsthand that a few days of life on the front made all infantrymen look alike. And his cartoons popularized a term for American soldiers that perfectly captured their grimy existence: dogface.

As Sakato and the rest of 442d headed into battle in the miserable cold and damp of the Vosges in mid-October, they would be just as filthy after a few days, and just as bloody, as any other American soldiers. The color of a man's face made no difference when it was covered with mud. So it was fitting that the code name for the VI Corps offensive in eastern France, in which the 442d would play a significant role, was also DOG-FACE.

★ ★ ★

Truscott, who had proved himself a general's general in Sicily, Italy, and southern France, had always been a soldier's soldier as well.* Just before Anzio, where the American troops would be stuck on the beachhead and under siege for four months, he noticed that "American soldiers in World War II did not sing as their fathers had done in World War I." Although he "had no wish to hear American soldiers sing as they tramped along," he had "always thought that good ballads are healthy for morale and for the souls of men."[4]

One night Truscott was entertained in his command post by three members of the 7th Infantry band, playing violin, accordion, and guitar.

---

*To Bill Mauldin, whose cartoons appealed to infantrymen partly because of their irreverence toward officers, Truscott was "somebody special . . . a hard-boiled old man who was incapable of planned dramatics. . . . Truscott spent half his time at the front—the real front—with nobody in attendance but a nervous jeep driver and a worried aide." (*The Brass Ring*, pp. 241, 272.)

They played and sang a tune that caught his ear, and he persuaded them to adapt it for the newly formed 3d Division band. The musicians were "vastly amused" when the general "sang the ditty for them and with them," as he did "each morning for several days." Eventually they "got it right" and made the tune "famous all over Europe and elsewhere." The perfect accompaniment to Mauldin's cartoons, the song was called "The Dogface Soldier."

★ ★ ★

DOGFACE was scheduled to begin the third week of October, with preliminary attacks the week before on the towns of Bruyères and Brouvelieures, at the gateway to the Vosges Mountains.

By the beginning of October, the Allied forces had rushed more than three hundred miles up the Rhône, propelled by Truscott's aggressive maneuvers from the moment DRAGOON/ANVIL had hit the beaches. Both German and Allied forces had moved so swiftly in September that Marty Higgins remembers his company had sometimes "lost contact with the enemy."[5] On one mission, he was assigned to reconnoiter a series of villages, leading a convoy of five jeeps. "The mission was to send back a jeep from each checkpoint," he remembers. "If I encountered the enemy, I was to return immediately with an estimate of the enemy strength." He was specifically ordered not to engage any Germans in a firefight.

Along the way, Higgins and his men were joined by random members of the FFI, the underground fighters organized as the French Forces of the Interior. So by the time they hit each town, Higgins was leading a small army. But instead of running into Germans, they were greeted again and again by cheering townspeople who waved American flags, showered the soldiers with flowers, and broke out bottles of wine they had been carefully hiding for the day of liberation.

Still, Higgins's cavalry training had taught him that an attack could come from any direction during rapid maneuvers. So in each town, while the celebrations continued, he sent out patrols to "eliminate the element of surprise by the Jerries." And, as a further precaution, "those that could participate in the celebration" were warned not to overdo it. "Thank God we never had to engage the Germans," Higgins says with relief today, perhaps thinking of all the wine that was consumed.

Celebration was mostly the order of the day between the Battle of
Montélimar and the arrival of VI Corps in the Vosges a month later. One
memorable photo taken on September 17, 1944, shows a smiling little
French girl in a hooded cape handing a bottle of wine to a passing American soldier—T/Sgt. Joe Trdenic, of F Company of the 141st Regiment—
while her father, a stocky man in a raincoat and beret, stands a few feet
away, puffing on a cigarette and looking on approvingly.[6]

Since the "second D-day," the American Seventh Army and the First
French Army had covered more distance in one month than the Allied
forces landing in Normandy on D-day had covered in three months.[7] "Indeed, by 14 September, D plus 30, the Seventh Army had achieved objectives that ANVIL planners had not expected it to attain until about D plus
120," according to Army historians.[8] The swift Allied successes and territorial gains after Montélimar are sometimes dismissed as resulting merely
from the hasty German retreat. While the German XIX Army was withdrawing ahead of the Allies up the east bank of the Rhône, the rest of the
German Army Group G was evacuating the entire southwest and west of
France.

But the enemy plan was not just to run, according to the Army's campaign history. It was to pick where to fight, as the Allies recognized at
the time:

> The German goal was to reach the area in front of the Reich border be-
> fore the Allied advance, join with Army Group B, and present a unified
> front to the invaders. As a result, from the last days of August to mid-
> September, the two opposing armies in southern France raced up the
> Rhône valley and proceeded northward one after the other—each often
> more concerned with reaching its objective than in impeding the
> progress of the other.[9]

The Germans were planning to make their last stand in eastern France
in the midst of one of the strongest natural barriers in the region—the
Vosges Mountains, which run roughly northeast to southwest through Alsace and Lorraine, border regions that had been contested by Germany for
centuries. In the heart of the Vosges, parallel to the Rhine, ran the infamous
Maginot Line, the elaborately fortified French defenses—with concrete
bunkers descending several stories underground, miles of underground

tunnels, and even subterranean train tracks—built after World War I. Although the Maginot Line has long been derided as providing only the illusion of defense, it did exactly what it had been designed to do: repel a German invasion through eastern France. At the beginning of World War II, the Germans had skirted to the north of the Maginot Line and invaded France through Belgium and Luxembourg, rather than fighting through Alsace, where the fortifications of the Line were most dense, or the Vosges, where the French had reinforced the natural barriers of the forests and mountains.

By the time VI Corps reached the Vosges, the Allied forces had become victims of their own success. In August, Toulon had fallen a week ahead of schedule and Marseille almost a month faster than originally anticipated in the planning for DRAGOON/ANVIL. But even though the port cities were under Allied control by the end of the month, another two weeks passed before they were able to handle the tens of thousands of tons of matériel—food, fuel, ammunition, and other supplies—required to support the rapid advance from Montélimar up the Rhône. The engineers had to clear up what the Germans had left in their wake: sunken ships blocking channel entrances, minefields in the harbors, damaged or destroyed jetties, cranes, and warehouses, and booby traps everywhere. "Minesweepers, mostly U.S. Navy vessels, cleared some 5,000 mines of various sizes and types from the main harbor and contiguous waters," according to the official campaign history, "while U.S. Army engineers removed well over thirty tons of explosives from the dock areas."[10]

Despite the heroic efforts of the engineers and minesweepers, it was not until September 15 that the first ship-to-shore unloading had taken place in Marseille. Commercial unloading had begun in Toulon on September 20.[11] By then, VI Corps, more than two hundred miles north up the Rhône, was almost literally running out of gas, after consuming about a hundred thousand gallons every day.[12]

And though Allied casualties were comparatively light, the three American divisions had been in combat almost continuously for more than a month, with few replacements. By the time they reached the Moselle, the men of the 3d, 36th, and 45th were exhausted. Brigadier General Butler, who had led the task force at Montélimar, had already noted a "declining aggressiveness of the front-line troop and a tendency to rely

more often on artillery and mortar fire in small combat engage-
ments."[13]

And the problem of command continuity continued to plague the
unlucky 141st, down to the company and platoon level. Captain James
McNeil, head of Higgins's A Company, had been killed shortly after
landing in southern France. Then 1st Lt. Ashburn Daughtrey had taken
over, but he died in a firefight a few days later. The company's third
commander—who Higgins says "shall remain nameless"—was relieved almost immediately. Then Higgins, though still a second lieutenant, assumed command of A Company. At the same time, T/Sgt. Ed Guy,
another Irish American, took over the weapons platoon of the company.
In the weeks ahead, he and Higgins would become close friends.

"I loved my men," Higgins says. They were the kind of soldiers who
were "real heroes" to Higgins, not the "movie version" but "the average
guy you grew up with who rose to spectacular heights due to a camaraderie forged in combat." It was only this kind of bond among smaller
units that would keep the regiment and the division functioning—as Higgins would find out all too soon. But he soon learned that leadership imposed limits on friendships forged in foxholes. The turnover from
casualties in his company was over two hundred percent while Higgins
was in it. "When I became C.O. [commanding officer], I did not want to
know my men too well," Higgins says with regret. "It hurt when they became KIAs or WIAs."[14]

As VI Corps left the Rhône Valley behind, it entered "hilly, often
wooded ground that gave many advantages to the defense." The problems
of "transportation, supply, fatigue, weather, and terrain" were all factors
that began to "blunt the edge of the Seventh Army's combat power."[15]
And Devers, Patch, and Truscott were in danger of losing the tactical flexibility, maneuver, and speed that had served them so well since the landing
in southern France.

★ ★ ★

But it was precisely at this point that the always aggressive Truscott had
seen an opportunity to strike fast and hard at the German heartland. VI
Corps was veering from the Rhône toward the Belfort Gap, a natural pas-
sageway through the Vosges, near Switzerland, to the Rhine. With a captured enemy map in hand, Truscott had "reason to hope that German

strength in the Belfort Gap was not too formidable," and he and Patch agreed that "the Belfort Gap is the Gateway to Germany."* But on September 14, Patch suddenly yanked the rug out from under him and canceled the plan to strike directly east. Instead, VI Corps would angle northeast toward Strasbourg, through the highest and most rugged parts of the Vosges.

Truscott was astonished at the change in plans and immediately wrote Patch an almost intemperate response for the record, although he "had no hope that it could have any effect upon the decision."[16] After making the case for attacking through the Belfort Gap, which he knew Patch already understood, Truscott explained with horrifying precision why the new line of attack was dangerous:

> The axis prescribed in F[ield] O[rder] 5 leads through the Vosges Mountains, where roads are limited, terrain rugged and easily defended. With the approach of weather in which rain and snow are to be expected, operations will be most difficult. As demonstrated in Italy last winter, the Boche can limit progress to a snail's pace and even stop it entirely, even against superior strength. . . . It would seem wasteful to employ the three most veteran divisions in the American Army [the 3d, 36th, and 45th] in an operation where they can be contained by a fraction of their strength and where their demonstrated ability to maneuver is so strictly limited.

In four sentences, Truscott had convincingly summarized the case against the plan that would become DOGFACE. In the Vosges, the Germans would have weather and terrain on their side, as well as time already spent fortifying defensive positions. The Allied forces included some of the very best and most experienced troops in the entire American Army, but no army in history had ever successfully crossed the Vosges against enemy opposition. And Adolf Hitler had personally ordered Army Group

---

Command Missions, p. 441. This was the route followed by Henri de La Tour d'Auvergne, vicomte de Turenne, maréchal de France, in his victorious winter campaign of 1674–75. One of the great French commanders, Turenne invaded Alsace from the south, took Turckheim, crossed the Rhine, and penetrated as far east as the Neckar River. B. H. Liddell Hart cited this campaign as a classic example of the "indirect approach" in *Strategy*, pp. 71–73.

G, consisting of the German First and Nineteenth Armies, to defend the Vosges down to the last man.

The Vosges campaign would be one of the few periods during the whole war "when the odds were even," as the historian Keith Bonn described it— with the Allies and the Germans "on a comparable operational and tactical footing."[17] Victory would not be determined by Allied air power or superior matériel; only sheer combat strength and proficiency would prevail.

Unfortunately, every doubt Truscott expressed would be confirmed by the grim events of the next two months. And the resulting toll on man- power and matériel would not be limited to the organic units of VI Corps. Hardest hit would be the 442d, only recently, and temporarily, attached to the 36th Division.

Truscott was analyzing the situation solely as a field commander, which was his proper role. But the "big picture" was not just about com- bat; among other things, it was about command. And Patch's Seventh Army, which included Truscott's VI Corps, was part of Devers's 6th Army Group, which in mid-September had fallen under the control of SHAEF (Supreme Headquarters Allied Expeditionary Forces) and Gen. Dwight D. Eisenhower, as the American and French forces moved from the Mediterranean theater to the European theater.

Pursuing a "broad front" strategy, Eisenhower now had what he had originally envisioned during the planning for OVERLORD: a continuous Allied front extending from the English Channel to the French border at the intersection of Germany and Switzerland—from Montgomery's 21st Army Group through Bradley's 12th through Devers's 6th. By this time, Marseille was fully operational and was processing more than eighteen thousand tons of supplies every day. It would be another two months be- fore Antwerp became a fully operational port on the Channel, and then only under heavy German bombing. In the meantime, a third of the sup- plies for the campaign in northern France would come through Marseille in the south. And fourteen more divisions would enter the war along the Rhône corridor during the fall.[18] But Eisenhower continued to believe that the sole function of the southern France operation was to support the drive across Belgium and Holland in the north. It never seemed to have oc- curred to Eisenhower and the SHAEF planners that a more flexible strat- egy, based on the kind of rapid maneuver that had succeeded in southern France, could find a different path into Germany.[19]

The Allied forces have always been criticized for choosing mass assault over maneuver, for relying on the brute strength of numbers and tonnage rather than exploiting their enemy's weaknesses.[20] Nowhere was this more apparent than in Eisenhower's decisions in northern France and Belgium in the late fall of 1944.

★ ★ ★

All of these strategic considerations were four to five levels of command removed from the 442d. The dogfaces in DOGFACE knew only that they had another hill to climb, another battle to fight, another town to take. But nothing they or their veteran counterparts in the 100th Battalion had experienced so far had prepared them for what lay ahead in the Vosges.

The 442d had left Italy at the end of September, packed aboard transport ships on the choppy Ligurian Sea. At first they had no idea where they were going; troop movements were classified information, and like foot soldiers everywhere, they were always the last to know. But when their ships, instead of turning left, toward Corsica, turned right, they realized they were heading toward combat in France.

After landing in Marseille, the 442d followed Highway 7 up the Rhône, traveling in trucks and boxcars to a bivouac area at Charmois-devant-Bruyères, near Épinal—where, tragically, many of them would later return to be buried in a cemetery reserved for Americans.

As Truscott had predicted, the weather was a negative factor from the very start. "Adverse conditions of rainy weather and slippery roads"[21] had followed the 442d all the way from the coast, and more wet and cold were forecast for the weeks ahead, enveloping ground troops and limiting or even curtailing air support.

On October 14, the 442d moved northeast to the Helledraye Forest. They were led by French scouts—among them, Sgt. Paul Charpin, an FFI veteran, and Paul Gérard, son of a local farmer. When the troops assembled near *Le Void de la Borde*, George "Joe" Sakato remembers the trucks, "half broken down" to begin with, could not negotiate the roads, which were "slick with mud." So the 442d hiked the final two miles to their jumping-off point, which was separated from their objective by another two miles of thick forest. A signal corps photo taken that day shows Sakato and his friend Pvt. Saburo Tanamachi at the head of a double column of soldiers tromping along a narrow unpaved road, with tall pines looming on one side and a muddy ravine on the other.[22] "Our coats were all wet and getting heavy," Sakato recalls. "We had our backpacks on and our rifles slogging in the mud." For someone weighing around 135 pounds, carrying all that weight in the rain—about 40 pounds of equipment, including an M1 rifle, which weighed 9.5 pounds—was "real tough."[23]

Accustomed to the subtropical weather of the islands, the Hawaiians were particularly susceptible to the cold and rain. France in the fall was nothing like Italy in the summer. But the Buddhaheads did bring an unexpected advantage to the battlefield. Over the radio, their rapid-fire pidgin was untranslatable by the Germans—though sometimes by their fellow soldiers as well. "Even we couldn't understand what they were talking about," recalls Pfc. Shuji Taketomo of I Company. The Buddhaheads were "really good at it."[24]

When the attack was launched the next morning, October 15, "the primary objective was the capture of the city of Bruyères, a city of four thousand population."[25] Although it was really more a small town than a city, Bruyères was a transportation and communications hub in the region, with three major roads and a railroad line radiating out from a central square and main street. One road led northeast to St. Dié and Strasbourg, and beyond that, Germany.

Nestled in a valley like a stone in the palm of an outstretched right hand, Bruyères is cupped by four hills, with the little finger pointing west to the Forêt de Faite, the ring finger designated by the Allies as Hill A, the middle finger Hill B, the index finger Hill C, and the thumb Hill D. As it was in Italy, the battle would be to capture the high ground, which gave artillery, mortars, tanks, and automatic weapons sweeping fields of fire over the valleys below. Control of the hills meant control of the whole territory.

From a distance, the hills look like gentle and inviting mounds fringed with green. Up close, they are harsh and forbidding. Many of the slopes are quite steep, forty-five degrees or more. The underbrush is knee high. And the trees are so tall and densely packed together that sunlight barely penetrates the canopy.[26] Army reports routinely compared the forests of the Vosges to a "jungle." And the 442d was facing only the foothills of the mountain chain. Higher and harsher climbs awaited them just miles away.

By this time, Dahlquist was concerned that his troops were "very low in spirits and determination." In addition to casualties, deserters and stragglers had depleted the ranks of the 36th Division, which was averaging only about 121 men per company (out of an authorized strength of 193).[27] The 442d, averaging around 180 men per company after its influx of replacements, was the freshest unit, so it would lead the assault on Bruyères, with the help of the 143d Regiment of the 36th Division. The rest of the "Texas" division would be temporarily in reserve or deployed in supporting attacks.[28]

At 0800 the 442d jumped off, with the 100th and 2d Battalions in the lead and the 3d Battalion in reserve. Young Oak Kim's old unit, B Company, spearheaded the drive against Hill A through the thickly wooded Forêt de Faite. The unit immediately ran into stiff resistance from two German companies, armed with artillery, automatic weapons, and a tank—even though, according to Kim, Maj. Gen. Dahlquist had said the 100th would take their objective with ease. Kim, by this time a captain and the battalion's intelligence officer, says the general was radioed about the enemy's strength but refused to believe it. "The battle we were fighting was a different battle than Dahlquist was fighting," Kim says, "and that's the way it was during the entire time [in the Vosges]. . . . We came to the conclusion we're in trouble. Not because of the Germans but because we had a commander who doesn't believe what we're telling him."[29]

In the middle of the afternoon a heavy artillery barrage rained down on A Company, causing one KIA and nineteen WIA. B Company "fought continuously throughout the day, took five prisoners, and suffered one KIA," according to the regimental journal. One of the company's bazooka men scored a hit on the German tank, but the shell failed to explode, and the tank escaped. All the while, C Company "exchanged small arms fire with the Germans in the woods and dug in during the afternoon."

On the right flank of the 100th, the 2d Battalion also ran into heavy opposition. Enemy artillery wounded three men in E Company, Sakato's unit. F Company ran into a firefight that lasted three hours. By midafternoon, "enemy resistance increased," and "the battalion dug in."[30]

By the end of the day, the 442d had not advanced far beyond the original line of departure. For the 672 replacements—including Sakato and his friend Saburo Tanamachi—who had just joined the 442d the previous month, the cold and rain and fear suffusing the black woods had added up to a brutal initiation into warfare. The 100th had suffered thirty-nine casualties, including two KIA. But the two attacking battalions had taken twenty German prisoners, who yielded important information during interrogation: the locations of the enemy command post and ration dump, which were quickly targeted by the 522d Field Artillery Battalion, and the locations and layouts of minefields along the road leading into Bruyères, which were passed along to the 232d Engineer Company.

The next morning, the 2d Battalion "advanced against infantry and machine gun nests," according to the regimental journal, and by the end of the afternoon advanced "to within 1000 meters of Bruyères." But at 1730, the Germans mounted a counterattack from Hill B, known as Le Château Col, after the ruins of an ancient castle looming directly over the center of town. Infantry and three tanks, supported by fire from mortars and SP (self-propelled) guns, assaulted the 442d for more than an hour. But the 2d Battalion held its ground against a downpour of bullets and shells. The hard lessons learned on the hills near Belvedere, Italy, where the veteran 100th Battalion had rescued the junior unit, now stiffened the resolve of the 442d.

On the left, the 100th Battalion was making steady progress— measured in yards—toward Hill A. T/Sgt. Al Takahashi, who had been an orderly shining shoes before getting the chance to carry a gun as a replacement in the 100th, remembers facing an open area that the 522d and division artillery had "shelled the hell out of." To his right, Capt. Young Oak Kim had arranged covering fire from a 36th Division tank. After hesitating for several long moments, Takahashi suddenly found himself, almost against his own will, yelling and charging across the clearing. "It's a good thing we were young and stupid," he says, still amazed today. Though bullets were buzzing everywhere, his momentum carried him, unscathed, all the way to the German line, where he literally stumbled into what he thought was an empty foxhole. To his astonishment, three German soldiers popped up, arms held high, and surrendered. "I thought I was dreaming," Takahashi says.

By the end of the day, the 100th had reached the base of the hill. The 442d had taken a total of twenty-one prisoners, along with documents revealing the enemy troop disposition.

That night, "a cold wind and soaking rain" introduced the 442d to the coldest and wettest fall that residents of the Vosges could remember. During the next two weeks, there would be only one day without rain.

Takahashi recalls thinking, "If the Germans don't get me, the weather will."[31] The troops, clad in the summer uniforms they had worn in sunny Italy, were "sopping wet, through and through," Kim recalls. "It was so cold, every muscle in your body shook. If you talked, you chattered. You couldn't hold your hands still, the muscles in your arms were shaking."[32]

One of Mauldin's cartoons shows Joe and Willie sitting in puddles under a tree in a rainstorm. One of them turns to the other and complains the tree is leaking.[33] Only, as the beleaguered troops were learning, rain was the least of the things to worry about under a tree.

In Italy, the 100th and 442d had learned a lot about the fine art of digging foxholes for shelter at night. It was not enough to burrow straight down—you had to dig sideways at the bottom, resulting in an L-shaped excavation. After all, your legs had to go somewhere, unless you wanted to spend the whole night with your knees to your chest. But then you had to decide what to do with your helmet. By the time you finished digging, water had already collected in a pool at the bottom, so you couldn't sit on the ground without getting soaked. A helmet made a good perch to squat on, but your head was then left uncovered. And that was a problem, not just because of the rain but because of the deadly showers of tree bursts.

Tree bursts were the hail of hot steel fragments and wood spikes from mortar and artillery shells exploding in the dense canopy of the forest overhead. Although the 100th and 442d had suffered tree bursts in Italy, the forests in the Vosges were much thicker and the trees taller, so the Germans had more opportunities to multiply the deadly effect of their shells. A single round that might miss a target in the open could become many times more lethal in the dense woods. As the Vosges campaign wore on, the 442d came to fear tree bursts as much as, if not more than, direct enemy fire.

So the burrowing soldiers learned to cover the openings of their foxholes with layers of branches and underbrush. "We cut down small trees, made logs of them to put over our foxholes, then spread pine boughs over them and threw sand and mud" over everything, Sakato recalls, to protect themselves from flying spikes of death. Finally, the weary soldiers could wrap themselves in a blanket and tent. Struggling under the weight of their backpacks, ammunition, and weapons, they had long since discarded the tent poles, since no one could actually remember ever pitching a tent in any previous combat. The tent cloth was better employed as an additional layer of cover.

Just before they fell asleep, the dogfaces found still other uses for their government-issue supplies. With a comic ingenuity that would have delighted Mauldin, they slipped condoms over their rifle barrels to keep the water out. And in the middle of the night, rather than leave their foxholes, some of them filled condoms with urine.

Digging, cutting, layering, bundling up, and coping with the demands of nature—these became the routine the men of the 442d would follow most nights during the next five weeks. Another Mauldin cartoon shows Joe digging a foxhole in the rain, turning to his buddy, and griping that he is becoming an authority on European soil.[34] It was a sentiment the 442d came to share.

Whatever physical protection it provided, their nightly routine was also a ritual to numb the terrors they had experienced during the day, and to ward off the fears that would pierce their dreams through the night, as shells continued to burst overhead, in dazzling displays of deadly fireworks. Despite their elaborate precautions, sheer luck was often, perhaps usually, the final arbiter of who would live and who would die. In Italy, Kim had often slept aboveground, figuring his chances of getting killed were about the same as belowground. In the midst of the continuous shelling outside Bruyères, Sakato recalls seeing one soldier who "got out of his foxhole to crawl over to the next foxhole to get a cigarette from his buddies." The next thing the soldier knew, "a shell hit the tree above his foxhole" and the tree "came down right down" where he had just been. His craving for a smoke had saved his life. For the rest of the night a stark reminder of his good fortune stuck out of his former foxhole "like a Christmas tree."[35]

Paul Charpin, the FFI scout, also miraculously escaped death when a white-hot mortar fragment struck his abdomen. His belt buckle melted, but it stopped the shrapnel.

Al Takahashi remembers being wide awake in his foxhole, unable to sleep after the adrenaline rush of battle. Combat had taken him a long distance, physically and emotionally, from his days as an orderly, restricted because of his parents' country of origin to shining shoes, typing requisitions, and dreaming of joining the Army Air Corps. Now he was so close to the Germans, he could hear them digging in for the night as well. Just for a moment, he thought, "I'd like to crawl over and talk to them"—and maybe find "another guy like me." Surely war was not the answer. But he quickly pulled himself out of his reverie. "When they start shooting, you forget all that," he recalls sadly. "The first thing I learned was 'Shoot him before he shoots you.' "[36]

Though nighttime brought some respite from combat, many of the men of the 442d found little comfort in thoughts of home. In another foxhole in the black woods, an F Company infantryman was "quietly sobbing" after reading a letter he had just received from his parents in a "relocation camp" stateside. They had learned their house left behind in rural California "had been burned down by the people of the community," according to 1st Sgt. Jack Wakamatsu. "We often wondered who our real enemies were, and why we were fighting here in France for a little town we'd never heard of," Wakamatsu wrote later, "risking everything trying to free this place from the enemies of freedom, while our own people in America imprisoned our families and now were destroying our homes there."[37]

The third day of battle, October 17, saw heavy German counterattacks in the early morning. Following a barrage by artillery and SP guns, two German infantry companies assaulted E and F Companies of the 2d Battalion, while another two companies hit B and C Companies of the 100th Battalion. With support from their heavy weapons companies, D and H, and from the 522d Field Artillery Battalion, the two battalions of the 442d fended off the Germans. But two hours later, the Germans regrouped on Hills A and B and once again charged down the slopes toward the 2d Battalion. This time the battalion's bazooka teams rose to the occasion and "drove the Germans back into the hills," as the regimental journal put it.[38]

In the afternoon, Dahlquist ordered A Company to wipe out the pockets of Germans between the 100th and 2d Battalions. The stone houses and commercial buildings in and around Bruyères were bristling with armaments. Fortified with automatic weapons at the base of Hills A and B, the Germans had pinned down the two battalions and halted their advance. One platoon of C Company near Hill A even had to withdraw "because of overwhelming enemy fire."[39] But the rest of the 100th pressed forward methodically and cleared house after house, where as many as fifteen German machine guns and two antitank guns had been concealed.[40] As night fell, C Company brought an "escaped British Indian in civilian clothes" to the command post. He told the officers at headquarters that "about 2,000 of his kind" had "escaped from the enemy" after being held at Épinal and were "roaming in the vicinity."[41]

Meanwhile, E and F companies had made it as far as the end of the woods, with the town lying before them across an open field. Wakamatsu, of F Company, heard directly from Dahlquist on a field telephone. The general "told me that only a few machine guns were stopping our advance," Wakamatsu wrote later, "and he ordered me to get on with it *now*. Since he was calling us from some place far behind, how could he know what the real situation was like?" Wakamatsu "invited the general to come up and lead the next attack; we would be happy to follow him." But then the line went dead.[42]

In the E Company sector, Sakato and his platoon "saw a German Tiger tank moving out of town" and into the field. The mechanical beast lumbered to a stop and turned its lethal snout toward the Americans. "Then I saw a puff of smoke coming from the gun," Sakato recalls, "and before we knew it, there was a big pow and shrapnel flying all over." Sakato "heard some yelling and screaming," but he was still standing there. "I was in shock, I guess." Then everyone ran for cover behind a ridge and tried to dig in, "but the soil was so hard and rocky that we could not dig more than six inches or so." Sakato didn't recognize the man frantically digging next to him.

Then German infantry attacked the ridge. With shells bursting in the trees overhead, Sakato was blazing away, "scared as hell . . . crying and praying at the same time." "I tried to crawl back into my helmet," Sakato recalls, hoping "I could get out of this hell hole."[43] For "the remainder of the day," as the regimental journal noted, "intense automatic and small arms fire coming across the open terrain from Hill B" kept E and F Companies pinned down.

It was only later, after the 442d had repelled the attack, that Sakato realized he had been fighting with F Company all along, and later still that he made it back to E Company.

★ ★ ★

In three days, the 442d had advanced barely two miles, yard by hard-fought yard, crouching, firing, crawling, firing, digging in, then starting all over again. It was an endless and exhausting cycle punctuated by long stretches of sheer terror. That night, there was more rain, and the dog-faces dug in once again.

The next morning, October 18, remained cold, with clouds and light rain. It was the day for an "all-out attack on Hills A and B." After the 522d had shelled the areas for a half hour, F and G Companies of the 2d Battalion and I and L Companies of the 3d Battalion hit Hill B, while the 100th Battalion assaulted Hill A. "All units met bitter opposition," according to the regimental narrative.

Following more than six hours of fierce fighting, the 100th Battalion finally took Hill A. B Company, Takahashi's unit, had silenced the Germans fortified in houses at the base of the hill and then struggled their way up the steep slope. A Company had circled to the left and knocked out a machine-gun nest, "taking nine prisoners, then dashed across the open flat and followed B Company up the hill." The 100th had taken sixty-six prisoners while suffering three KIA and twenty-three WIA.[44] With A and B Companies on the eastern slope, and C Company on the northern, the battalion dug in for the night to protect Hill A against German counterattack.

Meanwhile, Hill B fell to the 2d and 3d Battalions after "eight and a half hours of bitter fighting," according to the regimental history. F Company mortars had knocked out a machine gun at the foot of the hill that had been holding up the advance. But F and G Companies still faced a fierce firefight on the "steep side of the hill." At the same time, I and L Companies of the 3d Battalion circled around the foot of the hill, north of the road leading in the town. By 1630 the hill was in the hands of the 442d, and L Company "pushed into Bruyères, street-fighting and clearing the houses one by one."[45]

By 1830, L Company, coming down Rue Joffre toward Place Stanislas at the center of town, made contact with C Company of the 143d Regiment of the 36th Division, which had entered Bruyères from the south. Sergeant Paul Charpin, the FFI scout, became the first French soldier to set foot in the liberated town, and "by nightfall the town was under control."[46]

★ ★ ★

As blackness settled over the mountains, the people of Bruyères slowly emerged from their cellars. They had been living underground, without water or power, for more than two weeks, since the end of September, when American artillery had first started shelling the town and the surrounding area. "Days of long anguish," as one resident put it, had passed, "mingled with great hope." After the liberation of Épinal, the nearby town where the 442d had bivouacked, the people of Bruyères knew—from the German activity as well as from the escalating Allied bombardment—that it would "soon be their turn."[47]

The shelters they had shared were vaulted stone chambers, fortified long in advance, where they gathered when combat broke out. For the past eight days, the townspeople had been without meat, for the final three without bread. They had only dared to venture aboveground for their rations of *la soupe populaire* cooked at the local hospital and at a communal kitchen, and for biscuits that "smell of mold and are inedible," distributed from emergency supplies at the town hall.[48] Otherwise the streets of Bruyères had been empty of townspeople for two weeks, with Germans ghoulishly patrolling the deserted streets and lurking like vampires in the empty houses, which they had turned into machine-gun nests.

"If you had seen Bruyères at that moment" when the 442d arrived, "it wasn't pretty," recalls Paul Charpin, the FFI scout.[49] More than thirty-five thousand Allied shells had fallen on the area, fifteen thousand on the town itself, leaving more than three hundred houses damaged. Some structures that were still standing had been hollowed out by explosions. The walls of many buildings were blackened by smoke. Rubble littered the streets. Since fighting began, seventy-one civilians had been wounded and twenty killed, including a three-year-old girl who had been severed in half by a shell.[50]

One of the first civilians on the street was the local priest. He had opened the door to his cellar and was surprised to see "people of a certain height, with slanted eyes," according to Bernard Henry, then a teenager who had been working as a litter bearer in the local hospital. The priest "didn't know what was what." At first he thought they must be "Hindus who fought with the English"—like the Indian soldier brought to the 100th Battalion headquarters, who had escaped from the Germans at Épinal. But those "Hindus" had been British colonials. These soldiers marching into town were wearing American uniforms, and as Charpin explains, they did not have "the features of the big GIs" the townspeople were expecting.[51] "They didn't believe that we were American soldiers," recalls Pfc. Stanley Akita of C Company. "I don't think they knew what a Japanese looked like in the middle of France."[52]

"Devastated by the bombings," the town was at first "not very welcoming," says Charpin. The 442d did not initially enjoy the kind of reception Higgins had become accustomed to a month earlier, during the race up the Rhône. Both Charpin and Wakamatsu remember a man from the town complaining bitterly to the passing troops about the damage inflicted by the Allied shelling. He even threatened to "lodge a protest to the International Red Cross about our conduct." "We just stood there and looked at this Frenchman in amazement," Wakamatsu wrote later. "If this wasn't war . . . just what in hell was this all about?" But then German artillery started to hit the town, and Wakamatsu "asked this man what he was going to do now. He just turned and quickly walked away."[53]

Slowly, more townspeople emerged from underground, "cheering on their liberators." But the streets remained hazardous. Bruyères was still only "half liberated," as Charpin describes it. As the shelling continued, "everyone returned to his cellar" to wait out another night of "long anguish." But at least the soldiers patrolling the streets now were not Germans but "small yellow men."[54]

★ ★ ★

On Hill A, the 100th Battalion got "hot chow" for the first time in three and a half days. Along with fried chicken, Al Takahashi remembers a special treat that was a real morale builder. Somehow Service Company had managed to scrounge up the ingredients for vinegar-flavored rice balls, called *omusubi*, a Japanese dish that reminded this American soldier of home.

But the memory had a sour taste. If Takahashi thought about it, he didn't know exactly where his home was. His family was in the Poston Relocation Center. This dogface's only real home was the U.S. Army.[55]

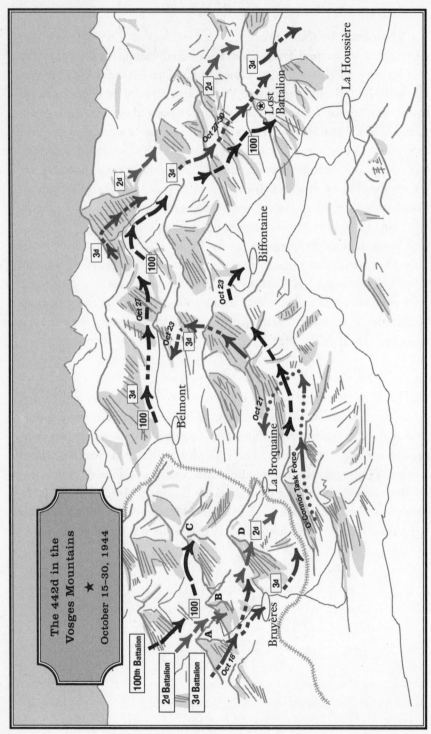

The 442d in the
Vosges Mountains
★
October 15–30, 1944

100th Battalion

2d Battalion

3d Battalion

Oct 18

A

B

C

D

2d

3d

100

Bruyères

La Broquaine

O'Connor Task Force

Oct 27

Belmont

Oct 23

3d

Oct 23

Oct 27

100

3d

100

Biffontaine

Oct 23

2d

3d

100

Oct 27

3d

3d

Oct 27–30

Lost
Battalion

2d

3d

La Houssière

Adapted from MTOUSA, *442nd Combat Team*, and Pierre Moulin, *U.S. Samurais in Bruyères*.

6

THE BATTLE FOR
THE HIGH GROUND

From Belmont to Biffontaine

Men who have been in battle know from first-hand experience that when the chips are down, a man fights to help the man next him, just as a company fights to keep pace with its flanks. Things have to be that simple.—S. L. A. MARSHALL[1]

The Vosges Mountains,
October 19–25, 1944

"In combat you almost never say no. That's a court-martial offense," says Young Oak Kim, whose journey from Bunker Hill in Los Angeles had led him to the Vosges Mountains in eastern France. A soldier on the front line is rarely in a position to defy his superiors. So Kim would follow his orders and nearly pay for his obedience with his life—in the service of what he considered, even at the time, a lost cause.

Sixty years later, he is still bitter about the offensive launched after the Battle of Bruyères, which would direct the 442d against a "worthless tactical objective"—Biffontaine. "We went into Biffontaine with great, great reluctance," Kim remembers.[2] After the successful attack on Bruyères, it would be a frustrating detour along the tortuous mountain path followed by DOGFACE in the Vosges.

* * *

Although the French would later celebrate October 18 as the day of liberation for Bruyères, Dahlquist was still not satisfied. He "wanted to do it all over again," according to Christopher Keegan, captain in command of

H Company, "so they could have movies." So the 2d Battalion retook the town, which the 3d Battalion had already captured, "for the benefit of General Dahlquist." "He had the cameras up there, the press taking pictures," Keegan says. "He put the regiment in some very embarrassing positions."[3]

On the 19th, L Company of the 3d Battalion remained on the streets, searching for the last pockets of German resistance and "mopping up," as the Army called it. Bernard Henry recalls watching the 442d pass and thinking, "These aren't Americans." They were "little men with yellow skin and slanted eyes . . . Chinese, Japanese, I didn't know."* But Henry's father and mother welcomed the American soldiers "with open arms, offering them a few sweets."[4]

George Oiye, called "Whitey" by the Buddhaheads, remembers seeing "an older lady with a long-handled, homemade stick broom, sweeping the street with real vigor, as if to be taking her frustrations out on the war."[5] And the town had other kinds of housekeeping chores. Private First Class Stanley Akita and Paul Charpin both recall the sight of Frenchwomen who had consorted with the Germans being dragged into the street. The townspeople "shaved them bald" and "threw things at them."[6]

* * *

Securing the town meant controlling Hill D, the Avison Massif, which overlooked the valley from the east. At its summit was the Mirador de l'Avison, an old watchtower visible from most of the surrounding area. During the previous days, American shelling by the 522d Field Artillery Battalion and 36th Division artillery had "almost entirely razed" the hill, according to Henry, exploding the trees "into the air like matches." The barrage had been so intense that the townspeople now called the hill Mont

---

*For the next sixty years, the residents of Bruyères—still confused—would refer to all of their Japanese American liberators, *kotonks* and Buddhaheads alike, as "les Hawaïens." After the war, the town of Bruyères became the sister city of Honolulu. Streets in the town were renamed Rue de Honolulu and Rue du 442e. And pineapple can still be found on the menus of local restaurants. To this day, "Japanese American" and "Hawaiian" are synonymous to residents of the area; there is little understanding that half of the soldiers of the 442d came from the mainland.

Pelé ("bare mountain") because "there wasn't a tree left." Yet somehow the Mirador remained standing.[7]

As the 2d Battalion and the rest of the 3d Battalion headed up the slopes, the Germans on Hill D rained heavy artillery down on them. But the attacking battalions swiftly succeeded in driving the Germans off the Avison before noon. The men of the 442d had no time to rest, however; in little more than an hour, they had regrouped and attacked again at 1300, according to the regimental journal, "with the objective of reaching the railroad embankment 2000 yards east of Bruyères on the edge of the Forêt de Belmont."[8] One branch of the railroad leading out of Bruyères turned north toward Rambervillers, and the front line of DOGFACE extended along this north-south axis.

E and G Companies of the 2d Battalion and I and K Companies of the 3d led the charge, but "enemy troops dug in behind the embankment," and German SP guns near Belmont, to the northeast, "held up the advance at 1600." Once again, the 442d called in artillery, and heavy fighting continued for another two hours.

Sakato remembers being pinned down with his platoon from E Company. "Crawling in the bushes," he ducked behind a fallen log and fired his Thompson submachine gun at some Germans in the distance. To his astonishment, two enemy soldiers he hadn't seen popped up, hands raised in surrender, on the other side of the very same log. "I was stunned in terror," Sakato recalls. But he came to his senses and took the Germans prisoner. "I captured my first machine-gun nest," he says.[9] It would not be his last.

He also confiscated a P-38 pistol from one of the prisoners. By now, after only a couple of days of battle, Sakato had become a master scrounger. He had already begun wrapping himself in bandoliers bristling with extra ammunition he had scavenged. And he had picked up his Tommy gun earlier from a wrecked Sherman tank as a replacement for his government-issue semiautomatic M1 rifle. Sakato figured a submachine gun was his best choice for combat in the Vosges. It was not so much accuracy that counted in the dense woods, he reasoned, but the ability to unleash a torrent of bullets against a shadowy and sometimes unseen enemy.[10] This was not the kind of marksmanship taught on the rifle range, where Sakato had been embarrassed by "Maggie's drawers." On his own, he had discovered the doctrine of firepower, which S. L. A. Marshall would popularize after the war.* Sakato's buddies in E Company now started to call him "Machine Gun Joe."

By the end of the day, the two battalions were in a thickly mined area jutting two thousand yards into the enemy lines. Barney Hajiro, of I Company, who had been transferred as a troublemaker from M Company, was positioned near the railroad embankment to secure his platoon's flank with his BAR. He had been firing the air-cooled, magazine-fed machine gun in support of an attack on some houses two hundred yards away, but when the assault failed, he had to cover the withdrawal of the unit. "He then noticed two snipers firing away at the friendly troops," according to eyewitnesses. Slinging the 18.5-pound BAR like a carbine, "he voluntarily ran twenty yards along the top of the embankment, to a shell hole where he could get a better field of fire." From there he opened up and "either killed or wounded both snipers, for there was no more harassing fire."[11] This was only the first of many times that Hajiro would utterly disregard his own safety to help his buddies.

Throughout the day and into the night, Bruyères fell under continuous German shelling. "Every building had suffered some demolition," according to the regimental narrative. But the 232d Engineer Company cleared the roads of mines and booby traps, and "the military value of the town was unimpaired."[12] After dark, the Germans infiltrated Hill D, and F Company and part of H Company were pulled back to reinforce the American position.

---

*See Marshall, *Men Against Fire*, pp. 82–83: "The broad inference to training is that it is unprofitable to put the accent on live targets or even on clearly defined targets such as those used for record. The moral effect on the rifleman is almost paralyzing when he is told to open fire on some apparently innocent feature of the landscape . . . we need to free the rifleman's mind with respect to the nature of targets." John Keegan agrees, in the *Face of Battle* (pp. 312–313):

[T]he underlying aim of weapon-training has now in many armies been changed: for the traditional object, that of teaching the soldier to hit a selected target, has been substituted that of teaching a group to create an impenetrable zone—akin in character to one of those meteorite belts which it is supposed will offer such hazards to travelers when and if men venture into deep space. . . . "Wasting ammunition," for decades the cardinal military sin, has in consequence become a military virtue; "hitting the target," for centuries the principal military skill, is henceforth to be left to the law of averages.

The next morning, October 20, saw more heavy rain. Under fire from the Germans who had crept up during the night, the engineers started sweeping for mines along the road wrapping around Hill D to the northeast, toward Belmont. Within hours, all three battalions of the 442d were "committed simultaneously in heavy fighting." The three rifle companies of the 100th were attacking Hill C. E and G Companies of the 2d Battalion and I and K Companies of the 3d were pushing back a German counterattack on the railroad embankment. And F and H Companies were still tied down on Hill D.

On the steep slopes of the Avison, S/Sgt. Robert Kuroda of H Company—whose mother had to sign his papers to enlist, because he was still underage when the 442d was formed—was on patrol with six men under his command. As they headed toward a ridge, Germans entrenched with automatic weapons fired at them from above. Unable to locate the enemy nest, Kuroda ordered his troops to cover him while he dodged forward alone. A hundred yards from the ridge, he spotted the Germans and, "disregarding the hostile fire," according to eyewitnesses, "ran forward using trees for cover until he was within twenty-five yards" of the enemy. Exposing himself to a hail of enemy bullets, he launched rifle grenades at the machine-gun emplacement, but it was well fortified, and his efforts "proved ineffective."[13] In the face of an unrelenting barrage from rifles, automatic pistols, and a machine gun, Kuroda "worked his way to within ten yards" of the enemy and lobbed four hand grenades. Two of them were on target, destroying the nest and killing three Germans. Kuroda then "directed clip after clip of M1 rifle fire on the supporting enemy riflemen, killing or wounding at least three."

As he ran out of ammunition, Kuroda saw another machine-gun emplacement open fire on a supply patrol advancing along a trail down Hill D. It was led by 1st Lt. Charles Farnum Jr., who had originally belonged to Capt. Christopher Keegan's H Company but had transferred to the 2d Battalion's headquarters company. Keegan had told Farnum the Germans had infiltrated between E and G Companies and warned him to "stay behind the trail, then attack down the trail."[14] But Farnum had apparently failed to follow Keegan's advice. Most of the patrol—unarmed, in order to carry the rations back—managed to leap into a ditch, while Farnum raced ahead, firing his Tommy gun.

As Kuroda watched, enemy fire cut down the young lieutenant.

Kuroda rushed to his side, but Farnum was already dead, shot through the throat. Kuroda "picked up the officer's submachine gun and all his clips of ammunition."[15] Clambering to within fifteen yards of the second nest and exposing himself to fire, He "emptied his submachine gun into the machine gun emplacement, killing the gunner, killing or wounding two of the crew, and destroying the nest." Kuroda "fought a battle all by himself," Keegan says. But as Kuroda turned to direct his troops' fire at the remaining Germans, fire from yet another sniper killed him instantly. He had told his mother Pearl Harbor would have to hire him after the war, because "I am an American." But now he would never get the chance that had been denied him less than three years earlier.

By noon, the 100th had seized Hill C, but "required several more hours of sharp fighting to completely clean the hill of the numerous enemy pockets." "For the first time in the whole war," Kim remembers with some satisfaction, he and his men were "sitting on top of the hill," with the Germans "attacking us, instead of the other way around." But then the 100th was ordered to reinforce the 2d Battalion on Hill D, potentially "costing the American Army another hundred lives," as Kim saw it, to recapture a hill "we already have."[16]

Allied aircraft broke through the clouds to strafe and bomb the enemy positions on Hill D, where fierce fighting continued through the afternoon. Leading his platoon, T/Sgt. Abraham Ohama of F Company risked his life to help a fallen soldier but was hit by a sniper and left exposed in an open area. His men rushed to help him but drew more enemy fire. As Ohama was being carried off the field under a white flag by aid men wearing the red cross brassard identifying them as noncombatants, "the Germans opened up again, killing him on the stretcher," according to the official narrative.[17] The German's shocking violation of the Geneva Convention protecting medical personnel[18] had an "unbelievable" effect on his company, as Jack Wakamatsu, of F Company, remembered fifty years later:

> Never had the men of our company been so shaken and angered by the death of a comrade. . . . After Abe died, our company began to move with a single purpose: to punish those responsible for his death.[19]

"In retaliation," says Pfc. Robert Katayama, one of the Hawaiians who had visited the Jerome Relocation Center, "our company formed a charge and attacked this hill shouting, *'Banzai.'*"[20] Enraged, the men of F and H Companies engaged the Germans "in hand-to-hand, tree-to-tree fighting," as the regimental journal put it. Wakamatsu recalls the Germans "had position and advantage over ours but lacked our anger and resolve." The "*banzai* charge" by F and H Companies was the first of what would be three nearly suicidal attacks by the 442d in October. After less than a half hour of furious combat, fifty Germans were killed and seven were captured. By the end of the day, another fifty German bodies were counted on the hill.

The attack by F and H Companies "brought home to us that while we are Americans, there are inherent aspects of Japanese culture or custom that still remain with us and gave us not only discipline but strength and courage as well," Katayama speculates. "Courage was very important, at least for those of us from Hawaii, because the rallying words were 'You can die, but don't embarrass yourself, your buddies, or your family.' And in Hawaiian pidgin it was, 'No bring shame.' "[21]

★ ★ ★

As the 442d headed only a few miles deeper into the Vosges, what Truscott had foreseen was becoming all too apparent. The Germans had been preparing their defenses for weeks, and reinforced bunkers and machine-gun nests lay behind elaborate mazes of minefields and booby traps. The route of DOGFACE to St. Dié, ten miles northeast of Bruyères, and then to Strasbourg, another twenty-five miles beyond that, grew ever more forbidding. The valleys were narrower, the ravines more twisted, the roads harder to negotiate as the farmlands west of Bruyères yielded to logging country east and north.

And with nearly constant rain and cold, the problem of nonbattle casualties became acute. Trench foot, in particular, took a great toll on the 442d. Although it sounds like a minor ailment, trench foot can be debilitating, even crippling. Bill Mauldin described its effect on infantrymen:

> The doggies found it difficult to keep their feet dry, and they had to stay in wet foxholes for days and weeks at a time. If they couldn't stand the pain they crawled out of their holes and stumbled and crawled (they couldn't walk) down the mountain until they reached the aid station. Their shoes were cut off, and their feet swelled like balloons. Sometimes

the feet had to be amputated. But most often the men had to make their agonized way back up the mountain and crawl into their holes again because there were no replacements and the line had to be held.[22]

And the Army's own graphic description is appropriately chilling:

Trench foot is a very serious nonfreezing cold injury which develops when skin of the feet is exposed to moisture and cold for prolonged periods (12 hours or longer). The combination of cold and moisture softens skin, causing tissue loss and, often, infection. Untreated, trench foot can eventually require amputation. Often, the first sign of trench foot is itching, numbness or tingling pain. Later the feet may appear swollen, and the skin mildly red, blue, or black. Commonly, trench foot shows a distinct "water-line" coinciding with the water level in the boot. Red or bluish blotches appear on the skin, sometimes with open weeping or bleeding.[23]

Treatment for the condition involved easing the discomfort with painkillers, drying and rewarming the feet, and doing whatever possible to fight infection and tissue death—all of which were difficult under battlefield conditions. And these were merely palliative measures. Wakamatsu, of F Company, would be hospitalized with trench foot a week after the end of the Battle of Bruyères. "I nearly lost all of my toes from both feet," he wrote later:

I know that if I had remained for a few more days in the field, I would have lost both of my feet to trench foot. . . . In my case, the pain was great enough to prevent any sleep. I was sleepless for ten days, and the only medication I received was aspirin. Near the end of ten days, the hallucinations became so severe that I could not distinguish between halfsleeping, dreams, or reality. . . . [24]

Of course, the key was to prevent trench foot in the first place, as the Army helpfully noted:

Extra care is required for cold-weather operations. Feet should be washed, dried and dusted with a dry, antifungal powder daily. Socks must be changed whenever they become wet from exposure to rain or snow, or from excess sweat. This may require changing into dry socks at least 2–3 times daily. Extra socks can be air dried and then carried under BDUs [battled dress uniforms] to warm.[25]

But in the Vosges, these recommendations verged on the comical. Corporal Sam Sasai of the 3d Battalion's Headquarters Company expressed the incredulity of the dogfaces to well-meaning medical advice:

> A stupid order the infantry received was "To avoid trench feet, take your boots off and massage your feet." I would defy that doctor who gave that order to sit on the front line, in a fox hole with inches of ice water, to take off his boots and massage his feet. You didn't know when the enemy attack would begin and you had to be ready to run—with your boots on![26]

The problem was exacerbated by the shortages that continued to plague DOGFACE, the downside of VI Corps's rapid race up the Rhône, which had left it far in advance of its supplies, almost from the time of the initial landing. The 350-mile pipeline from Marseille to the Vosges was not yet flowing at full capacity, and the men of the 442d were still fighting in the summer uniforms they had worn in Italy. The dogfaces were lucky to have even one spare pair of socks and, under the best of circumstances, it was all they could do to change their footwear once a day.

But they learned to improvise. A common practice was to wear one pair of socks, wash the other, and stuff the damp socks up the sleeves, under the armpits. Over the course of the day, body heat would eventually dry them and keep them warm until the next changeover.

Meanwhile, dogfaces who succumbed to trench foot remained stoical. "We were all in terrible pain," Wakamatsu recalled, but "no man cried out. We all suffered in silence."[27]

★ ★ ★

"Soldiers can endure hardship," S. L. A. Marshall wrote. "But no power on earth can reconcile them to what common sense says is unnecessary hardship which might have been avoided by greater intelligence in their superiors."[28] And this would be Kim's complaint about the attack on Biffontaine.

To begin the penetration northeast and east, the 442d deployed Felber Force on the afternoon of October 20. This was a special attack unit composed of tanks from the 753d Tank Battalion, tank destroyers, and engineers, along with the 3d platoon of A Company. With virtually no opposition, Allied air support bombed the road in front of Felber Force and scored "seven direct hits on the enemy column" of advancing enemy armor. The 522d Field Artillery Battalion and 36th Division artillery followed up with a barrage, and at 1710 the 2d and 3d Battalions finally hurdled the railroad embankment. But "the dug-in Germans and fields of antipersonnel S mines halted further progress."[29]

With Felber Force and the latest infantry thrusts temporarily stalled, Major General Dahlquist and Colonel Pence of the 442d "planned a surprise move to outflank the enemy." Under the command of Maj. Emmet O'Connor, executive officer of the 3d battalion, F and L Companies joined with wiremen and minesweepers from Headquarters Company of the 3d Battalion in another special unit, which became known as the O'Connor Task Force. Its mission was to "move south behind our lines during the night to a point opposite the ridge of the Bois de Boremont, to move along the top of the ridge at dawn," and then to "strike North at the enemy left flank." Like a wide receiver on a buttonhook pattern, the O'Connor Task Force would penetrate the line, make a long end run, and then circle back behind the German defenders.

At 0900 on October 21, when the Task Force struck the enemy from behind, the 2d and 3d Battalions would attack from the front. At the same time, the 100th Battalion would follow the same path as the Task Force. But instead of circling back, it would "push further along the ridge toward the town of Biffontaine."

It was a bold plan that mixed cunning with risk. The first part of the operation succeeded brilliantly. After a long night negotiating the high ground to the east of Bruyères, O'Connor and his men swept down the ridge to the open ground below and overpowered the Germans holed up in houses in the valley. They then turned back toward the enemy rear.

Meanwhile, the 2d and 3d Battalions crossed the railroad track once again and engaged the enemy in a firefight. This time, "attacked from both front and rear," the Germans "gave ground rapidly," according to the regimental history. By noon the Task Force was fighting the Germans "from house to house, killing and capturing many of the enemy foot troops" and driving back a tank with bazooka fire.[30]

By 1430, K Company joined forces with the Task Force, followed by the 2d Battalion. F and L Companies reunited with their battalions, and the special unit disbanded following its success. The 442d had broken through the logjam at the railroad embankment, and the road northeast toward the village of Belmont was opened.

But the second part of Dahlquist's plan ran into trouble almost immediately. The 100th Battalion moved rapidly up the trail blazed by the O'Connor Task Force, "cutting off Belmont from Biffontaine" to the east, and "completing a loop around the sector." But enemy patrols attacked B Company from behind, and by 1530 the 100th was stranded about a mile east of the rest of the 442d.[31]

It was a turn of events Kim had predicted before jumping off. On the morning the attack was launched, he remembers thinking, "The moment I take off from this ridge we have no more communications."[32] The mountains interfered with the line-of-sight signals of the radios and walkie-talkies. Although the 100th had "tied into the [telephone] wire laid by the [O'Connor] Task Force and extended it," as the battalion journal noted, there was "reason to believe that the Germans had tapped it."[33] And the 100th had no food, water, or ammunition beyond what the men carried with them into battle. "Most of us didn't even have a poncho to put over us in the rain overnight," Kim recalls.[34] Still, he and his battalion were "confident of their position and prepared to repulse any enemy attack," according to the unit's journal. As night fell, the 100th "dug in for defensive warfare."[35] The men of the 100th were used to being the aggressors; now they would have to be defenders.

The next morning, October 22, Christopher Keegan, H Company's commander, woke up and found he couldn't put his boots on. Returning from the O'Connor Task Force's jumping-off point the previous day, he had come under heavy German shelling and had to leap for cover from a ten-foot-high ridge. Now he discovered his left ankle was broken.

Meanwhile, I, K, and L Companies, the three rifle companies of the 3d Battalion, were moving steadily east into what the regimental journal called "the large pocket between Belmont and Biffontaine," roughly two miles east of Bruyères. In the advance, Barney Hajiro had volunteered for outpost security about fifty yards ahead of the rest of I Company. Concealed on a ridge with his squad leader, Sgt. Shigenori Matsumoto, Hajiro spotted a group of soldiers emerging out of the fog. He called out, "Hey, Buddhahead!" When there was no response, Hajiro opened fire on the patrol, wielding his heavy BAR like a carbine and immediately killing two and wounding another. Stunned by the ambush, the remaining fifteen Germans, though heavily armed, surrendered immediately.[36] Hajiro took an officer's Luger as a souvenir. Continuing to disregard his own safety to protect his mates, the former troublemaker was still trying to prove he was "not a bad guy."

Fighting through small arms fire and sporadic artillery, the 3d Battalion cleared the area by nightfall, but still remained short of the 100th Battalion, which was far ahead of the rest of the regiment.[37] The 100th had continued to press ahead aggressively during the day. A and C Companies, according to the battalion journal, "moved along the high ground north of Biffontaine," while B Company "went around the hills to the west of the town."

By 1330 the 100th confirmed the Germans had tapped its phone line and were tracing the battalion's location from the direction of the wire. The 100th was now exposed on three sides, and the Germans counterattacked with infantry and artillery. In the ensuing firefight, Capt. Sakae Takahashi, Kim's friend from Camp Shelby, was wounded in the arm and evacuated.

Felber Force had reached Belmont earlier, and the 3d platoon of A Company left at 1500 with five tanks to bring reinforcements, ammunition, and water to the isolated 100th. Along the Belmont-Biffontaine road, the infantrymen, including jeep drivers and kitchen workers, "dismounted and attempted to make contact by foot," hand-carrying ammunition and rations. Maurice Caël, who grew up near Belmont, was one of the local FFI scouts who led the reinforcements along a twisting route through "the dense unfamiliar forest and the impenetrable darkness which soon fell."[38] Suddenly, "there were shots everywhere," Caël remembers. The unit had run into a roadblock manned by fifty Germans.

In the ensuing firefight, the patrol suffered four KIA and four WIA. After an hour, Caël managed to make it back to safety with one of his comrades, negotiating a wilderness that was almost literally his backyard. But two other scouts who were not from the area were lost in the forest until much later.[39] And the reinforcements and supplies never reached the 100th.

Meanwhile, E and F Companies had run into around a hundred Germans on the right flank of the 100th. In close combat, the companies "destroyed the hostile force and took six prisoners."[40] From the base of a hill, "Machine Gun Joe" Sakato recalls shooting an enemy soldier coming down the slope. As he fell, the German called to the troops behind him and directed fire at Sakato and Saburo Tanamachi, who dived behind a pile of logs. A bullet ripped through Tanamachi's backpack, and the two friends quickly rolled aside to another log. Then they spotted the wounded German reaching for his gun, so Sakato shot him again in the chest. "This time it knocked him backward," Sakato recalls. "The .45 ammunition in the Tommy gun hits hard." As he and Tanamachi pulled back, they heard the dying soldier "hollering for help." The next thing they heard was an explosion.

After E Company took the hill, Sakato saw the dead German. He had ended his suffering by blowing off his own head with a grenade.

During the course of the day, the 100th had "cut the Belmont-Biffontaine road, cleared the hills around Biffontaine, and set up defensive positions on all sides," according to the regimental narrative. C Company, low on ammo, had to use captured enemy rifles and grenades. Then, after a house-to-house battle, the company "grimly hung on" to its position.[41]

By this time, Al Takahashi had become a "walking arsenal." Along with his M1 rifle, he carried a captured German pistol and hand grenades on his belt and wrapped himself in a bandolier, just as Sakato had. "I looked like Pancho Villa," he recalls with a smile. Even though his buddies laughed at him, he insisted on taking precautions. "If we get into a fight, I don't want to be caught short on ammunition." Perhaps as a result, Takahashi says, even in the darkest night of battle, "Never once did I think I wouldn't come back."

That evening, Bernard Henry remembers seeing the American flag atop what remained of the Mirador de l'Avison, "definitively marking the liberation of Bruyères." It had replaced the swastika that had flown there for four years. But heavy enemy shelling continued throughout the night.

★ ★ ★

The next morning, October 23, Dahlquist ordered the 100th to attack the town. Kim remembers, "It was no trouble taking Biffontaine"—it was not the fight but the objective that bothered him. But the records of both the regiment and battalion suggest more difficulty than Kim remembers. A and C Companies swept down the hill and "met bitter resistance," according to the regimental narrative, "fighting the Germans from house to house but pushing the attack despite their isolated position." The battalion was "forced to conserve ammunition" and was "low on water and with limited communications."[42]

To the rear, enemy patrols threatened to sever the 100th from the rest of the 442d. Even though the battalion occupied Biffontaine by 1715, the "situation outside of battalion positions" was "still hazy and indefinite."[43] There was little doubt, however, that the 100th had inflicted "tremendous damage" on the enemy, capturing around forty prisoners, a Panzer tank, four automobiles, two ambulances, a half-ton truck, dozens of pistols and rifles, ammunition, communications equipment, and various documents and maps.

Still, Kim's doubts about the tactical value of the town seem reasonable. Biffontaine lies in a valley through which one branch of the railroad runs east from Bruyères. But control of the valley, and thus the railroad, belonged more to whoever dominated the hills above, rather than the town below. The 100th had already cleared the surrounding heights. "The logical thing to do," Kim argues, would have been to trap the Germans between the 100th and the rest of the 442d outside Belmont, rather than descending into the valley to take Biffontaine.*

Or the battalion could have waited until reinforcements arrived and then hit the town with enough strength to maintain its flanks and supply routes. When a ration detail finally made it through, accompanied by a patrol from G Company, it brought food, water, ammo, and more than a hundred replacement infantrymen. But by that time the 100th was already

---

*A different appraisal of the value of objectives such as Biffontaine can be found in the "after action report" of the 36th Division, October 1944: "Holding the top of a hill or even what is ordinarily termed the military crest of a wooded hill does not necessarily give us control of the surrounding terrain. We must require all units engaged in capturing a hill covered with forests to continue down the forward slopes until the open country is under small arms fire and artillery observation." Quoted in Clarke and Smith, *Riviera to the Rhine*, p. 295.

occupying the town, so the only thing left to do was circle the wagons and dig in for the night. Enemy shelling had begun "promptly" after Biffontaine was seized, suggesting that the Germans realized it was easier to attack the town from above than to defend it from below.

With the 100th cut off in Biffontaine, Kim's chief concern was "How are we going to protect ourselves?" As S. L. A. Marshall wrote, "Co-equal with the security of flanks, the maintenance and full use of the line of communications to the rear are of major concern to the commander. It is his responsibility that the incoming supply is equal to the needs of his deployments."[44] Kim had no confidence that Dahlquist understood this concern. Over the past three days the 100th had been learning what Marty Higgins and the 141st Regiment would find out shortly—that the Germans were quick to take advantage of units that had outrun their flanks, their supplies, their communications links, and their artillery. A few days before the Lost Battalion of the "Alamo" Regiment would become famous, the 100th had nearly become a lost battalion itself.

In a house liberated from the enemy in Biffontaine, Kim was looking through a window when he spotted a German with a submachine gun. Suddenly a shower of bullets ripped through Kim's hand. He was as unprepared to be a casualty as the battalion was to treat him. The 100th had advanced so fast and so far ahead of the rest of the 442d that there were no "evacuation facilities for the wounded." Kim remembers being injected with morphine, which left him "woozy." The next thing he knew, he was being carried on a litter—by German prisoners of war, guarded by Americans.

This was "in distinct violation of Geneva convention," according to 2d Lt. Jimmie Kanaya, a 3d Battalion medic who was part of the relief team from the previous day. But "we wouldn't have been able to carry one" of the wounded men through the mountains, let alone a half dozen, without help. But Kanaya didn't feel he was in any position to object when the medical section of the 100th Battalion made litter bearers out of the prisoners. He had just earned his commission in combat, so he was junior in rank to the medical officers of the 100th, who were looking after their own battalion's men.[45]

As the litter train wended its way up a mountain path to the rear, following the supply route they had taken earlier to reach Biffontaine, the line of men stretched out over a hundred yards or so. Then, from the middle of the pack, Kanaya realized something strange was happening ahead. In a bizarre incident in which combat was suspended in a twilight zone of mutual restraint, the Americans had run into a German patrol—and, instead of shooting, the opposing forces were negotiating. Perhaps the only thing holding back the Germans from firing was the sight of their own soldiers under armed guard. Certainly the Americans knew they were in no position to resist. There were more than three dozen Germans in the patrol, and almost as many prisoners, covered by many fewer GIs.

As he watched the dispute play out, Kanaya "knew we were through." He watched the Germans disarming the "outgunned and outnumbered" Americans. Now "the tables were turned, and we had to carry the litters," Kanaya remembers.* But in the confusion of surrendering and handing over the weapons, he noticed Kim and one of the medics slipping off the side of the road.

"Just steady me and help me," Kim recalls telling the medic, T/4 Richard Chinen. "I'm not going to surrender." Without antibiotics, he remembers thinking, "I'll probably die in a German hospital." The two men pushed thirty yards or so through the thick underbrush and crouched down until the Germans left.[46]

To the astonishment of the troops in the rear, Kim, "although seriously wounded in the arm and suffering a loss of blood, managed to escape and made his way back, accompanied by a litter bearer." But, as the regimental journal put it, "it is believed that the wounded and medics were captured by the enemy, as no trace of them has been found."[47]

When he got to the aid station, Kim recalls, "I thought I was going to die." In a nearby bed, his friend Sakae Takahashi heard someone "moaning under the blankets." Takahashi, who had heard an erroneous report that Kim was already dead, was surprised to see him alive. The regimental chaplain was by Kim's side, "praying and crying and asking me to fight." But "an ice cold feeling came in my toes and came up my body, and I think

---

*Kanaya, *Hanashi* oral history. Another soldier taken prisoner was Pfc. Stanley Akita, of C Company, the Buddhahead who had wondered how anyone could think Japanese Americans were spies, since "we can't even speak Japanese" and "they wouldn't understand our pidgin anyway—nobody does." When Akita was eventually interrogated, the Germans said, "You're supposed to be fighting with us, not against us. What makes you think you're an American?" (Akita, *Hanashi* oral history.)

reached just past my navel and started up my fingertips and came up past my shoulders," Kim remembers. "I was just moments away from death. Then all of a sudden, for some unknown reason, the creeping . . . suddenly stopped."[48]

Without a dose of penicillin, only just beginning to be employed in combat, Kim might have died of blood poisoning from the bullets, or from shock. Instead, he recovered, though it would be more than two months before he returned to the 100th. But his days of combat were over, and he would be heading home shortly afterward.

Whatever the tactical value of taking Biffontaine, it had cost the 442d two of its most experienced leaders, Kim and Sakae Takahashi, who were also two of the last remaining frontline officers linking the pioneers in the 100th Battalion (Separate) to their successors in the larger regiment. Through his leadership and initiative, Kim had more than earned the nickname his men had given him—Samurai Kim. His courage had exemplified the spirit of the whole unit during the preceding year of combat. Though not Japanese, Kim was every bit as Asian, but also just as American, as his comrades in the 442d.

★ ★ ★

On the next day, October 24, halfway around the world from the Vosges, martial law was terminated in Hawaii, which had not even been categorized as a combat zone since April. But on the mainland, the West Coast was still designated an "exclusionary zone," and Japanese Americans remained in relocation camps because of "military necessity."

★ ★ ★

After the 141st Regiment relieved the 100th in Biffontaine, all three battalions of the 442d "had a momentary and much needed rest, billeted in houses around Belmont."

> Hot food was served and all personnel, by order of the Division Commander, shuttled back to Laval for a hot shower. Clean clothes and two pairs of wool socks per man were issued.[49]

"It was a great treat," F Company's Wakamatsu recalled. Everyone was "warm and very clean for a change."[50] "God, it felt good to take a shower and shave," Al Takahashi says. For most of the men of the 442d, it was their first hot shower since landing in France.

"Wherever the soldier may be and whatever he may be doing, his morale is still the product of his whole thought," S. L. A. Marshall wrote later. "A regiment, fretted to utter abjection by a protracted stay in the lines, may find its fighting spirit again in a six-hour respite, during which the men are deloused and given a change of underwear."[51]

In the days that followed, the men of the 442d would miss Kim's leadership by example. Yet when their period of rest and recuperation came to an abrupt end, they would find their own ways to rise to his level of heroic service. The citizen soldiers would face their greatest challenge when—as Al Takahashi puts it—"that damn stupid general got his battalion lost."[52]

DARK NIGHTS OF THE SOUL

The Lost Battalion

The battlefield is cold. It is the lonesomest place which men may share together. . . . The harshest thing about it is that it is empty. . . . It is the emptiness which chills a man's blood.—S. L. A. MARSHALL[1]

The Vosges Mountains, October 27–28, 1944

"We weren't really lost," Marty Higgins says today. "Our troops knew where we were. The Germans knew where we were. We were just cut off, with the Germans waiting for a rescue attempt."[2]

On Monday, October 23, the 1st Battalion of the 141st ("Alamo") Regiment of the 36th Division had passed through the 442d on the Belmont road.[3] Its mission was to seize the high ground above La Houssière, commanding the fields of fire over the main highway and railroad line east out of Bruyères, parallel to the Neune River.

The battalion had made rapid progress through the valleys and hills southeast of Belmont—"like a bat-out-of-hell," as Major General Dahlquist wrote, "making almost 8 kilometers against opposition."[4] But 1st Lt. Harry Huberth, commander of B Company, remembers worrying that the unit was "out ahead of our flanks," with "nobody on our right or left."[5] And Higgins, leader of A Company and by now a first lieutenant, had warned the commander of the battalion, Lt. Col. William Bird, that it was in danger of becoming dangerously overextended.[6] But Bird told the men to keep moving.[7]

By the end of the next day, October 24, Higgins's and Huberth's worst fears had been realized. "No one was following us," recalls Jack Wilson, staff sergeant of a machine-gun platoon.[8] During the late afternoon, a "strong enemy counterattack, supported by heavy artillery fire,"[9] had severed the tenuous supply lines to the battalion, isolating it in on Hill 645, known to locals as *Trapin des Saules* (the Willows). The 2d Battalion of the 141st had attempted to break through but "became heavily engaged," while the 3d Battalion had repelled a fierce, heavy counterattack "without loss of ground,"[10] but also without making any headway toward the stranded unit.

Fighting had continued overnight, with the Germans finally overwhelming the 1st Battalion command post. When the 2d and 3d Battalions of the 141st tried to punch through the enemy line the next day, heavy small arms and mortar fire held them up again. By the evening of October 25, "little progress had been made" toward reestablishing contact with the isolated 1st Battalion.[11] The only communication was through coded radio communication with 2d Lt. Erwin Blonder, attached to the unit as a forward observer from the 131st Field Artillery Battalion.

At this point Col. Carl E. Lundquist, who had been commander of the 141st Regiment only since early October, had to break the news to Dahlquist: the 1st Battalion was "out in front and cut off for 36 hours."[12]

The next day, Thursday, October 26, Dahlquist went up to the forward command post and "discovered [the] seriousness of [the] situation." As he noted in his diary, "Bn Comdr [Bird] or executive were not with the cut-off 1st Bn," and "no real attempt had been made to reach 1st Bn, give them orders, appoint a commander, or to use them in attacking rear of German positions."[13]

★ ★ ★

At 0300 on Friday, October 27, the men of the 442d began what would become their most famous battle. Their assignment was "to break through the reinforced German line of resistance and relieve the 1st Battalion, 141st Infantry,"[14] deep behind enemy lines in the Forêt Domaniale de Champ.

Rousing themselves in the dead of night, the men of the 442d stumbled around like zombies. The valleys of the Vosges were still smothered by a blanket of darkness, and dawn was still a distant dream away.[15] Sus Ito, assigned to I Company as a forward observer for the 522d Field Artillery Battalion, recalls the woods were so black that white toilet paper had been laid on the ground to mark a trail to and from the latrine. Just a day earlier, Ito had been promoted to second lieutenant. Along with his *kotonk* friends S/Sgt. George "Whitey" Oiye and T/4 Yuki Minaga, Ito had come a long way from Camp Shelby, where they had fought gangs of Buddhaheads in the barracks at night. Ito remembered his mother's warning him not to volunteer, and he wondered what he was getting himself into, now that he was an officer.[16]

As the soldiers set off into the hills, they grabbed the straps on the backpack of the man ahead, to keep from losing their way. If someone in front suddenly stopped, "there was a chain reaction," George "Machine Gun Joe" Sakato remembers, "all the way back."[17]

To this day, the men of the 442d blame Dahlquist for giving them this dangerous assignment, as if it had been a personal rather than a tactical decision. "I don't know if he was stupid or what, but how he got to be a major general, I'll never know," says Christopher Keegan, commander of H Company. "We didn't have much respect for Dahlquist . . . he put the 442d in positions they never should have been put in." But after a day and a half of rest in Belmont, they were the closest troops and, as they had been ever since joining the 36th Division in the Vosges, the freshest—and arguably the best available. Almost from the moment the 100th Battalion (Separate) had entered combat a year earlier, it had been almost continuously on the offensive, and the 442d had likewise served as an assault unit from the time it had joined the 100th in Italy. Like Truscott's Rangers, they knew they would be called upon to "lead the way."[18]

In any event, the choice had been approved one level up, the day before. As Dahlquist noted in his diary on the night of October 26, he "got authority to commit 442d from Corps Commander."[19] Still, his superior, Maj. Gen. E. H. Brooks, had been in charge of VI Corps just one day. Brooks's predecessor, Lucian K. Truscott Jr., always one of the 442d's strongest sponsors, had been promoted to lieutenant general and had left for a new command a day earlier.

The obstacles facing the 442d were formidable. The distance between the rest area at Belmont and the stranded men of the 141st was only about five miles on the map. But in the Forêt Domaniale de

Champ, that meant fighting up and down and around treacherous valleys and hills—exponentially increasing the amount of ground actually covered.

There were few signs of civilization in this part of the Vosges, unlike the populated areas they had just left. There was mostly an unending forest of sixty-foot pine trees looming above a "jungle-like"[20] catacomb of ravines and defiles. Where pathways existed at all, they were narrow dirt roads—actually, little more than old logging trails, hard to negotiate in the best of circumstances and now blocked and booby trapped. It was "excellent terrain for the German defense positions," Ito remembers with a shudder. The steep hillsides were pitched at forty-five degrees or more. And the weather forecast was "steady rain."[21]

Huddled against the elements in his field jacket, Ito still carried his Agfa folding camera, which he had been using since Camp Shelby to document the war. In one pocket of his jacket was a Bible, which he now confesses he didn't read very often. In another pocket was a gift he had received during one of his trips to see his family in Rohwer—a *senninbari*, a traditional Japanese waistband embroidered with a thousand red knots by his mother and sisters. It was supposed to have the power to ward off enemy bullets, but Ito was too embarrassed to wear it. And he didn't want it soiled, so he kept it tucked away, carefully folded and wrapped in cellophane.

In the center of the cloth was a tiger, symbolizing bravery and a cat's ability to find its way home. As Ito plunged into the blackness, his *senninbari* was a reminder that, if he returned from the war alive, the only home awaiting him was the Rohwer Relocation Center.[22]

* * *

To the stranded men of the 141st on Hill 645, attacking the enemy was out of the question. They barely had enough ammunition to protect themselves in a brief skirmish. By Thursday, three days after jumping off with only twenty-four hours' worth of supplies, they were cold, wet, hungry, and exhausted.

Still, without waiting to hear from headquarters, the isolated troops had already chosen a leader—Higgins, the most senior (by a few days) of the officers. Even though there were around 275 soldiers (less than a third of a full battalion) from four different companies stranded together,

Huberth recalls no disagreement about the choice among the officers or the enlisted men. Responding swiftly to the challenge, Higgins had "really started from the beginning"[23] to lead what would soon be known as the Lost Battalion.* Maybe it was the Irish in him, but "at age twenty-eight"—ten years older than the youngest of his men—Higgins says, "I had supreme confidence as a leader."[24]

Shortly after realizing they were cut off, Higgins had established a defensive perimeter, with machine guns anchoring the main line of resistance against the seven hundred Germans surrounding them. Higgins was personally relying on his Winchester carbine. He "had no faith" in his .45 caliber pistol, which had jammed on him once "in a rough situation," and he knew that close fighting in the woods demanded reliability and a high rate of fire more than anything else. Though it was less accurate than the standard-issue M1 Garand rifle, the carbine was much lighter (5.25 instead of 9.5 pounds) and had a greater magazine capacity (fifteen rounds instead of eight). With clips "taped back to back," Higgins recalls, he "could get *beaucoup* lead in the air."[25]

Higgins was impressed by his men's resolve. As they were fortifying their foxholes for the night, he saw them methodically using their knives to hack through gnarled branches four or five inches thick, for cover against tree bursts. It was the first time since landing in France, Higgins notes, that they had found a use for the government-issue knives, which were hardly designed for the task.[26]

Higgins had the men pool their resources—"everything from Coleman stoves to chewing gum."[27] "Everybody pitched in," recalls T/Sgt. Ed Guy, Higgins's friend, who was leading A Company's heavy weapons platoon. "The amount of stuff the GIs carried is amazing," says Higgins. "This kept us viable for another day."[28]

---

*There were actually many "lost" units during the war—they were a "common occurrence when attacking units sometimes outdistanced their companions and became isolated," according to Smith and Clarke in *Riviera to the Rhine*. Among the other "lost battalions" during World War II was the 551st Battalion during the Battle of the Bulge. Because of the high number of casualties and the role of the 442d in the rescue, the 36th Division's Lost Battalion became the most widely publicized: "The American media drew an obvious parallel to 'The Lost Battalion' of World War I, when some six hundred troops of the 308th Infantry, 77th Division, were cut off in the Argonne Forest during the period 3–7 October 1918."

The limited ammunition was carefully redistributed. "You couldn't afford to waste any," Guy remembers. "You don't fire unless you see something." But for the most part, the Germans "didn't want to waste time on us," says Huberth. "They never really made a concentrated attack."[29] "You'd only see them once in a while," Guy agrees. "Maybe two or three scouts."[30] The situation called to mind a classic tiger trap, with a goat tied to a tree as bait. The tiger on Sus Ito's *senninbari* would have to risk being snared before returning home.

Although the men on the hilltop were all too aware of their vulnerable position, they refused to dwell on it. "Everybody was joking, talking about getting back to eat," recalls Guy, "talking about pancakes and sausages and stuff, which you aren't going to get anyway."[31]

Shooting the breeze with the other men "about their wives and girlfriends, where they came from, what they did," Guy had learned they hailed "from all over—West Virginia, California, Texas, Kentucky." By the fall of 1944, replacements for the "Texas" Division had come from across the United States. And in shared foxholes, whatever differences once existed had long since disappeared under fire. "You get kind of close," says Guy. Higgins agrees: "Morale was high."

By Thursday, however, the strain was becoming evident. Some of the men had been scouring the area for mushrooms; others had tried trapping birds and small game.[32] But the pickings were slim. Everyone was now drinking from the same muddy waterhole—including the Germans. Higgins ordered his troops not to shoot any enemy soldiers nearby, for fear of contaminating the water supply.

Meanwhile, the Germans had cut the trail behind the Lost Battalion and established a roadblock reinforced with automatic weapons.[33] Higgins, ordered by radio to fight out of the trap, had dispatched a team of more than fifty volunteers down the slopes to attempt a breakthrough. But by Thursday evening, none of them had succeeded. And not one of them had yet returned to the hilltop.

1840—Higgins to headquarters: "Medical supplies low; no rations for three days . . . need ammunition."[34]

1920—Headquarters to Higgins: "We will drop supply to you . . . at 0800 [the next morning]."

2015—Higgins to headquarters: "Small clearing round our position. Will mark with white arrow and, if possible, yellow smoke at 0745. . . .

Request rations, ammo, fags [cigarettes], medical supplies, batteries. Have aircraft drop supplies so enemy will not observe and inform enemy our position."

As the Lost Battalion dug in for the fourth lonely night in the dark forest, Dahlquist made a grim entry in his diary: "Attacks today failed."[35] Now it was up to the 442d.

★ ★ ★

Friday, October 27, began badly for the Lost Battalion. Only five men returned from the patrol that had tried to connect with American forces, but instead walked straight into a German ambush.[36] And then came more bad news.

1220—Headquarters to Higgins: "Aircraft attempted at 1100 hrs. Weather did not permit dropping supply."

Higgins immediately asked, "Where is friendly force at?"

1250—Headquarters to Higgins: "Coming by your route."

★ ★ ★

That morning, Dahlquist showed up on the front line "at 10 o'clock and stayed all day." Impatient with Lundquist, he felt "the attack did not really get started until 2 o'clock."[37]

By then, the 442d was moving slowly through the Forêt Domaniale de Champ, with the 3d Battalion in the middle, between the 100th on the right and the 2d on the left. Tanks and mortars moved up alongside, attracting an intense German artillery barrage.[38] And fire from rifles, automatic weapons, and mortars rained down from about a hundred Germans entrenched on the high ground to the southeast.

When I Company found its left flank dangerously vulnerable to German fire from above, S/Sgt. Shiro Kashino, who had volunteered from the Minidoka Relocation Center and was now called "Kash" by his buddies, dashed fifty yards up a hill, "exposing himself to [the] enemy,"·in order to help the platoon pinned down in front of him. "We realized we had to watch both flanks," he recalled. "In the woods, you have nobody to protect you but yourself."[39] Then, "shouting to his comrades to follow,"[40] he covered their movement and directed their fire against a hostile machine gun, enabling the men to escape the kill zone. "Taking a machine gun nest, that was our job," he said simply. "We had the guts and the brains enough to do things without being asked by an officer."[41] Covering the withdrawal of his comrades with his Tommy gun, "Kash" was, characteristically, the last to leave, making sure everyone else was safe ahead of him.

At 1530, the Germans counterattacked in force. Peering around a tree, Al Takahashi of B Company, who had surprised himself by charging headlong across an open field in the battle of Bruyères, saw an enemy tank directly ahead, less than ten yards away. The muzzle of the tank's cannon flared, and he instinctively rolled to one side. A shell plowed into the ground inches away from him, and he felt a burning sensation in his thigh. It was only after the flash and the impact that the sound of the cannon firing caught up, a millisecond later. As the tank turned and rumbled off, Takahashi tentatively reached down his leg, expecting the worst. But his hand came up dry. His uniform was singed and his thigh was scorched, yet otherwise he was unhurt. The red-hot shell was a dud. But if he had rolled in the opposite direction, he would have been dead. It was his second miraculous escape from death.

* * *

While the 442d was holding its ground against the German counterattack, headquarters came up with another plan to supply the Lost Battalion.

1540—Headquarters to Higgins: "Will fire supply with artillery 1700 hours. Will transmit information at 1630. Where can you observe?"

The idea was to remove the chemical load from M84 smoke shells, fill them with D-rations, medicine, and other provisions, and fire them into the Lost Battalion's zone.

1730—Higgins to headquarters: "Fire one supply shell."

1800—Headquarters to Higgins: "Artillery will fire medical supply."

The fuses were timed to burst two hundred feet in the air. But although the Lost Battalion could hear the shell going overhead, by this time it was too dark to tell whether the range was correct, much less recover any contents.

1820—Higgins to headquarters: "Impossible to get supply shell tonight. Will you send aircraft tomorrow? Give me present location friendly force."

1935—Headquarters to Higgins: "Will send messages through the night."

1945—Higgins to headquarters: "Need Halazone [to purify drinking water]. Men weak. Nine litter. 53 MIA from patrol . . . 4 killed."

1950—Headquarters to Higgins: "Will use aircraft tomorrow. Friendly force near."

★ ★ ★

But "near" was a relative term in the mountains. By twilight on Friday, the 442d had stopped the German counterattack. On Takahashi's left, a K Company bazooka team had "knocked out one tank, one half track, and forced another tank to withdraw."[42] And the Americans had taken forty-three German prisoners before nightfall. But the total ground covered after another day of crushing combat was only about two miles as the crow flies.

As inky blackness once again flooded the Vosges, both the 442d and the Lost Battalion sank into their foxholes. German artillery kept shelling the Americans all night long, and the merciless tree bursts "increased the hazard of artillery against our advancing troops, while the German positions were elaborately prepared and roofed over." In the flooded American foxholes, "cases of trench-foot were becoming more numerous,"[43] as the weather kept taking its chilly toll. "It was a long night," Ito recalls. "Cold, damp and drizzly rain chilled our feet and legs to a stiff numbness."[44]

That night, Dahlquist's diary entry was terse: "1st Bn still holding on."[45]

★ ★ ★

On Saturday morning, October 28, as the Lost Battalion prepared for the long-awaited airdrop, Dahlquist "at noon got suspicious and went up to front line." Discovering once again that the "attacks had not really started,"[46] he sacked Col. Carl E. Lundquist and installed Col. Charles H. Owens as the fourth commander of the "hard luck" 141st in the two and a half months since the invasion of southern France in August.

1210—Higgins to headquarters: "Weather is clear now—please do something."

"We collected everything white we could find," recalls one of the men on the hill. "Linings from parkas and maps and even underwear were all stretched out in a long white strip. We bent the trunks of young trees and tied smoke grenades to them. Then when the planes came over we released the tree trunks and pulled the grenade pins, hoping that the smoke could be seen from above."[47]

Ten P-47s, two at a time, flew over *Trapin des Saules* and dropped provisions by parachute. But by 1405, Higgins had to report that the supplies had fallen into enemy hands. As fog obscured the sky once again, hope for another attempt faded along with the light.

★ ★ ★

Slogging through the dark valley below, the 442d ran into the first of a series of manned enemy roadblocks. Then the Germans unleashed "the worst barrage" the 100th Battalion ever remembered enduring "in the entire period of combat from Salerno on." Shells "came in like machine gun bullets."[48] At the same time, automatic weapon and mortar fire from "prepared positions selected to give best fields of fire"[49] sprayed down the hillsides, while "the jungle-like forest gave excellent concealment to the many German snipers"[50] who dispensed death with seeming impunity.

No one could escape the lethal shower, not even those who were supposed to be shielded as noncombatants. "Incidents of medical aid men being shot at, despite the fact that they wore the Geneva red cross brassard, were not rare," according to eyewitnesses.[51] In the 3d Battalion alone, three medics, all marked with red crosses, were shot "under circumstances that left no doubt that they were intentional."

But fear did not deter the medics. Spotting a wounded soldier in the middle of the killing field, T/5 James K. Okubo—whose family had been "relocated" to Tule Lake and Heart Mountain—left his cover and raced forward 50 yards to treat him. Then a second call for help came from even farther ahead. Evading small arms and machine-gun fire, Okubo "crawled and ran 150 yards toward the front," stopping only twice to cover up. He found the wounded man close to the enemy line, paralyzed by a grenade fragment.

Hoisting him over his shoulder, Okubo went back the same way he had come, darting across a stretch of flat terrain that provided little protection from enemy fire. "I saw him hit the ground twice to avoid the shell fragments from mortar and grenade bursts," said an eyewitness, Pfc. George Uchimiya of K Company. "He used his body to protect the wounded man" and then dropped him off safely in the rear.

Okubo returned to the front line. Still under continuous fire, he saw a wounded BAR man thirty yards away. As Okubo made his way forward, a grenade exploded ahead of him. Instead of seeking cover, he unhesitatingly ran and "picked up the BAR man and carried him to a depression nearby. As Okubo reached it and threw his body over the wounded man, [a] second grenade exploded a few yards away." "By some miracle he wasn't hit," Uchimiya said. "He treated the wounded man and had him evacuated."

"Throughout the attack, he continued to move from one wounded man to the next," Uchimiya continued, "though his personal safety was endangered at all times." When a tree burst rained shrapnel down on five soldiers a hundred yards away in another direction, Okubo sprinted to their aid, again without taking cover. During the long day, he treated seventeen men from K Company alone, as well as soldiers from adjacent units. "Under the same hazardous conditions, he carried on his work with complete disregard for his life, and with only the welfare and safety of his comrades in mind."

★ ★ ★

On the left side of the 442d's advance, the 2d Battalion had been making a sweeping maneuver toward Hill 617, just northeast of the Lost Battalion. Along the way, as E Company crossed a dirt road, George "Machine Gun Joe" Sakato noticed explosives tied to the base of trees on the hillside. They were designed to fall and explode on the road when trucks passed. Throughout the Vosges, the Germans had sprinkled minefields, barricades, and booby traps—ingenious death devices meant for unwary GIs.

Leaving the traps for the 232d Engineers to disarm, the 2d Battalion kept cautiously moving forward. By the end of the day they had cleared a few isolated farmhouses in their path and taken twenty German prisoners, "including the battalion commander of the 202d Mountain Troop Battalion, a newly arrived enemy unit."[52]

★ ★ ★

After the failed airdrop, 36th Division artillery at last began lofting supply shells to the Lost Battalion. The initial volleys were smoke shells, to fix the range. Second Lieutenant Blonder, the forward observer, heard the first round go over his head. He called fire command to decrease the range by two hundred yards. The next round was still long, requiring another adjustment. Finally he reported, "Range correct, fire for effect . . . all you've got."[53]

As the shells burst over the Lost Battalion, the contents spilled down through the trees, scattering all over the area. Other shells plowed into the ground. The men scrambled to recover what they could. The payload wasn't the pancakes and sausage they dreamed about, but to the famished men of the Lost Battalion, the D-rations were good enough. Nearly sixty years later, another soldier who had fought in the Vosges described the concentrated chocolate D-rations as "the nourishment of last resort . . . a block the size and consistency of a flattened brick." According to the novelist Tony Hillerman, who was an infantryman with the 410th Regiment of the 10th Division, which would follow the 442d into the Vosges, "given time, water, and a source of heat, one could soften this enough to bite it by boiling it in your canteen cup. Otherwise you had to hammer it into fragments and let it dissolve in your mouth."[54] But the D-bars "could hold you forever," according to Ed Guy.[55] More than just food, for the Lost Battalion it was the first material proof in five days that relief was truly close at hand.

At 1640, Higgins's message to headquarters was simple: "Keep firing."

* * *

Provisions were a problem for the 442d as well. As twilight surrendered to the suffocating blackness, "Kash" Kashino volunteered to lead a ration detail for the 3d Battalion. Reporting to the command post, he learned that the supply convoy had not yet arrived from the rear. "I knew the terrain would make it extremely difficult for the supply trucks to reach us, because we had just driven the enemy out of the same area," Kashino recalled. "It was so quiet that night you could hear a pin drop, and all of a sudden you could hear our supply trucks moving up."[56]

Kashino went around in the dark asking for volunteers. He had earned a reputation as a "go-getter," even a "reckless kind of guy," according to Tak Senzaki.[57] So at first Kashino found few willing to accompany him. "They say in the service never to volunteer for anything," says Sgt. Kenneth K. Inada of K Company. But Inada realized they "were all volunteers to begin with, and the impulse to volunteer was still there." Kashino told

Inada to bring up the rear of the detail—and to "travel light, to carry only a rifle and ammo belt in anticipation of a full load back."[58]

At 2000, the 3d Battalion commander, Lt. Col. Alfred Pursall, ordered the men to move down the hill to meet the convoy. But Kashino was concerned. He "told the colonel that the Germans could hear the moving vehicles and would know the exact route that our men and vehicles would use, and that it would be better for us to wait at least an hour before we moved out." Yet Pursall insisted, so Kashino, under protest, led his twelve men down to the road where the trucks were pulling up. "Sure enough," Kashino remembered, "the Germans threw a barrage right on top of us."[59] "We were only about 200 yards from where we started," says Inada, when it "came through the forest, lighting up brightly the whole area with a thunderous noise."[60]

"I remember vividly, as the last man of the detail, the thunderous noise and huge flames about 12 feet high engulfing and illuminating the entire detail," Inada continues. "I was knocked off my feet and blanked out for a moment." In the deadly chaos, eight men in the detail were casualties. "When I regained my senses, I was completely flat on my back and began to feel a cold sensation on my entire left arm and hand," Inada recalls. "My rifle was nowhere around me. I quickly found out that the cold sensation was caused by blood trickling down my arm." Despite the darkness, Kashino and the men who were still standing managed to get the wounded to the aid station. "The aid men expressed surprise that we had walked all the way from the front lines dripping in blood," Inada remembers. "They put us on a stretcher, dressed us up quickly, and put us on a jeep headed for the field [tent] hospital. There I was operated on immediately since gangrene was setting in, with my whole left arm bloated and the flesh ripping through the bandages."

When Kashino returned to battalion command, he did not hesitate to confront Pursall. "I told him in no uncertain words what I thought of him and his decision," Kashino recalled, "and told him any one of us would rather starve than suffer the casualties that occurred due to [his] orders." This was no way for a staff sergeant to speak to a lieutenant colonel. It was an encounter that would haunt Kashino for a long time to come.

★ ★ ★

Although they had taken ninety prisoners during the long day, the men of the 442d advanced less than a mile on Saturday. They were still about two miles from the Lost Battalion. That evening, Dahlquist wrote in his diary: "Situation is very blue."[61]

★ ★ ★

1835—Higgins to headquarters: "Need bandages, sulfur dizene and tape for other casualties. 1 man just died."

Taking stock of the supplies his men had recovered from the artillery shells, Higgins ended the evening's communication with guarded optimism.

2227—Higgins to headquarters: "Received only rations. Have not found everything as yet. Have water. Hope to see friends tomorrow."

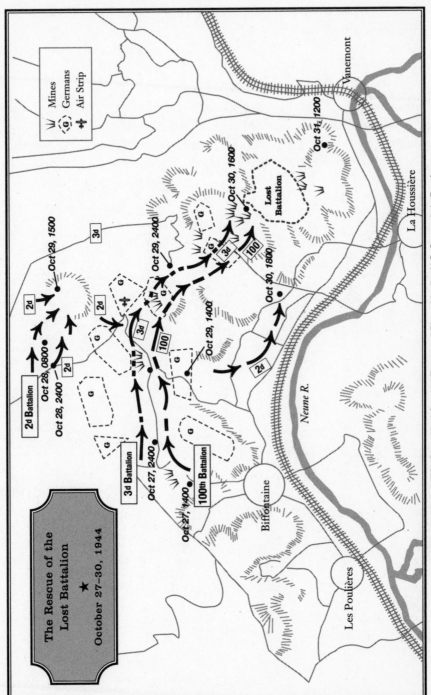

The Rescue of the
Lost Battalion

★

October 27–30, 1944

Mines
Germans
Air Strip

2d Battalion

Oct 28, 0800
Oct 28, 2400

Oct 29, 1500

2d

2d

2d

2d

3d

3d

3d

3d

Oct 29, 2400

Oct 29, 1400

Oct 30, 1600

Lost
Battalion

100

100

100

Oct 30, 1800

2d

Oct 31, 1200

Vanemont

La Houssière

3d Battalion

Oct 27, 2400

100th Battalion

Oct 27, 1400

Biffontaine

Les Poulières

Neune R.

Adapted from MTOUSA, *442nd Combat Team*, and Pierre Moulin, *U.S. Samurais in Bruyères*.

8

GO FOR BROKE

"What Others Fear to Attempt"

The near presence of death and the prospect of meeting it at the next moment move men in many curious and contrary ways. . . . The life of hardship and of danger gives new strength to the truly strong and greater weakness to the truly weak. . . . The backward man may come forward.—S. L. A. MARSHALL[1]

The Vosges Mountains,
October 29–30, 1944

"I'm not a bad guy." Six decades after the rescue of the Lost Battalion, Barney Hajiro's earnest plea continues to echo in the mind of his platoon commander, Sadaichi Kubota.[2] By the end of October it had been months since Hajiro's fistfight in Italy resulted in his transfer from M Company to I Company. He had already distinguished himself twice in action during the advance from Bruyères to Belmont. Yet Hajiro still thought of himself as a "goof-off."

But as daylight crept into the valleys of the Vosges, he and the rest of the 442d had little time for self-reflection. The inclement fall was edging into winter, and cold, gray fingers of early-morning fog and frost lingered in the twisting ravines.[3] Rising out of the mist, the *kotonks* and Buddha-heads steeled themselves for the third day of their rescue mission—and their greatest test as citizen soldiers.

Once again, Major General Dahlquist and his aide showed up at the front, right next to the riflemen. "Fatigue, weariness, and the terror of continuous combat in the dark forest was [sic] slowly overcoming our men. I could sense a failing futility among them," the general wrote several months later. "It was for that reason that Wells [Lewis, who was the son of the novelist Sinclair Lewis] and I were in the front line for three days in a row."[4]

A two-star general who would repeatedly join his men on the front line, rather than issuing orders from headquarters miles away in the rear, where senior officers were usually to be found, had to earn the respect of even the most grudging soldier. No one could doubt Dahlquist's courage. But not long after the attack began that Sunday morning, many would wonder about his judgment.

Dahlquist's plan was simple, a classic one-two punch. A left hook was aimed east by southeast against the German emplacements on Hill 617, which controlled the fields of fire sweeping down the valley leading to the Lost Battalion. This assault was to be mounted by the 2d Battalion of the 442d, with E and F Companies leading a surprise attack on the enemy rear.

Simultaneously, a straight right-hand blow, the main punch, was directed southeast at the German forces encircling the Lost Battalion on the *Trapin des Saules*, above La Houssière. The 3d and 100th Battalions of the 442d would make up the fist, with the knuckles of I Company on the left, K Company in the middle, and B Company on the right.

It was a plan faithful to U.S. Army doctrine[5]—an envelopment of the flank accompanying a penetration of the main line of resistance. Four months earlier, in Italy, the 442d had learned the hard way how important, and difficult, it was to seize a fortified hill. Only swift maneuvering by their older brothers in the 100th Battalion had saved the rookie regiment from veteran SS troops dominating the high ground of Belvedere.

But that was in sunny Italy in June, under conditions that permitted tactical flexibility and rapid movement. In the Vosges in late October, the ideal of "combined arms"—airpower, armor, and artillery in support of infantry—collided with the reality of narrow defiles, heavily wooded slopes, and incessant rain. Through Saturday the twenty-eighth, the continued bad weather had neutralized Allied superiority in the sky. Enemy tanks were already atop the hills, while American armor was bogged down on the muddy, serpentine mountain trails. And the heavily forested terrain favored German artillery and machine guns firing downhill from positions that had been fortified long in advance. By contrast, the high trajectory needed to fire shells at targets only a short distance away, but hidden by tall trees, left American artillery at a disadvantage. The gunners of the

522d Field Artillery Battalion were like tennis players aiming lob shots over a sixty-foot-high net—uphill. As the 442d drew closer to the Lost Battalion, American guns and mortars firing from below increasingly risked American lives above.

★ ★ ★

Two miles away, the men of the Lost Battalion readied themselves for their sixth day of confinement in the Forêt Domaniale de Champ. At 0910 on Sunday, October 29, Marty Higgins learned by radio from headquarters that "pals will be over this morning"[6]—another airdrop would be attempted as soon as possible.

For the most part, the Germans were directing their firepower downhill, toward the 442d, rather than back at the Lost Battalion. But even though the soldiers of the 141st were, at least temporarily, worth more as hostages than as casualties, German harassing fire and snipers continued to take their toll.

Intermittent shelling had also kept the men in their slit trenches. Higgins had left his trusty carbine near the edge of his foxhole, and a whirling shell fragment had shattered the wooden stock of the weapon—inches away from its owner. "I was one lucky SOB," Higgins says today.[7]

As Higgins made his morning rounds of the perimeter, he found still more corpses of American soldiers. With no graves registration unit to inter the dead, he had to weigh his regard for his fallen men against his lack of manpower and resources to give them the respect they deserved. Perplexed, he radioed headquarters at 1030: "We have three dead. Would like to bury. Would like advice." Headquarters responded with the only counsel that made sense under the circumstances: "Mark distinctly, keep record." Unless and until the living walked freely off the hill, the dead would lie where they fell, a lost battalion of souls.

Deep in their dark green prison, the desperate men of the 141st looked up for salvation. "We were just praying, that's all," said S/Sgt. Howard Jessup. "We just sat in our foxholes, listening hard, not saying a word . . . and we just prayed."[8] When the sky finally cleared above the Lost Battalion, their prayers were answered by the whir of propellers. By midmorning, like manna from heaven, supplies floated down by parachute from Allied aircraft, and the eager men below scrambled to retrieve the much-needed food, ammunition, and medicine before the Germans snared them. Higgins's friend Ed Guy, sergeant in charge of one of the heavy weapons platoons, remembers keeping a piece of one of the parachutes, which he later sent home to his mother.[9]

1100—Higgins to headquarters: "Pals did a good job."

Despite the pilots' best efforts, some of the provisions did land outside the Lost Battalion's perimeter. But Higgins personally led a patrol to retrieve them.[10] "He never asked you to do anything he wouldn't go out in front and do himself," Guy says of Higgins. "And he didn't have to. When you're a company commander you don't have to go out front. But he did."

Yet one item was missing from the airdrop. "Need batteries," Higgins continued in his 1100 message. Second Lieutenant Erwin Blonder's radio, the last link to the rescuers, was running out of power. And Higgins repeated himself at noon: "Need Halazone and batteries."[11]

After midday, fighting escalated on the hill, with scattered German attacks costing the Lost Battalion nine more casualties. Replying to headquarters' request, Higgins said he couldn't spare enough men for a "strong patrol" to meet the advancing 442d. Even after the airdrop, the Lost Battalion had only three thousand M1 rounds and eight hundred carbine rounds—an average of about sixteen bullets, or two clips, per man.[12] Higgins knew that wouldn't be nearly enough to repel a full-scale German assault.

Nonetheless, he sent scouts to explore a possible contact point. What the returning men reported was not encouraging—the rescuers were heading into a heavily fortified position. His message warning headquarters was terse.

1640—Higgins to headquarters: "Mined. Inform 442."[13]

★ ★ ★

Starting earlier that day, the 442d had already run into furious resistance. After jumping off at dawn, the 2d Battalion—the left hook of the assault—had met a "heavy concentration of small arms, machine gun, and mortar fire"[14] as it pushed southeast to circle behind the Germans entrenched on Hill 617. Although G Company was forced back to the base of the hill, it distracted enemy attention from the main thrust of E and F Companies.

In the fierce firefight that followed, "Machine Gun Joe" Sakato and the other men in his E Company platoon overran two enemy positions.

March 28, 1943: A crowd of 15,000 well-wishers jammed the grounds of Iolani Palace to salute the more than 2,600 Japanese American volunteers leaving Hawaii for basic training on the mainland. *Reprint courtesy of the Honolulu Star-Bulletin, from the Hawaii War Records Depository, University of Hawaii at Manoa.*

July 8, 1943: Japanese American women from the Rohwer and Jerome Relocation Centers in Arkansas traveled 250 miles to dance with 442d recruits at Camp Shelby, Mississippi. *Office of War Information, National Archives, Record Group 208-MO.*

March 3, 1944: Under the cover of darkness, draftees left the Heart Mountain Relocation Center for their pre-induction physical examinations. *War Relocation Authority, National Archives, Record Group 210-G.*

August 2, 1944: In Vada, Italy, Gen. Mark W. Clark, commander of the Fifth Army, awarded the 100th Battalion its first Distinguished Unit Citation. *Office of War Information, National Archives, Record Group 208-AA.*

September 17, 1944: A month after the "second D-Day" in France, T/Sgt. Joe Trdenic, of the 141st Regiment, 36th "Texas" Division, received a hero's welcome from the citizens of Luxeuil. During the months ahead in the Vosges, the Germans would be considerably less cordial. *U.S. Army Signal Corps, National Archives, Record Group III-SC.*

October 14, 1944: On the day before the Battle of Bruyères, Sgt. Paul Charpin (in beret) and Paul Gérard (far right), of the French Forces of the Interior, guided 2d Lt. Arthur MacColl (far left) and Pfc. William I. Soma (driving) to the 442d's jumping-off point in the Helledraye Forest. *U.S. Army Signal Corps, National Archives, Record Group 111-SC.*

October 14, 1944: Pvt. Saburo Tanamachi (first full figure on the left), Pvt. George "Joe" Sakato (second from left), and a long line of infantrymen from E Company of the 442d slogged through mud on the way to Bruyères. *U.S. Army Signal Corps, National Archives, Record Group 111-SC.*

October 19, 1944: During the "mopping up" after the Battle of Bruyères, the townspeople emerged from their hiding places to welcome "les Hawaïens" of the 442d. *Courtesy of Bernard Henry.*

Undated, but probably October 27, 1944: The men of the 442d marched out of Belmont on their fateful mission to rescue the Lost Battalion. *Courtesy of Susumu Ito.*

October 27, 1944: The 522d Field Artillery Battalion fired 105 mm howitzers in support of the 442d infantry. *U.S. Army Signal Corps, National Archives, Record Group 111-SC.*

October 30, 1944: As daylight faded on Hill 645, T/4 Yuki Minaga, one of the forward observers from the 522d Field Artillery Battalion who became a rifleman on "Suicide Hill," distributed cigarettes to the just rescued men of the Lost Battalion. *Courtesy of Susumu Ito.*

October 31, 1944: One day after the rescue, 2d Lt. Marty Higgins (left), leader of the Lost Battalion, shook hands with 2d Lt. Charles O. Barry, of the Medical Detachment of the 141st Regiment, 36th Division. There were no Japanese Americans in the photographs released to the press. *U.S. Army Signal Corps, National Archives, Record Group 111-SC.*

November 1, 1944: As the decimated troops of the 442d advanced farther and higher into the Vosges, the weather grew worse and the slopes more treacherous. *U.S. Army Signal Corps, National Archives, Record Group 208-AA.*

November 12, 1944: In their newly issued winter coats, "all that's left" of the 442d assembled on parade before Maj. Gen. John E. Dahlquist in the snow. *U.S. Army Signal Corps, National Archives, Record Group 111-SC.*

July 15, 1946: President Harry S Truman saluted the 442d at the Ellipse in Washington, D.C., and awarded the Combat Team its seventh Distinguished Unit Citation. *National Archives, Record Group 79-AR.*

May 27, 2004: After six decades, the Lost Battalion reunited with the 442d at the Library of Congress Pavilion during the dedication of the World War II Memorial in Washington, D.C. Left to right: Norman Ikari, E Company, 442d Regimental Combat Team; Kelly Kuwayama (wounded on Hill 617), medic, E Company, 442d; Marty Higgins, A Company, 141st Regiment, 36th "Texas" Division; Joseph Ichiuji, A Battery, 522d Field Artillery Battalion, 442d; Jack Wilson, D Company, 141st; George "Joe" Sakato (Medal of Honor winner), E Company, 442d; Terry Shima, Service Company, 442d; Gene Airheart, D Company, 141st. *Courtesy of Michaela McNichol, Library of Congress.*

September 2004: Wearing their Medals of Honor, Barney Hajiro (left) and Shizuya Hayashi (right) met in Hawaii with Gen. Peter Schoomaker, Army Chief of Staff (center), who displayed the patch of the 442d Regimental Combat Team. *U.S. Army photo (USARPAC).*

June 11, 2005: At a ceremony in front of the Go For Broke Monument in downtown Los Angeles, the late Young Oak Kim and Marty Higgins met for the first time, more than sixty years after they fought the Germans in the Vosges Mountains. *Courtesy of Shane Sato and the Go for Broke Educational Foundation.*

June 4, 1948: At Arlington National Cemetery, Lt. Gen. Jacob L. Devers offered his condolences to the parents of Fumitake Nagato. *U.S. Army Signal Corps, National Archives, Record Group 111-SC.*

June 4, 1948: Before a crowd of military and civilian dignitaries and "just Americans," the flag-draped casket containing the remains of Saburo Tanamachi reached its final destination at Arlington National Cemetery. *U.S. Army Signal Corps, National Archives, Record Group 111-SC.*

Prairie-dogging from one empty German foxhole to another for cover, Sakato killed five enemy soldiers and captured four single handedly. Nearby, T/4 Kelly Kuwayama, a medic with a red cross on his helmet, was working on a wounded soldier's leg. "Yet the German soldiers shot at him" anyway, Sakato remembers. "The bullet hit the side of his helmet and spun around inside [between the steel shell and the inner liner], then dropped out." Amazingly, though his skull was creased, "he was fine otherwise."

Sakato took advantage of a brief pause in the fighting to reload his machine gun's clips, and "threw a few hand grenades down at the Germans" below on the hillside, who were trying to circle around the advancing Americans. Then he happened to turn, and "saw some Germans running up the hill." A dozen enemy soldiers were counterattacking the platoon's left flank, supported by a frightening machine-gun and mortar barrage that forced Sakato and his mates to duck for cover.

When his good friend Saburo Tanamachi dared to rise up to spot the onrushing Germans, a bullet ripped through him. "I crawled over and picked him up," Sakato remembers. "I saw all the blood on my left hand and said, 'Why did you stand up?' He tried to say something, but it was just a gurgle and blood coming from his mouth. I held him close and cried. He went limp and I knew he was gone."[15] Tanamachi, from Texas himself, had just given his life trying to rescue the Lost Battalion of the 36th "Texas" Division.

Sakato grabbed his submachine gun and, ignoring enemy fire, leaped up and launched a one-man offensive. He was "mad as hell and crying." "I was going to get those Germans or die trying," Sakato recalls. "I was firing my Tommy gun from my hips and ran and hollered to the rest of the platoon to come on."

As E Company rallied behind him to block the enemy counterattack, Sakato quickly ran through both clips of his submachine gun. Once again he jumped into an enemy foxhole, this time grabbing a discarded rifle and using it to kill two Germans and wound a third. On the slopes below, the rest of the 2d Battalion was making its second *"banzai"* charge in nine days.

But Sakato was still ahead of the rest of his platoon, dangerously exposed to enemy fire. The Germans, "observing that he was the center of resistance, concentrated the attack upon him by throwing several grenades."[16] Returning fire with fire, Sakato once again exhausted his ammunition. Left with only the P-38 pistol he had snatched earlier from an enemy foxhole, he somehow kept his poise and "fired carefully,"[17] killing three Germans and wounding another as they were rushing toward him, less than ten yards away.

After the mayhem of the infantry charge, there was another momentary lull. And then the shelling finally started—friendly, not enemy. But the American troops were precariously close to the enemy targets. "We jumped into any hole that was open to keep from getting hit," Sakato remembers. Someone else leaped in with him—an acquaintance from Arizona. "We forgot about the shelling and began to talk about home." But when the barrage stopped, "we just had to crawl out of that old German foxhole, it stank so bad of body odor. So we had to dig our own foxholes."[18]

By midafternoon on Sunday, the left hook of the 2d Battalion, inspired by Sakato's one-man charge, had battered the enemy off Hill 617. The Germans lost one hundred dead and forty-one captured, while E and F Companies suffered eight dead and ten wounded. Through the end of Sunday's action, Sakato alone had killed twelve Germans, wounded two, captured four, and helped his platoon take thirty-four more prisoners.[19]

In the deathly calm after the barrage, Sakato surveyed the German position, a rocky area with no trees to hinder automatic weapons or artillery firing down the slopes. The enemy had enjoyed "a good view up and down the valley," Sakato recalls. The lives lost in seizing this vital high ground and eliminating the German threat to the American flank had not been in vain.[20]

★ ★ ★

The fierce resistance that the 2d Battalion met on Hill 617 was being matched by the furious German response to the main push by the 3d and 100th Battalions toward the Lost Battalion.

The first obstacle the American units faced was a mined roadblock at *Col de la Croisette* (the Crossroads), with enemy machine guns opening up from concealed and fortified nests. I Company killed scores of Germans in a firefight, freeing the 232d Engineers to clear the way for the three medium tanks and one light tank attached to the 3d Battalion.

As the troops kept inching ahead, "the enemy artillery unloosed a concentrated barrage on the battalion and heavy casualties ensued," according to the monthly regimental narrative. One of the dogfaces caught in the barrage was T/Sgt. Shig Doi, the recent replacement in the unit who had cut short his visit to his parents in Amache "because it was so depressing." As Doi ducked for cover, he was astonished to feel a tap on the back of his helmet. It was Dahlquist, urging I Company forward and saying, "Soldier, you can't do anything here." Doi remembers asking himself why the general and his aide were needlessly presenting themselves to enemy fire.[21]

T/Sgt. Tak Senzaki, who had left Rohwer by himself in the early morning to travel to Camp Shelby, also recalls thinking, "Get down, get down—we're pinned down," when Dahlquist, "making such a big target," approached, "stars on his helmet and everything." Then the general looked at him and asked, "Done any fighting today, soldier?"[22]

With 1st Lt. Wells Lewis in tow, Dahlquist continued along the front line to the 100th Battalion, which had advanced about six hundred yards "through heavy enemy resistance."[23] A skirmish had broken out when a German patrol split the seam between the 100th Battalion and the 36th Division on the right flank. Dahlquist ordered A Company of the 100th Battalion to the edge of the woods, to protect against further counterattacks.

By 1300, "terrific enemy fire" from a "prepared enemy line"[24] forced B Company to take cover. As the general was ordering an attack on the German position, a burst of small arms fire struck his aide. "He was standing alongside of me and fell into my arms," Dahlquist later wrote Lewis's mother. "He was dead before I laid him on the ground."[25] Lewis had been his aide for little more than three months, but "he had endeared himself . . . as a real man" to Dahlquist, by virtue of his "constant good nature, his keen mind, and his everlasting willingness to perform every task given him as a soldier. He was dependable and courageous."[26] But the men of the 442d wondered, not for the first time, who would be next to pay the price of the general's notion of courage.

Lewis's death did not stop Dahlquist from urging the two battalions to push forward at all costs. By this time, B Company was converging with I and K Companies on a narrow ridge with steep drop-offs on both sides. At the other end, still more than a mile away, was the crest of the hill, where the Lost Battalion was stranded. In between were seven hundred German defenders, with roving tanks, hazardous minefields (most of them concealed, though Higgins's scouts had identified some of them), and hidden mortar and machine-gun emplacements. Since "the terrain precluded a flanking movement," Dahlquist was forced to the "only alternative of a frontal attack against a strongly entrenched enemy."[27] Wearing steel helmets and carrying 9.5-pound rifles, ammunition, and backpacks, the American soldiers attacking uphill faced "physical stress that was literally hundreds of times greater than that created by fighting in the relatively flat terrain of Normandy, Belgium, or central France."[28] With limited Allied tank and almost no artillery support, the infantrymen of the 442d were making what the 100th Battalion journal later called an "almost suicidal" assault.

The common ground of attacker and defender was often less than half a football field in size—fifty or fewer yards of hillside pockmarked with shell craters and empty foxholes, scarred by treacherous defiles, clogged with knee-high underbrush springing out of soggy soil, and obscured by towering pine trees whose branches turned into flaming projectiles when shells exploded overhead.

Confusion reigned in this verdant hell. "Your enemy is ten or twenty feet away from you," says Shig Doi. "You hop from one tree to the next tree. We had them scattered so much, they might be in the back of us." Soldiers could barely trust their own senses to discriminate friend from foe. That shadowy figure behind a tree could be German or American. "The only reason I could fire at them is because the German has a white face," Doi remembers.* Even hearing was suspect. "The 36th Division took off and left a lot of their machine guns behind," Doi recalls. "So the Germans were firing our machine guns, and you couldn't tell the difference."[29] The *rata-tat-tat* of an American machine gun, easily distinguished from the chilling *brrrrrpp* of the faster German automatic weapons, might be fired not by a friend nearby, but by an enemy. And even if that man a few yards away was an American—a Japanese American—he might not belong to the same squad, the same platoon, the same company, even the same battalion.

"I had never seen men get cut down so fast, so furiously, caught in machine-gun fire," says Doi.[30] Near the crest of the ridge, unrelenting fire from automatic weapons and mortars kept the attacking Americans

---

*This is an unconsciously ironic refutation of the post–Pearl Harbor canard that "real" Americans could not trust Japanese Americans because they were physically indistinguishable from the enemy. To Japanese American eyes in the Vosges, the Caucasian officers of the 442d had the same skin color and features as the enemy, but the *Nisei* soldiers could nonetheless identify which white face to fire at.

sprawling facedown in the mud and underbrush. "You feel so helpless," says Tak Senzaki. "As soon as we made a move, they opened up." When one of his men was hit, "you want to help him but you can't," he recalls. "We were hoping he could crawl back, but he was already dead." Jim Yamashita, of I Company, remembers seeing one of the bazooka men of the 442d falling from a sniper's shot to his neck. "The life went out of him"[31] as blood spurted from his jugular vein. And after sixty years, several men are still haunted by the memory of hearing a dying soldier cry out, *"Okaasan"* (mother), over and over for many long minutes before falling silent.

Flattened on their bellies, hugging the cold earth, assaulted by the grisly sights and ghastly sounds of death everywhere, the men of the 442d came to the grim understanding that the only way to get off the razor ridge alive was to keep pressing forward—to attack the Germans on the slopes yards away from them. To stay where they were was to join the dead and dying.

So it all came down to lone men making the most difficult choices under the most extreme circumstances—just as they had done in Hawaii, while black smoke was still rising from Pearl Harbor, and in the "relocation camps," while their own government was questioning their citizenship. Without the support of air power, armor, or artillery, the men of the 442d were nakedly confronting not just an implacable enemy but their own individual and collective destiny. Facedown in the mud, with machine guns and minefields ahead of them and steep slopes to the side and rear, they knew their fates were literally in their own hands.

Steeling themselves for the assault on what they would later call "Suicide Hill," the soldiers began fixing bayonets to their M1s. A bullet whizzed by Barney Hajiro's ear. The assistant BAR man, Takeyasu Onaga, made one last check of the larger, heavier automatic weapon he and Hajiro had worked so hard to master in Italy. Just then, "Kash" Kashino crawled over to join them. But Hajiro noticed his platoon leader had been wounded and urged him to get medical attention. "I'm a private, and I'm telling a sergeant to go back," Hajiro remembers. It was Kashino's third wound in almost as many days. "I got hit in the back," Kashino remembered. "I felt blood running down." Before, he had always returned to the front line as soon as possible. "You got to go back," he said. "As long as you're alive, you have to fight." But this time the aid station would not let him rejoin the battle.

Grabbing extra ammunition, Hajiro turned to Onaga, who said, "Take my P-38 if I get shot." Hajiro remembers wondering why Onaga "looked sad" when he said that. But Hajiro had also "committed himself to a course of action which he did not expect to survive," according to his superiors.[32] He "saw mounting casualties," said his commander, 1st Lt. Sadaichi Kubota. "For him, death was apparent. Yet he saw the need of a job to be done."[33]

Three years later, S. L. A. Marshall would write about soldiers like Hajiro in *Men Against Fire:* "There were many men who had been consistently bad actors in the training period, marked by the faults of laziness, unruliness, and disorderliness, who just as consistently became lions on the battlefield, with all of the virtues of sustained aggressiveness, warm obedience, and thoughtfully planned action."[34]

To this day, Kubota believes Hajiro's action was "calculated."[35] But at the time, what the men on the ridge saw was not premeditation but simply courage beyond comprehension. Hefting his BAR, Hajiro suddenly stood up. "I didn't think about dying," he recalls, adding what still strikes him as obvious: "Automatic weapons go first." The BAR, which would provide the firepower to lead the attack, would also make him the prime target of the enemy. But Hajiro knew someone had to act—there were no officers left standing. "Me, a buck private," he says. "I had to do the job."

"Loudly shouting expletives," Hajiro began charging uphill alone, seemingly oblivious to the rain of bullets. "You cannot go backward," Hajiro remembers thinking. "I was mad."[36] Knowing they "couldn't let Hajiro attack by himself," the rest of the 442d rose, man by man, and clambered up behind him in waves, "firing and attacking with crazed-like shouts."[37] "We were swearing at the Germans," Hajiro remembers, "Hawaiian style."

"You know, we swear naturally," says S/Sgt. Joe Shimamura of K Company, who was leading a squad of eleven riflemen. "And then we just walk. We shoot from the hip."[38] But the lethal fire, slicing in overlapping arcs from machine guns carefully positioned in the thick woods, began systematically felling them like saplings—among them, the assistant BAR man, Onaga, killed in Hajiro's wake.

Yet somehow Hajiro kept pushing forward, only once dropping to his knee to reload his BAR. "You spin the BAR around," Hajiro says. "Once you pin them down, you wipe them out. . . . This is not a Hollywood movie." Meaning there was no time to take prisoners.

Miraculously still on his feet after agonizingly long seconds, Hajiro deliberately made himself a target in order to get the hidden German gunners to reveal themselves. When a machine gun opened up about twenty yards away, Hajiro traded bursts with the enemy and killed three Germans with his BAR.

Not far away, the forward observers from the 522d Field Artillery Battalion—Sus Ito, George Oiye, who had been called "Whitey" by the Hawaiians, and Yuki Minaga, who had been jumped by the Buddhaheads in the barracks—found themselves together again, watching one another's backs as they had been almost constantly since their days at Camp Shelby. Only this time, it was not a fistfight. Though originally assigned to different units as spotters, they were now within a few yards of one another, scrambling for cover in the chaos that was funneling I, K, and B Companies toward the waiting Germans on the hilltop. According to the 100th Battalion journal, artillery was "conspicuous by its absence" in the drive toward the Lost Battalion. So the three friends did not have their designated roles to play. They were no longer observers. Now they were riflemen.

As the earth around him exploded from the impact of mortar shells, Minaga joined the rush up the ridge—the 442d's third *"banzai"* charge in the Vosges. He swept up a fallen soldier's weapon and, risking murderous enemy fire, worked his way forward.[39] Ito and Oiye climbed right behind him. Minaga remembers Lieutenant Colonel Pursall, 3d Battalion commander, right behind him, waving a shiny pistol and yelling, "First one up the hill gets a Silver Star!" Oiye recalls Minaga rushing forward to find a large boulder for protection so he could operate his radio. Ito today claims he doesn't remember anything at all about "Suicide Hill."

But through the fog of war, Oiye had a clear view of an amazing sight: an unarmed medic, with a red cross on his helmet, running alongside them, darting from one fallen soldier to another, administering aid to those still living. Once again it was James Okubo, who before daylight faded would treat eight wounded men while disregarding his own safety.[40]

Also swept along in the charge up the hill was Pfc. Mickey Akiyama, who had been the first of the hundred volunteers from Manzanar. After "Kash" Kashino was wounded, Akiyama had taken his place as platoon leader. But by then, it was less a platoon (normally three dozen soldiers) than a squad (usually twelve men). Casualties from the nearly continuous firefight had left Akiyama with only three other I Company men, though another three soldiers from K Company joined his depleted band.

As Akiyama neared one of the minefields in front of the German position, he was suddenly knocked off his feet, unconscious. From a few yards behind, Shig Doi had seen one soldier after another picked off by a well-concealed German sniper. Akiyama was the third soldier Doi remembers falling. The enemy's carefully aimed round had pierced Akiyama's helmet and gouged his skull. The impact had blown the helmet off his head.

Yards away, Barney Hajiro was still in the lead, with the rest of I, K, and B Companies now charging headlong behind him. Hajiro "realized the odds were mounting against him, but without a thought for his safety, he headed through the heavily booby-trapped area" lying before him.[41] Moving steadily forward, he took out another machine-gun nest about twenty-five yards away. But in doing so, he drew fire from still another automatic weapon about forty yards to his right.

This time, Hajiro's breathtaking advance between oncoming bullets came to a brutal halt. Four rounds riddled his arm and pierced his side. "My helmet went flying, my BAR went flying," he remembers, "but if I had a gun, I would have shot again."[42]

As Hajiro fell, the men of the 3d and 100th Battalions, "shouting at the enemy and firing from their hips,"[43] hurled themselves at the remaining Germans, at first blazing away point blank, then rushing in with "bayonets and grenades," and finally engaging in "savage hand-to-hand combat."[44] "We yelled our heads off and charged and shot the head off everything that moved," according to Pfc. Ichigi Kashiwagi of K Company. "We didn't care anymore . . . we acted like a bunch of savages."[45]

"Very few prisoners were taken," the 100th Battalion journal noted laconically, echoing Hajiro's understanding of the situation. "The enemy fought back fanatically, and countless number were found dead at their posts in dugouts."[46] Some dead Americans joined them, "sprawling over the enemy positions they had just neutralized,"[47] but even more of the living carried their spirit forward.

On his own, Hajiro had killed seven Germans in two key machine-gun nests and also knocked out two snipers. But his heroism, like "Machine Gun Joe" Sakato's on Hill 617, was measured not by numbers but by the example he set. "The great victories of the United States have pivoted on the acts and courage and intelligence of a very few individuals," S. L. A.

Marshall wrote in another context. "Every worthwhile action comes of some man daring what others fear to attempt."[48]

★ ★ ★

By 1700 on Sunday, the carnage on "Suicide Hill" temporarily ceased, as darkness descended on the Vosges. The exhausted men of the 3d and 100th Battalions dug in, still over a mile short of the Lost Battalion, with enemy mortar and artillery fire continuing to rain down on them.

Since daybreak, I Company saw five men killed and forty wounded in action—a third of the unit's frontline strength knocked out in less than a day. K Company had no officers left. Colonel Pence, the founding commander of the 442d, was among the wounded. He had "fought tooth and nail for the 442d,"[49] Christopher Keegan remembers, and his leadership would be missed. Lieutenant Colonel Virgil Miller took his place. Young Oak Kim's mentor, Lt. Col. Gordon Singles, became executive officer of the whole regiment, and Maj. Alex E. McKenzie took his place leading the 100th Battalion. Casualties had finally integrated the senior command structure of the 442d and 100th, which had been combined on paper since the summer and unified under fire since entering the Vosges.

That night, the Antitank Company, Frankie Seto's unit, which had finally rejoined the 442d after serving in gliders during the invasion of southern France, guarded transport bearing supplies for the weary soldiers and served as litter bearers for the wounded. Incredibly, Mickey Akiyama had not only survived the shot to his head but had bandaged himself while lying on the battleground, in clear view of the enemy. Somehow, he found his helmet, inside of which he had a photo of his daughter, Mariko Ann, who had been born shortly before he had volunteered from Manzanar. Though he was bleeding and dizzy, Akiyama even managed to accept the surrender of four German soldiers. It was not until night that he was evacuated to the field hospital, along with Barney Hajiro, who characteristically insisted that the thirty-nine other wounded men of I Company go ahead of him. "I'm okay," he said, though he was in fact seriously wounded. "Help the others first."[50] Hajiro walked down "Suicide Hill," bleeding all the way. But at least "the Germans gave me a break," Hajiro recalls. No one shot at him as he made his way to safety.[51]

Before falling asleep on his cot, Dahlquist wrote in his diary: "Late in

[the] evening a furious fight developed which I believe was the crisis." He continued in a handwritten letter to his wife:

> The past week has been a very difficult and anxious one and the strain will not be over for several days yet. . . . It astounds me how these men are able to stand the physical and mental strain under which they are constantly living. It is almost beyond comprehension that the human being can stand so much.[52]

★ ★ ★

October 30, 0900: With a relatively stable front established overnight, instead of the rapidly shifting battle lines from the previous day, American artillery was finally able to direct a heavy barrage at the top of the ridge separating the 442d from the Lost Battalion.

Following the bombardment, the cautiously advancing soldiers found "large amounts" of enemy clothing and supplies littering the area just beyond "Suicide Hill." The scene was a tragicomic reminder of the horror and fury of the day before. Apparently "unnerved" by their heavy losses, the Germans had fled their original fortified positions "in confusion."[53]

Although they didn't know it at the time, the deserted landscape meant the worst was over for the 442d. But it was still to come for the Lost Battalion.* Since daybreak, the enemy had been turning its fire on the trapped men. Headquarters ordered Higgins to "be prepared to attack" and to "check in every fifteen minutes for further instructions."

0950—Higgins to headquarters: "German patrols harass our position."

1011—Headquarters to Higgins: "Remain in position. Await orders."

1025—Higgins to headquarters: "Harassed by enemy patrols. . . . Do not want pals to fly over today."

Though unsure when the rescuers would break through, Higgins believed enough supplies were on hand. And he feared that further airdrops would pinpoint the Lost Battalion's position in the woods.

---

*My interview with Higgins. John Keegan points out that usually the "eerily empty" battleground, "to an experienced twentieth century soldier, is a prime indicator that danger lies all about." (*The Face of War,* p. 312.) S. L. A. Marshall makes the same point in *Men Against Fire,* pp. 44–48.

1120—Higgins to headquarters: "Situation here gets worse. 22 litter casualties. 11 trench foot casualties. 10 wounded. . . . Enemy patrols active on flank and front. Automatic weapons, mines . . ."

Higgins assured headquarters he was "not trying to beg off" by maintaining a tight defensive posture rather than launching a counterattack. Instead, he proposed a smaller patrol to scout the enemy rear.

1232—Headquarters to Higgins: "Send patrol. We are coming to relieve you as fast as we can. 442 now about one mile away."

By this time, E and G Companies of the 2d Battalion had moved down from Hill 617 to clear the valley below, establish roadblocks, and connect with the 3d and 100th Battalions to protect the regiment's flank. Along the way, E Company came under heavy mortar fire. "Machine Gun Joe" Sakato remembers hitting the ground twice when shells exploded nearby. The third time, the explosion was just behind him, hurling him six feet from the spot where he had been ducking for cover.

"I ached all over," Sakato recalls, "but we had to start digging a foxhole." He got his shovel from his backpack and tried to use it, but found he couldn't raise his arm. Disoriented, he took off his pack and saw a hole in it. He shrugged off his jacket and saw it had been punctured as well. Then he felt something oozing down his back, and he knew his tour of duty was about to end.

Above on the hillside, the 100th Battalion ran into "heavy enemy small arms fire," but managed to cover another two hundred yards toward the Lost Battalion. On the left flank, the 3d Battalion moved ahead to a mined roadblock manned by fifty Germans in an area known to locals as *La Baignoire des Oiseaux* (the Birdbath). After a swift firefight, the Americans overwhelmed the obstacle and carefully pushed forward.

Leading the advance were three I Company scouts, Pfc. Matsuji "Mutt" Sakumoto, from Hawaii, Pfc. Henry Nakada, whose family was in the Gila River Relocation Center, and T/Sgt. Tak Senzaki, whose early-morning departure from Rohwer had led him to this mountaintop in the Vosges. Crawling slowly through an open patch of ground ringed by dense forest, the three friends "all took turns" on the point, Senzaki recalls, "to be fair about it." Unsure whether Germans or Americans were hiding in the trees ahead, the trio silently exchanged hand signals across the field. After yesterday's carnage, the battleground was preternaturally still.

"It was a pretty nice day," recalls Ed Guy of the Lost Battalion. "It's all misty in those woods, but you could see out there." On lookout duty in the late afternoon, he remembers peering around a tree and "seeing three fellows with American uniforms on."

"And that's when I hollered," Guy remembers. "I actually ran down the hill." Perhaps nonplussed by Guy's sudden appearance, Sakumoto could not think of anything to say except "You guys need cigarettes?"

"I might have hugged him, I don't know," says Guy. "I was just excited to get out of there."[54]

Around the same time, the 100th Battalion made contact on the right flank. (To this day, Al Takahashi believes B Company made it to the Lost Battalion before I Company did.[55]) According to the 100th Battalion journal, "The happiness and relief expressed on the faces of those relieved made up a little for the hardship and suffering, as well as losses."[56]

"The chills went up our spines when we saw the *Nisei* soldiers," says Higgins. "Honestly, they looked like giants to us."[57]

Waiting anxiously at headquarters, Dahlquist heard the news by radio.

1600—Lost Battalion to headquarters: "Patrol 442 here. Tell them we love them."

9

CASUALTIES

"Let Them Loose"

Every action large or small is decided by what happens up there on the line where men take the final chance of life or death. . . . One man must go ahead so that a nation may live.—S. L. A. MARSHALL[1]

The Western Front and the Western Defense Command, November–December 1944

On November 7, 1944, an Associated Press wire story on the Lost Battalion appeared on page three of *The New York Times,* under the headline "Doughboys Break German Ring to Free 270 Trapped Eight Days." The "rescuing Yanks" were called "doughboys" in the body of the story as well as in the headline. There was no mention of the 442d, *Nisei* soldiers, or Japanese Americans.

One of the pictures accompanying the article showed D-rations and Halazone tablets "placed in a wrapper before being stuffed into a 150-mm. howitzer shell." The other photo showed Marty Higgins, bearded and grimy, his trusty carbine, with its shattered wooden stock, slung over his shoulder. Smiling broadly, Higgins was shaking hands with a clean-shaven "Lieut. C. O. Barry, Williamstown, Pa., of the relief unit," while an unidentified soldier—Caucasian, like Higgins and Barry—looked on.

There was no Lieutenant Barry in the 442d. And there were no Japanese Americans shown in the original Signal Corps photos.*

---

*There was a 2d Lt. Charles O. Barry from Williamstown, Pennsylvania, in the Medical Detachment of the 141st Regiment (see the reproduction of the 36th Division

★ ★ ★

But the Lost Battalion knew who had come to its rescue. "We had heard they were on their way," recalls T/Sgt. Ed Guy, Marty Higgins's friend, who had first learned about the 442d when it was attached to the 34th Division in Italy. "There were no finer soldiers," says Jack Wilson. "They had a lot to prove and they certainly did."[2]

As the 442d approached, the men of the Lost Battalion "peered out of their fantastic, deep, deep foxholes that were more like small caves," Sus Ito remembers. "They came out with much grime and looked shocked but obviously happy."[3]

"I'm glad to see you Japs," one soldier told Ichigi Kashiwagi of K Company. "I know he didn't mean it," Kashiwagi says. "It just came out that way."[4]

"I saw a wounded soldier in a foxhole (4' x 8') partially covered with logs for protection from tree bursts caused by artillery shells," recalls Hiroo Endo of K Company. "I either hugged him or shook his hand. He emptied his canteen of chocolate, I thought. However, it was muddy water scooped from rainwater in the foxhole. I offered him my canteen of water and I saw tears rolling down his cheeks."[5]

In the momentary hush that enveloped the hill, Ito remembers most of all "a strange feeling of numb stupor and relief." He and his friends George Oiye and Yuki Minaga—the three *kotonks* from Camp Shelby, forward observers turned riflemen—had made it up "Suicide Hill" unscathed. "God was really looking after us," Ito recalls, "and I like to think that perhaps my *senninbari*"—his hand-stitched waistband, still wrapped in cellophane—"may also have played a role." He would not tell his mother he had volunteered for frontline duty until after the war, when he got back home and his family had been released from Rohwer.[6]

---

roster at http://www.lettersfromthewar.com/14.html). Commenting on the identification of Barry as belonging to "the relief unit," Marty Higgins says, "Glad they did not say rescuers" (my correspondence with Higgins).

A day later, on November 8, 1944, the headline of the United Press wire story on page three of *The Honolulu Advertiser* was "Local Troops in Daring Dash Rescue Beleaguered Texans." Of course by this time roughly half of the soldiers in the 442d were not "local" to Hawaii, they were from the mainland. And by the fall of 1944, the 36th Division, though it began as a Texas National Guard unit, included men from across the United States. "I'm from New Jersey," Marty Higgins notes. The photos are from a series of six at the National Archives in College Park, Maryland, numbered SC-196052-S through SC-196057-S.

Ito and his friends were the lucky ones. After two weeks of bloody combat, climaxing with the rescue of the 211 men of the Lost Battalion, the 100th and 3d Battalions combined had lost more than sixty percent of their authorized strength of 193 men per company. (Most of the 442d's companies entered the Vosges with less than their authorized strength. Since an infantry company typically had a significant "overhead," the loss as a percentage of frontline soldiers was actually much higher.) A Company had 65 men standing; B Company, Al Takahashi's unit, only 55; C Company, 75; D Company, 74; I Company, Barney Hajiro's unit, 71; K Company, 78; L Company, 85; M Company, 102.[7] K Company had no officers left; it was being led by Sgt. Chester Tanaka.

But the dazed men on the hill, rescued and rescuers alike, had little time to mourn the dead or to celebrate the rescue. Minaga handed out some cigarettes to the grateful men of the 141st, but the 442d and the Lost Battalion were together for "two or three minutes, that's all," Guy recalls. "We went back, and they went forward."[8]

Although everyone in the surrounding woods understood the 442d had achieved a significant and bloody victory, the rescue of the Lost Battalion was, at the end of the day, just one more hilltop captured in the wearying Vosges campaign. There was practically no rest for the exhausted soldiers. "I could never figure out why the Germans never attacked us right after we got to the Lost Battalion," says Shig Doi. "They could have run us right off, but they must have been hurt just as bad as we were. We were so tired. The next morning we would have been all dead."[9]

As October and the fall faded into November and an early winter, Operation DOGFACE continued along its grim mountain path. Anticipating a strong German counterattack, the 442d dug into the high wooded ground—recently occupied by the Lost Battalion—above La Houssière. Under constant artillery fire, the 442d's patrols forayed south and east toward the railroad tracks stretching from Bruyères toward Germany. All the while, the cold continued to inflict "a great hardship on the wounded especially," according to the regimental narrative, "and a steady rain impeded operations and filled the slit trenches."[10]

On November 4, after three weeks of shivering in lightweight uniforms, the 442d finally got its winter gear: overcoats or heavy field jackets, wool sweaters, thick socks, and "shoe-pacs" (rubberized boots).* That same day, General Dahlquist once again visited the front, where he complained the 442d "had done practically nothing to clear its positions and get a defensible position." Lieutenant Colonel Virgil Miller "started to faint" while talking to him, Dahlquist noted. "He is apparently in very bad physical condition."[11]

While Dahlquist was visiting, I and L Companies were advancing northeast of La Houssière with three medium tanks in support. Crossing a flat open ridge, they ran into a barrage of small arms, machine gun, and mortar fire from Germans fortified in the dense woods ahead. As one of the tanks "stopped to maneuver into a firing position clear of the trees," Pfc. George Uchimiya of K Company remembered, "it was hit by an enemy bazooka, wounding two of the occupants. One of the crew was fatally hit, while the other was seriously wounded and was frantically calling for help."[12]

Once again James Okubo risked his life to aid the wounded, as he had repeatedly during the previous weeks. "Somehow he wasn't hit," said Uchimiya, amazed. Okubo ran fifty yards under fire, climbed onto the burning tank, pulled the crewman out of the hatch, and carried him to safety. The tank was so far in enemy territory that the Germans later used it as a roadblock when they counterattacked.

It was not until the following day that Dahlquist belatedly acknowledged the general condition of the troops. "The 442d is in terrible shape," he noted on November 5.[13] By this time, six days after the rescue of the Lost Battalion, B Company, Al Takahashi's unit, had only forty-three men standing; I Company, Barney Hajiro's unit, was down to forty-two. Staff Sergeant Joe Shimamura had led a squad of twelve men to rescue the Lost Battalion. When his unit, K Company, was finally relieved, only one man in his squad remained standing. Shimamura himself could not even walk, because of trench foot. He had been "carried off the mountain" two days before.[14]

But even these stark figures didn't tell the full story. Counting only riflemen, L Company had seventeen on line; I Company, just four.[15]

---

*About seventy-five percent of the infantry in the Vosges had already received their winter gear by the end of October, according to Clarke and Smith, *Riviera to the Rhine*, p. 294.

★ ★ ★

On November 7, when the *New York Times* story on the Lost Battalion ran, Pfc. Joe Nishimoto of G Company—whose family had been "relocated" to Jerome—and his squad were locked in the third day of a struggle to dislodge entrenched Germans from a ridge overlooking La Houssière. Fortified machine gun and bazooka emplacements commanded the hillside, and the only approaches were through a fifty- to seventy-five-yard no-man's-land strewn with mines and booby traps. Right next to Nishimoto on the front line, in the same squad, was his brother-in-law, Pvt. Sam Ishida, who had volunteered along with him from Ohio.

After the Germans had repeatedly repelled American assaults, Nishimoto turned to Sgt. Bill Okutsu and told him "the quickest and easiest way to break through was to sneak behind and give them hell." "Several men in his platoon volunteered to go with him," said S/Sgt. Akira Ishimoto, "but he ordered them to remain behind and cover his advance."[16] Nishimoto crawled through the minefield, "carefully cut trip wires, and used the cover of bushes and rocks whenever possible."[17] Fifteen yards from one of the machine-gun nests, he lobbed a hand grenade and knocked it out. Spotting another emplacement forty more yards away, "he circled to the rear of the position and stood up in full view of the enemy to fire his Thompson submachine gun at pointblank range, wiping out the nest, killing one enemy and wounding another."[18]

On his left, two German riflemen started shooting at Nishimoto. "Joe kept advancing toward his foes as he fired his Thompson," said Okutsu. "When he had hit one of them the other must have decided it was too hot—he took off." Nishimoto kept circling the hill. Thirty yards away he spotted yet another machine-gun nest. When he started firing, the Germans, "seeing that they had been hit from the flank, also joined their comrades in flight," said Ishimoto. It was only then that G Company could negotiate the route through the minefield that Nishimoto had single-handedly cleared, breaking the three-day stalemate.

★ ★ ★

On Sunday, November 12, two weeks after the charge up "Suicide Hill," the 442d assembled on parade before Major General Dahlquist near Bruyères. Starting a few days earlier, on November 8, the depleted 442d had finally been taken off line. The 100th Battalion was the first to be relieved. Through heavy snow, the troops traveled forty miles southwest to the Army Rest Center at Bains les Bains, where they were treated to hot baths in what had been a resort before the war. The morale of the men was "exceptionally high."[19]

The next day, relief continued for the remaining troops. After three weeks of sleeping in muddy foxholes, the soldiers of the 442d were "billeted in buildings" well behind the front line—the 2d Battalion in Fays, the 3d in Lépanges, headquarters company and medical detachment in Fiménil, and service and antitank companies in Bruyères. The men collected their October paychecks, Special Services showed a movie, and the troops gratefully took advantage of their beer rations. And, long after it could have made a difference, "special attention was given to instruction in the prevention of trench foot."[20]

As a light snow fell over the parade ground, the men of the 442d stood at attention in their newly issued boots and long coats.[21] It was only while he was reviewing the troops that Dahlquist was finally forced to acknowledge the heavy casualties suffered by the 442d. Turning to Lt. Col. Virgil Miller, who had nearly fainted when he saw the general at the front a week earlier, Dahlquist looked at the nearly empty ranks and files and asked where the rest of the men were. Miller replied, "That's all that's left."*

Among those missing from the ceremony was Robert Kuroda, killed in action in the Battle of Bruyères. Also absent was Joe Nishimoto, killed in action a few days after breaking the three-day stalemate at the minefield overlooking La Houssière.

From his hospital bed, Shiro "Kash" Kashino sent a letter to his fiancée, Louise Tsuboi: "I'm not lonesome in the hospital," he wrote, "there are a lot of boys." He added, "In fact it's full." The price of taking the high ground in the Vosges had been paid in shattered limbs, shredded flesh,

---

*This exchange has taken on legendary status among the 442d. Many of the men I interviewed were on parade that day, and most of them told me about it, though it seems likely they were out of earshot. Both Dahlquist and Miller are deceased, so there is no way to confirm the exact wording of the conversation.

Dahlquist awarded two Silver Stars, ten Bronze Stars, and sixteen Division Citations to the men standing in the snow. He also posthumously awarded four Distinguished Service Crosses, four Silver Stars, and one Bronze Star to absent members of the 442d. All the medals were for bravery shown in combat months before but only now acknowledged after the normal administrative lag.

and blood. Also hospitalized were Young Oak Kim, who had been wounded near Biffontaine, Barney Hajiro, whose heroism on "Suicide Hill" had led to the rescue of the Lost Battalion, and George "Machine Gun Joe" Sakato, who had led the charge up Hill 617. Swathed in bandages, Sakato learned his life had been saved by his overcoat, which he had folded and stuffed into his backpack. It had absorbed the shock of exploding shrapnel that otherwise would have sliced through his spine.

Sakato, Hajiro, Kuroda, and Nishimoto were all recommended for the Congressional Medal of Honor. Hajiro was incredulous when his commander, 1st Lt. James Wheatley Jr., gave him the news. "I thought he was joking," he says. Hajiro believes to this day that Wheatley wanted him to get the award "for the Japanese Americans in the camps."[22]

It would be months before the surviving heroes learned their honors had been downgraded one level, to Distinguished Service Crosses. Sakato would hear the news much later in a hospital in Vancouver, Washington, where he would spend months in rehabilitation after being flown back to the United States.

James Okubo's recommendation for a Medal of Honor was also turned down. But instead of a Distinguished Service Cross, he would eventually be awarded a Silver Star, another grade lower, which the Army somehow deemed "more appropriate"[23] for a medic who had risked his life dozens of times under fire to save his wounded comrades. More than a half century would pass before he and the other heroes of the 442d finally earned the recognition they deserved.

But if individual valor was not properly acknowledged at the time, the astonishing collective bravery of the 442d could not be ignored.* Although the actual awards would not be made until many months later, all

---

*The awarding of medals to individuals can be skewed by subjective considerations, by the number of approvals required at levels of command increasingly far removed from the actions described, by the credibility of eyewitnesses (assuming there are any who survive), even by the quality of the writing in the original recommendations. "The personnel at higher headquarters who approve [or disapprove] the awards have no personal knowledge of the action," wrote Lt. Col. James M. Hanley, commander of the 2d Battalion of the 442d, in his memoir, *A Matter of Honor* (p. 66). "The result is that many who deserve awards do not receive them, and many receive awards to which they are not strictly entitled." Citations for units, however, are more likely to result from measures such as attainment of objectives and levels of casualties inflicted and sustained, which can be assessed more accurately and fairly at higher levels.

of the frontline units of the 442d, and one of its support units, won Distinguished Unit Citations for their service in the Vosges.

The 100th Battalion was cited for its "extraordinary heroism, daring determination, and esprit de corps . . . during the period 15 to 30 October, 1944, near Bruyères, Biffontaine, and in the Forêt Domaniale de Champ, France." The specific actions noted were the capture of "the strongly fortified Hill A, dominating Bruyères, from a fanatically resisting enemy," the "bitter fighting at close range" that "resulted in the capture of the entire town" of Biffontaine, and the fight "without respite for four days against a fanatical enemy that was determined to keep the 'lost battalion' isolated."[24]

Companies F and L of the 2d Battalion were cited for their "fearless determination, daring, and intrepidity" in the O'Connor Task force, "a plan brilliantly conceived and expertly executed" that "secured the high ridge which dominates Belmont."[25]

The entire 2d Battalion was cited for its "courage, determination, and esprit de corps" in the attack on Hill 617: "In the face of intense enemy barrages and numerous counterattacks, the infantrymen of this battalion fought their way through difficult jungle-like terrain in freezing weather and completely encircled the enemy."[26]

The 3d Battalion was cited for its "intrepidity, fearless courage, and complete disregard for personal safety" in the rescue of the Lost Battalion: "After repeated frontal assaults had failed to drive the enemy from the hill, Companies I and K, then leading the attack, fixed bayonets and charged up the slope, shouting at the enemy and firing from their hips, while the enemy fired point-blank into their ranks. . . . Completely unnerved by the vicious bayonet charge, the enemy fled in confusion after making a desperate stand."[27]

Finally, and notably, the 232d Engineer Combat Company was cited "for heroism, esprit de corps and extraordinary achievement in combat from 23 October to 11 November 1944 near Bruyères, France." The engineer company of the 442d Regimental Combat Team had built "a supply road out of a mountain trail which rose 1,000 feet above the valley floor. . . . Almost continuous rain and snow made their task more difficult, yet by sheer determination and grit, these men accomplished this magnificent feat of engineering. Without this road, the division operation could not have succeeded."[28]

These five Presidential Unit Citations, earned by the 442d in less than a month of combat in the Vosges, represented an unparalleled achievement among American Army troops in World War II.*

★ ★ ★

The day after the parade, Dahlquist ordered the depleted 442d back to the front. Operation DOGFACE had already ended three days earlier for the 36th Division, which still had not reached its original objective, the hills above St. Léonard, five miles south of St. Dié. Since its start a month earlier, DOGFACE had advanced only ten miles through the mountains, across a fifteen-mile front—a distance that "seemed insignificant," as VI Corps headquarters put it, "when compared with the lightning-like advances during the preceding six weeks,"[29] which covered more than three hundred and fifty miles, from the landing near Nice on August 15 to the foothills of the Vosges at the beginning of October.

The 442d's final role in the campaign was to maintain defensive positions and patrol the forward areas. It was not until November 17 that the combat team was finally relieved of its duty in the Vosges. It was Lieutenant General Devers, commander of the 6th Army Group, four levels of command higher than the 442d, who personally ordered the unit taken off line. And it was not until then that 382 new Japanese American replacements arrived, along with 62 RTUs, soldiers "returned to units" from hospitals. The exhausted 442d was reassigned to southern France, for what they would call the "champagne campaign," a four-month respite of light combat in patrols along the France-Italy border in the mountains above Nice.

In a farewell letter to the 442d, Dahlquist described its role in Operation DOGFACE as "one of hard, intense fighting through terrain as difficult as any army has ever encountered." He thanked the officers and men

---

*According to the "combat chronicles" in *The Army Almanac*, only four of the Army's infantry divisions, each with three times as many men as the 442d, earned proportionately more Distinguished Unit Citations than the 442d won just in the Vosges, and those units earned their awards over the entire course of the war, not just a month. When the two Distinguished Unit Citations the 100th/442d earned in Italy are added to the five won in the Vosges, only one division—the 9th—earned proportionately more Distinguished Unit Citations, and it was in combat fifty percent longer than the 442d.

for their "courage, steadfastness, and willingness," which "were equal to any ever displayed by United States troops."

"Every officer and man of the Division joins me in sending best personal regards and good wishes to every member" of the 442d, Dahlquist continued, "and we hope that we may be honored again by having you as a member of our Division."[30]

The general did not mention the 442d's sacrifices in rescuing the Lost Battalion, which VI Corps headquarters acknowledged had been the main focus of the entire 36th Division at the end of October.[31] From October 1 through November 17, the 442d infantry had shrunk by twenty-five percent, from 3,313 to 2,484 enlisted men, and from 193 to 122 officers and warrant officers. But those figures included replacements and RTUs. During the twenty-six days actually spent in combat, the 442d suffered 140 deaths and 1,800 other casualties, battle and nonbattle.[32] That is, in less than a month, more than half of the men in the unit were casualties. Even more remarkable, many of the casualties returned to the front line—some of them, like Shiro "Kash" Kashino, over and over again.

"We were not aware of the tremendous losses," Marty Higgins says today. "No one will ever be able to convince me that the men killed and wounded in our rescue can be justified. We should have been bypassed."

★ ★ ★

But it was not just the sacrifices of the 442d that had been squandered in the Vosges. By the end of the year, the whole Allied strategy in eastern France was undermined, both by command decisions and by an unanticipated—but preventable—turn of events.

On November 25, shortly after the 442d had departed for the south of France, General Dwight D. Eisenhower, supreme commander of the Allied Expeditionary Forces, visited Devers, commander of the 6th Army Group. Under Devers were the French First Army and the American Seventh Army, which, led by Lt. Gen. Alexander Patch, was poised to sweep down the Alsatian plains and cross the Rhine into Germany.

But rather than take advantage of the gains made by the Seventh Army, Eisenhower was concerned about the "flagging offensive" of the Third Army, commanded by Lt. Gen. George C. Patton, which was advancing north of the Vosges toward the forests of the Ardennes. By late 1944, the Allies' "broad front" strategy had become focused on delivering a decisive blow through the northern lowlands toward the industrialized areas of the Rhine in Germany. The first attempt had been the abortive Market Garden offensive through Holland in September, which would be remembered as the failure to hold "a bridge too far." By November, the main thrust was intended to be Patton's drive east through northern France and Belgium toward the heavily defended Saar Basin.

But when Devers, Patch, and the energetic Truscott were pushing Operation DOGFACE through the Vosges in October, new possibilities had emerged: entering a back door to Germany through the Belfort Gap, near Switzerland, which Truscott had argued for, or through the Saverne Gap, farther north. Weather, terrain, and a determined and fortified enemy had slowed Operation DOGFACE to a crawl. Still, by mid-November, shortly after the 442d had left the area, the 6th Army Group had captured St. Dié and Strasbourg and become the first Allied troops to reach the Rhine.

So Devers was astonished when Eisenhower ordered him to stop preparing to invade Germany and instead to turn north, to protect the right flank of Patton's Third Army as it headed east toward the Saar. Devers vehemently objected that Patch's Seventh Army, not Patton's Third, should spearhead the drive into Germany. He argued forcefully that the Seventh Army could still support Patton by driving east across the Rhine and circling the Saar Basin with a left turn, northeast through Germany. It would be a classic enveloping maneuver, straight out of the field manual—reminiscent of the last stage of Turenne's famous winter campaign of 1674–75, which the famous French leader launched across the Rhine from Strasbourg.[33] It would hit the enemy where he was weakest, instead of striking head-on, as Patton was aiming, against the main line of defense farther north.

"The decision not to cross the Rhine was a blow to both Patch and myself," Devers wrote in his diary, "for we were really poised and keyed up to the effort, and I believe it would have been successful."[34] Devers was so frustrated that he wondered if he was even "a member of the same team" as Eisenhower.[35] But the supreme commander, upset at being second-guessed by his subordinate, whom he had long regarded as a personal rival, prevailed in the end. In December, the French First Army and parts of the Seventh Army were consigned to "mopping up west of the Rhine," so that Devers could "hurriedly throw his strength to the north"[36] in support of Patton's advance. And the precious momentum gained by the 6th Army Group slowly disappeared under the winter snow.

So while Patton's Third Army headed toward a fateful encounter in the Ardennes Forest to the north, Eisenhower wasted the Seventh Army's drive through the Vosges Mountains and lost a chance to end the war sooner, farther south. Devers's 6th Army Group had achieved something no other army in history had: defeating an entrenched opposition in the Vosges Mountains, "without the vaunted air support available to American units elsewhere in the European theater," as the military historian Keith Bonn put it, "and without the benefit of significant numerical superiority in the most difficult terrain on the western front."[37] But the heroic successes and sacrifices of Operation DOGFACE, including those of the 442d, would be relegated to a footnote rather than filling the main chapter in the history of the Allied advance on Germany.

* * *

On December 11, with the Seventh Army "mopping up" the Alsatian plains instead of crossing the Rhine, Marty Higgins was once again cut off behind enemy lines. "This time we really were a lost battalion," Higgins recalls, and this time no one came to his rescue. "It was my worst experience of the war," Higgins says today. "Much worse than when we were cut off before."[38]

Captured by the Germans at Sigolsheim, down the eastern slope of the Vosges, Higgins and his fellow officers were segregated in a small hotel, where they were "well fed and well treated" by the Germans. After dinner, they learned why: they were to be personally questioned by Heinrich Himmler.

As it turned out, Higgins was not so much interrogated as berated by Himmler. "At no time was I asked any questions concerning our mission," Higgins remembers, "nor threatened to reveal any military information." Instead, Himmler was "very belligerent." He castigated Roosevelt as "an evil Jew" and pretended not to understand English, "but I'm sure he knew every word I spoke," Higgins recalls. Finally, Himmler said something in German that his aide translated to Higgins: "You are fortunate that you will survive the war."

Higgins immediately shot back, "I would not have minded dying for my country." But he instantly wished he had held his tongue—that was "not the kind of remark to make to Heinrich Himmler."

Less than a week after Higgins's capture, one of the Roosevelt administration's darkest fears about immigrant groups in America came true. After Pearl Harbor, the War Department had argued that Japanese
Americans could not be trusted to serve in the Pacific theater because it
was difficult, if not impossible, to distinguish friend from foe—the "sheep
from the goats," in the words of Lieutenant General DeWitt.[39] Japanese
Americans should be kept out of the U.S. Army, because Japanese soldiers
could wear American uniforms and pass as Japanese Americans—and who
could tell one Oriental from another?

As 1944 drew to a close, the extent to which looking like the enemy
was a genuine problem became shockingly apparent—though not as anyone had ever imagined, and in the context of an even greater threat than
anyone had ever dreamed. On December 16, specially trained teams of
enemy soldiers—many of whom had been born or raised or educated in
the United States—infiltrated Allied positions. They were physically indistinguishable from American soldiers. They spoke fluent English and
wore American uniforms. Their mission was to create confusion and dis-
order behind the lines, disrupt communications, and seize key targets in
advance of the counteroffensive.

But these enemy soldiers disguised as Americans were not exploiting
the blood ties between Japanese and Americans of Japanese ancestry,
which the Roosevelt administration had so feared. These counterfeit
Americans were actually Germans—members of Operation *Greif* (Grif-
fin), led by the notorious *Waffen SS* Colonel Otto Skorzeny. They were
the spearhead of the final German counteroffensive of the war, code-
named *Wacht am Rhein*—Hitler's last desperate gamble on the western
front, a massive Panzer counterattack through the Ardennes Forest in
Belgium and Luxembourg that soon became known as the Battle of the
Bulge.

Of course "there would have been no Bulge" in the first place, had
Eisenhower not stopped Devers and Patch from crossing the Rhine in
November. "We had an excellent plan, had the equipment ready, knew
what was in front of us on the other side of the Rhine (which was nothing)," Devers continued to insist, "and undoubtedly would have forced the
Germans to use the armies which caused the debacle of the Bulge against
us"[40]—forty thousand casualties and months added to the war.[41]

The clandestine Operation *Greif* was only possible because most

American and British soldiers were physically indistinguishable from their German enemies. But if the difficulty of distinguishing the "sheep from the goats" had truly justified segregating Japanese Americans, then the same logic would have implied that Caucasian Americans were unsuitable as American troops in the European theater. After all, Caucasian Americans, the racial majority in the United States, looked just as much like the German enemy as Japanese Americans looked like the Japanese enemy.

Yet the Allies had not barred German Americans or Americans of Anglo-Saxon descent from service—let alone "relocated" them and their families to camps in the United States or Great Britain. Operation *Greif* should have exposed once and for all the sham of "military necessity," which boiled down to nothing more than the fear of Japanese Americans because they looked like and were related to Japanese and looked different from the white majority. But "military necessity" was never meant to be applied to white Americans, or Anglo-Saxon Americans, or even German Americans, who looked like and were actually related to Germans. It was always, and only, a rationale for discrimination against Japanese Americans.

As the Battle of the Bulge strained the manpower of the Allied Armies, Lt. Gen. Mark Clark's warnings from nearly three years earlier proved alarmingly prescient. On December 15, just one day before the Germans launched Operation *Greif*, General Eisenhower had cabled the War Department about taking steps to "prevent a complete breakdown in the machine due to the concentration of these shortages [of manpower] in the infantry element."[42] After the war, Gen. George C. Marshall, Army chief of staff, admitted that "the narrow margin on which we were compelled to allocate our resources so that Germany might be defeated at the earliest possible moment required superhuman effort by troops and commanders."[43] In fact, the demands of the western front for manpower meant the Pacific would receive no additional troops until victory had been assured in Europe. Yet for more than two and a half years, vast resources had been squandered on transporting, housing, feeding, and guarding 120,000 Japanese Americans in the "assembly" and "relocation" camps instead of properly training and outfitting an equivalent number of soldiers.

Now, with the Germans threatening to burst through Belgium to the English Channel, recently mobilized and poorly prepared Allied troops that had just arrived in Europe were hastily thrown into battle, suffering horrific casualties. The ill-fated 106th Division, for example, which had landed on the continent only ten days before the launch of Operation *Greif*, would lose two thirds of its strength—more than 9,200 KIA, WIA, died of wounds, or POW—during the Battle of the Bulge.[44]

As Clark had warned, the "evacuation" of Japanese Americans from the West Coast exemplified irrational security measures on the home front that almost caused "our entire offensive effort to be sabotaged" abroad. The question had never boiled down to "military necessity" versus civil rights in the abstract. It had always been a question of which policies made *military* sense and which did not—which decisions properly weighed the "advantages and disadvantages" and which did not.[45] And in the Battle of the Bulge, Gen. George C. Marshall nearly lost his famous "ninety-division gamble"—for want of personnel and other resources wasted on ill-conceived missions such as the forced "relocation," which could not be justified by military logic, let alone "military necessity."[46]

The United States has always prided itself as a "nation of immigrants"—an ideal President Roosevelt had underscored in a celebrated speech in which he reminded the conservative Daughters of the American Revolution that "all of us, and you and I especially, are descended from immigrants and revolutionists."[47] But some immigrants were more equal than others, more likely to be regarded by their own president as his fellow Americans.

★ ★ ★

The day after Operation *Greif* began, the War Department announced that Japanese Americans would no longer be "excluded" from the West Coast. For the first time in nearly three years, since Roosevelt had signed Executive Order 9066, Japanese Americans finally had the right to live and work where they chose to, just like other American citizens. But many of the Japanese Americans in the camps no longer had homes or jobs to return to in the former "exclusionary zones" of California, Oregon, Washington, and Arizona. Their rights had been restored, but not the lives they had been forced to abandon after Pearl Harbor.

The unusual timing of the announcement—a Sunday—lent credence to the suspicion that the forthcoming Supreme Court decisions in *Korematsu* and *Endo*, the two cases challenging the legal basis of the "exclusion" of Japanese Americans from the West Coast, had been leaked (perhaps by Justice Felix Frankfurter) to Roosevelt in advance. Thus the administration could announce the closing of the camps without appearing to have had its hand forced by the Supreme Court.[48]

In any event, on the next day, Monday, December 18, the War Relocation Authority announced its schedule for closing the camps where around 120,000 Japanese Americans* had been incarcerated during the past two and a half years. On the same day, the Supreme Court handed down its historic decisions in *Korematsu* and *Endo*.

Fred Korematsu had been convicted of violating Lt. Gen. John L. DeWitt's order "excluding" Japanese Americans from California. In *Korematsu*, the Supreme Court delivered what is generally regarded as one of the worst decisions ever (ranking right below *Dred Scott*, the pre–Civil War decision that denied citizenship to Black Americans, "a subordinate and inferior class of beings . . . emancipated or not").[†] A six-to-three majority gave constitutional blessing to the government's rationale of "military necessity," a power that was as sweeping as it was arbitrary.

---

*The number of people who passed through the camps increased from more than 110,000 to around 120,000 because of births and transfers from other camps under different jurisdictions (such as the Department of Justice) and from other territories (such as Hawaii).

†Bruce Ackerman, Sterling Professor of Law and Political Science, Yale University, recently wrote of the *Korematsu* decision: "It is bad law, very bad law, *very*, *very* bad law. . . . The result is the normalization of emergency conditions—the creation of legal precedents that authorize oppressive measures without any end." (*Yale Law Journal*, 113 (2004), p. 1043.) However, as Eric Muller, professor of law at the University of North Carolina, reminds us, in *Adarand Constructors, Inc. v. Peña*, Certiorari to the United States Court of Appeals for the Tenth Circuit, No. 93–1841, argued January 17, 1995, decided June 12, 1995, eight of the nine Justices of the Supreme Court repudiated the federal government's discrimination against Japanese Americans in *Korematsu*. Writing for the majority, with the concurrence of Chief Justice William Rehnquist and Justices Clarence Thomas, Antonin Scalia, and Anthony Kennedy, Justice Sandra Day O'Connor noted the "illegitimate racial classification" of *Korematsu* and called the decision an "error." Although they dissented from the majority, Justices Stephen Breyer and Ruth Bader Ginsburg nonetheless referred to *Korematsu* as having "yielded a pass for an odious, gravely injurious racial classification" that "will never again survive scrutiny: such a classification, history and precedent instruct, properly ranks as prohibited." Justice John Paul Stevens dissented from the majority because he believed that "an attempt by the majority to exclude members of a minority race from a regulated market is fundamentally

Writing for the majority, Justice Hugo Black declared:

Korematsu was not excluded from the Military Area because of hostility to him or his race. He was excluded because we are at war with the Japanese Empire, because the properly constituted military authorities feared an invasion of our West Coast and felt constrained to take proper security measures, because they decided that the military urgency of the situation demanded that all citizens of Japanese ancestry be segregated from the West Coast temporarily, and finally, because Congress, reposing its confidence in this time of war in our military leaders—as inevitably it must—determined that they should have the power to do just this. There was evidence of disloyalty on the part of some, the military authorities considered that the need for [323 U.S. 214, 224] action was great, and time was short. We cannot—by availing ourselves of the calm perspective of hindsight—now say that at that time these actions were unjustified.[49]

In his dissent, Justice Owen Roberts stated that "the indisputable facts exhibit a clear violation of Constitutional rights." And Justice Robert Jackson gave an impassioned and logical rejoinder to the reasoning of the majority:

Korematsu . . . has been convicted of an act not commonly a crime. It consists merely of being present in the state whereof he is a citizen, near the place where he was born, and where all his life he has lived.

Even more unusual is the series of military orders which made this conduct a crime. They forbid such a one to remain, and they also forbid

---

different from a subsidy that enables a relatively small group of newcomers to enter that market." But even he called *Korematsu* an "invidious" decision that "imposed special burdens . . . on the members of a minority class defined by racial and ethnic characteristics." (See Muller, "Inference or Impact? Racial Profiling and the Internment's True Legacy.")

The qualified dissent of the liberal justices in *Adarand* highlights the ambivalent legacy of *Korematsu*, which established "strict scrutiny" ("rigid scrutiny" was the original wording) and "suspect category" as standards in antidiscrimination suits for the next six decades. Although eight of the nine justices in *Adarand* regarded *Korematsu* as a mistaken application of those standards, apparently none of them wanted to overturn the decision that established them.

him to leave. They were so drawn that the only way Korematsu could avoid violation was to give himself up to the military authority. This meant submission to custody, examination, and transportation out of the territory, to be followed by indeterminate confinement in detention camps.

A citizen's presence in the locality, however, was made a crime only if his parents were of Japanese birth. Had Korematsu been one of four—the others being, say, a German alien enemy, an Italian alien enemy, and a citizen of American-born ancestors, convicted of treason but out on parole—only Korematsu's presence would have violated the order. The difference between their innocence and his crime would result, not from anything he did, said, or thought, different than they, but only in that he was born of different racial stock.

Now, if any fundamental assumption underlies our system, it is that guilt is personal and not inheritable. Even if all of one's antecedents had been convicted of treason, the Constitution forbids its penalties to be visited upon him, for it provides that "no Attainder of Treason shall work Corruption of Blood, or Forfeiture except during the Life of the Person attained." Article 3, 3, cl. 2. But here is an attempt to make an otherwise innocent act a crime merely because this prisoner is the son of parents as to whom he had no choice, and belongs to a race from which there is no way to resign. If Congress in peace-time legislation should [323 U.S. 214, 244] enact such a criminal law, I should suppose this Court would refuse to enforce it.

But the "law" which this prisoner is convicted of disregarding is not found in an act of Congress, but in a military order. Neither the Act of Congress nor the Executive Order of the President, nor both together, would afford a basis for this conviction. It rests on the orders of General DeWitt.

... But a commander in temporarily focusing the life of a community on defense is carrying out a military program; he is not making law in the sense the courts know the term. He issues orders, and they may have a certain authority as military commands, although they may be very bad as constitutional law.

But if we cannot confine military expedients by the Constitution, neither would I distort the Constitution to approve all that the military may deem expedient.

If "military necessity" became enshrined as precedent, Jackson warned, "The principle then lies about like a loaded weapon ready for the hand of any authority that can bring forward a plausible claim of an urgent need." In short, "military necessity" could now be invoked to justify literally anything, as Justice Frank Murphy emphatically noted in his dissent:

> This exclusion of "all persons of Japanese ancestry, both alien and non-alien," from the Pacific Coast area on a plea of military necessity in the absence of martial law ought not to be approved. Such exclusion goes over "the very brink of constitutional power" and falls into the ugly abyss of racism. . . . The main reasons relied upon by those responsible for the forced evacuation, therefore, do not prove a reasonable relation between the group characteristics of Japanese Americans and the dangers of invasion, sabotage, and espionage. The reasons appear, instead, to be largely an accumulation of much of the misinformation, half-truths, and insinuations that for years have been directed against Japanese Americans by people with racial and economic prejudices—the same people who have been among the foremost advocates of the evacuation.

Even at the time, legal analysts branded the *Korematsu* decision "a disaster."[50] More than sixty years later, it remains on the books, "still aimed at the members of any racial or national minority held hostage to the acts of their country of origin," according to the constitutional scholar Peter Irons.

And the accompanying decision in *Endo* merely affirmed legally what had already been taking place politically. Mitsuye Endo was a California state employee who had been suspended from her job and "evacuated" to the Tanforan "assembly center." Her case was a habeas corpus petition that "forced the Supreme Court to confront the internment issue directly."[51]

Even before the Court decisions, more than thirty thousand Japanese Americans had already been granted "leave" from the camps after being "cleared"—to marry, to attend school, to work on farms and in war-related industries, and to volunteer for, and to be drafted into, the Army. In *Endo*, the Court rubber-stamped the "leave clearance" process, concluding that "whatever power the War Relocation Authority may have to detain other classes of citizens, it has no authority to subject citizens who are concededly loyal to its leave procedure."[52] But *Endo* begged the question of whether the government had the right to "evacuate" and "relocate" them in the first place, and then to subject them to its "leave procedure." Even though it formally put an end to the "relocation," *Endo* was merely a fig leaf for *Korematsu*. Left unchallenged was the government's naked power of "military necessity."

★ ★ ★

Yet despite the attention paid to the Supreme Court decisions at the time and increasingly during the following decades, it was not lawsuits that won the freedom of the Japanese Americans on the mainland. (*Korematsu* ended in defeat; *Endo* was at best a stalemate.) Nor was it public protest, the effectiveness of which is easy to overestimate from the perspective of the civil rights movement two decades later. The demonstrations at Tule Lake, Heart Mountain, and elsewhere had done little besides provoke nativist fears and lend spurious justification for the mass incarceration of Japanese Americans.

The real key to unlocking the gates of the camps was political and military, not constitutional. More than a month before the Court handed down its decisions in *Korematsu* and *Endo*, Franklin D. Roosevelt had won an unprecedented fourth term as president of the United States. Election Day was November 7, 1944, the same day *The New York Times* ran the wire story on the rescue of the Lost Battalion, and the same day Joe Nishimoto single-handedly broke the three-day stalemate on the hill overlooking La Houssière. Three days later, on November 10, with key congressional seats in California safely in the hands of the Democrats, Roosevelt finally met with Secretary of the Interior Harold Ickes, Attorney General Frances Biddle, and Secretary of War Henry Stimson to discuss the fate of the Japanese Americans.

For months the president had ignored Ickes, who had favored closing the camps from the moment the Interior Department took charge of them earlier that year. Now, at the first cabinet meeting following the elections, Roosevelt was finally prepared to address the recommendation that Major General Bonesteel of the Western Defense Command had made three months earlier, in August, to Stimson and Chief of Staff George C. Marshall—that Americans of Japanese ancestry on the mainland be released "from internment."*

---

*The word "internment" is Stimson's, in his memo of November 10, 1944.

After more than two and a half years, "we all agreed that it was time to let them loose," Stimson noted after the meeting—in candid language that was meant not for the public but only for officials within the administration. Although the *Korematsu* and *Endo* cases were still pending, Stimson did not mention constitutional concerns.

The first consideration he cited was military: "The war necessity no longer exists for keeping them interned." As swiftly and arbitrarily as it had been invoked, "military necessity" was now being revoked—even though the Supreme Court had not yet spoken on the matter.[53]

On the most cynical reading, this was the president's bow to military and political reality. Assured of an unprecedented fourth term, Roosevelt now had little to worry about from a nativist backlash against Democrats on the West Coast. The tide had long since turned in the Pacific, and any fear of a Japanese invasion, which had not even been a remote possibility since the Battle of Midway in 1942, two and a half years earlier, could be completely discounted. Almost exactly at the same time the 442d was entering the Vosges, Gen. Douglas MacArthur had returned, as he had promised, to the Philippines.

Around the same time, Eisenhower had bet Montgomery five pounds that the war in Europe would be over before Christmas. (Neither of them had anticipated the Battle of the Bulge.) And the 6th Army Group, following the rescue of the Lost Battalion, was only miles away from the German border.

From a more generous perspective, Roosevelt's decision was an overdue though still unspoken acknowledgment of the injustice that he, more than anyone else, had personally brought about by signing Executive Order 9066.

The "second point" Stimson cited in favor of closing the "relocation camps" belatedly but explicitly recognized an achievement that undermined the whole illogic of "military necessity" and Lt. Gen. DeWitt's repugnant notion that "a Jap's a Jap."* Stimson simply acknowledged the Japanese Americans' "good record as soldiers."[54]

---

*Recently some defenders of the "exclusion" and "evacuation" have tried to acquit DeWitt of the charge of racism. For example, Keith Robar notes that the general's notorious statement in a phone conversation with McCloy—"Out here [California], Mr. Secretary, a Jap is a Jap to these people now"—indicates that DeWitt was

So in the end, it was the Japanese Americans in uniform whose heroism had shamed their own government into doing the right thing. After fighting their way up the slopes of the Vosges, the 100th/442d had unarguably occupied the moral high ground. It was the liberators of Bruyères, Belmont, and Biffontaine who finally opened the gates of Manzanar and Poston. It was not demonstrations in the camps (which had only strengthened the government's case that Japanese Americans were disloyal) or arguments in the courts (which had not only failed to overturn the notion of "military necessity" but had actually enshrined it as precedent), but bullets on the battleground that won the fight for civil rights. As it was for the "colored troops" Frederick Douglass recruited for the Union Army during the Civil War, the "true course" to Japanese Americans' "freedom and citizenship was over the battlefield." The rescuers of the Lost Battalion were the saviors of Rohwer.[55]

Despite Eisenhower's decisions in November, which squandered the successes in the Vosges, the casualties on "Suicide Hill" had helped put an end to the sacrifices on Heart Mountain. The victory on the home front had been won in combat abroad.

---

actually describing the attitude of "these people" in California, not his own beliefs. (Robar, *Intelligence, Internment, and Relocation*, p. 63.) But later in the same conversation, DeWitt said to McCloy, ". . . if they are allowed to remain where they are, we are just going to have one complication after another, because you just can't tell one Jap from another. They all look the same." This clearly shows DeWitt was expressing his own opinion, not attributing it to other people. And then he told McCloy, "Give a sentry or an officer or troops any job like that, a Jap's a Jap, and you can't blame the man for stopping all of them." This just as clearly shows that DeWitt was agreeing with—not merely describing—the attitude of "a sentry or an officer or troops" whom "you can't blame" for thinking "a Jap's a Jap." (McCloy, phone conversation with DeWitt, February 3, 1942, Archives II, RG 107.)

Chinese Americans on the West Coast were worried about being mistaken for Japanese Americans—to the point where they were wearing buttons identifying themselves as Chinese Americans. But apparently the fact that "a Jap's a Jap" and "they all look the same" meant that even "a sentry" could distinguish one group from the other. Otherwise, even after the Japanese were "relocated," "one complication after another" would have continued, because all those Chinese Americans would still have been living on the West Coast.

VETERANS

10

HOMECOMING

"Americans First Class"

One of the first shocks I got when I went to live in California after being discharged was the attitude among many residents toward the Japanese Americans on the West Coast. . . . The Nisei came home loaded with medals and covered with scars and minus limbs and eyes, and they found themselves getting kicked out of Arizona barbershops and San Francisco restaurants just as if they had never left home. —BILL MAULDIN[1]

Italy, Germany, and the United States, 1945–1948

Throughout 1944, long before the decision to close the camps, public speculation had been building about the return of Japanese Americans to the West Coast. The *Korematsu* and *Endo* cases had been slowly wending their way through the courts, and it was clear that some change in government policy was in the works.

By September, Maj. Gen. E. H. Bonesteel, head of the Western Defense Command, had noted that requests from individuals in "relocation centers" for leave clearance to travel, work, and reside in prohibited areas of the West Coast had been "rapidly increasing" since the beginning of summer. "We are soon going to be 'snowed under,'" he said, "with requests for exemption." He added:

A considerable portion of the requests are coming from United States citizens of Japanese ancestry who have either been inducted into the reserve army or have been given notice that they are eligible for military service and subject to induction at any time.[2]

It seemed reasonable that Japanese Americans in the military would have the same right to travel anywhere any other servicemen could. But anticipating the influx of Japanese Americans in general, many local governments and civic organizations in the region expressed fear of racial conflict and even publicly warned of riots. And in late 1944, some of them decided to take preemptive action.

In November, while the 442d was still in the Vosges, the American Legion post in Hood River, Oregon, erased the names of sixteen Japanese American soldiers from a memorial honoring servicemen from the area.[3] Hood River—which the federal government called "a hotbed of anti-Japanese sentiment"[4]—was the birthplace of Minoru Yasui, whose defiance of the curfew imposed on Japanese Americans in early 1942 had been the first constitutional challenge to what turned into the "exclusion" and "evacuation."

The official reaction to the Legion's action was swift. At a press conference, Secretary of War Henry L. Stimson denounced the actions of the Hood River post as "unworthy discrimination" that was "wholly inconsistent with American ideals of democracy," and praised the heroism of Japanese American soldiers.[5]

Even other Legion posts condemned their comrades in Hood River. The members of Post 591 in Hollywood called the removal of the soldiers' names "a shameful act which discredits and humiliates the name of the American Legion."[6] It was also "particularly ill-timed," as the WRA noted:

> It came at a time when there was a growing knowledge in this country of the fighting record made by Nisei troops in Italy. Stories of their exploits had been recorded in War Department dispatches and published in newspapers everywhere. Because of the dramatic injustice and flagrant racial basis of the local Legion action, it was possible to stimulate the interest of the press in general. For three months, columnists, editorial writers, and radio speakers across the country condemned the Hood River Legion post.[7]

But the Hood River post initially refused to back down. In fact, the local Legionnaires were merely spearheading an all-out campaign by significant elements of the larger community. Before the war, the small minority of Japanese American farmers in Hood River County had been producing "90 percent of the county's asparagus, 80 percent of the strawberries, 35 percent of the pears, and 30 percent of the apples."[8] Now, faced with the return of what the government described as a "competitive threat,"[9] local residents announced that Japanese Americans would be kept from purchasing agricultural equipment and supplies. Others plotted to buy up farmland and refuse to sell or lease it to Japanese Americans, civilian or military. Full-page newspaper ads signed by local citizens helped to reignite the black embers of prejudice, which had only been smoldering while Japanese Americans were absent from the area, locked up in the camps.[10]

It would not be until early 1945, after the camps were officially closed, that the Legionnaires in Hood River finally bowed to pressure and restored the names of Japanese American soldiers to the post's honor roll. But this was just the first skirmish in what would develop into open hostilities. As the conflict in Europe drew to an end, the war at home was just beginning.

★ ★ ★

Through early 1945, the 442d had been enjoying their "champagne campaign" of light action in patrols along the border of France and Italy in the Maritime Alps. After fifty-three days in the hospital, Barney Hajiro had recovered from his wounds enough to rejoin his comrades, but was given light duty in the kitchen. "In M Company I was rubbish," he remembers even today. "In I Company they treat me like a VIP." He still thought of himself as a bit of a "goof-off," and was amazed at the hero's welcome he received.

But Shiro "Kash" Kashino, who had been wounded three times in the Vosges, had fared less well than Hajiro, his I Company mate. In southern France Kashino was busted from staff sergeant to private after being arrested for taking part in a bar brawl, although he argued he had been trying to act as a peacemaker. He could not shake the suspicion that he had actually been punished for telling off his commander after the shelling of the supply detail he had led during the rescue of the Lost Battalion. But when the "champagne campaign" drew to an end, Kashino was released from the stockade and returned to active duty. The 442d was on its way back to the front line in Italy, and a bar fight would not keep soldiers off the front line. Kashino's only thought was "Oh, God, I don't want to miss the battle."* As much as any other soldier in the 442d, Kashino had proved his worth where it counted—in combat. "The 100th had Kim," Barney Hajiro says simply, "the 442nd had Kashino."[11]

Attached in April 1945 to the 92d Division, the 442d found itself in familiar company and on familiar ground. The 92d was made up of Negro (as they were called then) troops, who had indirectly continued the lineage of the "colored troops" in the Union Army and the "buffalo soldiers" in the post–Civil War West.[12] Poised to attack the fortified German defenses known as the Gothic Line, the 92d was part of the Fifth Army, now led by Lucian Truscott Jr., former head of VI Corps in the Vosges. After earning a promotion to lieutenant general, Truscott had taken over command of the Fifth Army from Gen. Mark Clark, the enthusiastic sponsor of the 100th and the 442d during their first tour of duty in Italy. Now Clark was once again Truscott's superior, but this time as commander of the 15th Army Group in the Mediterranean.

It had been upon Clark's "personal appeal" to Eisenhower that the 442d was reassigned to Italy.[13] On April 3, Clark welcomed the troops when they arrived, telling them "how proud he was to have this fine regiment and old friends back again with the Fifth Army and 15th Army Group."[14] He inspected the bivouacs and messes and spoke to officers and enlisted men. When he asked a group of 442d infantrymen whether they liked Italy better than France, "most of the men gave Gen. Clark a hearty 'no.'"[15] After four months of light duty on the Riviera, they were now back in a shooting war.

By this time, the reputation of the 442d had spread far and wide among both friends and foes. General George C. Marshall, chief of staff, declared, "The Japanese regiment was spectacular." A German commander in Italy (interrogated after the war) said the 442d was "an excellent unit, absolutely trained for mountain warfare" (which would have been news to the 442nd, since their "training" took place in combat).

---

*See S. L. A. Marshall, *Men Against Fire*, p. 60: "Some of the most gallant single-handed fighters I encountered in World War II had spent most of their time in the guardhouse."

They were "feared by the Germans, since it was rumored by the Germans that they were not in the habit of taking prisoners."*

The 442d returned to almost the same spot it had left six months earlier. During the winter, Allied progress in Italy had slowed to a crawl. Just as Churchill had predicted and Clark had feared, the loss of three key divisions—the 3d, 36th, and 45th—had weakened the American drive up the west coast of the Italian peninsula. Though they were north of Rome, Allied troops were still short of the industrial regions of Italy near the Swiss border, and even farther from the Balkans, Churchill's and Clark's favored target all along.

And in February, the Allied Combined Chiefs of Staff had further depleted the campaign by transferring five divisions from the British Eighth Army in Italy to Montgomery's 21st Army Group in Western Europe. Faced with the "appalling undertaking" of advancing up "steep mountain slopes" that were "sheathed in ice," which "would have handicapped the movement of infantry enormously, and made the movement of supporting weapons all but impossible," Clark's 15th Army Group had been put on hold for the rest of the winter. "It was a sad blow to our hopes," Truscott wrote. The American role was reduced to preventing a German advance south until a concerted Allied offensive could be mounted in the spring of 1945, when weather and terrain permitted "an attack through the most heavily defended portion of the German lines."[16]

---

*General Marshall was another commander who called Japanese Americans "Japanese" or "Japs." He unflatteringly compared the 92d to the 442d in a bet he made with Lt. Gen. Clark almost two months before the 442d returned to combat in Italy:

> At this time I made a dicker—a wager with Clark: that he could take those three regiments of the 92d Division and form one regiment out of them, take the one regiment made up of AAA [anti-aircraft artillery] troops who had already been converted to infantry and I would bring back the Japanese regiment, the 442d from Southern France. He was to put the Negroes in front and the Japs in reserve behind them. The Germans would think the Negro regiment was a weak spot, and then would hit the Japs.

Though apparently made in jest, this wager describes fairly well what actually turned out to be the organization and tactics of the spring offensive. Marshall's quote is from his interview with Dr. Sidney T. Matthews, Dr. Howard M. Smyth, Maj. Roy Lemson, and Maj. David Hamilton. The quotes from *Generalleutnant* Otto Fretter-Pico, commander of the 148th Grenadier Division, are in Ulysses Lee, *The Employment of Negro Troops*, p. 572, where Marshall's quote can also be found.

A limited assault by the 92d Division in February had failed to breach German defenses southeast of Genoa in the Apennine Mountains, overlooking the Ligurian Sea. It was here that Truscott and Clark positioned the 442d at the start of the spring offensive. In the cover of night on April 4–5, the 3d Battalion made a daring climb up the sheer ridge between Mount Folgorito and Mount Carchio and circled behind the German line. At 0500 the battalion attacked from the rear, while the 100th Battalion struck from the front.

"We got on top of the ledge way up there and we caught them napping," recalls Shig Doi, who had dodged sniper fire in the rescue of the Lost Battalion. "And it's a good thing because they would have mowed us down like nothing . . . the hill that we went up, a machine gun had the whole side covered." By the next day the two battalions had made contact on Mount Cerreta. The ridge line was so steep that Doi remembers the wounded couldn't be safely evacuated in the dark and had to wait until the next day.[17]

Meanwhile, the 2d Battalion, which had followed in the steps of the 3d on the following night, turned north and attacked Mount Belvedere. Within two days, the 442d had captured "a position which had resisted the 92d Division for six months."[18] As the Fifth Army burst through the Gothic Line, the 442d and the 473d, an antiaircraft regiment that had recently been converted to infantry, sparked the advance of the 92d Division, which went on to capture La Spezia and Genoa. Though the whole effort by the division was only a diversionary attack, with the main Allied thrust occurring inland, Truscott called the coastal offensive "wholly successful" and praised the "courage, endurance, and heroism" of the 442d and 473d.[19]

By this point in the war, the Germans were putting up much more of a fight in Italy than they were in their own homeland. Soviet troops were rushing toward Berlin from the east, and American troops had crossed the Rhine and were racing across Germany from the west. But in the Po River Valley, north of the Gothic Line, the Germans were still fiercely resisting the Allied advance.

On April 12, 1945, President Franklin D. Roosevelt died in Washington, D.C. When news of his death reached the 442d, 2d Lt. Daniel K. Inouye recalled thinking, "Every *Nisei* who had been invested with first-class citizenship by virtue of the uniform he wore" knew that Roosevelt "had given us our chance and we had a lot of *aloha* for that man."[20] Inouye, of course, was a Buddhahead. *Kotonks* remembered Roosevelt as the author of Executive Order 9066.

By April 21, "the beginning of the end was in sight," as Clark put it.[21] Inouye and his platoon of E Company were assigned to attack Colle Musatello, a "high and heavily defended ridge."[22] Jumping off at first light, Inouye and his men overcame German opposition so easily that they outran the rest of the attacking troops. As a result, they were "right under the German guns, 40 yards from their bunkers and rocky defense positions." They were so close, Inouye "had to call off our artillery," for fear of casualties from friendly fire.

The platoon now "had a choice of either moving up or getting the hell out of there." As soon as Inouye decided to advance, "three machine guns opened up on us," and he got up to throw a grenade. Then, as he recalled in his autobiography:

> Somebody punched me in the side, although there wasn't a soul near me, and I sort of fell backward. Then I counted off three seconds as I ran toward that angry splutter of flame at the mouth of the nearest machine gun.

Though Inouye didn't realize it, he had been shot in the stomach. But he kept climbing the hill. The grenade he threw three seconds after pulling the pin blew up the enemy machine-gun nest, and when the crew staggered out, Inouye shot them with his machine gun. He kept staggering up the hill, lobbing two more grenades into a second nest.

Then his legs failed him. "Somehow they wouldn't lock," he wrote later. "I couldn't stand and I had to pull myself forward with one hand." He remembered hearing someone yell, "Come on, you guys, go for broke!" as they headed toward yet another machine-gun nest.

Inouye kept hauling himself up the slope. When he was close enough to the Germans, he pulled the pin on his last grenade. Just as he was about to lob it, an enemy soldier stood up in the bunker ahead of him, aimed at Inouye from only a few yards away, and fired a rifle grenade that exploded into Inouye's right elbow, turning his arm into "a few bloody shreds of tissue." Inouye's own grenade, set to detonate in seconds, was "still clenched in a fist that suddenly didn't belong to me any more."

Inouye "swung around to pry the grenade out of that dead fist" with his other hand. He hurled it into the third machine-gun nest and lurched to his feet, firing his machine gun with his left hand, his "useless right arm slapping red and wet" against his side.

While his men ran past him and overwhelmed the bunker, "some last German, in his terminal instant of life, squeezed off a final burst from the machine gun" and hit Inouye's right leg, finally knocking him out of combat.[23]

The end of hostilities in Italy was less than two weeks away. Germany would formally surrender on May 7, 1945.

★ ★ ★

After the 442d Infantry had returned to the Mediterranean, one element of the original combat team had remained behind in the European theater. The 522d Field Artillery Battalion was assigned to the 45th Division, Bill Mauldin's old unit, which had fought next to the 442d as part of VI Corps in the Vosges. "When we separated from the 442d to go into Germany, we of the 522d felt like orphans," says Pfc. Manabi Hirasaki, who had always thought a segregated unit "would feel more like home."[24]

By March, Eisenhower had amassed all three of his army groups in Europe—Montgomery's 21st to the north, Bradley's 12th in the center, and Devers's 6th to the south—for a final assault on Germany across the Rhine. Though Devers had reached the Rhine three months earlier, strategic miscalculations, intelligence errors, indecision, excessive caution, supply-chain delays, and the onset of winter had stalled the Allied advance, leaving it vulnerable to the German counteroffensive in the Battle of the Bulge and to the *Nordwind* attack on Alsace. It was not until March 7 that the First Army captured the first Rhine bridgehead at Remagen, and not until March 19 that Eisenhower shifted the strategic focus from Montgomery's sector to Bradley's, finally unleashing Patton's Third Army for what would be, on March 23, the first modern assault crossing of the Rhine.

In early April, while the 442d Infantry was storming the Gothic Line in Italy, the last major pocket of German resistance was sealed off in the Ruhr Valley, and "the campaign to finish Germany was transitioning into a general pursuit."[25] The Germans' resistance was much weaker in their homeland than in Italy. By mid-April, the Ninth Army, part of Bradley's group, had pushed three hundred miles from the Rhine and was only fifty miles from Berlin.

In the south, the divisions in Devers's 6th Army Group were heading toward southeastern Germany and western Austria, where Allied intelligence believed—incorrectly, as it turned out—Hitler would make his last desperate stand in the "National Redoubt," a natural fortress in the Alps.

Sweeping across Germany, Major General Dahlquist's 36th Division captured *Generalfeldmarschall* Gerd von Rundstedt, Admiral Miklós Horthy (the regent of Hungary), and Leni Riefenstahl. But after capturing *Reichsmarschall* Hermann Göring—whose hand he shook, and whom he treated to a cordial interview, followed by lunch—Dahlquist was savaged in newspaper editorials and cartoons (showing a bloody handshake), and Eisenhower took the extraordinary measure of formally reprimanding him.

As the rapidly advancing American troops neared Munich at the end of April, the 522d Field Artillery Battalion made a gruesome discovery. Alongside a road, Sus Ito, Yuk Minaga, and George Oiye—the three *kotonks* who had all been decorated for their heroism in the rescue of the Lost Battalion—and T/4 Tahae Sugita stumbled onto what looked like "many lumps in the snow." These turned out to be "emaciated bodies of human beings that were starved, frozen, beaten, exhausted." Some of them were wearing striped uniforms. Others were naked. Many were "just skeletons."[26]

The 522d had entered one of the dozens of satellite camps surrounding Dachau, the oldest concentration camp in Germany. It had originally been established to detain Communists, Socialists, Social Democrats, and other political prisoners, as well as Roma (Gypsies), religious groups such as Jehovah's Witnesses, and violators of the 1935 Nuremberg Laws governing "racial purity." By the late 1930s, Dachau had become a slave-labor camp, and the number of Jewish prisoners had increased significantly. It had also become the site of horrific medical experiments, a training camp for the SS, and "the model for all Nazi concentration camps."[27]

In April, there were more than sixty thousand prisoners in Dachau, a third of them Jews. On the twenty-sixth, just before Allied troops arrived, the Germans forced more than seven thousand prisoners, most of them Jews, out of Dachau on a death march to the south.

A young woman named Yanina Cywinska recalled being herded out of the camp and "standing with a blindfold on, waiting to be shot, but the shot didn't come."

> So I asked the woman next to me, "Do you think they're trying to make us crazy, so we'll run and they won't have to feel guilty about shooting us?" She said, "Well, we're not going to run. We'll just stand here." So we stood and stood, and suddenly someone was tugging at my blindfold. . . . I saw him, and I thought, "Oh, now the Japanese are going to kill us."[28]

It was, of course, an American soldier, a member of the 522d, who eventually managed to convince Cywinska that she was free.

"We weren't supposed to give the Jewish survivors any food because they were weak and their stomachs could not handle anything solid," remembers Hirasaki. "One day, after cleaning our mess kits, I noticed some Jews were picking leftover food out of the soapy dishwater we had thrown out. They were that hungry." Hirasaki, who had grown up in the small town of Gilroy, California, "didn't even know what a Jew was" before the 522d entered Dachau.

Another survivor, Josef Erbs, was "eighteen years old, seventy-six pounds at the time, barely alive." He had been "on the ground" and "couldn't walk"—one of those lumps in the snow that Ito and his comrades had seen. The next thing Erbs remembered was "a big Oriental man" who had picked him up and saved his life. "Never before had I seen an Asian man," he recalled. On the shoulder of his rescuer was "an emblem—blue, with a white hand and white torch."[29]

It was the regimental patch of the 442d.

★ ★ ★

On May 8, officially declared V-E ("Victory in Europe") Day, bullets were fired into the house of a Japanese American named S. G. Sakamoto in Fresno, California. He had lived there for more than fifty years and had only recently returned with his family from the Poston Relocation Center. "A sincere effort had been made to identify the perpetrators of the shooting," according to an Army intelligence report, but "no hope is held for solving it."[30]

★ ★ ★

"A lot of people don't realize we could have failed," Shiro "Kash" Kashino reflected after the war. "If we weren't at the right place at the right time, I think we would have never made a name for ourselves." Guarding German POWs in Italy, Kashino—still a private, never having regained his rank as staff sergeant after being court-martialed for that bar brawl in southern France—had a disconcerting sense of déjà vu as he looked at the barbed wire, armed guard towers, and rows of huts. "This was exactly what they had built for us in Idaho," he said.[31] The layout of the POW compound was almost identical to that of the Minidoka Relocation Center, where Kashino had volunteered for the 442d two long years before.

★ ★ ★

Even before the end of the war, some members of the 442d were finding their way home. But the price they had paid for leaving combat early was measured in blood.

Barney Hajiro, who had led I Company's "*banzai*" charge up "Suicide Hill," could not return to his old job as a stevedore when he finally made it back to Hawaii. His wounds left him unable to perform manual labor. Although he landed a position as a supervisor on a plantation, a lengthy labor strike put an end to his "easy job." He eventually found work as a security guard.[32]

George "Machine Gun Joe" Sakato, who had led the 2d Battalion's assault on Hill 617, spent several months in hospitals and rehabilitation clinics in Birmingham, England; Vancouver, Washington; and San Diego. Following his discharge, he attended a trade school for automotive and diesel engineering and drove a truck at night to supplement his disability pension from the Army. After marrying Bess Saito, he worked for a while near Phoenix, converting marine diesel engines into water pumps for farmers. But he lost his job when more convenient electrical pumps took over the market. He and Bess moved to Denver, where he tried to find work with trucking companies and the railroad, but all the jobs were unionized, and he found he was not welcome. Eventually Sakato passed a civil service examination and got a job with the Post Office. He and Bess grew strawberries on a small plot to raise the money for a down payment on their first house. He would come home at night and pack strawberries and then get up early the next morning to sell them at the market before he went to his job as a mail carrier.[33]

Daniel Inouye spent the next two years in hospitals, recovering from his wounds, undergoing multiple operations, and struggling through painful physical rehabilitation. He had received seventeen transfusions of blood from the Negro troops of the 92d Regiment. Inouye's company commander had promoted him to first lieutenant on the day he was wounded and also recommended him for a Congressional Medal of Honor. He received the Distinguished Service Cross instead, just as Hajiro and Sakato had.[34]

In July 1945, when Inouye was finally able to make a long-distance phone call to Hawaii, his father could not talk to him. Although Germany had surrendered, the war against Japan was still going on, and resident aliens in the islands—even if, like Inouye's father, they had lived there for decades—were not permitted to make or receive long-distance calls.

In one rehabilitation center, Inouye got to know the only other Japanese American there—Capt. Sakae Takahashi, former commander of B Company and Young Oak Kim's friend from the 100th Battalion, who, like Kim, had been wounded at Biffontaine. Inouye and Takahashi were together "until the small hours of the morning talking of home and of our hopes for Hawaii and ourselves." What the two men came to believe was that "the time had come for us to step forward":

> We had fought for that right with all the furious patriotism in our bod-
> ies and now we didn't want to go back to the plantation. Times were
> changing. The old patterns were breaking down. We wanted to take our
> full place in society, to make the greatest contribution of which we were
> capable. . . . [35]

This was just the latest installment of the long-running "bull session" that had begun around the campfires and in the barracks at Camp Shelby in 1943, when Kim had joined the 100th Battalion (Separate). But now it included the larger 442d as well. Though Inouye and Takahashi had only hopes, not even plans, at this stage, their conversations would bear fruit in postwar Hawaii sooner than they, or anyone else, could have imagined. Japanese Americans, a little less than forty percent of the population of the islands, had made up sixty percent of Hawaii's fighting forces—and eighty percent of the casualties.[36] Their sacrifices would give them a moral authority and political credibility that they would not squander.

Finally discharged in May 1947, Inouye traveled back to Hawaii via San Francisco. It was there that he stopped at the barbershop where he was told, "You're a Jap, and we don't cut Jap hair."[37]

★ ★ ★

An Army intelligence report written at the end of 1944 had grimly predicted the response of people in many areas of California who "do not desire the return of Japanese to their community":

> There are still nearly 100 Salinas boys in Japanese prison camps, and the Salinas Valley mothers of those sons are somewhat bitter against the order permitting the Japanese to return and have stated that the Japanese know what happened on Bataan and won't want to face us any more than we will be able to stand meeting them. The commander of the Salinas Post 31, American Legion, has stated, "We don't want Japanese here and we said so bluntly in a recent resolution. There appears nothing we can do about it however." . . . The settlement of Oliverhurst, south of Marysville, has a population composed of many former Oklahoma people who have many sons in the Pacific area, and these persons may feel a particular resentment against the Japanese. . . . From the information available to this office as outlined above, it appears that the majority opinion in all of the area covered by the Central Security District was decidedly against the return of Japanese to this area and that such opinion has not changed radically since the announcement by the War Department of the possible return of certain Japanese.[38]

"When my parents returned" to Venice, "no neighbors came to greet them," remembers Sgt. Jack Wakamatsu, of F Company, who had been temporarily disabled by trench foot after the Battle of Bruyères. "It was fortunate we returned to California when we did, because my father's land was already up for delinquent-tax sale. Our friends, who were supposed to manage our land, did not pay taxes as part of the agreement." Although the family was able to save the land and their home, Wakamatsu "wondered, again, who my real enemies were."[39]

Within the first five months after the announcement that the "relocation centers" would be closed, incidents of violence against returning Japanese Americans "had reached such proportions that Secretary Ickes issued a public statement denouncing the perpetrators and demanding more effective protection for the returning evacuees," according to the WRA. On May 4, 1945, Ickes "indicated that 24 incidents of violence or open intimidation had been recorded—15 shooting attacks, one attempted dynamiting, three arson cases, and five threatening visits." He emphatically denounced what he called "terrorism":

> In the absence of vigorous local law enforcement, a pattern of planned terrorism by hoodlums has developed. It is a matter of national concern because this lawless minority, whose actions are condemned by the decent citizens who make up an overwhelming majority of West Coast residents, seems determined to employ its Nazi storm trooper tactics against loyal Japanese Americans and law-abiding Japanese aliens in spite of the state laws and constitutional safeguards designed to protect the lives and property of all of the people of this country. . . . [Japanese Americans] are far more in the American tradition than the race-baiters fighting a private war safely at home.[40]

After his discharge, Shig Doi, of I Company, whose helmet Dahlquist had rapped during the rescue of the Lost Battalion, returned to his home in Placer County, California, which he regarded as "a hotbed of prejudice and discrimination."[41] While Doi was still overseas, his family had returned from the Amache Relocation Center to their farm, where some local citizens had planned a welcome home party. The Western Defense Command of the Army covered the incident in a periodic report:

> Sheriff Charles Silva of Placer County reported an attempt by night riders to blow up with dynamite the packing shed on the farm of Summio Doi, Japanese American who recently returned to his place near Newcastle from Lamar, Colorado. Doi called the sheriff to report that several carloads of persons were on his property and shots were being fired at the house to force him and his family to remain indoors. The cars sped away as a patrol car arrived. Deputies found nine sticks of dynamite and a litter of burned matches in the shed. Doi said that the shed had been soaked with gasoline and set afire the night before, but that he and his father had put out the flames. The Sheriff and District Attorney

announced that all Japanese-owned property would be patrolled in the future. The State Attorney General's office is investigating.[42]

When Shig Doi got home, his mother showed him the holes from the shotgun pellets.

I was getting shot at from the enemy, and then at home in my own country, people were shooting at my dad. I was risking my life for this country, and my government was not protecting my folks. And they came home from camp with nothing.[43]

A white soldier who was absent without leave from Camp Knight, Oakland, later confessed to the crime and implicated two civilians.[44] Meanwhile, Doi found work as a medical technician for Contra Costa County. One day he bumped into a veteran he thought he recognized.

I was looking at his head, and he had a scar right up here. "Jesus," I said, "Goddammit, I know where you got hit. You got hit in that *banzai* hill going after that Lost Battalion. He said, "How'd you know?" I said, "You went after that guy with a Tommy gun and the other guy was already shot and you got shot by the sniper. I went after you, and I don't know why to this day that sniper didn't shoot me."[45]

It was Mickey Akiyama, who had led his depleted I Company platoon up "Suicide Hill" until a sniper's bullet blew off his helmet and creased his skull. Akiyama had returned to a home he had never set foot in before. His wife, Mary, and his baby daughter were waiting for him. Mariko Ann, who had been born in Manzanar shortly before Akiyama volunteered for the 442d, and whose picture he had kept inside his helmet, didn't recognize her father. The wound in Akiyama's head would cause headaches, dizziness, nausea, and other symptoms for decades to come.[46]

In the postwar peace, wounded Japanese American veterans were a living reproach to those who had doubted their loyalty and favored their "exclusion" and "evacuation" after Pearl Harbor. One Californian who could barely contain his resentment told the WRA, "The worst mistake the government made was to let them into the Army. They come back with an arm gone, or a leg gone, and you have to show them consideration."[47]

Wilson Makabe, another I Company veteran and Placer County resident, called his brother when he returned stateside. His brother told him
the family house in Loomis, California, had been set on fire within hours
after the closing of the camps was announced on the radio.

When he told me that . . . oh, you can't describe the feeling. I remember
the pain and the hurt, the suffering in the hospitals in Italy—that was
nothing compared to this. I cried for the first time. All the time in the
hospital I don't remember shedding a tear, but I cried that night. You
wonder if it was worth going through all that.

Makabe had spent two and a half years in hospitals, much of the time
in a full body cast, after being wounded in Italy. He had lost a leg to gangrene. His other leg was in a long brace. He could walk only with agoniz-
ing difficulty, but he had made up his mind he wasn't going to spend his
life in a wheelchair. When he got back to Loomis, he drove to a local gas
station.

I knew the family. The fellow's father was one of the old settlers in
Loomis and knew my father well. When he saw me at the service station
getting out, struggling to get out of the car, to fill it with gas, he came
out. After I was all through he said, "I'd like to talk to you." I said, "Hop
in." He traveled with me down the road from the station. He said,
"Y'know, I was one bastard. I had signs on my service station saying 'No
Jap trade wanted.'" He said, "Now when I see you come back like that,
I feel so small." And he was crying.[48]

* * *

But the government of the United States and people on the East Coast
were more hospitable than the state of California and people on the West
Coast were to the homecoming 442d.

"The postwar reaction of Congress and the public generally, suddenly
so favorable to the Japanese in the United States, was caused chiefly by the
gallant manner in which they fought in our armies, in substantial numbers," Francis Biddle—Roosevelt's attorney general, who had argued in
vain against the "evacuation" and "relocation"—wrote years later.

But it came also, I suspect, from a feeling of guilt for the way we had treated them, and a desire to make up for it. The Army, who had been keen to evacuate, was particularly laudatory of the behavior of Japanese soldiers. If not much lasting harm was done to the relation of the Japanese to other persons in their communities it was because of the courage and decency of a majority of the Japanese, and in spite of the attitude of those who favored their internment.*

On July 2, 1946, more than a year after the end of the war in Europe, "Bones" Fujimoto, who had been drafted from Rohwer after finishing high school, returned with the rest of the 442d to a hero's welcome in New York City. "Carrying battle honors unsurpassed by any unit of comparable size, the much-decorated combat team arrived off the narrows at 3 P.M. on the transport *Wilson Victory*," according to *The New York Times*, which belatedly gave the 442d the recognition in its pages that had been missing after the rescue of the Lost Battalion. "They were escorted up the Hudson River to Pier 84 by an Army tug carrying a band and a welcoming group of Japanese Americans." When they arrived at the pier, "the men were delighted when four young women in Hawaiian costumes danced the 'hula hula' and attempted to toss paper leis to the returning veterans."[49]

The 442d's landing on American soil was filmed for newsreels shown in movie theaters across the country. The press asked for six soldiers to pose disembarking from the ship. After all the time they had spent in the Army, the dogfaces knew better than to volunteer. So three Buddhaheads and three *kotonks* were "volunteered." One of them was Fujimoto.

Later, a friend's sister recognized him on the big screen at a theater in Los Angeles. By that time, Fujimoto's family had returned from Rohwer to their farm in Bell, California. Most of the items of value they had left with friends for safekeeping had been sold. Their friends "didn't think the

---

*Francis Biddle, *In Brief Authority*, pp. 224–25. As late as 1962, when this book was published, Biddle was still referring to Japanese Americans as "Japanese." And, twenty years after the fact, he was blurring the distinction between "internment" and the incarceration of Japanese Americans resulting from their forced "exclusion," "evacuation," "assembly," and "relocation"—a distinction he, more than anyone else, had been keenly aware of when he was arguing against the "exclusion" and "evacuation."

Japanese were ever coming back." Family pictures, books, records, radios, cameras, and guns had all been sold, confiscated, destroyed, or lost.[50]

Fujimoto and his comrades traveled to Washington, D.C., where they trained at nearby Fort Belvoir for a ceremony at the White House. As honored as the men felt, they were also a little embarrassed. By this time, almost all of the soldiers in the 442d were replacements; many of them had never even seen combat. Most of them felt the original members of the 100th Battalion (Separate) and the 442d should be bringing home the colors and parading before the president.

It was raining on July 15, 1946, when they marched in formation down Constitution Avenue to the Ellipse. Standing in the shower, their uniforms soggy, the men of the 442d received their seventh Presidential Unit Citation. But this time it was from a new president, Harry F. Truman, who recognized, as his predecessor had not, where the buck stopped. Just two weeks earlier, he had issued Executive Order 9742, which terminated the War Relocation Authority.[51] Now the talk among the press corps was that aides had advised the president to cancel his appearance because of the weather. Among the press corps, Truman was said to have snapped back: "Hell, no, after what these boys went through, I can stand a little rain."*

Wearing a modest hat and trench coat, Truman reviewed the troops and addressed the assembled crowd.[52] Behind him were four wounded veterans in seats of honor. One of them, in a wheelchair, was Wilson Makabe. Affixing the unit citation banner to the regiment's colors, Truman declared:

> You are to be congratulated on what you have done for this great country of ours. I think it was my predecessor who said that Americanism is not a matter of race or creed, it is a matter of the heart. . . . You are now on your way home. You fought not only the enemy, but you fought prejudice, and you have won. Keep up that fight, and we continue to

---

*According to Terry Shima, who was the public relations representative in Service Company of the 442d. His predecessor, Mike Masaoka (the JACL leader and author of the "Japanese American Creed"), told Shima what Colonel Pence had told him: "Remember that your most important job is to publicize the heroics of the RCT." (My correspondence with Shima.)

win—to make this great Republic stand for just what the Constitution says it stands for: the welfare of all the people all the time.[53]

★ ★ ★

Two years later, on June 4, 1948, there was another ceremony in the nation's capital. Two members of the 442d who had died in the Vosges were finally coming home to America. After more than three and a half years in the cold earth of the American cemetery at Épinal—the town where the 442d had bivouacked before the Battle of Bruyères—their bodies were being transferred to Arlington National Cemetery. In the eighty-four-year history of the cemetery, they would be the first persons of Japanese ancestry to be buried there.

One of the soldiers was Fumitake Nagato, of G Company, who had been killed during the Battle of Bruyères. The other was Saburo Tanamachi of E Company—brother of Jerry Tanamachi, who had married Kikuko Nakao in the Rohwer Relocation Center—who had died in the arms of his friend "Machine Gun Joe" Sakato during the assault on Hill 617, during the rescue of the Lost Battalion.

In an impressive gathering of dignitaries, the honorary pallbearers from the military included Maj. Gen. John E. Dahlquist, former commander of the 36th Division and now deputy director of personnel and administration of the Army General Staff; Gen. Jacob L. Devers, former commander of the 6th Army Group and now chief of the Army Ground Forces; Col. Charles W. Pence, former commander of the 442d, who had been wounded during the rescue of the Lost Battalion; Col. Virgil R. Miller, who had succeeded Pence as commander of the 442d; Lt. Col. James M. Hanley, former commander of the 2d Battalion of the 442d, in which both Nagato and Tanamachi had served; and Col. Charles H. Owens, former commander of the 141st Infantry Regiment, to which the Lost Battalion had belonged. General Mark Clark had been invited but sent his regrets because of prior commitments.

Honorary pallbearers who were civilians included Joseph R. Farrington, congressional delegate from the Territory of Hawaii; Representative Ed Gosset of Texas; Dillon S. Myer, former director of the War Relocation Authority; and John J. McCloy, former assistant secretary of war and now head of the World Bank, whom the 442d remembered as its sponsor in the War Department, but whom residents of the "relocation centers" remembered as the prime mover in Washington behind the "exclusion" and "evacuation" of Japanese American civilians from the West Coast.

At 3:00 P.M., under a bright spring sky, General Devers spoke. He read a message from Clark, who wrote: "Valor has won the *Nisei* a historic place in the annals of American arms."[54] Then Devers delivered a simple but eloquent eulogy. In five brief paragraphs, quoted in their entirety below, he summed up the achievement not only of the two soldiers being buried but of all Japanese Americans in the European, Mediterranean, Pacific, and China-Burma-India theaters during World War II:

There is one supreme, final test of loyalty to one's native land . . . readiness and willingness to fight for, and if need be to die for, one's country.

These Americans, and their fellows, passed that test with colors flying. They proved their loyalty and devotion beyond all question.

They volunteered for Army combat service, and they made a record second to none. In Europe, theirs was the combat team most feared by the enemy. In the Pacific, they placed themselves in double jeopardy, chancing the bullets of friend as well as foe. Everywhere, they were the soldiers most decorated for valor, most devoted to duty. Their only absences without leave were from hospitals which they quit before they recovered from their wounds, in order to get back into the fight for what they knew to be the right.

These men, to two of whom we pay our heartfelt respects today, more than earned the right to be called just Americans, not Japanese Americans. Their Americanism may be described only by degree, and that the highest.

The United States Army salutes you, Privates First Class Fumitake Nagato and Saburo Tanamachi. You, and your compatriots, will live in our hearts and our history as Americans First Class.[55]

AFTERWORD

"Here We Admit a Wrong"

Blood that has soaked into the sands of a beach is all of one color. America stands unique in the world: the only country not founded on race but on a way, an ideal.—RONALD REAGAN[1]

California, 1945, and Washington, D.C., 1988

Gensuke and Tamae Masuda, who spent two and a half years in the Poston Relocation Center, were among the first Japanese Americans to return to Orange County, California. Just before they came back, some local vigilantes visited their daughter Mary, who had left camp before her parents, and tried to terrorize her into leaving. Although she reported the incident and even identified the men, the local sheriff took no action.

Four of the Masudas' sons (out of eleven children) had served in the U.S. military. Mitsuo had recently been discharged from the Army, Masao was in the MIS, and Takashi had been wounded during the rescue of the Lost Battalion. Kazuo, a staff sergeant with the 442d, had distinguished himself in combat during the Italian campaign by advancing two hundred yards through enemy fire and single-handedly laying down a mortar barrage on the enemy for twelve hours. On August 27, 1944, while leading a night patrol through a minefield, he had sacrificed his own life to save his men from being surrounded. When his parents tried to bring his body back home after the war, the town of Westminster refused to open the gates of the local cemetery.

On December 8, 1945, Gen. Joseph W. Stilwell, former commander in chief of American forces in the China-Burma-India theater and now commander of the peacetime Sixth Army at the Presidio, visited the Masudas at their modest house in Talbert, a small farm community in Orange County. A legendary leader who had earned the nickname "Vinegar Joe" for his candor, Stilwell had harshly criticized his superior, Lieutenant General DeWitt, four years earlier, following the attack on Pearl Harbor. And two months before visiting the Masuda family, Stilwell had told *The Washington Post* that "we soldiers ought to form a pickax club to protect Japanese Americans who fought the war with us."

> You're damn right those *Nisei* boys have a place in the American heart, now and forever. . . . They bought an awful hunk of America with their blood. Anytime we see a barfly commando picking on these kids or discriminating against them, we ought to bang him over the head with a pickax.

"I've seen a good deal of the *Nisei* in service and never yet have I found one of them who didn't do his duty right up to the handle," Stilwell declared.[2]

Now, saluting the Masuda family, Stilwell pinned Kazuo Masuda's posthumously awarded Distinguished Service Cross on his sister Mary. While she was "struggling to keep back the tears," according to the *Los Angeles Times*, Mary Masuda said, "In accepting this distinction for my brother, I know that he would want me to say that he was only doing his duty as a soldier of our beloved country."[3]

After leaving the Masudas, Stilwell expressed his outrage over the treatment of Japanese Americans before a large crowd at a rally called "United America Day," in the nearby Santa Ana Municipal Bowl. A contingent from Hollywood was also on hand at the gathering, including Robert Young and Will Rogers Jr. Louise Allbritton, an actress who had grown up in Texas and Oklahoma, spoke about a certain Texas battalion rescued by Japanese Americans in France. And another young Hollywood star, wearing the uniform of an American Army Air Force captain, made his first political speech, declaring, "Not in spite of but because of our polyglot background, we have had all the strength in the world. That is the American way."[4]

★ ★ ★

The veterans of the campaigns in southern and eastern France followed many different roads out of the dark woods of the Vosges.

General John E. Dahlquist led the 36th Division through the end of the war, by which time it had become one of the most highly decorated units of the Army in World War II. He later served as deputy director of personnel and administration at the War Department, 1947–49, and eventually rose to four-star general and commander in chief of the Continental Army Command before retiring in 1956. He died in 1975 and was buried at Arlington National Cemetery, the resting place of Saburo Tanamachi and Fumitake Nagato of the 442d.

General Jacob L. Devers, commander of the 6th Army Group in France and Germany, won his fourth star in March 1945 and went on to command the U.S. Army Ground Forces after World War II. He retired from active duty in 1949. In 1959 he succeeded Gen. George C. Marshall as chairman of the American Battle Monuments Commission, an independent agency of the executive branch of the federal government in charge of memorials, markers, and monuments honoring the war dead of the U.S. Armed Forces, as well as American burial grounds abroad (including the American Cemetery and Memorial in Épinal, in the Vosges). Devers died in 1979 and was buried at Arlington National Cemetery.

Shig Doi, whose family's farm had been the target of night riders, operated the free mobile X-ray unit for the Tuberculosis Control Program of Contra Costa County, California, for more than a quarter century. Before Proposition 13 put an end to the service, Doi had X-rayed more than 750,000 people, processing the film and servicing the equipment himself, while working out of a 1948 truck he had purchased from the federal government for one dollar. After a trip to Biffontaine in 1984, on the fortieth anniversary of the rescue of the Lost Battalion, Doi said, "I will never go back to that place again." Too many bad memories lingered in the mountains. Doi still lives in Contra Costa County with his wife, Yo.

Barney Hajiro continued working as a security guard until his retirement. Asked to explain how a self-described "goof-off" could lead the heroic charge up "Suicide Hill," Hajiro says today he was worried about being court-martialed for the third time if he didn't keep moving forward, as ordered: "I had to be a good boy." (There is no reason to regard this explanation as anything but absurdly modest.) By his own admission, he is still a lousy gambler, but he occasionally enjoys a trip to Las Vegas. For a half century, he says, "I never thought about the military."[5] Then, in 1998, "they said it [the upgraded Medal of Honor] was going to happen," he told the *Honolulu Star-Bulletin*, "but nothing came." He "nearly gave up hope."[6] Hajiro and his wife, Esther, have been married for sixty years. When they traveled to the White House for the Medal of Honor ceremony, they invited Shiro "Kash" Kashino's widow, Louise, to accompany them.

Marty Higgins found being a POW far worse than anything he had experienced in combat. After the war, he came back to the New York City area and took a personnel screening test at Macy's, which revealed he would have a problem with discipline and following orders. He worked for many years as a sales representative in the playing-card industry, eventually and reluctantly becoming an executive, no happier giving orders than following them. In 1952, Higgins wrote a series of letters urging congressmen to support legislation granting first-generation Japanese American immigrants (*Issei*) the citizenship they had been denied for decades. After his retirement, he went back to school and earned a master's degree in education and worked as a youth counselor in South Carolina. His beloved wife of more than fifty years, Marge, died shortly before he gave his speech at the Punchbowl. Now, with his new computer, he maintains active e-mail relationships with friends and comrades all around the country.

Daniel K. Inouye, who couldn't get a haircut in San Francisco after returning with a Distinguished Service Cross and a hook in place of the arm he lost in Italy, graduated from George Washington University Law School and went on to help the Democratic Party in Hawaii win the 1954 territorial elections. The "quiet revolution" of that year ended decades of Republican Party control and fulfilled the dreams arising from the barracks room and campfire discussions at Camp Shelby, led by **Sakae Takahashi,** who became the first Asian in the territorial cabinet and went on to be majority leader of the State Senate. Another veteran of the 100th's visionary bull sessions was **"Spark" Matsunaga,** who was elected U.S. representative from Hawaii in 1962 and U.S senator in 1976. When Hawaii won statehood in 1959,* Inouye became the former territory's first U.S.

---

*Statehood for Hawaii was by no means a foregone conclusion. U.S. senators and representatives from the South opposed admitting the Territory because it would become the first, and only, state with a nonwhite majority. Although it is not usually recognized today for what it represented at the time, Hawaii's becoming a state was an important chapter in the history of the civil rights movement.

representative. "If we had not done what we did" as soldiers, Inouye says, "Hawaii would still be struggling for statehood."[7] Shortly after he took office, he was invited to speak at the Citadel, by **Gen. Mark Clark,** who had become president of the military academy after retiring from the Army as a four-star general in 1953. In 1962, Inouye became U.S. senator from Hawaii. In 2004, he was reelected to his eighth consecutive term of office.

Sus Ito, one of the three *kotonks* who watched one another's backs from Camp Shelby to "Suicide Hill," followed the tiger on his *senninbari* and made his way safely home. He attended Western (now Case Western Reserve) University on the GI bill and eventually became a world-renowned authority on electron microscopy. He retired from Harvard University as emeritus professor of medicine but still conducts research and maintains a laboratory on campus, where he goes every weekday at 5:00 A.M. Colleagues, students, friends, and acquaintances who know his international reputation as a scholar are always surprised to learn of his wartime heroism. After the Japanese American National Museum opened in Los Angeles in 1992, he donated his *senninbari* and the dozens of rolls of photographs he took with **George Oiye** ("Whitey") at Camp Shelby and in Italy, France, and Germany. Ito and Oiye both won Bronze Stars for their heroism during the rescue of the Lost Battalion. True to Lieutenant Colonel Pursall's word, their friend **Yuki Minaga,** the "first one up the hill," won a Silver Star. Although they live on different coasts, Ito remains close friends with Oiye, who had a long career as an engineer for the Jet Propulsion Laboratory at the California Institute of Technology and at companies including Borg Warner and Philco Ford, and as an operations manager for ILC, a laser technology firm. Ito still tinkers with cars, and even provides emergency repair service to his neighbors on the suburban street where he has lived for four decades.

Shiro "Kash" Kashino, the "go-getter" who volunteered from one detention camp, Minidoka, then served time in the stockade for a bar brawl, and finally guarded German POWs at another camp in Italy, worked for decades as a car dealer in Seattle. When his youngest daughter was growing up, she was always self-conscious in school on Pearl Harbor Day, because all of her classmates would look at her—and she didn't even know what side her father fought on during the war. When he finally realized what his daughter was going through, Kashino said, "I was quite embarrassed." From then on, he and his wife, Louise, made an effort to educate not just their own children but the larger community in Seattle about Japanese Americans in the "relocation centers" and the military. Over the years, his former comrades in arms urged him to try to get his court-martial reversed, but he insisted it was an experience long past that he wanted to forget. Then, in 1985, while attending a reunion in Maui, former I Company officer Sadaichi Kubota told Kashino that he had written Senator Inouye about reopening the case. For the next twelve years, Kashino, Louise, and their many friends persisted against long odds and considerable obstacles, including the Army's discovery that many of his files were damaged, destroyed, or missing as a result of a fire at the National Personnel Records Center, Military Personnel Records, in St. Louis. Finally, on December 9, 1997, Maj. Gen. Walter Huffman, the judge advocate general of the U.S. Army, wrote: "Mr. Kashino's appeal is granted and his court-martial is set aside."[8] But it was a bittersweet vindication, for Kashino had died of cancer six months earlier. To his official letter, Major General Huffman added a handwritten postscript to Louise: "Your husband was an American Hero—and that is how he should be remembered."

Young Oak Kim traveled a long way from Bunker Hill in Los Angeles, only to return home after six decades. He served thirty years in the Army and rose to the rank of colonel before retiring as the most decorated Asian American in the U.S. military. In Korea he was the first Asian American ever to command a regular combat battalion in war. He still maintained strong ties with the Japanese American community. "I may not see somebody for many, many years," he said, but "when I see them, it just seems like yesterday."[9] Though a Korean American, Kim was one of the founders of the Japanese American National Museum as well as the Go For Broke Educational Foundation, which has a grant from the government of California to develop classroom materials on the *Nisei* experience for high school students throughout the state. In 2000–2001, he served on the official Department of Defense panel reviewing charges of American war crimes at No Gun Ri during the Korean War. In February 2005, the consul general of France awarded him the Legion of Honor in a ceremony at the Go For Broke Monument in downtown Los Angeles. Kim died in December 2005, as this book was being finished.

S. L. A. Marshall, who had been present at the birth of the 442d during the "registration" in the camps, wrote several best-selling books, including *Pork Chop Hill.* He retired as a brigadier general after helping to revolutionize the writing of military history. In an editorial for *The Detroit News* in 1959, headlined "We Join Hawaii," Marshall praised Congress for passing the Admissions Act, granting statehood to the territory.[10]

> So doing, the U.S. paid off a debt to the islands' largest population group—the Americans of Japanese blood—for having saved its declared national policy in a fateful clutch during wartime.
>
> One of the sacred principles of the Constitution—the right of citizens to be free and equal—was at stake and they, by their voluntary action, revitalized it. . . . They responded because they love the flag and, more solidly than any other population bloc under it, they uphold the lofty standard that the privileges of life there attending must be paid for by the citizen through full acceptance of proportionate responsibility.[11]

Three years later, in 1962, the 442d Veterans Club in Honolulu asked him to invite Eleanor Roosevelt to the forthcoming twentieth anniversary of the founding of the unit, but she had to decline, for reasons of health. Marshall remained an admirer of what he called "the great *Nisei* fighting outfit"[12] until his death in 1977. He was buried with full military honors at Fort Bliss National Cemetery, and his posthumously published autobiography, *Bringing Up the Rear,* appeared in 1979.

General Alexander M. Patch, commander of the Seventh Army in France and Germany, returned to the United States in August 1945 to take command of the Fourth Army, which at the time of Pearl Harbor had been under the Western Defense Command and Lt. Gen. John DeWitt. Three months later, in November 1945, Patch died of pneumonia.

George "Joe" Sakato, the "tiny runt" who had transformed himself into "Machine Gun Joe," worked for the U.S. Post Office (as it was called then) for thirty years before retiring in 1980. In the spring of 2000, he received a call from the Pentagon inviting him to Washington to receive the Medal of Honor. He was so speechless that the caller thought Sakato was having a heart attack. But when he was told each recipient could only bring a party of ten, Sakato replied that if the White House couldn't accommodate all of his family and many of his friends, the Pentagon might as well put his Medal of Honor in the mail. The White House relented, and Sakato stood proudly at attention, before a large crowd of his relatives and loved ones, to receive the Medal of Honor from President Clinton. To this day, he believes he was chosen to win the Medal of Honor because he is the only surviving honoree from the mainland. So he makes a point of talking about the "relocation" as well as about the 442d in the appearances he has made before schools, civic organizations, and the Military Academy at West Point.

Al Takahashi, who went from shining officers' shoes stateside to one miraculous escape from death after another in France and Italy, had a long career as an engineer in the aerospace industry. After retiring, he continues to live not far from where he worked, and only a short drive from the Go For Broke Educational Foundation, where he is a board member. Still an aviation enthusiast after more than six decades, he has been building a light airplane in his garage. The nose cone keeps the door propped open at an angle. He is planning to attach the wings (which are too wide for the garage) at the local airport after he finishes the fuselage. Now in his mid-eighties, he's determined to fly the plane while he can still qualify for his pilot's license.

General Lucian K. Truscott Jr., commander of VI Corps in France and the Fifth Army in Italy, retired as a four-star general after a long and distinguished career that never quite received the attention from military historians, or the acclaim of the general population, that it deserved. His son, Col. Lucian K. Truscott III, served as a company commander in Korea and a battalion commander in Vietnam, and his grandson, Lucian K. Truscott IV, is a graduate of West Point and the best-selling author of *Dress Gray* and other novels. General Truscott's battlefield memoirs, *Command Missions*, originally published in 1954, remain a model of the genre—clear, candid, insightful, and well written. Truscott died on September 12, 1965, and was buried at Arlington National Cemetery.

★ ★ ★

On August 10, 1988, four decades after Saburo Tanamachi and Fumitake Nagato were honored at Arlington, another ceremony took place in Room 450 of the Old Executive Office Building in Washington, D.C. The occasion was the signing of a bill providing redress to the 80,000 surviving Japanese Americans of the 120,000 who had been "evacuated," "relocated," or detained during World War II.* One of the driving forces behind the bill was California congressman Norman Mineta. In 1942, he had worn his Cub Scout uniform on the long train ride from San Jose to the Santa Anita Assembly Center.

The young actor who had spoken at the rally in Santa Ana in 1945 was now the president of the United States. As he signed the bill into law,[13] Ronald Reagan told those present they were here "to right a grave wrong":

> More than forty years ago, shortly after the bombing of Pearl Harbor, 120,000 persons of Japanese ancestry living in the United States were forcibly removed from their homes and placed in makeshift internment camps. This action was taken without trial, without jury. It was based solely on race, for these 120,000 were Americans of Japanese descent.

---

*The amount of restitution—up to $20,000 per individual—did not cover the losses suffered. (Twenty thousand in 1988 dollars would have been worth about $1,150 in 1942, per capita GDP, which was about two thirds of what an average employee made in a year [according to Bureau of the Census, *Historical Statistics of the United States, Colonial Times to 1970*]—without taking into account real property.) Earlier settlements of claims, beginning in the late 1940s, had covered less than a quarter of the individuals involved, and less than a fifth of the real property losses (estimated at $200 million in 1942 dollars). According to the WRA after the war, Japanese Americans' "material losses had already reached disturbing proportions . . . the loss of hundreds of property leases and the disappearance of a number of equities in land and buildings were among the most regrettable and least justifiable of all the many costs of the wartime evacuation." (*WRA: A Story of Human Conservation*, pp. 145–51.) Considerable farm, commercial, and residential property was lost in prime real-estate areas such as the San Francisco Bay Area, Santa Monica, and Orange County, where small lots are often worth millions of dollars each today, far outstripping any adjustment for inflation.

In "The Emergency Constitution," *Yale Law Journal*, 113 (2004), Bruce Ackerman notes:

> It took almost half a century before the Japanese-American victims of wartime concentration camps gained financial compensation, and then only by a special act of Congress that awarded incredibly tiny sums.
>
> Such callousness suggests a deeper distortion in the law of just compensation. When a small piece of property is taken by the government to build a new highway, the owner is constitutionally guaranteed fair market compensation, even if owed a relatively trivial sum.
>
> But when an innocent person is wrongly convicted by the criminal justice system, he or she is not guaranteed a dime when the mistake is discovered afterward, despite the scars of long years of incarceration.

Yes, the Nation was then at war, struggling for its survival, and it's not for us today to pass judgment upon those who may have made mistakes while engaged in that great struggle. Yet we must recognize that the internment of Japanese Americans was just that: a mistake.*

But he also reminded the gathering that "throughout the war, Japanese Americans in the tens of thousands remained utterly loyal to the United States."

Indeed, scores of Japanese-Americans volunteered for our Armed Forces, many stepping forward in the internment camps themselves, The 442d Regimental Combat Team, made up entirely of Japanese Americans, served with immense distinction to defend this nation, their nation. Yet back at home, the soldiers' families were being denied the very freedom for which so many of the soldiers themselves were laying down their lives.

Reagan recalled the remarks he had made more than four decades earlier about the color of "blood soaked into the sands." "Here we admit a wrong; here we reaffirm our commitment as a nation to equal justice under the law," he declared. "The ideal of liberty and justice for all—that is still the American way."

Then he concluded the ceremony by noting that HR 442, which offered amends for the "relocation," had been "so fittingly named in honor of the 442d."†

---

*Like many before and after him, Reagan mistakenly referred to the "relocation" as "internment." And the number of Japanese Americans "relocated" after Pearl Harbor was not 120,000, which was roughly the total number of individuals who passed through the camps during their roughly two and a half years of existence.

†Reagan, "Remarks on Signing the Bill Providing Restitution for the Wartime Internment of Japanese-American Civilians." Characteristically, Young Oak Kim was much more blunt: "If it wasn't for the 100th/442d there would have been no redress."

EPILOGUE

Hill of Sacrifice

Hawaii, 2000, and
Texas, 2004–2005

Just a mile north of downtown Honolulu is the vast crater of an extinct volcano. To Hawaiians, this hollow expanse of more than a hundred acres is known as the Punchbowl. To the Armed Forces, it is the National Memorial Cemetery of the Pacific, gravesite of more than forty thousand soldiers, sailors, and airmen who died in World War II, Korea, and Vietnam. To the ancient islanders, it was *Pu'owaina*, the "consecrated hill" or "hill of sacrifice."[1]

On March 25, 2000, Marty Higgins stood at the bottom of the steps leading up to the Honolulu Memorial, capped by the towering figure of Lady Columbia, overlooking the Punchbowl and symbolizing grieving mothers everywhere. Gazing out over the seemingly endless ranks and files of flat granite headstones, Higgins could see the promontory of Diamond Head rising beyond the eastern end of Waikiki Beach. Behind his right shoulder, Pearl Harbor, less than ten miles away, provided a blue backdrop to the skyscrapers of Honolulu. And in front of him, framed by the mountains on one side and the Pacific on the other, were more than three hundred people—most of them, like Higgins, men in their late seventies and eighties, veterans of World War II.[2]

They were gathered for a memorial service at the Punchbowl, honoring their fallen comrades and celebrating the fifty-seventh anniversary of the founding of the 442d. Though he had never met most of the men standing before him, Higgins was going to speak about that moment in history when his fate and theirs had been joined forever.

Earlier that morning, Higgins had been jolted awake in his hotel room by a vision of rippling red flags in an open field. Afraid that he would be unable to deliver his speech, he was wracked with tears before falling asleep again. Now, seated on the dais next to U.S. senator Daniel Inouye, Higgins was apprehensive for another reason. He had heard that Inouye did not have fond memories of the 36th Division after the 442d's rescue of the Lost Battalion, which some thought had never been properly recognized after more than five decades.

But something amazing happened as Higgins listened to the speakers scheduled ahead of him. Just before his name was announced, Higgins felt a soothing warmth spread throughout his body. It came not from the brilliant Hawaiian sun but from somewhere deep within. When he stood up and started to speak, he found himself strangely transformed. Instead of talking in his rapid-fire New Jersey Irish cadence, he spoke calmly, enunciating every word.

"At age eighty-four," Higgins began, "I am experiencing the most awesome moment of my life. Thank you for sharing it with me. *Aloha pumehana!*" The audience burst into applause at his use of Hawaiian. His son-in-law, who had attended college in Hawaii, had carefully added phonetic spellings (*poo-may-hah'-nah*, meaning "warm" or "affectionate") to the draft of Higgins's speech, so he would pronounce the words correctly.[3]

"This may be hard to believe, but at the time of the rescue, we were not aware of the losses you sustained in getting us out," Higgins told the Japanese American veterans. "For some unbelievable reason, you were never identified by the American press, other than as 'soldiers.'"

Despite their shared history, Higgins had first met some of his rescuers only two years earlier. In 1998, he had been introduced to Sus Ito at a reunion of the 141st Regiment of the 36th Division. Ito, one of the three *kotonks* who had changed from forward observers to riflemen on "Suicide Hill," had persuaded the 442 Veterans Club to invite Higgins to speak at the Punchbowl.

"It is an honor to stand before you," Higgins declared, "to offer my regrets for your losses, to give you thanks for your bravery and sacrifice, for myself, for the others in the Lost Battalion, and for the country for which you fought." He continued:

The bureaucrats of the United States government imposed despicable and unconscionable acts on your parents. They lost their homes, places of business, and farms; they were imprisoned in relocation centers. I am not sure if I could have done what you did: to volunteer to fight for the country that took away your constitutional rights. In my lifetime, no other group was ever persecuted as badly as you were. Every one of you deserves the Distinguished Service Award. You distinguished yourselves in combat, and as loyal citizens of the United States of America. We are forever thankful and indebted to you.

When he finished, still awash in serenity, he sat down. Senator Inouye leaned over, and with his left hand, his only hand, clasped Higgins's hand in gratitude. A debt of honor had been gracefully discharged to the old men standing before Higgins in the Punchbowl, men who had climbed a very different "hill of sacrifice" in France fifty-six years earlier. As the crowd cheered, Higgins cried, for the second time that day. But this time he was not afraid, and he was not alone.

★ ★ ★

Jefferson County, Texas, 2004

Four years later, Higgins found himself once more in combat alongside the men of the 442d. Again they were fighting a common enemy, but this time it was the Lost Battalion that came to the aid of the 442d.

Although Sandra Tanamachi had been in Lake Jackson for seven years by this point, she had not given up her lonely battle to change the name of Jap Road in Beaumont, 140 miles away. And during the intervening years she had slowly gained many allies.

Foremost among them was a helicopter pilot named Thomas Kuwahara. An Army veteran who was still active in the Reserves, Kuwahara was an EMS pilot who had worked in Colorado, Louisiana, and Georgia. On a trip through Texas in 1999, he had spotted a sign for the catfish restaurant on Jap Road. "It startled me at first," he said. He couldn't believe such a slur could be so publicly displayed, "not in the state that had made the men of the 100th/442d honorary Texans" for rescuing the Lost Battalion. So he "turned and backtracked to see the sign again." But "to my sorrow," he realized, "my eyes were fine."

A third-generation Japanese American like Tanamachi, Kuwahara had grown up in Hawaii. "The men of the 100th/442d are my role models, my heroes," he was proud to declare. "They are of my mother's, father's, aunts', and uncles' generation, many of whom served in the U.S. Army." He knew "they wouldn't put up with this slur," and neither would he.[4]

Kuwahara learned of Tanamachi's efforts and offered to help. Together they contacted prominent Japanese American veterans in advance of a meeting scheduled for July 19, 2004. Senator Daniel Inouye wrote the Jefferson County commissioners: "I was in the same company, Company E, as Kelly Kuwayama, who is testifying at your hearing in Beaumont, and Saburo Tanamachi, a resident of Beaumont, who was killed in the rescue [of the Lost Battalion]. With his life, Saburo honored his family, Jefferson County, the Great State of Texas, and the United States of America." Inouye urged the commissioners to change the name of Jap Road and "replace it with one that is not offensive to anyone. . . . Japanese American men served in the European and Asia Pacific theaters of war to prove their loyalty, to erase racial slurs," he reminded the commissioners, "and to be treated as Americans."[5]

Tanamachi got in touch with another E Company veteran, her old family friend George "Machine Gun Joe" Sakato. In a letter of support, Sakato described how—just before he led the charge up Hill 617 that would earn him the Medal of Honor—he had held Sandra's uncle Saburo, dying of a bullet wound, in his arms. After the rescue of the Lost Battalion, Sakato had been proud of another honor—being a Texas citizen by official state proclamation. But now, he said, "It feels like an embarrassment."[6]

Among the organizations Kuwahara and Tanamachi contacted were the Go For Broke Educational Foundation and the Japanese American Veterans Association (JAVA) in Washington. And the rescue of the Lost Battalion came full circle after sixty years, when JAVA helped mobilize the veterans of the 36th Division.

Jack Wilson, who had led a machine-gun platoon in the Lost Battalion, asked the Jefferson County commissioners to change the name of Jap Road, "in honor of these brave and loyal Americans" who "gave so much for our country."[7]

When he learned of the controversy, Marty Higgins wrote to remind the commissioners of the debt Texas owed to Japanese Americans. "I was the commander of that 1st Battalion, 141st Regiment, 36th Texas Division, rescued in the Vosges Mountains, October 30, 1944," he wrote. He would have flown to Beaumont to deliver his message in person, Higgins said, but he was suffering from congestive heart failure. A few weeks earlier he had been in Washington, D.C., for the dedication of the World War II Memorial. Even though he was wheelchair bound, he had spoken on a public panel with 442d veterans and then made time for well-wishers at the JAVA booth in a sweltering tent on the Mall.

Now he was asking the commissioners to act out of consideration for "what these men accomplished." "If it were not for the 442d we would have been killed, wounded, or captured," he stated flatly. "I think we owe them."[8]

One of Higgins's comrades in the Lost Battalion, Gene Airheart, went even further in his letter to the commissioners. "I owe my life, and my daughter's life, and my grandson's life, and his lineage into the future, to the self-sacrificial service of these Japanese American patriots." Unlike Higgins, Airheart had had no contact with anyone from the 442d for sixty years, assuming that he "would never see them again this side of heaven." But he, too, had been in Washington, D.C., in May, along with thousands of other World War II veterans on the Mall. There he "stood shoulder to shoulder" with 442d vets, and he "shook hands and hugged those men." His heart "almost burst with emotion, knowing what they had done" in those black woods so many years before. He urged that Jap Road be renamed because it was "offensive to an honorable segment of our population who have served and sacrificed honorably, despite prejudices against them."[9]

★ ★ ★

As July 19 drew near, the controversy had spread throughout Jefferson County and beyond. On the night before the meeting, more than a hundred local residents packed the Pine Tree Lounge on Taylor Bayou. An informal survey had claimed that around forty of the fifty-five residents of the 4.3-mile road opposed changing the name of Jap Road. And a thousand of their neighbors in the county had signed a petition asking the commissioners "not to bow to pressure from outside sources." "Most of the protests on the name are coming from Louisiana, California, and Hawaii," one resident told *The Port Arthur News*. "Changing the name would be losing part of who we are."

But who did they think they were? "If you live in this country, you are American, not Japanese-American, African-American or Italian-American," another resident told the *News*, employing the classic tactic of blaming the victim. "It is the 'hyphenated' Americans that are the racists. If some think Jap Road is offensive, it is offensive to me to have outsiders come in and change part of our history."[10]

Others complained about the cost in time, effort, and money of changing the name on street signs and legal documents. Most believed the matter should be put on the ballot for voters to decide.

By the next day, media coverage had focused attention from around the country, not to mention around the world. Outsiders were everywhere. CNN and *The New York Times* had already started covering the story days earlier. The *Houston Chronicle* reported that one of the commissioners had just been to New York City. There he saw a story on Jap Road in *The New York Times* and "felt ashamed." A local judge feared the country would "believe we're a bunch of racists," but "that is so, so, so far from the truth."[11]

When the commissioners finally convened, more than 150 people showed up at the county offices. The crowd was so large that the meeting was moved to a larger room used to empanel jurors, and speakers were limited to three minutes each, alternating voices for and against the name change. A crew from nearby Lamar University was on hand to tape the session for the local television station. But Sandra Tanamachi, who was eager to have a complete record of the proceedings, was told the equipment wasn't set up properly, so no copies were available later.[12]

One resident of the road began by sounding the note that had been heard from the start—that there was "nothing racial" about the name. Taking offense at Jap Road was like being outraged by the White House, he said, apparently identifying the color of the paint on the walls with the color of its occupants' skin. Others stressed again the origin of the name, claiming it was meant to honor the Mayumi family, which had never been offended. (Or at least they had not said so if they were.) Many of the opposition speakers complained about the expense and inconvenience and decried the influence of "outsiders." Everyone denied he or she was a racist.[13]

One speaker in favor of changing the name was an outsider named Micki Kawakami, who had traveled to Beaumont from her home state of

Idaho—"a state with a reputation of racism," she admitted, "though not entirely warranted," as she hoped would be the case in Texas. Her family had been in the "relocation camps" and her uncles had served in the 442d. Kawakami tried to sound a conciliatory note. "The people here are not bigots or racist. May I suggest you *inherited* a road named a racist name?" She suggested that there was "common ground here. Most speakers want to honor the Mayumi family." But "whoever said words can't hurt you has never stood in a person of color's shoes, never been judged by appearance alone and found less than his fellowman." It was often difficult to do the right thing, she declared, but "removing this pejorative name" would be the only correct decision. "We are not Japs."[14]

Willie Tanamachi, Saburo's brother and Sandra's uncle, agreed. "I was called names when I was a little kid" in Beaumont, he said, "and Jap was one of them." Far from being a way to honor someone, "it was always used to put me down."[15]

Kelly Kuwayama—whom "Machine Gun Joe" Sakato had seen shot by the Germans, even though he was wearing the red cross of a medic— retold the story of Saburo Tanamachi's death on Hill 617. Like Kawakami, Kuwayama accepted at face value the professed intention of honoring the Mayumi family. But then why not change the name, he asked, to Mayumi Road?[16]

Finally Sandra Tanamachi had her chance to speak, for which she had been waiting more than a dozen years. She reminded the commissioners and the audience that she was not an "outsider." She spoke of her family's roots in the area and identified her uncle Willie as a native son of Beaumont. She spoke warmly of her teaching experience at Blanchette Elementary School and of her colleagues and neighbors.

She did not mention the anonymous notes and phone calls, or the night riders who shot up her mailbox. She said instead that "the only thing in Jefferson County which caused me pain and anguish" was the name "Jap Road." The word "Jap" was used, she said, when her "mother and her family were forced out of their homes and placed in horse stalls . . . then placed in trains and taken clear across the country to live in an internment camp in a desolate place in Arkansas." "The word 'Jap' was also used," she said, when she herself was a child. And she "knew that it wasn't meant to be any type of compliment."

Tanamachi appealed to the commissioners' wisdom, courage, and leadership. And she expressed hope that "simply changing the name of Jap Road" would lay to rest the concerns of the rest of America about Jefferson County's ability to "respect diversity and appreciate the dignity of all."[17]

After twelve years, three minutes were hardly enough time for her to make her case. But after fighting almost alone for so long, she had now been joined, in person and in spirit, by a band of brothers—with their own brothers and sisters and sons and daughters and nephews and nieces—who had found common ground with other Americans on a "hill of sacrifice" in France sixty years earlier.

★ ★ ★

When the vote was finally called after three hours of contentious debate, the outcome was exactly the opposite of the original decision. This time the lone dissenter among the commissioners was an opponent, not a supporter, of the name change. He had told *The Port Arthur News* that he wished the commissioners had "had the backbone" to resist "political correctness." "I believe that if the county sticks with the name and educates and honors the history, then twenty years from now people will be glad." But when his name was called, he said nothing—not opening his mouth to vote no or even to abstain. So with his silence, the vote was not just a majority decision—it was unanimous. Jap Road would be Jap Road no longer.[18]

After more than twelve years, the victory had been achieved not through the courts, or through the media, or through protest marches. It had been won by individuals investing their faith in politics, speaking as citizens in a public meeting, and putting democracy into action.

As soon as the tally was announced, Sandra Tanamachi jumped up and embraced her son and her mother. They all cried tears of joy. "I immediately thought of my father and my grandparents," she said, "and of course Uncle Saburo."[19]

★ ★ ★

After their decision, the Jefferson County commissioners announced that residents of the former Jap Road could choose a new name, as long as it wasn't offensive. Over the next week, the locals expressed a variety of preferences, but little enthusiasm emerged, if it had ever existed at all, to honor the Mayumi family by naming the road after them. "I don't know of anyone of this road that would like it," one resident told *The Beaumont Enterprise*. "It's being changed because people that don't live here want it changed." "I definitely would not want to name it a Japanese name," another said.[20]

More than a decade earlier, Sandra Tanamachi had asked her second-grade students what the road should be renamed. "They said we should call it 'American Road,'" she told the *Houston Chronicle*, "because we're all Americans now."[21]

But after several more days of discussion, the locals chose a different name, with sixty percent of them writing it in as their first choice. Rather than honoring the Mayumi family, they decided to name the road after the catfish restaurant that the Tanamachi family had decided not to enter— even though it had been closed for a decade. By majority will, the establishment's name became the road's: Boondocks.

This was the victory Tanamachi won after more than twelve years of struggle. It was, to be sure, a battle worth fighting, though it was only over a word on a sign. It was not a world war between democracy and fascism. Still, the struggle over what it means to be an American must be fought anew with each generation of our fellow immigrants, as President Roosevelt reminded us. If it did nothing else, the conflict over Jap Road reawakened the memories, and reestablished the bonds, of old men who thought they had triumphed in their just cause years ago.

Today as in 1944, they had won a battle that represented at best a small victory in a larger war—and at worst a sacrifice that could be squandered. And, as Shiro Kashino noted, the hard-won victories of the Japanese American soldiers are too easily taken for granted: "A lot of people don't realize we could have failed."[22] But the significance of the rescue of the Lost Battalion, then as now, was not just military. It had united men as Americans, not as hyphenated Americans. "We were brothers in arms," George "Machine Gun Joe" Sakato says, "fighting a similar enemy." The 442d had freed their fellow unhyphenated Americans from a German ambush on a hillside bristling with booby traps. In so doing they had helped liberate their own families and loved ones from camps surrounded by barbed wire in their own country. And sixty years later, the circle was closed when Army veterans joined forces again as just Americans.

But even the most deviously designed landmines and cleverly concealed traps in wartime cannot match the insidious workings of narrow minds. The most high-minded appeals to tradition and history, regional culture and local politics—not to mention "military necessity"—can mask the basest impulses. Bigotry can flatter itself as resistance to "political correctness." And prejudice can be found in all corners of America. Not just in the boondocks of East Texas but in the White House, the one in Washington whose name is as inoffensive as Jap Road. The one that was occupied in World War II by a revered president who signed Executive Order 9066—and then authorized the formation of the 442d Regimental Combat Team.

★ ★ ★

Two weeks after Jap Road disappeared from the map in Jefferson County, officials in Fort Bend County, 130 miles away, met to change the name of another Jap Road in Texas. "We decided to do something before it causes a controversy," one of the commissioners told *The Houston Chronicle*.[23] This Jap Road used to be called Moore Road. Nobody knows, or is willing to say, when the name changed, but the commissioners decided the original name should be restored.

The former Jap Road, now rechristened Moore Ranch Road, is less than a mile away from 36 Memorial Highway. The highway was named in honor of the 36th "Texas" Division.

At the time of this writing, there is still a Jap Lane remaining in another Texas town, Vidor, in Orange County. In 1993, *Texas Monthly* had called Vidor "the most hate-filled town" in the state. There were at least five Ku Klux Klan factions active in Vidor. But after the name changes in Jefferson and Fort Bend counties, Orange County commissioners recently asked residents of Jap Lane to submit recommendations for a new name.

As far as Sandra Tanamachi knows, there are no remaining Jap Roads or Jap Lanes in her home state. But Texas is very large. And so is the United States of America. We can only hope it is big enough in spirit for all of its diverse citizens to be recognized not as hyphenated Americans but as just Americans.

APPENDIX

Pearl Harbor and 9/11

Fear is often expressed of the power of the majority in a democracy. This mass evacuation [of Japanese Americans] illustrates the influence that a minority, uncurbed and substantially unopposed, can exercise. It shows, too, the power of suggestion which a mystic cliché like 'military necessity' can exercise on human beings.—FRANCIS BIDDLE[1]

A sneak attack by a hostile power that leaves thousands of Americans dead. A minority group in America harassed for its racial, ethnic, and religious ties to an enemy thousands of miles away and sometimes generations removed. A worldwide conflict that tests our soldiers' resolve in combat and our nation's commitment to democracy, justice, equality, and liberty—abroad and at home.

This is not just the story of Japanese Americans after the bombing of Pearl Harbor. It is also, of course, the story of a very different minority in a very different time—Arab and Muslim Americans following the attacks on the World Trade Center and the Pentagon. While the ruins of the Twin Towers were still smoldering, pundits were already comparing September 11, 2001, to December 7, 1941.

"We would do well to pursue the analogy, because the Pearl Harbor attack led to the most massive government-sponsored human rights violation in the United States since the end of slavery," wrote Eric L. Muller, professor of law at the University of North Carolina and author of *Free to Die for Their Country: The Story of the Japanese American Draft Resisters in World War II*, shortly after 9/11.

Within a few months of Pearl Harbor, the federal government uprooted all 110,000 people of Japanese ancestry from the West Coast,
aliens and U.S. citizens alike, and jailed them in desolate camps in the
U.S. interior.

With upwards of three million people of Arab descent living in
America, we must now ask ourselves: Could it happen again?

The early indications are worrisome. Mosques have been defaced.
Arab-owned businesses have been shot at. Arab Americans have faced
verbal and physical abuse in the streets. Internet message boards burst
with anti-Arab and anti-Muslim slogans and threats. . . .

The risk of a replay of 1942 is clear. In the public's mind, today's enemy is not so different from the enemy of sixty years ago. His religion
is foreign, we tell ourselves. His devotion to it is suicidal. He is secre-
tive. He is barbaric. His skin is of a different color. And so on.[2]

Four years after 9/11, no such "replay of 1942" has taken place—or seems
even remotely possible.

Yet some commentators thought it might have been an appropriate response by the government. Even civil libertarians who had decried "racial
profiling" before 9/11 had second thoughts after. On September 15, 2001,
a headline in *The New York Times* declared "Last Week, Profiling Was
Wrong," and the author of the story, Joyce Purnick, continued: "But that
was then and this is now. . . . It doesn't seem simple anymore."[3] And three
years later, Michelle Malkin, a conservative columnist, published a book
called *In Defense of Internment: The Case for "Racial Profiling" in World War
II and the War on Terror.*

But historical comparisons are rarely simple, whether between 1941
and 2001, or between "racial profiling" pre-9/11 and realistic threat assessment post-9/11. Confusion (sometimes deliberately sown) over terminology, misconceptions about "military necessity," present-day concerns
imposed on past events, and ignorance of or disregard for individual responsibility have all obscured our understanding of what actually happened to Japanese Americans, and America, after Pearl Harbor—and what
some Japanese Americans in the U.S. Army did for themselves and their
country. What was at stake for them was citizenship. What is at stake for
us is not just historical relevance but truth.

★ ★ ★

Our contemporary culture does not particularly honor military valor. As Walter Russell Mead, a senior fellow at the Council on Foreign Relations, recently told *The New York Times*, "the cult of celebrity has cheapened fame," adding, "What's a war hero to do? Go on *Oprah*?" The author of the same *Times* article, Damien Cave, suggested that even the U.S. military might be leery of publicizing its heroes:

> After the heroic tales of Pfc. Jessica Lynch and Sgt. Pat Tillman were largely debunked—with Private Lynch shown to have never fired a shot during her capture and rescue in Iraq, and Sergeant Tillman killed accidentally by fellow Americans, not the enemy, in Afghanistan—the Pentagon may have grown cautious.[4]

And the story of the 100th Battalion and 442d Regimental Combat Team is not one that satisfies the current agendas of either liberals or conservatives. The right, particularly on its nativist fringe, is too preoccupied with downplaying the "evacuation" and "relocation" in order to disparage Japanese Americans' successful campaign for redress in the 1980s. Some conservative commentators, who might have been expected to celebrate the upgraded Medals of Honor in 2000, actually attacked them instead. Rather than acknowledging Japanese Americans' patriotism and heroism, which would seem to be conservative virtues, these commentators were more intent on dismissing the overdue Medals as "politically correct" posturing by Bill Clinton, the right's bête noire.* Meanwhile, the left—typically uncomfortable with military valor and war in general—remains focused on the story of Japanese Americans in the "relocation camps" rather than in combat.

---

*The 442d was called the "most decorated unit in American military history for its size and length of service" decades before the upgraded Congressional Medals of Honor. But critics have characterized the recent awards as the product of "affirmative action." Of course, the number of individual decorations is not a fair or full measure of a unit's valor; it is impossible to quantify heroism. But in order to answer critics, some statistical comparisons are required, to put the upgraded awards in the proper context.

Relative to its size, the 442d won more Distinguished Service Crosses (the second highest award for valor) than any other unit in the Army won during World War II—and this was long before the era of "political correctness." *The Army Almanac* has no record of any infantry division, with three times as many men as the 442d, winning three times as many Distinguished Service Crosses. But before the review, the 100th/442d's ratio—1:47—of Medals of Honor to Distinguished Service

The achievements of Japanese Americans in the Army were not always so neglected. Throughout the 1940s and 1950s, their exploits were well publicized. In 1951, there was even a Hollywood movie that climaxed with the rescue of the Lost Battalion—*Go for Broke!* starring Van Johnson, produced by Dore Schary, and featuring Lane Nakano, a former member

---

Crosses was *more than five times lower* than the ratio among American troops in general throughout World War II, which was about 1:9. In some highly decorated divisions, the ratio was 1:3 or higher. By this measure alone, the 442d could have expected to have won five to twelve Medals of Honor (and correspondingly fewer Distinguished Service Crosses) during the war, instead of the single Medal actually awarded—especially since the unusually high number of Distinguished Service Crosses and Distinguished Unit Citations awarded already indicated that the overall heroism of the 442d was not in question.

More than three decades ago, the historian Roger Daniels—who cannot be characterized as anything but sympathetic to Japanese Americans—criticized even the general claim that the 442d was the "most decorated" unit in the Army:

> Without in any way detracting from the superb performance of these men in combat, the historian must insist that this particular accolade is largely meaningless. The whole system of decorations in the United States Army is farcical, and within larger units they are usually awarded on a quota basis. (*Concentration Camps USA*, pp. 152–153.)

If there had been a quota for the 442d, it might have been necessary because, as Gen. George C. Marshall told John P. Sutherland after the war, "There was great opposition to decorations being given these men because of jealousy from other outfits." Marshall said he "forced this on Gen. Clark. 'If you don't decorate them, I will,' but it was better for Clark to do it." But the disproportion between the other awards received and the sole Congressional Medal of Honor suggests the 442d actually did not benefit from any preferential treatment.

In any event, the point is not that medals should be awarded according to quotas, but that glaring statistical anomalies require attention. The upgrade for Japanese Americans "was not a case of apology or redress," according to James McNaughton, Kristen Edwards, and Jay Price, the historians who conducted the research on the upgrades for the Army (but were not involved in the final decision to make the awards):

> The army agreed simply to reexamine previous cases using its established procedures and criteria. Neither the legislation nor the funding agency called for any broad study of historical discrimination. Any new awards would be based solely upon 'incontestable proof of the performance of the service' . . . the soldiers under consideration had already been decorated for valor; in some cases they had been recommended originally for the Medal of Honor. The army was merely giving their cases a second look. (" 'Incontestable Proof Will Be Exacted': Historians, Asian Americans, and the Medal of Honor," *The Public Historian*, 24, 4 Fall 2002, pp. 11–33.)

of the 442d, and dozens of other Japanese American veterans. Although some of the period characterizations and pidgin dialogue make it almost embarrassing to watch today, the film is remarkably true to events and even acknowledges the injustice of the "relocation camps," which were not widely discussed at the time. Prejudice against Japanese Americans at home and the heroism of *Nisei* soldiers abroad were the mainspring of the plot of *Bad Day at Black Rock*, also produced by Schary, which earned Spencer Tracy an Academy Award nomination in 1955. And as late as 1959, James Michener celebrated Japanese American soldiers in his best-selling novel *Hawaii*, in which the rescue of the Lost Battalion by the fictional "222" is a minor subplot.

But after the general shift in public attitudes against the Vietnam War and toward the concerns of ethnic minorities, attention to Japanese Americans in the 1960s and later began to focus more on victims in the camps than on heroes in the military. As the valor of the 100th/442d began to fade from memory, the history of the "evacuation" and "relocation" became the subject of popular books and movies throughout the next three decades.[5]

Jeanne Wakatsuki's *Farewell to Manzanar*, a memoir of her childhood spent in a "relocation camp," became a staple of recommended reading lists during the 1970s and was made into a television movie in 1976 that was nominated for two Emmy Awards. And as recently as the mid-nineties, David Guterson's novel *Snow Falling on Cedars*, which centered on the "evacuation" and its aftermath in the Pacific Northwest, became a best seller; in 1999 it was made into a feature movie.

Meanwhile, the story of the 100th/442d has been found mostly in books from small presses and houses specializing in military history. The veterans themselves have produced unit histories, collections of oral histories, and memoirs. But most of them have been self-published, with limited exposure. And except for Civil War history, military history in general remains mostly a backwater of academic history.

For all these reasons, it is hardly surprising that the exploits of the 100th Battalion and 442d Regimental Combat Team are far less familiar today than the plight of Japanese Americans in the camps.

★ ★ ★

One of the peculiarities of our post-9/11 culture is that many contemporary conservatives have rushed to defend a sweeping policy undertaken six decades ago by New Dealers, while modern-day liberals have tended to attack it as an aberration of the New Deal rather than an example of its paternalism. But as the sociologist William Petersen argued more than three decades ago, the "evacuation" of Japanese Americans could only have taken place because liberal and progressive supporters of Roosevelt, including the American Civil Liberties Union, failed to oppose it and in some cases actually supported it—under the influence of the Communist Party, which had shifted overnight, after the collapse of the Stalin-Hitler pact, from isolationism to superpatriotism. As Petersen puts it,

Most commentators accuse California reactionaries—"certain agricultural and business groups," in the euphemism that [Morton] Grodzins uses—and the military, or specifically General DeWitt. But the Army acted under civilian directives, and the reactionaries (however much noise they made) were in control of nothing.

This was an era dominated by liberals, among whom one counts virtually every civilian significantly involved in the action against Japanese Americans. . . . And at each stage the officials were encouraged to go forward not only by the anti-Japanese clamor but—more significantly— by the absence of meaningful resistance to incarceration of thousands of Americans whose only crime was their race.[6]

The constitutional scholar Peter Irons, who played a key role in the redress movement and represented Fred Korematsu, Gordon Hirabayashi, and Min Yasui in their petitions to vacate their original convictions after Pearl Harbor, is particularly blunt about the failings of the ACLU:

The ACLU lawyers initially attacked the constitutionality of the presidential order that authorized the internment [sic] program. My research in the files of the ACLU and its West Coast branches disclosed that personal and partisan loyalty to Franklin D. Roosevelt, who signed this order, led the ACLU's national board to bar such a constitutional challenge in subsequent appeals.[7]

The socialist leader Norman Thomas was virtually alone among liberals and progressives in calling attention to what he called "a horrible indictment of our democracy":

It is the "liberals" who lead in demanding more aggressive action from the administration against those whose opinions they do not like. . . . In an experience of nearly three decades I have never found it harder to arouse the American public on any important issue than on this. Men and women who know nothing of the facts . . . hotly deny that there are concentration camps. Apparently that is a term to be used only if the guards speak German and carry a whip as well as a rifle.[8]

Writing for the majority in *Korematsu*, Justice Hugo Black deemed it "unjustifiable to call them concentration camps, with all the ugly connotations that term implies," even though the term was widely used at the time. But in his dissent, Justice Owen Roberts pointedly referred to the "so-called Relocation Centers, a euphemism for concentration camps."[9] Today, conservatives who disparage "political correctness" tend to deride the use of the term "concentration camps" in describing the "assembly centers" and "relocation centers," just as liberals tend to insist on the term and condemn what they regard as Orwellian doublespeak.

What's lost in this debate is the full impact of the words used at the time. The real point is not that words such as "exclusion," "evacuation," "assembly," "relocation," "registration," "segregation," and "distribution" are euphemisms (although they were then and still are today, which is why they are in quotes throughout this book) but that most of them are military jargon. Wounded soldiers, for example, are "evacuated" to field hospitals; troops "assemble" on parade grounds for review; young men "register" for the draft.* The terminology suggests how the whole process, from Executive Order 9066 on, authorized by the commander in chief and carried out by the Army, was actually a military campaign—though on American soil, directed against Japanese Americans who were mostly U.S. citizens.

This campaign, often referred to as "internment" today, actually had almost nothing to do with the commonly understood and accepted power

---

*The term "exclusion" had its own distinct and ignoble lineage. The Chinese Exclusion Act of 1882 was the first U.S. law aimed at limiting immigration of "Orientals." The term continued to have nativist and racist connotations for the next sixty years. A leading nativist group was the Japanese Exclusion League of California, founded in 1920. When the War Department drew up "exclusionary zones" on the West Coast after Pearl Harbor, it was using politically freighted terminology whose meaning was impossible to misconstrue.

of sovereign states to treat foreign nationals and resident aliens differently from their own citizens, particularly during wartime.[10] Many who now condemn the treatment of Japanese Americans during World War II mistakenly believe that substituting "internment" for the very different stages of "exclusion," "evacuation," "assembly," and "relocation" will expose the truth behind the euphemisms and military jargon. But this linguistic maneuver actually plays right into the hands of those who want to argue "in defense of internment." For if Executive Order 9066 had truly authorized the internment of Japanese Americans, then it would have been a perfectly routine, uncontroversial policy.

But it did not, and it was not. The roundup of Japanese Americans that Roosevelt delegated through the War Department to DeWitt went far beyond the accepted powers of the government to intern foreign nationals and resident aliens. Most of the 110,000 "evacuees" from the West Coast could not have been interned under any interpretation of U.S. law—because they were citizens. And the *Issei* (the first generation of immigrants) among the larger group—who were not citizens, even though they had lived in the United States for decades—had been barred from citizenship by law for decades. In this key respect they differed from German and Italian immigrants, who faced no such barriers to citizenship.

Even the late chief justice William Rehnquist, who in 1998 offered a partial defense of the "exclusion" and "evacuation" of Japanese American resident aliens,* had to concede:

> Both federal and state restrictions on the rights of Japanese emigrants had prevented their assimilation into the Caucasian population and had intensified their insularity and solidarity. . . . There is a considerable irony [sic], of course, in relying on previously existing laws discriminating against Japanese immigrants to conclude that still further disabilities should be imposed upon them because they had not been assimilated into the Caucasian majority.[11]

In other words, even to a contemporary apologist, there was "irony" in the government's using the fact that Japanese American resident aliens were

---

*Rehnquist did *not* defend the "exclusion" and "evacuation" of Japanese American citizens.

not citizens as a reason for "excluding" and "evacuating" them—when they had been forbidden by statute and treaty from becoming citizens in the first place. This was using bad law to justify worse.

Executive Order 9066 actually gave the government even greater authority than martial law. Unlike internment, which had well-defined legal procedures and boundaries, and unlike martial law, which was meant to apply universally rather than single out Japanese Americans, the "exclusion," "evacuation," "assembly," "relocation," "registration," "segregation," and "distribution" of Japanese Americans were almost completely open-ended and unconstrained. Policies and procedures were invented month-to-month and enforced with an arbitrariness that should have alarmed, and should continue to alarm, both civil libertarians on the left and opponents of big government on the right.

And it bears emphasizing that martial law in Hawaii did not require the islands' 137,000 Japanese Americans—unlike their "evacuated" counterparts on the mainland—to give up their jobs, businesses, homes, and personal property and move to camps, hundreds of miles away, in remote and desolate areas.

★　★　★

Our understanding of the past is further confused by the contemporary debate over "racial profiling." To law enforcement agencies, a profile is a hypothesis about a criminal's background, behavior, and physical characteristics (one of which might be race), based on actual crime-scene evidence and intended to help narrow down the universe of suspects.

Whatever else can be said of the "exclusion" and "evacuation" of Japanese Americans after Pearl Harbor, they did not involve "racial profiling." To begin with, race was not the most important factor—Chinese Americans, for example, were not discriminated against, because China was an ally, and Japan an enemy, of the United States.* Nevertheless, race was certainly one of the factors tipping the scales against Japanese Americans

---

*However, the term "race" was used much more loosely in the 1940s than in our times. Japanese were frequently referred to as a distinct "race." Still, all Asians apparently did look alike to Caucasian Americans—so much so that Chinese Americans wore buttons identifying themselves as "Chinese," and businesses in Chinatowns in metropolitan areas posted signs to the same effect.

on the West Coast, yet not against German Americans or Italian Americans on the West or East Coasts.

More important, the mass "exclusion" and "evacuation" did not involve any "profiling" at all. Rounding up 110,000 Japanese Americans, including women, children, and old people, was the opposite of "profiling." It far exceeded any reasonable threat assessment. Rather than enumerating and evaluating criteria of potential spies and saboteurs, Lieutenant General DeWitt simply assumed, and declared, that this disproportionate response was required because it was impossible to distinguish the "sheep from the goats." This is why he and the Western Defense Command opposed the "registration" and "loyalty questionnaire" a year after Pearl Harbor—because these proved the assumption wrong, and thus undermined the whole rationale for the "exclusion."

The FBI had actually undertaken systematic "profiling" (though it was not called that at the time) of Japanese foreign nationals and resident aliens before Pearl Harbor. The Bureau had identified Japanese language teachers, Shinto priests, martial arts instructors, *Issei* community leaders, employees of Japanese businesses and the Japanese government, and other representatives of Japan and Japanese culture in America. It had monitored resident aliens' bank accounts in Japan as well as Japanese-language newspapers and fraternal groups in the United States. As a result, it had extensive files on individuals and organizations that enabled the swift identification and internment (properly understood) of more than a thousand Japanese nationals and resident aliens immediately after Pearl Harbor.

For the past two decades, revisionist writers on the right have tried to argue that MAGIC intercepts, the top secret Japanese diplomatic cables decoded and decrypted by U.S. signals intelligence, were the basis of Executive Order 9066—that the alleged revelations about the network of potential saboteurs and spies among Japanese American resident aliens and citizens were convincing enough to make "the case for 'racial profiling' in World War II."[12] The revisionists' claim is that Roosevelt and the War Department had access to top secret information not available to the FBI—therefore the limited internment of Japanese nationals and resident aliens by the Justice Department was an inadequate response to the widespread threat revealed by the MAGIC intercepts. As Malkin puts it:

The three highest-ranking government officials who approved the decision to evacuate ethnic Japanese from the West Coast—President Roosevelt, Secretary of War Henry Stimson, and Assistant Secretary of War John McCloy—all had full access to MAGIC. McCloy later stated that he reviewed the MAGIC messages every day and night.

By contrast, none of the prominent government figures who opposed the evacuation knew about MAGIC. Not FBI Director J. Edgar Hoover. Not Attorney General Francis Biddle. Not Office of Naval Intelligence officer Kenneth Ringle. Not special State Department representative Curtis Munson.[13]

According to this line of argument, MAGIC confirmed the belief of those who were privy to it that "exclusion" and "evacuation" of all Japanese Americans, resident aliens and citizens alike, were the only appropriate response, for reasons of "military necessity."

But the revisionists are much too credulous about the secrecy surrounding MAGIC. Early in the war, Chief of Staff Gen. George C. Marshall was in a "state of despair . . . when top-secret documents were lost for days at the White House." "I took a call from one of my junior assistants," Marshall said. "He started talking about one of the Japanese messages we had intercepted and told me what interesting reading it was. He wasn't supposed to know anything about it. . . . I checked up on this and found that at one time over 500 people were reading messages we had intercepted from the Japanese. I learned that at the White House these messages were being passed back and forth. Everybody seemed to be reading them.

"I asked for an appointment with the president and made him promise to restrict these messages," Marshall recalled. "I called in high officials and told them that if they didn't stop this they would never see another message."[14]

In any event, there is no evidence, and no reason to believe, that General DeWitt had access to MAGIC when he "prescribed" the "military zones" and issued the specific orders of "exclusion" and "evacuation," which were at the discretion of the Western Defense Command, not the War Department. And there is no documentary evidence, and little reason to believe, that Secretary of War Stimson or Assistant Secretary McCloy regarded MAGIC as decisive factors supporting mass "exclusion" and "evacuation," especially since there is a wealth of documentary evidence showing exactly the opposite—that they opposed the policies until almost the very moment when President Roosevelt urged them, "Be as reasonable as you can,"[15] and then dumped the whole problem of formulating a policy back onto their laps.*

There is little dispute that Roosevelt took MAGIC seriously, but also little reason to believe that it made a significant difference in his decision to issue Executive Order 9066. The MAGIC revelations did not even lead him to indicate just *how* Executive Order 9066 was to be implemented. Claims of an extensive network of saboteurs and spies did not, by themselves, support the "military necessity" of a mass "exclusion" and "evacuation" of a whole population, including women, children, and old people. Such a response was disproportionate to the threat, even if it was genuine. And raw intelligence reports are not the end of the process but the beginning; their truth and utility must be evaluated just like any other input in the policy process. Presented with options ranging from a "lesser step such as the establishment of restricted areas around airplane plants and critical installations" all the way to "100 percent withdrawal" of Japanese Americans, the president explicitly did *not* instruct the War Department to carry out the latter policy, even though contemporary revisionists now argue that his knowledge of MAGIC required it.

As the late Chief Justice Rehnquist pointedly noted:

> Such information [from MAGIC] might well have justified exclusion of Nisei, as opposed to other citizens, from work in aircraft factories without strict security clearance, but it falls considerably short of justifying the dislodging of thousands [sic] of citizens from their homes on the basis of ancestry.[16]

---

*The revisionists argue there is no documentary evidence because of security restrictions intended at the time to prevent compromising the "sources and methods" behind MAGIC. But an entire Record Group (457) at the National Archives now consists of declassified intelligence documents, including well over a hundred thousand MAGIC messages, many of them declassified for more than twenty years, and the revisionists have not uncovered a single document showing that MAGIC played *any* role in the decisions of Roosevelt, Stimson, or McCloy regarding the "exclusion" and "evacuation" of Japanese Americans.

Malkin's arguments have been been painstakingly and devastatingly refuted by Eric Muller and Greg Robinson at http://www.isthatlegal.org/Muller_and_Robinson_on_Malkin.html#IDOI%201.

Instead of taking any direct action or even indicating any policy preference, Roosevelt framed Executive Order 9066 as simply a transfer of authority from the Justice Department to the War Department and then washed his hands of the entire matter—until the time came to end the "exclusion" two and a half years later, when all pretense of "military necessity" had long since disappeared. Then what was really important to him became clear, as he continued to insist on a rationale that had never had any connection to the defense of America: the "distribution" of Japanese Americans across the country, which was a matter of social policy, not "military necessity."

Roosevelt's underlying reason had been political, not military, all along, and the term "relocation"—which neither defenders nor opponents of Executive Order 9066 have focused on—accurately described his ultimate goal. Rather than being just a euphemism, the term was a chillingly appropriate expression of New Deal paternalism. Government could, and should, use its vast, coercive powers to force people to give up their jobs, businesses, homes, personal property, and communities, and "relocate" elsewhere—for their own good and for the good of the country.*

But regardless of the underlying political motive, the documentary record shows that fear of compromising "sources and methods" did *not* keep the War Department from sharing information derived from

---

*For a thorough critique of this paternalistic approach, see Edward Banfield's *Government Project*, a history and analysis of a New Deal rural cooperative established in 1938 that embodied many of the social-engineering ideas behind the "relocation."

Although liberals have tended to support the recent Supreme Court decision in *Kelo et al. v. City of New London et al.*, No. 04-108, argued February 22, 2005, decided June 23, 2005—which affirmed the sweeping power of "eminent domain," the right of government to take private property for whatever it deems public use—it should disturb not just defenders of private property on the right, but civil libertarians on the left. *Kelo* is a grim reminder that, in principle, anyone—not just minority groups—can be "relocated." In practice, of course, it is only the socially, economically, and politically vulnerable, like Japanese Americans in World War II, or inhabitants of urban areas today that are allegedly in need of "renewal" by expansive local governments in alliance with real-estate developers.

Liberal support for *Kelo* is less surprising when it is seen as consistent with paternalistic government claiming to act in the interest of urban minorities. In this regard, the excuse for exercising "eminent domain" today is little different from Eleanor Roosevelt's rationale for breaking up those "little German or Japanese or Scandinavian island[s]" after Pearl Harbor.

MAGIC with the Justice Department—or even from sharing, or at least indicating beyond doubt, the source of the information. One "summary" the FBI received from the War Department General Staff, Military Intelligence Division, on "Reorganization of Japanese Intelligence Service," for example, was a virtually word-for-word copy of the original MAGIC message. And since it openly referred to "the salient points of the directive sent to the Embassy in Washington"—and even to "an intelligence organ in the Embassy"—the "summary" clearly identified diplomatic cables as the source. According to a copy of a subsequent letter from the FBI to Assistant Secretary Adolph Berle, "it is further averred that reports on this material are to be sent to Japanese embassies." So Hoover knew the information came from diplomatic cables, even if he wasn't authorized to see MAGIC or even to know its name.

But since he knew not just what MAGIC revealed but also where it came from, there is no reason to believe that Hoover "could never fully appreciate just how reliable the information was," as Malkin puts it—or that the Justice Department's narrowly focused internment of Japanese nationals and residents missed any threats that Roosevelt and those privy to MAGIC knew about independently. The revisionists' argument about the role of MAGIC in the decision-making behind Executive Order 9066 and the "exclusion" and "evacuation" is thus nothing but an elaborate red herring resulting from selective review and citation of the primary source material.*

---

*Colonel C. H. Mason, memo for the Chief, Counter-Intelligence Branch, on "Reorganization of Japanese Intelligence Service in the United States," February 12, 1941, with letter of transmittal by Brig. Gen. Sherman Miles, Acting Chief of Staff, G-2, War Department General Staff, to J. Edgar Hoover, Federal Bureau of Investigation, February 18, 1941. In addition to the letter from the FBI to Berle on February 19, 1942, there is also a memo from P. E. Foxworth to Hoover on April 14, 1941, stating that "a voluminous report" that the Office of Naval Intelligence had on "the material which the Japanese are seeking in this country" was information "the FBI had already been furnished." Mason's memo, the cover memos, and the letters are in Archives II, RG 65.

Mason's memo virtually duplicates MAGIC message #44, cited by David Lowman in *MAGIC: The Untold Story of U.S. Intelligence and the Evacuation of Japanese Residents from the West Coast during WW II*, p. 122, as having a "wide-ranging nature and significance." (He even reproduced the memo three times in his book.) Lowman claimed that the original MAGIC material was "sanitized"—"paraphrased to prevent any possible comparisons with the original" in order to "avoid disclosing its true origin" (p. 62). But a side-by-side comparison of the material in the FBI files with

★ ★ ★

As a result, current defenders of Executive Order 9066 have little else to fall back on, except the rhetorical ploy of posing the policy question as one of "military necessity" versus civil liberties. And to them, the choice—particularly post-9/11—seems simple. "In war, desperate times sometimes call for disparate measures," Malkin writes. "But any inconvenience, no matter how bothersome or offensive, is preferable to being incinerated at your office desk by a flaming hijacked plane."[17]

Of course, one woman's "inconvenience" is another woman's loss of job, business, farm, home, personal property, and two and a half years of life. It is easy to minimize how "bothersome" or "offensive" a policy is when someone else—not you—suffers the effects. Besides, this way of framing the issue is nothing but a debased version of Pascal's famous, or infamous, wager. To choose between believing and not believing in God,

---

MAGIC message #44 shows only insignificant paraphrasing. And the source of the material—though it was of course not known as MAGIC to those who were not privy to it—was nevertheless obvious to anyone who wrote or read the words "sent to the Embassy in Washington" in the original War Department memo or "sent to Japanese embassies" in the FBI's letter to Berle.

In any event, despite Lowman's claim that MAGIC message #44 has a "wide-ranging nature and significance," in fact it reveals only the intentions of Japanese intelligence more than ten months before Pearl Harbor. It says nothing about what the Japanese actually achieved in the United States. It is clearly as much a wish list as it is a concrete plan of action.

In her book, Malkin, unlike Lowman, does not deny the strong similarity between what the FBI saw and the original MAGIC message #44. In fact, she contradicts Lowman by acknowledging that memos to and from various government agencies and departments "clearly derive, sometimes verbatim, from MAGIC." She even reproduces both Mason's memo and a later memo from Hoover as examples of how the "rigorous attention that military intelligence and FBI officials were paying to Japan's espionage operations and activities in the United States and elsewhere" was "all based on MAGIC" (pp. 209–210). But like Lowman, she believes that "those outside the MAGIC loop could never fully appreciate just how reliable the information was since they didn't know it came straight from high-ranking Japanese diplomats" (p. 41). The copy of Mason's memo in the FBI files and the letter to Berle show otherwise. Both the content and the source of MAGIC message #44, with its "wide-ranging nature and significance," were readily apparent even to those who were not privy to the original intelligence.

My thanks to Peter Wakamatsu, who drew may attention to these documents—particularly the cover memos, letters of transmittal, and other accompanying letters—and the significance of comparing them to the MAGIC intercepts.

the seventeenth-century mathematician and philosopher challenged us to consider the prospect of salvation on the one hand and eternal damnation on the other, and then urged us to wager in favor of belief. "Compare the two chances: if you win, you win everything; if you lose, you lose nothing. Don't hesitate, then. Make a bet that god exists."[18]

The problem with this kind of argument is that it can be used to justify anything, and it therefore justifies nothing. If it is a choice between requiring all airline passengers to wait in long lines and take off their shoes, or risk dying "by a flaming hijacked plane," who would choose the latter? But the same could be said of the choice between interrogating every passenger and examining every vehicle at every entrance to every bridge and tunnel across the United States, at every minute of every hour of every day, or risking death by truck bomb. (There were plans to blow up the Hudson River tunnels into Manhattan at the time of the 1993 bombing of the World Trade Center.) Or between inspecting every handbag and briefcase and bag of every passenger on every train of the Washington Metro or New York subway, at every minute of every hour of every day, or risking death by explosives concealed in backpacks. (The recent bombings in London proved the vulnerability of subways.) Or between frisking every passenger and checking every package on every bus on every route in every major city, at every minute of every hour of every day, or risking death by backpack bomb. (One of the London bombs destroyed a bus and killed thirteen passengers.)

The list could be extended indefinitely, which is the point: we do not and cannot assess threats in isolation, and in the abstract. Our response to a given danger, actual or potential, must always be weighed against other choices confronting us, and must always consider the constraints—military and nonmilitary—of manpower, money, and time. And homeland security is the *last* line of defense against an attack. Real security depends upon, among other things, timely and reliable intelligence from abroad about possible threats, a strong military that deters our enemies and defeats them if deterrence fails, carefully calibrated foreign policies that build alliances to help us fight the growth and export of terror, and rational immigration and naturalization policies that balance security with other concerns (such as economic and technological growth). All of these demand resources as well, entailing more, and more complicated, trade-offs.

We do not measure the true cost of our policies by the "inconvenience" that could result. The problem with most airport security measures now in place is not that they cause "inconvenience" (although they do), but that they do not reflect realistic threat assessments and sensible cost-benefit analyses. Every dollar and man-hour spent on making little old ladies and small children take off their shoes in airport lines is a dollar not spent on securing our bridges and tunnels, and especially our ports, which are far more vulnerable to terrorist attacks that could cripple or even destroy (with smuggled biochemical weapons or nuclear devices) entire metropolitan areas. We also have thousands of miles of lightly patrolled borders to the north and south. (A would-be bomber with a car full of explosives was arrested at the border crossing at Port Angeles, Washington, and later convicted of plotting to blow up Los Angeles International Airport.) We could mobilize entire Army divisions to interdict any illegal crossings in the wilderness or desert, but how would we pay for them? At just the relatively few official points of entry, inspecting every package and every passenger in every vehicle, sixty minutes an hour, twenty-four hours a day, would still consume enormous resources that could be devoted to other equally important, perhaps more important, security measures elsewhere.

To believe that the "requirements" of national defense and homeland security trump everything else is to surrender to what Attorney General Francis Biddle called the "mystic cliché" of "military necessity." But just saying something is "military necessity" does not, and cannot, make it so. There actually is no such thing as "military necessity." Even the fundamental "requirements" of manpower and matériel must be placed on the familiar scales weighing guns and butter. In wartime, people still have to work at nonmilitary jobs, pay their rent or mortgage, feed and clothe themselves and their families. It is surely true that without strong national defense and homeland security, there would be nothing left to defend. But the opposite is equally true—that without a strong, nonmilitary political and economic order, there would be nothing to support and sustain national defense and homeland security. All those tax dollars to pay for our protection have to come from somewhere—and there will never be enough money to guard against every possible threat, every minute of every day. We must always weigh trade-offs and make choices, and Pascal's wager tells us nothing about how to do so.

The "requirements" of national defense and homeland security are subject to policy judgment and the political process, just like any other government expenditures. No specific policy results from "military necessity." Whether at the tactical, operational, or strategic level, trade-offs are the only things that could actually be called "military necessity." Time and logistics, not to mention the demands for manpower and matériel elsewhere around the globe, make every military action contingent upon decisions—stretching all the way up the ladder of command and around the world—that weigh possibility, not necessity.

Far from being the consequence of "military necessity," the full-scale "evacuation" of Japanese Americans from the West Coast actually made very little military sense, as Gen. Mark Clark pointed out at the time, and as events revealed very quickly afterward. Quite apart from the affront to civil liberties and the human toll it exacted at home, it was a diversion of resources desperately needed to fight the war abroad. The "bothersome or offensive" costs were borne not just by the 110,000 Japanese Americans "evacuees" from the West Coast but by hundreds of thousands of American soldiers in Europe and the Pacific who had fewer supplies and reinforcements when they most needed them—because $80 million or more (more than $2.5 billion in current dollars, per capita GDP) had been squandered on the "relocation."

In fact, the "evacuation" made so little military sense that it can only be understood as the beginning stage of a sweeping social policy of "relocating" a politically vulnerable minority group from a part of the country where much more powerful forces, reaching all the way to the White House, regarded its members as unwelcome. The "evacuation" of Japanese Americans was not a "military necessity" but a social policy implemented and enforced by the military.*

---

*"The point that has bothered me, as an Army historian, has been the official justification of this Order [9066] on grounds of military necessity as determined by the responsible Army commanders," Stetson Conn wrote to James Rowe on October 3, 1955 (Archives II, RG 319). "The evidence I've seen, and the comments from participants I've received, do not support this contention." After drafting his essay on the "evacuation," which would appear in different form in *Guarding the United States and Its Outposts* and *Command Decisions*, Conn had solicited comments from the principal figures involved in the decision to "evacuate," including McCloy and DeWitt. The latter told Conn, who quoted the general's remarks in the same letter to Rowe, that Conn's "reconstruction of the events leading up to the President's signature of Executive Order 9066 on 19 February was accurate, to the best of his knowledge."

* * *

More than anything, the distorted view of Pearl Harbor and its consequences for Japanese Americans results from looking through the wrong end of the historical telescope, backward to World War II from the perspective of the civil rights movement and its aftermath. All of us in the early twenty-first century are so accustomed to the concepts and language of race, ethnicity, and rights that we unreflectively use them to frame earlier eras, when they had less or different significance.

Through the 1950s and 1960s, the civil rights movement followed a political strategy of challenging unjust laws and institutions by publicly identifying and voicing grievances, enlisting the media to publicize nonviolent demonstrations, lobbying for remedial federal legislation, and focusing the attention of an activist Supreme Court on violations of constitutional protections. This strategy achieved its successes because of the undeniable moral claim it made on the conscience of all Americans.

But as the ideal (no matter how illusory) of integration later gave way to separatism, as other minority groups copied the civil rights strategy, and as a post-civil-rights grievance culture became institutionalized in group preferences, the political arena became overcrowded, the moral claims of successive groups appeared weaker, and a backlash was almost inevitable.

Today, significant elements on the right are so upset by what they regard as "political correctness" that they regard complaints about the "exclusion" and "evacuation" of Japanese Americans as little more than an excuse advanced by yet another minority group to demand (and receive) redress. As a result, especially among revisionists on the nativist fringes of the right, the whole point of reexamining Pearl Harbor and its aftermath is to discredit the claims that Japanese Americans made before the Commission on Wartime Relocation and Internment of Civilians, established by Congress in 1980, which led to Ronald Reagan's signing of HR 442 in 1988.

At the time of the "evacuation," the Posse Comitatus Act (18 USC 1385) of 1878, a product of the Reconstruction era, had considerably more force in proscribing use of American military forces to "execute the laws" within the United States (except when expressly authorized by the Constitution or Congress, as in Public Law 503) than it does today. For the past quarter century, court cases and legislation involving the war on drugs and terrorism have reduced the force of the Posse Comitatus Act to mostly a procedural formality.

To these neonativists, truth and history are not the point. They want to downplay the real costs (monetary and human) of the "evacuation" and "relocation," muddy the waters by comparing them to "racial profiling," suggest (by analogy to post-9/11 security measures, by reproducing pictures of smiling children in "relocation camps," and by other rhetorical maneuvers) that Japanese Americans suffered little more than an "inconvenience, no matter how bothersome or offensive," invoke the alleged revelations of MAGIC as trumping every other consideration, and frame the issue as "military necessity" versus civil liberties, rather than analyzing the complex contingencies and trade-offs of wartime. These revisionist strategies are designed not to uncover the truth but to stake out a position in current debate over homeland security and racial, ethnic, and religious minorities.

On the left, critics of the treatment of Japanese Americans after Pearl Harbor are sometimes equally misled by their own contemporary agendas. In the post-civil-rights grievance culture, protest is often regarded as a sign of virtue. This has led to the celebration of some rather unlikely figures such as Japanese American draft resisters in the "relocation camps."

For example, the historian Roger Daniels—to whom students of Japanese Americans in particular and Asian Americans in general owe an enormous debt of gratitude—has argued that the "nature and scope" of what he calls the " 'loyal' Japanese American resistance" (i.e., those in the camps who supported the United States against Germany and Japan but resisted the draft) is "highly significant," because it "calls into question the stereotype of the Japanese American victim of oppression during World War II who met his fate with stoic resignation and only responded with superpatriotism." Daniels continues, "There are those who will find more heroism in resistance than in patient resignation."[19]

But "resistance" to the draft and "patient resignation" were not the only choices open to Japanese Americans in the camps. There was at least one other option: volunteering for the Army, a year before the draft even became an issue. Although Daniels's motives and scholarship are beyond reproach, by collapsing "stoic resignation" and "superpatriotism" into one category, he is blurring the crucial distinction between the overwhelming majority of Japanese Americans in the camps, who endured in "patient resignation," and the tiny minority of volunteers for the 442d, whose complex motives cannot be reduced to "superpatriotism."

It was not the draft resisters but these volunteers from the camps who truly defied the stereotype of "stoic resignation" by affirming their citizenship through their actions. In the face of the passive and active disapproval of many, if not most, of their parents and peers, these men (and a few women) consigned themselves to an even smaller minority than the draft resisters. There were eighty-five convicted draft resisters at Heart Mountain, for example, but only fifty-four volunteers for the Army—the third lowest number from all of the camps.

And whatever the philosophical merits of draft resistance are in the abstract, in World War II, a total war against ruthless fascist and imperialist powers, draft resisters resembled what economists call "free riders." Somewhat like turnstile jumpers who can ride subways for "free" because everyone else pays full fare, draft resisters could exercise their rights only because others were willing to die to defend them. Of course, unlike fare beating, dissent is a constitutional right in our democracy, even in wartime. But even if their motives were completely pure, the moral claim of all draft resisters in World War II—not just Japanese American resisters—was relatively weak. It would be very difficult to make the case that they were refusing to fight in the war against Nazi Germany and Imperial Japan because it was unjust, as protestors and draft resisters later argued the Vietnam War was. And the government's unjust treatment of Japanese Americans was not, in itself, sufficient reason to resist taking arms in a global war against fascist imperialism.

Eric L. Muller, at the University of North Carolina, has correctly, and wisely, cautioned:

> Those who resisted the draft were not all patriots. Neither were all of those who complied with it. They were, instead, imperfect human beings, and young ones at that, trying their best to deal with an impossible set of conditions not of their making. Neither group is honored by pretending that all were heroes or all were villains.[20]

But there is an important difference between the two groups. Those who resisted the draft risked a prison sentence. Those who complied with it—and especially those who volunteered for their Army—risked their lives.

★ ★ ★

No one seems comfortable acknowledging that the real "activists" in the camps were the soldiers of the 442d. Many on the left prefer victims or protestors. Many on the right regard Japanese Americans as just another "politically correct" minority group advancing a grievance.

But regardless of the strategies used by the redress movement in the 1980s during the Commission on Wartime Relocation and Internment of Civilians, Japanese Americans who served in World War II nearly four decades earlier were very far from what we would call "politically correct" today. Their actions did not follow from the familiar categories of race, ethnicity, and rights that both left and right use in viewing World War II from the post-civil-rights perspective, which conservatives reject and liberals embrace. Japanese Americans who volunteered in Hawaii after Pearl Harbor did not have a constitutional complaint, since they were not in "relocation camps." Japanese Americans who volunteered from the camps on the mainland may have had a grievance, but they did not pursue it, and instead acted as individuals, often against the will of the larger group. Far from embodying the "identity politics" (to use another contemporary term) of most mainland Japanese Americans, the volunteers from the camps were affirming a civic identity that transcended their race and ethnicity. Along with their counterparts from the islands, they were putting duties before rights and acting as American citizens first, not simply as Japanese Americans.

Understanding the significance of their actions requires abandoning the post-civil-rights perspective. Conservatives need to stop looking at individuals as merely grievance-pursuing representatives of the racial or ethnic groups to which they belong. Liberals need to stop looking at individuals as merely rights-bearing representatives of the racial or ethnic groups to which they belong. The right needs to acknowledge that racial, ethnic, religious, and nativist intolerance continues to be a real problem in America. The left needs to surrender its faith in "identity politics" and the grievance culture as the best way to combat it.

All of us need to stop judging and misusing history from a post-civil-rights perspective—and to stop regarding the political strategy of grievance, demonstrations, remedial legislation, and constitutional claims as the proper model for politics. The civil rights movement was one of the noblest struggles of twentieth-century America, but it does not necessarily correspond to realistic political action in the twenty-first century. Post-

9/11, the changing American population, with the pressure and promise of immigration, includes new people and poses new problems that have nothing to do with the terrible legacy of slavery. The fight for civil rights continues, as it should and as it must, but it is only one of many battles the United States faces in this century and beyond.

What is needed is an understanding of politics that returns moral and political agency to individuals—not as representatives of groups, or bearers of rights, or pursuers of grievances, but as members of a civil society and political order founded on free choice. Liberals who deride "necessity" when it comes to the military often embrace essentialism when it comes to individuals, whom they tend to see as little more than the inevitable product of predetermined group identities. But racial and ethnic identities are created through politics as much as, or more than, they are discovered.[21] "Necessity" is a metaphysical fantasy, whether applied to the military or to "identity politics."

The most important lesson we can learn from the 100th Battalion and 442d Regimental Combat Team is that individuals and their free choices matter—they are the driving force of history. This sounds like an embarrassing truism, but in telling the story of Japanese Americans after Pearl Harbor, writers and historians have been blinded by abstractions and missed the significance of what specific people actually did in making concrete choices. Liberals have been too busy defending Roosevelt and the New Deal, and conservatives too busy rationalizing "military necessity," to see the truth for what it is.

"Military necessity" never compelled anyone to do anything, or dictated any particular policy over another. Roosevelt freely made the decision to authorize the deliberately vague and open-ended Executive Order 9066. Secretary of War Stimson freely (and reluctantly) delegated policy-making power to DeWitt, who freely (even wildly) exercised it in collaboration with Assistant Secretary McCloy, who freely followed the political winds, managing the "evacuation" one day and championing the 442d the next.

At the same time, Japanese Americans from Hawaii and the mainland who served in the Army advanced the cause of all Japanese Americans during the difficult days of World War II—not by pursuing grievances, not by demonstrating, not through legislation, and not through the courts—but by freely assuming the heaviest burden of citizenship. Whether it was

George "Joe" Sakato on Hill 617, or Barney Hajiro on "Suicide Hill," or Saburo Tanamachi in Arlington Cemetery, they undertook as individuals "what others fear to attempt," as S. L. A. Marshall put it. "One man must go ahead so that a nation may live."[22]

As just Americans, not Japanese Americans, they risked their lives, and gave their lives, for their country in wartime—and in so doing helped make a better country for themselves and everyone else.

ACKNOWLEDGMENTS

This book could not have been written without the help of the following individuals and organizations:

The veterans of the 100th Battalion (Separate), 442d Regimental Combat Team, and 36th Division, and their families, who were all so generous with their archives and libraries, and especially their time. My special thanks to Shig and Yo Doi, Barney and Esther Hajiro, Marty Higgins, Ed Ichiyama, Susumu and Minnie Ito, Louise Kashino, Young Oak Kim, George and Mary Oiye, George "Joe" Sakato, Al and Connie Takahashi, Ted and Fuku Tsukiyama, Ed Yamasaki, and Jim Yamashita.

Stanley Akita, Evelyn Honda, Amanda Stevens, and the staff and members of Club 100/100th Infantry Battalion Veterans, Honolulu, HI.

Eichi Oki, Claire Mitani, and the staff and members of the 442nd Veterans Club/ 442nd RCT Archives and Learning Center, Honolulu, HI.

Al Dietrick, Walter Holcomb, and the 36th Division Association, San Antonio, TX.

Maurice Cäel, Paul Charpin, Bernard Henry, Pierre Moulin, Pierre Poix, and the citizens of Belmont, Biffontaine, Bruyères, Épinal, Gérardmer, Granges, and La Houssière, France.

Sandra Tanamachi, Willie Tanamachi, Kikuko Nakao Tanamachi, Ikuko Nakao Kitayama, Judy Tanamachi, Diana Parr, and Laura Corkill.

Christine Sato-Yamazaki, Executive Director/President, Diane Tanaka, Associate Director, and the volunteers, staff, and board of directors of the Go For Broke Educational Foundation (GFBEF), Torrance, CA.

Irene Y. Hirano, President/CEO, Japanese American National Museum (JANM), and Toshiko McCallum, Marie Masumoto, Cris Paschild, and the staff of the Manabi & Sumi Hirasaki National Resource Center at JANM, Los Angeles, CA.

The staff of the National Archives and Records Administration at College Park, MD (Archives II), and Washington, D.C. (Archives I).

The staff of the National Personnel Records Center, Military Personnel Records (NPRC-MPR), St. Louis, MO.

The staff of the U.S. Army Military History Institute (USAMHI), Carlisle, PA.

Colonel John P. Mikula and the staff of the U.S. Army Human Resources Command, Alexandria, VA.

James C. McNaughton, Command Historian, U.S. Army, Pacific (USARPAC), Fort Shafter, HI.

Joseph Frechette and the staff of the U.S. Army Center of Military History (CMH), Fort Lesley J. McNair, D.C.

Jane Yates, Director, The Citadel Archives & Museum, The Citadel, SC.

Lila Fourhman-Shaull, Assistant Librarian, and the staff of the York County Heritage Trust Library & Archives, York, PA.

Marshall Adams and Thomas Burdett, Curator, Military History Collection, C. L. Sonnichsen Special Collections Department, The University of Texas at El Paso Library.

Bob Vietrogoski and the staff of the Archives and Special Collections of the A. C. Long Health Sciences Library, Columbia University Medical Center.

Dennis Vetock, Assistant Director, Collection Management, U.S. Army Heritage and Education Center, Carlisle Barracks; Martin Andresen, Friends of the Omar N. Bradley Foundation; John Blumenson.

Anneleisa Behrens, Helen Dalrymple, and Michaela McNichol of the Library of Congress.

Noriko Sanefuji, National Museum of American History, the Smithsonian Institution.

James Cartwright, University Archivist, the University of Hawaii at Manoa.

Terry Shima, Vice President, David W. Buto, Secretary and Webmaster, and Marcia Mau of the Japanese American Veterans Association (JAVA), Washington, D.C.

George J. Hirasaki, President, Houston chapter, Japanese American Citizens League, TX.

Frank Bridgewater, editor, *Honolulu Star-Bulletin*.

Fred Hirayama, Yuki Minaga, Andrew Ono, Peter Wakamatsu, and Maj. Nathan Watanabe.

Roger Daniels, the Charles Phelps Taft Professor Emeritus of History, the University of Cincinnati.

Jack Tchen, Director, Laura Chen-Schultz, Deputy Director, and the faculty, staff, and students of the Asian/Pacific/American Studies Program & Institute, New York University.

The staff of the Law Library, New York University.

Martha Bayles, Anne Easley, Mariko Gordon, Aiko Herzig, Stacey Hirose, Judy Soo Hoo, Lucia Hwong-Gordon, Ken Iwagaki, David Louie, Dale Minami, Judy Niizawa, Lewis Opler, Carole Sullivan, Catherine Tanaka, Lucian K. Truscott IV, Linda Upton, and Fumie Yamamoto for helpful suggestions and references.

Christopher DeMuth, the American Enterprise Institute, Washington, D.C.

Frank Fukuyama, the Paul H. Nitze School of Advanced International Studies, Johns Hopkins University.

Marc Plattner, the National Endowment for Democracy, Washington, D.C.

Claire Lerognon, for her assistance in translation and her personal knowledge of the Vosges.

Savannah Ashour, my stepdaughter, for her precise translation and meticulous editorial suggestions.

Suzanne Gluck, Joni Evans, Emily Nurkin, Erin Malone, Georgia Cool, and the staff of the William Morris Agency.

William Shinker, Lauren Marino, Brendan Cahill, Erin Moore, Jessica Sindler, and the staff of Gotham Books and Dutton.

Peter Skerry, Boston College, to whom I owe an immeasurable intellectual debt.

Linda Phillips Ashour, my wife, for her indispensable assistance in translation, her invaluable editorial judgment, and her unfailing support.

SOURCES

Research for *Just Americans* drew on the following sources, in groups I have organized in roughly descending order, according to generally accepted canons of historical evidence regarding time, place, and bias.

I. U.S. GOVERNMENT ARCHIVES RELATING TO THE MILITARY

A. Primary source material on the 100th Battalion (Separate), the 442nd Regimental Combat Team, the 141st Infantry Regiment, the 36th Division, VI Corps, the Fifth Army, the Seventh Army, the Sixth Army Group, the Wartime Civilian Control Administration, and the Western Defense Command and Fourth Army in World War II can be found at the U.S. National Archives and Records Administration in College Park, MD (known as Archives II), which organizes its holdings by record group (RG), corresponding to the organization that created or maintained them:

RG 80: Department of the Navy, 1798–1947
RG 107: Office of the Secretary of War
RG 165: War Department General and Special Staffs
RG 208: Office of War Information
RG 319: Army Staff
RG 331: Allied Operational and Occupation Headquarters, World War II
RG 338: U.S. Army Operational, Tactical, and Support Organizations (World War II and thereafter)
RG 389: Office of the Provost Marshal General, 1941–
RG 407: Adjutant General's Office, 1917–
RG 499: U.S. Army Defense Commands (World War II)

B. Photographs of the Army in World War II are found in the Still Picture holdings of Archives II:

RG 111-SC: Office of the Chief Signal Officer, 1860–1982
RG 208-AA: Office of War Information, 1926–1951

C. Photographs of the presidency are found in Archives II, RG 79-AR: National Park Service, 1785–1990, Series AR, "White House Photographs Taken by Abbie Rowe."

D. Army personnel files, including unit morning reports, are at the National Personnel Records Center, Military Personnel Records (NPRC-MPR), in St. Louis.

E. Primary source material on the military can also be found at the U.S. Army Military History Institute (USAMHI) at Carlisle, PA, which the Army describes as "the primary facility where researchers study Army history."

F. For the original medal recommendations, supporting affidavits, approvals or disapprovals, citations, and general orders for the medals awarded in the Vosges Mountains, as well as the reconstructed recommendations and citations for the upgraded Congressional Medals of Honor, I filed a Freedom of Information Act (FIOA) request with the Department of the Army, which was granted on January 9, 2004. (Department of the Army, U.S. Army Human Resources Command, Alexandria, VA.)

II. U.S. GOVERNMENT ARCHIVES
RELATING TO JAPANESE AMERICANS

A. Primary source material on the "exclusion," "evacuation," "assembly," "relocation," "registration," "distribution," and "dissemination" can be found at the U.S. National Archives and Records Administration in Washington, D.C. (known as Archives I), RG 210: War Relocation Authority. The material is also available on microfilm at the University of Hawaii, Manoa, and other libraries across the nation. Copies of some of the material can be found in the Harry S. Truman Library and Museum in Independence, MO, administered by the National Archives and Records Administration.

In 1946, the War Relocation Authority (WRA), which had become part of the Interior Department in 1944, published an eleven-volume history of the Authority's activities during and after World War II. The Final Report of the Director of the WRA was issued independently as *WRA: A Story of Human Conservation*, and one of the other volumes, *Impounded People: Japanese-Americans in the Relocation Centers*, was also edited and published independently. The last volume in the series, *People in Motion: The Postwar Adjustment of the Evacuated Japanese Americans*, was published by the successor to the War Relocation Authority. All volumes can be found in RG 210, as well as in many libraries across the nation. In 1975, AMS Press published photo-offset reproductions of the original volumes.

War Agency Liquidation Unit (formerly War Relocation Authority), United
    States Department of the Interior. *People in Motion: The Postwar Adjustment of*

the Evacuated Japanese Americans. Washington, D.C.: U.S. Government Printing Office, undated (but internal references and the change in the Authority's name suggest a publication date of 1947).

War Relocation Authority. *Administrative Highlights of the WRA Program.* Vol. 1. Washington, D.C.: U.S. Government Printing Office, 1946.

———. *Community Government in War Relocation Centers.* Vol. 2. Washington, D.C.: U.S. Government Printing Office, 1946.

———. *The Evacuated People: A Quantitative Description.* Vol. 3. Washington, D.C.: U.S. Government Printing Office, 1946.

———. *Legal and Constitutional Phases of the WRA Program.* Vol. 4. Washington, D.C.: U.S. Government Printing Office, 1946.

———. *The Relocation Program,* U.S. Government Printing Office. Vol. 7. Washington, D.C.: U.S Government Printing Office, 1946.

———. *Token Shipment: The Story of America's War Refugee Shelter.* Vol. 8. Washington, D.C.: U.S. Government Printing Office, 1946.

———. *Wartime Exile: The Exclusion of the Japanese Americans from the West Coast.* Vol. 10. Washington, D.C.: U.S. Government Printing Office, 1946.

———. *The Wartime Handling of Evacuee Property.* Vol. 11. Washington, D.C.: U.S. Government Printing Office, 1946.

———. *WRA: A Story of Human Conservation,* Final Report of the Director of the War Relocation Authority, transmitted July 10, 1946.

Spicer, Edward H.; Hansen, Asael T.; Luomala, Katherine; Opler, Marvin K. *Impounded People: Japanese-Americans in the Relocation Centers,* University of Arizona Press, 1969.

B. Additional primary source material on the "exclusion," "evacuation," "assembly," "relocation," "registration," "distribution," and "dissemination" can be found at Archives II:

RG 65: Federal Bureau of Investigation
RG 107: Office of the Secretary of War
RG 394: U.S. Army Continental Commands, 1920–1942
RG 499: U.S. Army Defense Commands (World War II)

Lieutenant General John L. DeWitt's final report on the "evacuation" can be found in RG 499 and elsewhere in Archives II:

Headquarters Western Defense Command and Fourth Army. *Final Report: Japanese Evacuation from the West Coast,* 1942.

C. The Commission on Wartime Relocation and Internment of Citizens (CWRIC) was established on July 31, 1980, and ended its work on June 30, 1983. Its holdings are found in RG 220.18.25: Commission on Wartime Relocation and

Internment of Civilians. The material is also available on microfilm at the Law Library of New York University and at other libraries across the nation. The summary report of the Commission was published separately in 1982:

Commission on Wartime Relocation and Internment of Civilians. *Personal Justice Denied.* Washington, D.C.: U.S. Government Printing Office, December 1982.

III. OTHER ARCHIVES

A. Papers of Army generals involved with the 100th/442d can be found at the following:

Gen. Mark W. Clark papers, 1916–1984, The Citadel Archives & Museum, Charleston, SC.

Gen. John E. Dahlquist papers, U.S. Army Military History Institute (USAMHI), Carlisle, PA.

Gen. Jacob L. Devers, York County Heritage Trust Library/Archives, York, PA.

Gen. George C. Marshall, the Marshall Foundation Library and Archives, Lexington, VA.

S. L. A. Marshall Papers, 1900–1979, MS 186, C. L. Sonnichsen Special Collections Department, University of Texas at El Paso Library, El Paso, TX.

B. The *Hanashi* Oral History Video Archive of the Go For Broke Educational Foundation (GFBEF), in Torrance, CA, includes more than six hundred (as of the time of this writing) videotaped interviews of veterans of the 100th Battalion (Separate), the 442d Regimental Combat Team, the Military Intelligence Service, and the 1399th Engineers Construction Battalion, as well as Japanese American veterans who served individually in nonsegregated units. The Foundation also maintains a library and resource center and provides material for teachers and students.

C. The Manabi & Sumi Hirasaki National Resource Center of the Japanese American National Museum (JANM) in Los Angeles maintains an archive of primary documents, personal papers, artifacts, diaries, photographs, oral histories, and other material on the history of Japanese Americans.

D. After the war, the 100th Battalion and the 442d Regimental Combat Team established veterans' organizations, which maintain archives of primary source materials and artifacts as well as oral histories and secondary source material:

Club 100, Honolulu, HI

The 442d Veterans Club, Honolulu, HI

E. The Archives & Manuscripts Department of Hamilton Library, at the University of Hawaii, Manoa, maintains extensive archives in the Hawaii War Records Depository (HWRD) and the Japanese American Veterans Collection (JAVC).

F. The Houston chapter of the Japanese American Citizens League (JACL) maintains an archive of government documents, letters, press clippings, and other material relating to the "Jap Road" controversies in Texas.

G. The Archives and Special Collections of the A. C. Long Health Sciences Library, Columbia University Medical Center, is the repository of the papers of Marvin Kauffman Opler, 1914–1981. Opler was a WRA Community Analyst at Tule Lake and one of the coauthors of *Impounded People*.

IV. U.S. GOVERNMENT PUBLICATIONS AND OFFICIAL HISTORIES

The U.S. Army Center of Military History (CMH), Fort Lesley J. McNair, Washington, D.C., records the official history of the Army and advises the Army Staff. Its seventy-nine volumes on the U.S. Army in World War II (the "green books") are the authoritative histories of the campaigns, operations, organizations, and administration of the war.

Bedessem, Edward N. *Central Europe*, The U.S. Army Campaigns of World War II. United States Army, Center of Military History Publication 72-36.

Clarke, Jeffrey J. *Southern France*. The U.S. Army Campaigns of World War II. United States Army, Center of Military History Publication 72-31.

Clarke, Jeffrey J., and Smith, Robert Ross. *Riviera to the Rhine*, United States Army in World War II: The European Theater of Operations. Washington, D.C.: United States Army, Center of Military History, U.S. Government Printing Office, 1993.

Conn, Stetson. "The Decision to Evacuate the Japanese from the Pacific Coast," in *Command Decisions*, edited with introductory essay by Kent Roberts Greenfield. Washington, D.C.: United States Army, Center of Military History, U.S. Government Printing Office, 2000.

Conn, Stetson; Engelman, Rose C.; Fairchild, Byron. *Guarding the United States and Its Outposts*, United States Army in World War II: The Western Hemisphere. Washington, D.C.: Office of the Chief of Military History, Department of the Army, U.S. Government Printing Office, 1964.

Kirkpatrick, Charles E. *Defense of the Americas*. The U.S. Army Campaigns of World War II. United States Army, Center of Military History Publication 72-1.

Lee, Ulysses. *The Employment of Negro Troops*, United States Army in World War II: Special Studies. Washington, D.C.: United States Army, Center of Military History, U.S. Government Printing Office, 1966.

Leighton, Richard M. "Overlord versus the Mediterranean at the Cairo-Tehran Conferences," in Kent Roberts Greenfield, ed., *Command Decisions*, Washington, D.C.: Center of Military History, 2000.

Mahon, John K., and Danysh, Romana, *Infantry*, Part I: Regular Army. Army Lineage Series. Washington, D.C.: United States Army, Office of the Chief of Military History, 1972.

Marshall, Gen. George C. *Biennial Reports of the Chief of Staff of the United States Army to the Secretary of War, 1 July 1939–30 June 1945.* Washington, D.C.: Center of Military History, 1996.

Matloff, Maurice. "The ANVIL Decision: Crossroads of Strategy," in *Command Decisions*, edited with introductory essay by Kent Roberts Greenfield. Washington, D.C.: United States Army, Center of Military History, U.S. Government Printing Office, 2000.

———. "The 90-Division Gamble," in *Command Decisions*, edited with introductory essay by Kent Roberts Greenfield. Washington, D.C.: United States Army, Center of Military History, U.S. Government Printing Office, 2000.

Order of Battle of the United States Army, World War II. European Theater of Operations: Divisions. Paris, France: Office of the Theater Historian, United States Army, December 1945. Reproduced by United States Army, Center of Military History.

Williams, Mary. *Chronology: 1941–1945*, United States Army in World War II: Special Studies. Washington, D.C.: United States Army, Center of Military History, U.S. Government Printing Office, 1994.

Other government publications include the following:

442nd Combat Team. Information-Education Section, MTOUSA (Mediterranean Theater of Operations, U.S. Army). Undated (probably late 1945).

The Army Almanac: A Book of Facts Concerning the Army of the United States, Department of the Army, U.S. Government Printing Office, 1950. Commercial edition, revised and updated, Stackpole, 1959.

Army Life, War Department Pamphlet 21-13, 10 August 1944, U.S. Government Printing Office.

Bureau of the Census, U.S. Department of Commerce. *Historical Statistics of the United States, Colonial Times to 1970,* Parts 1 and 2. Washington, D.C.: U.S. Government Printing Office, 1975.

Burton, Jeffrey F.; Farrell, Mary M.; Lord, Florence B.; Lord, Richard W. *Confinement and Ethnicity: An Overview of World War II Japanese American Relocation Sites.* Seattle: University of Washington Press, 2000. (Originally released in 1999 as Publications in Anthropology 74 of the Western Archeological and Conservation Center, National Park Service, U.S. Department of the Interior. The Department of the Interior continues to maintain the sites of the "relocation camps.")

Director of Selective Service (Lewis B. Hershey). *Selective Service in Peacetime.* First Report of the Director of Selective Service, 1940–41. Washington, D.C.: U.S. Government Printing Office, 1942.

————. *Selective Service in Wartime.* Second Report of the Director of Selective Service, 1941–1942. Washington, D.C.: U.S. Government Printing Office, 1943.

————. *Selective Service as the Tide of War Turns.* The 3rd Report of the Director of Selective Service, 1943–1944. Washington, D.C.: U.S. Government Printing Office, 1945.

————. *Selective Service and Victory.* The 4th Report of the Director of Selective Service, 1944–1945, with a supplement for 1946–1947. Washington, D.C.: U.S. Government Printing Office, 1948.

FM 21-00, *Soldier's Handbook,* War Department Basic Field Manual, July 23, 1941, including C1, May 4, 1942. Washington, D.C.: U.S. Government Printing Office.

FM 23-7, *U.S. Carbine Caliber .30 M1 and M1A1,* War Department Basic Field Manual, 23 April 1944. Washington, D.C.: U.S. Government Printing Office.

FM 100-5, *Operations,* War Department Field Manual: Field Service Regulations, 15 June 1944. Washington, D.C.: U.S. Government Printing Office, 1944.

FM 100-15, *Larger Units,* War Department: Field Service Regulations, June 29, 1942. Washington, D.C.: U.S. Government Printing Office, 1942.

FM 101-5, *The Staff and Combat Orders,* War Department: Staff Officers' Field Manual. Washington, D.C.: Superintendent of Documents, 1940.

FM 101-10, *Organization, Technical, and Logistical Data,* War Department: Staff Officers' Field Manual, June 15, 1941. Washington, D.C.: U.S. Government Printing Office, 1941.

Historical Section, Army Ground Forces. *Ground Forces in the War Army: A Statistical Table.* Study No. 3, 1946.

Selective Service System, *Special Groups,* Special Monograph No. 10, Vol. I: Text, 1953.

Sustaining Health & Performance in the Cold: Environmental Medicine Guidelines for Cold-Weather Operations, Technical Note No. 92-2, U.S. Army Research Institute of Environmental Medicine (July 1992).

The War Reports of General of the Army George C. Marshall, Chief of Staff; General of the Army H. H. Arnold, Commanding General, Army Air Forces; Fleet Admiral Ernest J. King, Commander-in-Chief, United States Fleet and Chief of Naval Operations. Philadelphia and New York: J. B. Lippincott, 1947.

War Relocation Authority. *What We're Fighting For: Statements by United States Servicemen about Americans of Japanese Descent.* Department of the Interior, Washington, D.C., undated (probably late 1944).

V. AUTHOR'S INTERVIEWS (IN PERSON AND BY TELEPHONE) AND CORRESPONDENCE (MAIL AND E-MAIL) FOR *JUST AMERICANS*

A. 100th/442d veterans

George Aki
Stanley Akita
Mickey Akiyama
Ken Akune
Gungi Asahina
Tets Asato
Al Binotti
Shig Doi
Kiyoshi Fujimoto
Barney Hajiro
Katsumi Hikedo
Ed Ichiyama
Susumu Ito
Young Oak Kim

Christopher Keegan
Sadaichi Kubota
Yuki Minaga
Henry Nakada
Ray Nosaka
Ron Oba
Ted Ohira
George and Mary Oiye
Tokuji Ono
Ken Otagaki
Lawson Sakai
George "Joe" Sakato
Matsuji "Mutt" Sakumoto
Don Seki

Takashi Senzaki
Frankie Seto
Goro Sumida
Al Takahashi
Willie Tanamachi
Bill Thompson
Martin Tohara
Rudy Tokiwa
Tadd Tokuda
Isamu "Mike" Tsuji
Ted Tsukiyama
Ed Yamasaki
Jim Yamashita

B. 36th Division veterans

Ed Guy
Bill Hawkins
Marty Higgins

Harry Huberth
Ted Rodriguez
Jack Wilson

C. Other veterans

Shoichi Asahina
Rusty Kimura
Carl Miyagashima

Bacon Sakatani
Lou Weiss

D. French citizens

Maurice Cäel
Paul Charpin
Bernard Henry
Pierre Moulin

E. Japanese American civilians

Yo Doi
Sachiye Ito Itaya
Ikuko Nakao Kitayama
Louise Kashino

Sandra Tanamachi Nakata
Kikuko Nakao Tanamachi
Fuku Tsukiyama

VI. AUTOBIOGRAPHIES, INTERVIEWS, MEMOIRS, ORAL HISTORIES, PAPERS, AND SPEECHES

Biddle, Francis. *In Brief Authority*. Garden City, NY: Doubleday, 1962.

Bruyere, Walter III. Oral history. Interviewed by G. Kurt Piehler and Elise Krotiuk; transcript by Rebecca Karcher, Sean Harvey, Walter Bruyere III, and Sandra Stewart Holyoak. Rutgers Oral History Archives of World War II, November 7, 1997.

Charpin, Paul. "The Battle of Bruyères." Speech at the Bruyères town hall on the fifty-second anniversary of the town's liberation, October 1996. Translated by Savannah Ashour.

Churchill, Winston S. *Triumph and Tragedy*, The Second World War, Volume VI. Boston: Houghton Mifflin, 1985.

Clark, Gen. Mark W. *Calculated Risk*. New York: Harper & Brothers, 1950.

Douglass, Frederick. *Life and Times of Frederick Douglass: His Early Life as a Slave, His Escape from Bondage, and His Complete History to the Present Time*, electronic edition. Chapel Hill: University of North Carolina, 1999.

Eisenhower, Dwight David. *The Papers of Dwight David Eisenhower*, The War Years: IV and V. Baltimore: The Johns Hopkins Press, 1970.

Eisenhower, Milton S. *The President Is Calling*. Garden City, NY: Doubleday, 1974.

Hanley, James M. *A Matter of Honor: A Mémoire*. New York: Vantage Press, 1995.

Hillerman, Tony. *Seldom Disappointed: A Memoir*. New York: Perennial, 2002.

Hirasaki, Manabi, with Hirahara, Naomi. *A Taste for Strawberries: The Independent Journey of Nisei Farmer Manabi Hirasaki*. Los Angeles: Japanese American National Museum, 2003.

Inouye, Daniel K., with Lawrence Elliott. *Journey to Washington*. Englewood Cliffs, NJ: Prentice-Hall, 1967.

Marshall, George C. Interview with Dr. Sidney T. Matthews, Dr. Howard M. Smyth, Maj. Roy Lemson, and Maj. David Hamilton, July 25, 1949, The Pentagon, Room 2E844. George C. Marshall Foundation Library and Archives.

———. Interview with John P. Sutherland, March 29, 1954, Pinehurst, NC, and April 6, 1955, Leesburg, VA. George C. Marshall Foundation Library and Archives. Published as " 'The Story Gen. Marshall Told Me': Hitherto Unpublished Views on Fateful Decisions of World War II," *U.S. News & World Report* 47 (November 2, 1959), pp. 50–56.

Marshall, S. L. A., *Bringing Up the Rear: A Memoir*, edited by Cate Marshall. San Rafael, CA: Presidio Press, 1979.

Masaoka, Mike, with Hosokawa, Bill. *They Call Me Moses Masaoka: An American Saga*. New York: William Morrow, 1987.

Mauldin, Bill. *Back Home*. New York: William Sloane Associates, 1947.

———. *The Brass Ring*. New York: W. W. Norton, 1971.

———. *Up Front*. New York: Henry Holt, 1945.

The Men of I Company, 442nd Regimental Combat Team. *And Then There Were Eight*. Honolulu, Hawaii: Item Chapter, 442nd Veterans Club, 2003.

Myer, Dillon S. *Uprooted Americans: The Japanese Americans and the War Relocation Authority During World War II.* Tucson: University of Arizona Press, 1971.

O'Donnell, Patrick K. *Beyond Valor: World War II's Rangers and Airborne Veterans Reveal the Heart of Combat.* New York: Touchstone, 2001.

Patton, Gen. George S. *War as I Knew It.* Boston: Houghton Mifflin, 1995.

Rosario, Carina A. del, editor. *A Different Battle: Stories of Asian Pacific Veterans.* Seattle: Wing Luke Asian Museum, 1999.

Safire, William, editor. *Lend Me Your Ears: Great Speeches in History,* updated and expanded edition. New York: W. W. Norton, 1992.

Stilwell, Gen. Joseph W. *The Stilwell Papers,* edited by Theodore White. New York: William Sloane Associates, 1948.

Stimson, Henry L., and Bundy, McGeorge. *On Active Service in Peace and War.* New York: Harper & Brothers, 1947, 1948.

Tateishi, John. *And Justice for All: An Oral History of the Japanese American Detention Camps.* Seattle: University of Washington Press, 1999.

Truscott, Lt. Gen. L. K., Jr. *Command Missions: A Personal Story.* New York: E. P. Dutton, 1954.

———. *The Twilight of the U.S. Cavalry: Life in the Old Army,* 1917–1942. Lawrence, KS: University Press of Kansas, 1989.

Wakamatsu, Jack K. *Silent Warriors: A Memoir of America's 442nd Regimental Combat Team.* New York: Vantage Press, 1995.

Wilson, Jack. *Living on the Edge.* Privately published, 2005.

VII. MILITARY HISTORIES, UNIT HISTORIES, AND BIOGRAPHIES

Americans of Japanese Ancestry World War II Memorial Alliance. *Echoes of Silence: The Untold Stories of the Nisei Soldiers Who Served in World War II.* CD-ROM, 2004.

———. Memorial Dedication, February 19, 2000.

Blumenson, Martin. *Mark Clark: The Last of the Great World War II Commanders.* New York: Congdon & Weed, 1984.

Bonn, Keith E. *When the Odds Were Even: The Vosges Mountains Campaign, October 1944–January 1945.* Novato, CA: Presidio, 1994.

Chang, Thelma. *"I Can Never Forget": Men of the 100th/442nd.* Honolulu: Sigi Productions, 1991.

Crost, Lyn. *Honor by Fire: Japanese Americans at War in Europe and the Pacific.* Novato, CA: Presidio, 1994.

Dupuy, Trevor N.; Bongard, David L.; Anderson, Richard C. *Hitler's Last Gamble: The Battle of the Bulge, December 1944–January 1945.* New York: HarperCollins, 1994.

Duus, Masayo Umezawa. *Unlikely Liberators: The Men of the 100th and 442nd.* Honolulu: University of Hawaii Press, 1987.

Ellis, John. *Brute Force: Allied Strategy and Tactics in the Second World War.* New York: Viking, 1990.

———. *The Sharp End: The Fighting Man in World War II*. New York: Charles Scribner's Sons, 1980.

Go For Broke: 1943–1993. Fiftieth anniversary commemorative booklet.

Grossman, Lt. Col. Dave. *On Killing: The Psychological Cost of Learning to Kill in War and Society*. Boston: Little, Brown, 1996.

Halloran, Richard. *Sparky: Warrior, Peacemaker, Poet, Patriot*. Honolulu: Watermark, 2002.

Historical Album Committee of the 522 Field Artillery Battalion of the 442 Regimental Combat Team. *Fire for Effect: A Unit History of the 522 Field Artillery Battalion*. Honolulu: Fisher Printing Company, 1998.

Ichinokuchi, Tad, with Aiso, Daniel. *John Aiso and the M.I.S.: Japanese-American Soldiers in the Military Intelligence Service, World War II*. Los Angeles: MIS Club of Southern California, 1988.

Ito, Susumu, and Oiye, George. *Charlie Battery, A Legend: 522 FABN, 1943–1945*, Roberts Press, 2003, reprinted for the Japanese American National Museum (Los Angeles) from the original 1991 edition.

Kanazawa, Tooru Joe. *Close Support: A History of the Cannon Company of the 442d Regimental Combat Team*. Cannon Company, 442 RCT, 1993.

Kashiwa, Genro, and Yamamoto, Jun. *Collection of Memoirs, Company L, 3rd Battalion, 442nd Regimental Combat Team*. Honolulu: Privately published.

Keegan, John. *The Face of Battle*. New York: Penguin, 1978.

———. *The Second World War*. New York: Penguin, 1990.

Liddell Hart, B. H. *History of the Second World War*. New York: Perigee, 1971.

———. *Strategy*, second revised edition. New York: Signet, 1974.

Markey Michael A. *Jake: The General from West York Avenue*. York, PA: Historical Society of York County, 1998.

Marshall, S. L. A. *Men Against Fire: The Problem of Battle Command in Future War*. Gloucester, MA: Peter Smith, 1978, reprint of 1947 edition.

Matsuo, Dorothy. *Boyhood to War: History and Anecdotes of the 442nd Regimental Combat Team*. Honolulu: Mutual Publishing, 1992.

———. *Silent Valor: The Story of the 442nd Medics*. Honolulu: Honolulu Chapter of the 442nd Medics, 2002.

Moulin, Pierre. *U.S. Samuraïs in Bruyères*. Luxembourg: rapidpress, 1993.

Murphy, Thomas D. *Ambassadors in Arms: The Story of Hawaii's 100th Battalion*. Honolulu: University of Hawaii Press, 1954.

Oba, Ronald. *The Men of Company F*. Privately published, 1993.

The 141st Infantry Regiment Association. *Five Years, Five Countries, Five Campaigns . . . with the 141st Infantry Regiment*. Edited by Clifford H. Peek Jr., layout by Alfred H. Ellis, map work by George D. Harney, illustrations by John E. Pretsch, Munich, Germany, 1945. Reproduced by the Texas Military Forces Museum, 1998.

Schrijvers, Peter. *The Crash of Ruin: American Combat Soldiers in Europe during World War II*. New York: New York University Press, 1998.

Shirey, Orville C. *Americans: The Story of the 442nd Combat Team*. Washington, D.C.: Infantry Journal Press, 1946.

Sons & Daughters of the 100th Infantry Battalion. *Remembrances: 100th Infantry Battalion 50th Anniversary Celebration, 1942–1992*, revised edition. Honolulu, 1997.

Steidl, Franz. *Lost Battalions: Going for Broke in the Vosges, Autumn 1944*. Novato, CA: Presidio, 2000.

Stouffer, Samuel A.; Suchman, Edward A.; DeVinney, Leland C.; Star, Shirley A.; Williams, Robin M., Jr. *The American Soldier: Adjustment During Army Life*. Vol. 1. New York: John Wiley, 1965.

———. *The American Soldier: Combat and Its Aftermath*. Vol. 2. New York: John Wiley, 1965.

Tanaka, Chester. *Go For Broke: A Pictorial History of the Japanese American 100th Infantry Battalion and the 442nd Regimental Combat Team*. Novato, CA: Presidio, 1997.

The 36th Division Association. *A Pictorial History of the 36th Division*, compiled by the 36th Division Pictorial History Team, Austin, Texas, 1945. Reproduced by the Texas Military Forces Museum, 2000.

Tsukano, John. *Bridge of Love*. Honolulu: Hawaii Hosts, 1985.

Vezina, Meredith. "Defending the Border: The Cavalry at Camp Lockett," *The Journal of San Diego History*, 39, 1–2 (Winter–Spring 1993).

Weigley, Russell F. *Eisenhower's Lieutenants: The Campaigns of France and Germany 1944–1945*. Bloomington, IN: Indiana University Press, 1981.

VIII. OTHER SECONDARY SOURCES

Banfield, Edward C. *Government Project*. Glencoe, IL: The Free Press, 1951.

Biddle, Francis. *Democracy and Racial Minorities*. New York: Institute for Religious Studies, 1943.

Bosworth, Allan R. *America's Concentration Camps*. New York: W. W. Norton, 1967.

Cohen, Eliot A. *Citizens and Soldiers: The Dilemmas of Military Service*. Ithaca, NY: Cornell University Press, 1985.

Daniels, Roger. *American Racism: Exploration of the Nature of Prejudice*. Englewood Cliffs, NJ: Prentice-Hall, 1970.

———. *Asian America: Chinese and Japanese in the United States Since 1850*. Seattle: University of Washington Press, 1988.

———. *Concentration Camps USA: Japanese Americans and World War II*. New York: Holt, Rinehart and Winston, 1971.

———. *The Decision to Relocate the Japanese Americans*. Philadelphia: J. B. Lippincott, 1975.

———. *The Politics of Prejudice: The Anti-Japanese Movement in California and the Struggle for Japanese Exclusion*. Berkeley: University of California Press, 1962.

———. *Prisoners Without Trial: Japanese Americans in World War II*. New York: Hill and Wang, 1993.

Fischer, David Hackett. *Historians' Fallacies: Toward a Logic of Historical Thought*. New York: Harper Perennial, 1970.

Fuchs, Lawrence H. *Hawaii Pono: A Social History*. New York: Harcourt, Brace & World, 1961.

Girdner, Audrie, and Loftis, Anne. *The Great Betrayal: The Evacuation of the Japanese Americans During World War II*. New York: Macmillan, 1969.

Grodzins, Morton. *Americans Betrayed*. Chicago: University of Chicago Press, 1949.

Herzig, John A. "Japanese Americans and MAGIC," *Amerasia Journal*, 11, 2 (Fall/Winter 1984), pp. 47–65.

Higham, John. *Send These to Me: Immigrants in Urban America*, revised edition. Baltimore: Johns Hopkins University Press, 1984.

Huntington, Samuel P. *The Soldier and the State: The Theory and Politics of Civil-Military Relations*. Cambridge, MA: The Belknap Press of Harvard University Press, 1957.

Irons, Peter. *Justice at War: The Story of the Japanese American Internment Cases*. Berkeley: University of California Press, 1993.

Janowitz, Morris. *Military Conflict: Essays in the Institutional Analysis of War and Peace*. Beverly Hills, CA: Sage, 1975.

———. *The Reconstruction of Patriotism: Education for Civic Consciousness*. Chicago: University of Chicago Press, 1983.

Leighton, Alexander H. *The Governing of Men: General Principles and Recommendations Based on Experience at a Japanese Relocation Camp*. Princeton: Princeton University Press, 1968.

McNaughton, James C.; Edwards, Kristen E.; Price, Jay M. " 'Incontestable Proof Will Be Exacted': Historians, Asian Americans, and the Medal of Honor," *The Public Historian*, 24, 4 (Fall 2002), pp. 11–33.

Miller, Merle. *Plain Speaking: An Oral Biography of Harry S. Truman*. New York: Tess Press, 2004, reprint of Berkley edition, 1974.

Mullar, Eric L. "An Arab American Internment?" from the *Pacific Citizen*, reprinted in *The Days After*, essays written in the aftermath of September 11, 2001, University of Chicago Press, http://www.press.uchicago.edu/News/911muller.html.

———. *Free to Die for Their Country: The Story of the Japanese American Draft Resisters in World War II*. Chicago: University of Chicago Press, 2001.

———. "Inference or Impact? Racial Profiling and the Internment's True Legacy," University of North Carolina–Chapel Hill, School of Law, Public Law and Legal theory Research Paper No. 03–6.

———. "To Resist or to Comply: A Human Dilemma," *Nichi Bei Times*, May 2, 2002.

Novick, Peter. *The Holocaust in American Life*. Boston: Houghton Mifflin, 1999.

Odo, Franklin. *No Sword to Bury: Japanese Americans in Hawai'i during World War II*. Philadelphia: Temple University Press, 2004.

Park, Robert E., and Miller, Herbert A. *Old World Traits Transplanted*. Chicago: Society for Social Research, University of Chicago, 1925.

Petersen, William. *Japanese Americans: Oppression and Success*. New York: Random House, 1971.

Pickus, Noah. *True Faith and Allegiance: Immigration and American Civic Nationalism*. Princeton: Princeton University Press, 2005.

Rehnquist, William H. *All the Laws but One: Civil Liberties in Wartime*. New York: Vintage, 2000.

Robinson, Greg. *By Order of the President: FDR and the Internment of Japanese Americans*. Cambridge, MA: Harvard University Press, 2001.

Rostow, Eugene V. "The Japanese American Cases—A Disaster," *Yale Law Journal*, 54 (1945).

Skerry, Peter. *Mexican Americans: The Ambivalent Minority*. New York: The Free Press, 1993.

Smith, Page. *Democracy on Trial: The Japanese American Evacuation and Relocation in World War II*. New York: Simon & Schuster, 1995.

tenBroek, Jacobus; Barnhart, Edward N.; Matson, Floyd W. *Prejudice, War and the Constitution: Causes and Consequences of the Evacuation of the Japanese Americans in World War II*. Berkeley: University of California Press, 1970.

Thomas, Dorothy S., and Nishimoto, Richard. *The Spoilage: Japanese-American Evacuation and Resettlement During World War II*. Berkeley: University of California Press, 1969.

Walls, Thomas K. *The Japanese Texans*. San Antonio: University of Texas Institute of Texan Cultures at San Antonio, 1987.

Weglyn, Michi. *Years of Infamy: The Untold Story of America's Concentration Camps*. New York: Morrow, 1976.

IX. VIDEOS

The 442nd: Duty, Honor & Loyalty, documentary, Video Rights Corp.

442 for the Future: An American Story, documentary, Pacific Film Currents.

Beyond Barbed Wire, documentary, written and directed by Steve Rosen, Sunwood Entertainment, 1997.

The Color of Honor, documentary, Vox.

Go for Broke!, Madacy Music Group, Inc., feature film, produced by Dore Schary, written and directed by Robert Pirosh, 1951.

Honor Bound: A Personal Journey, documentary, Flower Village Films.

Looking Like the Enemy, documentary, Japanese American National Museum.

The Nisei Legacy: Sharing the Promise of America, documentary, Japanese American National Museum.

Nisei Soldier: Standard Bearer for an Exiled People, documentary, Vox.

The Silent Glory, documentary, Zed Merrill & Associates.

A Tradition of Honor, documentary, written by David Yoneshige, directed by Craig Yahata, Go For Broke Educational Foundation, 2002.

Yankee Samurai: The Little Iron Men, documentary, MPI Home Video.

WWII Memorial Dedication Ceremony, February 19, 2000, documentary, Americans of Japanese Ancestry WWII Memorial Alliance.

WWII 100th Battalion: TV News Coverage, 6/24/2002–7/4/2002, compilation, Dateline Media, Inc.

IX. FICTION

Guterson, David. *Snow Falling on Cedars*. New York: Vintage, 1995.

Michener, James. *Hawaii*. New York: Ballantine Books, 1982.

Shirota, Jon. *Lucky Come Hawaii*. Honolulu: Bess Press, 1988. Originally published by Bantam in 1965, this is a novel about Japanese Americans just before, during, and just after the attack on Pearl Harbor. Much of the dialogue is in pidgin, which the author spoke growing up.

Yates, Richard. "The B.A.R. Man," in *Eleven Kinds of Loneliness*. New York: Delta, 1982.

X. REVISIONIST HISTORIES

The allegations and "revelations" in these works must be regarded with considerable skepticism.

Baker, Lillian. *American and Japanese Relocation in World War II;* [sic] *Fact, Fiction & Fallacy*. Medford, OR: Webb Research Group Publishers, 1996.

———. *Dishonoring America: The Collective Guilt of American Japanese*. Medford, OR: Webb Research Group, 1988.

Lowman, David D. *Magic: The Untold Story of U.S. Intelligence and the Evacuation of Japanese Residents from the West Coast During WWII*. Athena Press, 2001.

Malkin, Michelle. *In Defense of Internment: The Case for "Racial Profiling" in World War II and the War on Terror*. Washington, D.C.: Regnery, 2004.

Robar, Keith. *Intelligence, Internment & Relocation: Roosevelt's Executive Order 9066: How Top Secret "MAGIC" Intelligence Led to Evacuation*. Seattle: Kikar Publications, 2000.

NOTES

EPIGRAPHS

1. Harold Ickes, in *Lend Me Your Ears: Great Speeches in History*.
2. Barack Obama, Knox College, http://www.knox.edu/x9803.xml.

PROLOGUE:
JAP ROAD

1. "Talk to Japanese American Citizens League" July 1, 1972, Gen. Mark W. Clark papers, The Citadel Archives & Museum, box 338.
2. My interview with Sandra Tanamachi. See also: *Beaumont Enterprise*, December 2, 3, and 16, 2003, and January 11 and 17, July 3, 15, 18, 20, 21, and 28, and August 3, 2004.
3. HB No. 1756, passed by the House on May 22, 1991; the House concurred in Senate amendments to HB No. 1756 on May 26, 1991, Houston JACL archive.
4. 99th Congress, 2d Session, H. Con. Res. 290, July 24, 1986, Houston JACL archive.
5. Esther Wu, "Slur in Road Name Challenged," *Dallas Morning News*, July 14, 2004, Houston JACL archive.
6. *Riviera to the Rhine*, by Jeffrey J. Clarke and Robert Ross Smith, is the final volume in the Army's official series of operational histories of World War II, published nearly a half century after the war ended. According to the Foreword by Brig. Gen. Harold Nelson, Chief of Military History, it "examines the least known of the major units in the European theater, Gen. Jacob L. Devers' 6th Army Group," to which the 442d was attached in France.
7. October 21, 1963, signed by Governor John Connally. Houston JACL archive.
8. Quoted by Gen. Mark W. Clark, "Statement to the Commission on Wartime Relocation and Internment of Citizens," July 14, 1981, Gen. Mark W. Clark papers, The Citadel Archives & Museum, box 31, folder 2.
9. Selective Service System, *Special Groups*, Special Monograph No. 10, Vol. l: Text, p. 141.
10. General Mark W. Clark papers.
11. Dillon S. Myer, Director, "Nisei in Armed Forces," War Relocation Authority

Administrative Notice No. 322, October 29, 1945. This is the total "who served with the Army of the United States between July 1, 1940 and June 30, 1945." U.S. National Archives and Records Administration II (hereafter, Archives II), Record Group (hereafter, RG) 389.

12. General Mark W. Clark papers.

13. My interviews with Barney Hajiro, Louise Kashino, and George "Joe" Sakato. See "Remarks by the President at Ceremony Honoring Asian American Medal of Honor Recipients, The White House," Office of the Press Secretary, June 21, 2000; "22 Medals of Honor Awarded to Asian-Pacific Americans," Center of Military History, 21 June 2000; "Becoming Part of Legend, History: America at Last Honors 22 Asian-American Heroes with the Nation's Highest Award for Valor in Combat," *Honolulu Star-Bulletin*, June 21, 2000; "21 Asian American World War II Vets to Get Medal of Honor," U.S. Department of Defense, American Force Press Service, May 19, 2000; "21 Asian-Americans Receive Medal of Honor," *The New York Times*, May 14, 2000. There was an initial disparity in the number of Medals of Honors because one of them, for T/5 James K. Okubo, required congressional waiver of the statutory time limit on making the award.

14. James C. McNaughton, Kristen E. Edwards, and Jay M. Price, "'Incontestable Proof Will Be Exacted': Historians, Asian Americans, and the Medal of Honor," *The Public Historian*, 24, 4 (Fall 2002), pp. 11–33.

15. Roger Daniels, *Asian America: Chinese and Japanese in the United States Since 1850*, p. 225.

16. Daniel K. Inouye, *Journey to Washington*, p. 224.

17. A ceremony I attended during *"Nisei* Week" in Los Angeles, August 3–5, 2001.

18. Remarks at funeral ceremonies for Japanese Americans, Arlington National Cemetery, June 4, 1948. Jacob L. Devers papers, York County Heritage Trust Library & Archives, box 48.

CHAPTER 1:
ONE PUKA PUKA

1. Bill Mauldin, *Back Home*, pp. 164, 166.

2. This account is based on my interview with Young Oak Kim, his oral history at the Japanese American National Museum (hereafter, JANM), and his oral history for the *Hanashi* project of the Go For Broke Educational Foundation (hereafter, *Hanashi*). For details concerning Jerome, Rohwer, and the other "relocation centers," see Jeffrey F. Burton, Mary M. Farrell, Florence B. Lord, and Richard W. Lord, *Confinement and Ethnicity: An Overview of World War II Japanese American Relocation Sites*. See also, *WRA: A Story of Human Conservation*, as well as *Administrative Highlights of the WRA Program, Community Government in War Relocation Centers, The Evacuated People: A Quantitative Description, Impounded People: Japanese-Americans in the Relocation Centers, Legal*

and Constitutional Phases of the WRA Program, People in Motion: The Postwar Adjustment of the Evacuated Japanese Americans, The Relocation Program, Token Shipment: The Story of America's War Refugee Shelter, Wartime Exile: The Exclusion of the Japanese Americans from the West Coast, and *The Wartime Handling of Evacuee Property.*

3. *WRA: A Story of Human Conservation,* p. 102.
4. Kim, JANM oral history.
5. *Community Government in War Relocation Centers,* pp. 4, 6.
6. *WRA: A Story of Human Conservation,* pp. 25 ff.
7. *Federal Register,* 7, 38 (February 25, 1942), p. 1407.
8. Lt. Gen. John L. DeWitt, Headquarters Western Defense Command and Fourth Army, *Final Report: Japanese Evacuation from the West Coast, 1942,* p. 9.
9. Quoted in Martin Blumenson, *Mark Clark: The Last of the Great World War II Commanders,* p. 55.
10. Mark Clark in Stetson Conn papers, quoted in Roger Daniels, *Concentration Camps USA: Japanese Americans and World War II,* pp. 65–67.
11. William H. Rehnquist, *All the Laws but One: Civil Liberties in Wartime,* p. 209.
12. Stetson Conn, "The Decision to Evacuate the Japanese from the Pacific Coast," p. 138. See also Conn, *Guarding the United States and Its Outposts,* p. 147.
13. Francis Biddle, memo to Henry Stimson, February 12, 1942, Archives II, RG 107.
14. Quoted by Peter Irons, *Justice at War,* pp. 49–50. Lt. Col. Karl Bendetsen, memo to Maj. Gen. Allen W. Gullion, Provost Marshal General, February 4, 1942, Archives II, RG 389.
15. Henry Stimson, diary entry, February 10, 1942, Commission on Wartime Relocation and Internment of Citizens (hereafter, CWRIC) 19649 (the internal locator number for holdings).
16. According to John J. McCloy. Phone call from Lt. Col. Karl Bendetsen to McCloy, February 11, 1942, Archives II, RG 499. A draft of the options presented to the president, dated February 11, 1942, can be found in Archives II, RG 107.
17. Stimson, memo to Lt. Gen. John L. DeWitt, February 20, 1942, Archives II, RG 107.
18. Quoted by Stetson Conn, "The Decision to Evacuate the Japanese from the Pacific Coast," p. 132. Lt. Gen. John L. DeWitt, telephone conversation with Maj. Gen. Allen Gullion, January 24, 1942, Archives II, RG 499.
19. Quotes in this section are from Gen. Joseph W. Stilwell, *The Stilwell Papers,* pp. 5, 7, 8.
20. DeWitt, *Final Report,* pp. 43–44.
21. Stetson Conn, Rose C. Engelman, and Byron Fairchild, *Guarding the United States and Its Outposts,* Chapter V, footnote 45, and Conn, "The Decision to Evacuate the Japanese from the Pacific Coast," p. 148.
22. My interviews with Kikuko Nakao Tanamachi and Ikuko Nakao Kitayama. See also Thomas K. Walls, *The Japanese Texans.*

23. *WRA: A Story of Human Conservation*, p. 145.

24. The author's grandparents and their children.

25. From a speech by Norman Mineta in San Jose, quoted in *The Washington Post*, June 12, 2005.

26. My interview with Sachi Itaya.

27. See Michi Weglyn, *Years of Infamy: The Untold Story of America's Concentration Camps*, pp. 84–86. For the story of a New Deal undertaking that suggests the roots of the "relocation" in the politics of the New Deal, see Edward C. Banfield, *Government Project*.

28. *Confinement and Ethnicity*, pp. 38–39.

29. DeWitt, *Final Report*, pp. 43–44.

30. Quoted in Richard Halloran, *Sparky: Warrior, Peacemaker, Poet, Patriot*, p. 38.

31. "Reorganization of 100th Infantry Battalion (Separate) (Japanese)," July 7, 1942, Archives II, RG 165.

32. See John K. Mahon and Romana Danysh, *Infantry*, Part I: Regular Army.

33. Kim, *Hanashi* oral history and JANM oral history.

34. Thomas D. Murphy, *Ambassadors in Arms*, p. 68.

35. See S. L. A. Marshall, *Men Against Fire: The Problem of Battle Command in Future War*, pp. 83–84. "Fire superiority is the thing and . . . movement is its physical and psychological derivative, along with all other acts of the initiative. . . . Fire is the key to mobility. To fire is to move. Weapons when correctly used will invariably bring decision." General George S. Patton Jr. put it even more succinctly around the same time in *War as I Knew It:* "Battles are won by fire and by movement."

There is no question that Marshall sometimes played fast and loose with the facts, even regarding his own life and career. But unless and until Marshall's critics address the real arguments of *Men Against Fire*, the sniping over the "ratio of fire" will remain, at best, an academic exercise rather than a substantive debate.

The chapter on the "ratio of fire" amounts to only thirteen and a half pages in a thirteen-chapter, 211-page book. Lost in the obsessively close focus on the "ratio of fire" is the larger argument Marshall was making. And, far from being controversial, at the time of this writing Marshall's concern with "future war" more than a half century ago seems uncannily prescient.

The overall point of *Men Against Fire*, which does not depend on any specific "ratio of fire," is the danger of believing that discipline, perfection in drills, mastery of marksmanship, and mechanical rule-following are the key components of soldiers' training. Just after the United States had ushered in the nuclear era at Hiroshima, Marshall was warning there was no such thing as a "push-button war." Likewise, he warned, thinking a nation could triumph over its enemies by relying on industrial power—epitomized by his hometown, Detroit—was an "illusion." And appeals to morale and patriotism were just bromides.

The point of *Men Against Fire* was to prepare soldiers for "future war" by trying to understand the war the U.S. had just fought in Europe and the Pacific.

Marshall was concerned about training soldiers for combat as it had actually been experienced by soldiers on the front line—sometimes chaotic, usually confusing, and always dangerous. He tried to analyze the horrific conditions of battle from the point of view of living, fearful, and sometimes heroic soldiers.

This was not the perspective of an armchair strategist or an academic historian. He was writing as a reporter, talking to men just after they had confronted the enemy, and death. He was interested in making clear the isolation they felt in battle, the lack of communication—not just between front line and rear but across the front to the flanks—that could paralyze troops, the frustration of trying to sort out relevant information under fire, the "tactical cohesion" that bound soldiers together in extreme circumstances, the barriers that exist to issuing clear commands in combat. Most of all, he was concerned with the difficulty of developing the "aggressive will" required to overcome the natural fear of death, and of killing, in war.

Even one of his most severe critics, Roger J. Spiller, the George C. Marshall Professor of Military History at the U.S. Army Command and General Staff College, recognized that S. L. A. Marshall's "real contribution" was his "insistence that modern warfare is best understood through the medium of those who actually do the fighting," which "stands as a challenge to the disembodied, mechanistic approaches that all too often are the mainstay of military theorists and historians alike."

Marshall's critics include Harold P. Leinbaugh and John D. Campbell, in *The Men of Company K: The Autobiography of a World War II Rifle Company* (1985); Roger J. Spiller, in "S. L. A. Marshall and the Ratio of Fire," *RUSI* [Royal United Services Institute for Defence Studies] *Journal* (Winter 1988), Fredric Smoler, in "The Secret of the Soldiers Who Didn't Shoot," *American Heritage* (March 1989); and John Whiteclay Chambers II, in "S. L. A. Marshall's *Men Against Fire:* New Evidence Regarding Fire Ratios," *Parameters* (Autumn 2003). Marshall's defenders include Gen. William E. DePuy, in "Insights," *Military Review* (July 1989), and Lt. Col. Dave Grossman, in *On Killing*, 1995. In *The Face of Battle*, John Keegan calls *Men Against Fire* a "masterpiece" (p. 71) but also warns that it "is a useful corrective but it is not a cure-all for the ills of military history" (p. 73).

36. Kim, *Hanashi* oral history.
37. Kim, JANM oral history.

CHAPTER 2:
KOTONK V. BUDDHAHEAD

1. S. L. A. Marshall, *Men Against Fire*, pp. 150, 153.
2. Barney Hajiro, *Hanashi* oral history, my interview with Hajiro.
3. Inouye, *Journey to Washington*, pp. 54–57.
4. John Keegan, *The Second World War*, p. 278.
5. My interview with Kikuko Tanamachi. See also Thomas K. Walls, *The Japanese Texans*.

6. Letter from Stimson to Maj. Gen. Lewis B. Hershey, Director, Selective Service System, June 17, 1942, Archives II, RG 107. See also Selective Service System, *Special Groups*, p. 118, referring to Selective Service Regulations, Section 622.43 (a), as amended September 14, 1942. Local Board Release No. 112, effective September 30, 1942.

7. See War Relocation Authority, "Army and Leave Clearance Registration at War Relocation Centers," Community Analysis Section, June 1943. Papers of Philleo Nash, Harry S. Truman Museum and Library.

8. Franklin D. Roosevelt, letter to Henry L. Stimson, February 1, 1943, Archives II, RG 107.

9. See the letters from John J. McCloy to Milton Eisenhower and to Brig. Gen. Donald Wilson, both on August 24, 1942; the transcript of a conversation between Col. Tate and Dillon Myer on September 4, 1942; the letter from Mc-Cloy to Eisenhower on October 15, 1942, which notes Elmer Davis's letter to Franklin D. Roosevelt on October 2, 1942; the memo from McCloy to Henry L. Stimson on October 15, 1942, which mentions Davis's "suggestion" to "permit Japanese-Americans to enter the armed forces" and attaches the original letter along with Eisenhower's letter from October 13, 1942; and the memo from Col. Moses W. Pettigrew to McCloy, November 17, 1942. All references to Archives II, RG 107.

10. *WRA: A Story of Human Conservation*, p. 103.

11. DeWitt, *Final Report*, p. 9.

12. *WRA: A Story of Human Conservation*, p. 103.

13. S. L. A. Marshall, *Bringing Up the Rear: A Memoir*, p. 53.

14. Marshall, *Bringing Up the Rear*, pp. 53–54.

15. DSS Form 304A, from War Relocation Authority, "Army and Leave Clearance Registration at War Relocation Centers," Archives II, RG 499.

16. Kim Muromoto, oral history in *A Different Battle: Stories of Asian Pacific American Veterans*, p. 78.

17. S. L. A. Marshall, "Report on the Tulelake Registration," unpublished manuscript, S. L. A. Marshall Papers, Special Collections Department, MS 186, University of Texas at El Paso Library. Hereafter, S. L. A. Marshall papers.

18. John J. McCloy, phone conversation with Lt. Gen. John L. DeWitt, January 18, 1943, Archives II, RG 499. My thanks to Peter Wakamatsu for pointing out this conversation to me.

19. DeWitt, letter to McCloy, January 7, 1943, Archives II, RG 499.

20. Quoted by Roger Daniels, *Concentration Camps USA: Japanese Americans and World War II*, p. 147. Lt. Col. Karl Bendetsen, telephone conversation with Col. William P. Scobey, Executive Officer, General Staff, February 17, 1943, Archives II, RG 394.

21. Mark Clark in Stetson Conn papers, quoted in Roger Daniels, *Concentration Camps USA: Japanese Americans and World War II*, pp. 65–67.

22. *The Evacuated People*, Section X.

23. S. L. A. Marshall papers.

24. War Relocation Authority, *Semi-Annual Report*, January 1–June 30, 1943, Washington, D.C., Hamilton Library, University of Hawaii.

25. Tom Kawaguchi, oral history in John Tateishi, *And Justice for All*, p. 181.

26. Shiro Kashino, interview with the Sons and Daughters of the 442, Honolulu, March 27, 1995.

27. Quoted in Thelma Chang, *"I Can Never Forget": Men of the 100th/442nd*, p. 105.

28. Shiro Kashino, "True Colors," Komo TV and KCTS TV, Seattle, February 25, 1997.

29. My interview with Rudy Tokiwa.

30. Quoted in Dorothy Matsuo, *Boyhood to War*, p. 56.

31. Don Matsuda, JANM oral history.

32. Shiro Takeshita, personal history in the Historical Album Committee of the 522 Field Artillery Battalion of the 442 Regimental Combat Team, *Fire for Effect*, p. 179.

33. Frank Seto, oral history in Patrick K. O'Donnell, *Beyond Valor: World War II's Rangers and Airborne Veterans Reveal the Heart of Combat*, pp. 191–193.

34. Mike Masaoka, *They Call Me Moses Masaoka*, p. 50.

35. Hajiro, *Hanashi* oral history; my interview with Hajiro.

36. Isamu "Mike" Tsuji, "My Life as a Dog Face (Soldier)," unpublished manuscript.

37. Gregg K. Kakesako, "Honoring a War Hero: A Ship Is Named After Isle Soldier Robert T. Kuroda, Killed in Action in WWII," *Honolulu Star-Bulletin*, August 31, 2003.

38. Hajiro, *Hanashi* oral history; my interview with Hajiro.

39. Mickey Akiyama, oral history in The Men of I Company, 442nd Regimental Combat Team, *And Then There Were Eight*, p. 117; my interview with Akiyama.

40. Takashi Senzaki, *Hanashi* oral history; my interview with Senzaki.

41. Shig Doi, oral history in *And Justice for All*, p. 161.

42. Memo from S. L. A. Marshall to Col. William P. Scobey, April 8, 1943, Archives II, RG 107.

43. Memo from S. L. A. Marshall to Col. William P. Scobey, April 9, 1943, 442 Club archives.

44. Manabi Hirasaki with Naomi Hirahara, *A Taste for Strawberries*, p. 65.

45. Kim, JANM oral history, *Hanashi* oral history; my interview with Kim.

46. Don Seki, *Hanashi* oral history.

47. Inouye, *Journey to Washington*, p. 100. Bureau of the Census, U.S. Department of Commerce, *Historical Statistics of the United States: Colonial Times to 1970*, Part 1, Series F 17-30.

48. Soldiers' correspondence in the Hawaii War Records Depository, Hamilton Library, University of Hawaii, Manoa.

49. Hajiro, *Hanashi* oral history; my interview with Hajiro. For a fictional representation of pidgin-speaking Japanese Americans in the Pearl Harbor period, see Jon Shirota, *Lucky Come Hawaii*.

50. Christopher Keegan, *Hanashi* oral history.

51. Susumu Ito, *Hanashi* oral history; my interview with Ito.

52. Keegan, *Hanashi* oral history.

53. Quotes in this section are from Ito, *Hanashi* oral history, and my interview with Ito.

54. My interview with Sachi Itaya.

55. Inouye, *Hanashi* oral history.

56. My interview with Ikuko Nakao Kitayama. Also, Inouye, *Hanashi* oral history, and oral history in *Boyhood to War*, pp. 71–73.

57. Robert Katayama, JANM oral history.

58. Hajiro, *Hanashi* oral history.

59. Keegan, *Hanashi* oral history.

60. Hirasaki, *A Taste for Strawberries*, p. 63.

61. Kawaguchi, oral history in *And Justice for All*, p. 182; Kashino, "True Colors."

62. Keegan, *Hanashi* oral history; my interview with Keegan.

63. Kawaguchi, oral history in *And Justice for All*, p. 181.

64. Stanley Akita, *Hanashi* oral history.

65. DeWitt, *Final Report*, p. 17.

66. Robert E. Park and Herbert A. Miller, *Old World Traits Transplanted*, pp. 178–180.

67. Ted Tsukiyama, *Hanashi* oral history, my interview with Tsukiyama.

68. Kawaguchi, oral history in *And Justice for All*, p. 181.

69. Quoted in Hirasaki, *A Taste for Strawberries*, p. 63.

70. Tsuji, "My Life as a Dog Face (Soldier)."

71. James M. Hanley, *A Matter of Honor*, pp. 16–17.

72. Col. Karl R. Bendetsen, memo to Commanding General, Western Defense Command and Fourth Army, notes on conferences with Assistant Secretary of War John J. McCloy, May 3, 1943, Archives II, RG 499.

73. Col. D. H. Cowles, for the Quartermaster General, memo to Commanding Officer, 442d Combat Team, July 31, 1943, Archives II, RG 107.

CHAPTER 3:
"WHAT WE'RE FIGHTING FOR"

1. Mark W. Clark, "Statement to the Commission on Wartime Relocation and Internment of Civilians," July 14, 1981. Mark W. Clark Papers, The Citadel Archives & Museum, box 31, folder 2.

2. Quotes in this section are from George "Joe" Sakato, unpublished autobiographical notes. See also Sakato, *Hanashi* oral history; my interview with Sakato.

3. Keegan, *Hanashi* oral history.

4. Clark, Headquarters Fifth Army to Commander in Chief, AFHQ, 15th Army Group, October 8, 1943. The Citadel Archives & Museum, Mark W. Clark papers, box 3, folder 1.

5. Hayashi, Medal of Honor Citation, U.S. Army Center of Military History.

6. Ohata, Medal of Honor Citation, U.S. Army Center of Military History.

7. Mark W. Clark, *Calculated Risk*, p. 220.

8. Clark, *Calculated Risk*, p. 418.

9. Quoted by Lt. Gen. Jacob L. Devers in a message to the War Department, January 23, 1944, Archives II, RG 165.

10. Harold Ickes, Department of the Interior release, April 13, 1944, Archives II, RG 389.

11. Stimson diary, Archives II, RG 319.

12. John J. McCloy files, Archives II, RG 107.

13. "Subsistence Homesteads, Sec. 208," National Industrial Recovery Act (1933), Archives I, RG 11. See Edward Banfield, *Government Project*, which has a foreword by Rexford Tugwell, administrator of the Resettlement Administration.

14. Eleanor Roosevelt, "To Undo a Mistake Is Always Harder Than Not to Create One Originally," original draft of article in *Collier's Magazine* (October 10, 1943), reproduced in *Confinement and Ethnicity*.

15. See Conn et al., *Guarding the United States and Its Outposts*, Chapter IV, and United States Army Center of Military History, *Defense of the Americas*, pp. 10–11.

16. Conn et al., *Guarding the United States and Its Outposts*, p. 96.

17. War Relocation Authority, *People in Motion: The Postwar Adjustment of the Evacuated Japanese Americans*, p. 57.

18. Quotes in this section are from *People in Motion*, pp. 59–61.

19. *People in Motion*, p. 60.

20. John J. McCloy, transcript of phone call to Emmons, June 13, 1944, Archives II, RG 499.

21. McCloy, phone conversation with Lt. Gen. John L. DeWitt, January 18, 1943, Archives II, RG 499.

22. Ickes, Department of the Interior release, April 13, 1944, RG 389.

23. Quotes in this section are from War Relocation Authority, "What We're Fighting For: Statements by United States Servicemen about Americans of Japanese Descent," Department of the Interior, Washington, D.C., not dated (although individual entries carry dates as late as September 1944). Author's personal files.

24. Quoted in Halloran, *Sparky*, p. 49.

25. Selective Service System, "History and Records: Induction Statistics," http://www.sss.gov/induct.htm.

26. See *The Papers of Dwight David Eisenhower: The War Years IV*, pp. 2182–83, 2347–48. See also Maurice Matloff, "The 90-Division Gamble," in Kent Roberts Greenfield, *Command Decisions*, pp. 365–381.

27. Among the other inductees was the late Gungi Asahina, the author's uncle.

28. My interview with Willie Tanamachi.

29. My interview and correspondence with Sandra Tanamachi.

30. Memo from Lt. Col. Merritt B. Booth to Col. William P. Scobey, January 25, 1943, Archives II, RG 107.

31. Doi, oral history in *And Justice for All*, pp. 157–158; my interview with Doi.

32. My interview with Takahashi.
33. My interview with Kiyoshi and Shiz Fujimoto.

CHAPTER 4:
DRAGOON

1. Bill Mauldin, *Up Front*, p. 198.
2. What follows is based on my interviews and correspondence with Marty Higgins, his unpublished autobiographical notes, and the records in his personal files.
3. *The Army Almanac*, second edition, p. 18; *The Army Almanac*, first edition, p. 591.
4. See Meredith Vezina, "Defending the Border: The Cavalry at Camp Lockett." See also The California State Military Museum (http://www.militarymuseum.org/CpLockett.html).
5. See USAF Museum, http://www.wpafb.af.mil/museum/history/wwii/ce9.htm.
6. Clarke and Smith, *Riviera to the Rhine*, p. 14.
7. See Winston S. Churchill, *Triumph and Tragedy*, The Second World War, Vol. VI, Chapters IV and VI.
8. *Southern France: The U.S. Army Campaigns of World War II*, U.S. Army, Center of Military History publication 72–31.
9. Clarke and Smith, *Riviera to the Rhine*, p. 33.
10. L. K. Truscott Jr., *Command Missions: A Personal Story*. Also, *The Army Almanac*, first edition.
11. Clarke and Smith, *Riviera to the Rhine*, p. 38.
12. Distinguished Unit Citation, 100th Battalion, War Department General Orders 66, August 15, 1944, Center of Military History.
13. Barney Hajiro, *Hanashi* oral history.
14. My interview with Sadaichi Kubota; Kubota, oral history in *And Then There Were Eight*, p. 108.
15. Memo from Gen. George C. Marshall to Lt. Gen. Jacob L. Devers, July 2, 1944, Archives II, RG 107.
16. Mark W. Clark, Letter to Gen. George C. Marshall, August 17, 1944. The Citadel Archives & Museum. Mark W. Clark papers, box 1, folder 4.
17. Clarke and Smith, *Riviera to the Rhine*, p. 78.
18. Quotes in this section are from Truscott, *Command Missions*, pp. 413–414.
19. Frank Seto, oral history in Patrick K. O'Donnell, *Beyond Valor: World War II's Rangers and Airborne Veterans Reveal the Heart of Combat*, Touchstone, 2001, pp. 191–193.
20. Clarke and Smith, *Riviera to the Rhine*, p. 122.
21. Quoted in Clarke and Smith, *Riviera to the Rhine*, p. 122.
22. Quotes in this section are from Truscott, *Command Missions*, pp. 416–417.
23. Higgins, autobiographical notes.
24. Truscott, *Command Missions*, p. 425.

25. Higgins, autobiographical notes.
26. Quotes in this section are from Truscott, *Command Missions*, pp. 427, 430–31.
27. Clarke and Smith, *Riviera to the Rhine*, p. 165.
28. Quotes in this section are from Higgins, autobiographical notes.
29. Clarke and Smith, *Riviera to the Rhine*, pp. 167–69.
30. Truscott, *Command Missions*, pp. 432–433.
31. John E. Dahlquist papers, Military History Institute (hereafter, Dahlquist papers).

CHAPTER 5:
DOGFACES

1. Bill Mauldin, *Up Front*, Henry Holt, 1945, pp. 146–47.
2. The following is based on my interview with George "Joe" Sakato, his unpublished autobiographical notes, and his *Hanashi* oral history.
3. Quotes in this section are from Mauldin, *Up Front*, pp. 1, 5, 8, 11, 15, 39.
4. Quotes in this section are from Truscott, *Command Missions*, pp. 295–297.
5. Martin Higgins, autobiographical notes.
6. U.S. Army Signal Corps photo SC-195295, National Archives.
7. Clarke and Smith, *Riviera to the Rhine*, p. 197.
8. *Southern France*, p. 30.
9. Clarke and Smith, *Riviera to the Rhine*, p. 171.
10. Clarke and Smith, *Riviera to the Rhine*, p. 204.
11. Clarke and Smith, *Riviera to the Rhine*, p. 204.
12. Clarke and Smith, *Riviera to the Rhine*, p. 169.
13. Clarke and Smith, *Riviera to the Rhine*, p. 195.
14. My correspondence with Higgins.
15. Clarke and Smith, *Riviera to the Rhine*, p. 197.
16. *Command Missions*, pp. 441–444.
17. See Keith E. Bonn, *When the Odds Were Even: The Vosges Mountains Campaign, October 1944–January 1945*, Presidio, 1994.
18. See Clarke and Smith, *Riviera to the Rhine*, pp. 226–228, and Gen. George C. Marshall, *Biennial Reports of the Chief of Staff of the United States Army to the Secretary of War, 1 July 1939–30 June 1945*.
19. Clarke and Smith, *Riviera to the Rhine*, pp. 229–230.
20. See, e.g., Russell F. Weigley, *Eisenhower's Lieutenants: The Campaigns of France and Germany 1944–1945*, and John Ellis, *Brute Force: Allied Strategy and Tactics in the Second World War*.
21. 442d narrative of events, October 1944. Archived copies of this monthly report can be found at Archives II, RG 407, INRG-442, and at the Military History Institute, the Hawaii War Records Depository, the Center of Military History, and elsewhere. Hereafter, narrative of events.
22. U.S. Army Signal Corps photo SC-253983, RG 111-SC, Archives II.
23. Sakato, unpublished autobiographical notes.

24. Shuji Taketomo, *Hanashi* oral history.

25. Narrative of events, October 15, 1944.

26. My personal impressions of the region on a trip in October 2001 match the description of soldiers during the war and years later, as well as photographs from the period. Climbing Hills A and D on winding roads to the summit left me a little breathless. I found it difficult to imagine what it would have been like to scale the side of the hills with a full field pack, a helmet, and a rifle—all the while dodging bullets. See U.S. Army Signal Corps photo 208-AA-104-S, RG 208-AA, Archives II.

27. Diary, Dahlquist papers. See also Clarke and Smith, *Riviera to the Rhine*, pp. 291–292.

28. Clarke and Smith, *Riviera to the Rhine*, p. 313.

29. My interview with Kim.

30. Narrative of events, October 15, 1944.

31. My interview with Al Takahashi.

32. Kim, *Hanashi* oral history; my interview with Kim.

33. Mauldin, *Up Front*, p. 148.

34. Mauldin, *Up Front*, p. 149.

35. Sakato, autobiographical notes.

36. My interview with Takahashi.

37. Jack Wakamatsu, *Silent Warriors*, pp. 181–182.

38. Narrative of events, October 17, 1944.

39. 100th Battalion journal, October 17, 1944, Club 100 archives. Hereafter, 100th Battalion journal.

40. Narrative of events, October 17, 1944.

41. 100th Battalion journal, October 17, 1944.

42. Wakamatsu, *Silent Warriors*, p. 185.

43. Sakato, autobiographical notes.

44. Narrative of events and 100th Battalion journal, October 18, 1944.

45. Narrative of events, October 18, 1944.

46. Narrative of events, 100th Battalion journal, October 18, 1944.

47. My interview with Bernard Henry, former deputy mayor of Bruyères.

48. My interview with Paul Charpin, former FFI member; my interview with Bernard Henry.

49. My interview with Charpin.

50. My interview with Henry.

51. My interview with Charpin.

52. Stanley Akita, *Hanashi* oral history.

53. My interview with Charpin and his speech at the Bruyères town hall, October 1996; Wakamatsu, *Silent Warriors*, p. 189.

54. My interview with Charpin, Charpin's speech.

55. My interview with Takahashi.

CHAPTER 6:
THE BATTLE FOR THE HIGH GROUND

1. S. L. A. Marshall, *Men Against Fire*, p. 161.
2. Quotes from Young Oak Kim are from his JANM oral history.
3. Keegan, *Hanashi* oral history, my interview with Keegan.
4. My interview with Henry.
5. George Oiye, unpublished autobiography.
6. My interview with Charpin; Akita, *Hanashi* oral history.
7. My interview with Henry.
8. Narrative of events, October 19, 1944.
9. Sakato, autobiographical notes.
10. My interview with Sakato.
11. Medal citation, affidavits, and supporting documentation for Barney Hajiro, from my Freedom of Information Act (FOIA) request. Hereafter, Hajiro, medal citation.
12. Narrative of events, October 19, 1944.
13. Medal citation, affidavits, and supporting documentation for Robert Kuroda, from my FOIA request. Hereafter, Kuroda, medal citation.
14. Keegan, *Hanashi* oral history; my interview with Keegan.
15. Kuroda, medal citation.
16. Kim, *Hanashi* oral history; my interview with Kim.
17. Narrative of events, October 20, 1944.
18. "Amelioration of the Condition of the Wounded on the Field of Battle" (Red Cross Convention), Geneva Conventions of 1864, 1906, 1929, reproduced at http://www.yale.edu/lawweb/avalon/lawofwar/geneva04.htm.
19. Wakamatsu, *Silent Warriors*, pp. 192–193.
20. Robert Katayama, JANM oral history.
21. Robert Katayama, JANM oral history.
22. Mauldin, *Up Front*, pp. 35–37.
23. *Sustaining Health & Performance in the Cold: Environmental Medicine Guidelines for Cold-Weather Operations*, Technical Note No. 92-2, U.S. Army Research Institute of Environmental Medicine (July 1992).
24. Wakamatsu, *Silent Warriors*, pp. 179–180.
25. *Sustaining Health & Performance in the Cold: Environmental Medicine Guidelines for Cold-Weather Operations*.
26. Quoted in Dorothy Matsuo, *Boyhood to War*, p. 111.
27. Wakamatsu, *Silent Warriors*, p. 180.
28. Marshall, *Men Against Fire*, p. 159.
29. Narrative of events, October 20, 1944.
30. Narrative of events, October 21, 1944.
31. Narrative of events, 100th Battalion journal, October 21, 1944.
32. My interview with Kim.
33. 100th Battalion journal, October 21, 1944.

34. My interview with Kim.
35. 100th Battalion journal, October 21, 1944.
36. Hajiro medal citation; my interview with Hajiro; Hajiro, *Hanashi* oral history.
37. 100th Battalion journal, October 22, 1944.
38. My interview with Maurice Caël; Narrative of events, 100th Battalion journal, October 22, 1944.
39. 100th Battalion journal, October 22, 1944.
40. Narrative of events, October 22, 1944.
41. 100th Battalion journal, October 22, 1944.
42. Narrative of events, 100th Battalion journal, October 23, 1944.
43. 100th Battalion journal, October 23, 1944.
44. Marshall, *Men Against Fire*, p. 191.
45. Jimmie Kanaya, *Hanashi* oral history.
46. Kim, *Hanashi* oral history; JANM oral history; my interview with Kim.
47. Narrative of events, October 23, 1944. Kanaya became a POW.
48. Kim, *Hanashi* oral history; JANM oral history; my interview with Kim.
49. Narrative of events, October 23, 1944.
50. Wakamatsu, *Silent Warriors*, p. 203.
51. Marshall, *Men Against Fire*, pp. 158, 179.
52. Takahashi, *Hanashi* oral history; my interview with Takahashi.

CHAPTER 7:
DARK NIGHTS OF THE SOUL

1. Marshall, *Men Against Fire*, pp. 44–45.
2. My interview with Higgins.
3. 36th Division narrative, Archives II, RG 338.
4. Letter to Truscott, January 7, 1945, Dahlquist papers.
5. My interview with Huberth.
6. Higgins, unpublished autobiographical notes; my interview with Higgins.
7. My interview with Huberth.
8. My interview with Wilson.
9. 36th Division narrative, October 24, 1944.
10. 36th Division narrative, October 24, 1944.
11. 36th Division narrative, October 25, 1944.
12. S-3 reports, 36th Division, National Archives II, RG 338, October 25, 1944.
13. Dahlquist papers.
14. Narrative of events, October 27, 1944.
15. My trip to the Vosges confirmed the blackness of the area at night.
16. My interview with Ito; Ito, *Hanashi* oral history.
17. Sakato, unpublished autobiographical notes.
18. The motto of the Rangers. Keegan, Hanashi oral history; my interview with Keegan.
19. Dahlquist papers.

20. Distinguished Unit Citation, 100th Battalion, War Department General Orders 78, September 12, 1945, Center of Military History.

21. 36th Division G-2 reports, Archives II, RG 338, October 7, 1944.

22. My interview with Ito; Ito, *Hanashi* oral history.

23. My interview with Huberth.

24. My correspondence with Higgins.

25. My interview with Higgins. See also *FM 23-7: U.S. Carbine Caliber .30 M1 and MA1*, and *FM 21-100: Soldier's Handbook.*

26. My interview with Higgins; Higgins, unpublished autobiographical notes.

27. The 141st Infantry Regiment Association. *Five Years, Five Countries, Five Campaigns . . . with the 141st Infantry Regiment*, Chapter IX. Hereafter, 141st Regiment unit history.

28. My interview with Higgins.

29. My interview with Huberth.

30. My interview with Guy.

31. My interview with Guy.

32. The 36th Division Association, " 'Lost Battalion' Story," in *A Pictorial History of the 36th Division*. Hereafter, 36th Division unit history.

33. Narrative of events, October 26, 1944.

34. All quotes of radio messages are from the 36th Division narrative and from the 141st Regiment narrative, Archives II, RG 338. Also see personal files of Marty Higgins. In some cases, the recorded times of the messages differ in the two narratives. In general, I have cited the earlier recorded times, when they are consistent with other data, treating the difference as the lag in relaying information from field artillery or regiment to division headquarters. I have used "headquarters" to describe the recipients of 2d Lt. Blonder's coded messages, which are all described as coming from Higgins.

35. Dahlquist papers.

36. 36th Division narrative, October 27, 1944.

37. Diary, Dahlquist papers.

38. 100th Battalion narrative, October 27, 1944.

39. Shiro Kashino, oral history, Sons and Daughters of the 442, March 27, 1995.

40. Medal citation for Shiro Kashino, General Orders No. 24, Headquarters Sixth Army Group, April 1, 1945. Courtesy of Louise Kashino.

41. Shiro Kashino, oral history, Sons and Daughters of the 442, March 27, 1995.

42. Narrative of events, October 27, 1944.

43. Narrative of events, October 28, 1944.

44. Sus Ito, oral history in *Fire for Effect*, p. 85.

45. Dahlquist diary, Dahlquist papers.

46. Dahlquist diary, Dahlquist papers.

47. 141st Regiment unit history.

48. 100th Battalion narrative, October 28, 1944.

49. Medal citation, affidavits, and supporting documentation for James Okubo, from my FOIA request. Hereafter, Okubo, medal citation.

50. Narrative of events, October 28, 1944.
51. All quotations in this section are from Okubo, medal citation.
52. Narrative of events, October 28, 1944.
53. Headquarters 131st Field Artillery Battalion, "Report of Artillery Activities in connection with 'Lost Battalion,'" November 2, 1944, Dahlquist papers.
54. Tony Hillerman, *Seldom Disappointed*, p. 82.
55. My interview with Guy.
56. Shiro Kashino, memo to the U.S. Army, September 8, 1985, requesting review of his 1945 court-martial. Courtesy of Louise Kashino. Hereafter, Kashino memo.
57. My interview with Tak Senzaki.
58. Kenneth K. Inada, "A Soldier's Final Cries for Mother," in *Echoes of Silence: The Untold Stories of the Nisei Soldiers Who Served in World War II.*
59. Kashino memo.
60. Kenneth K. Inada, "The Ill-Fated Ration Detail," in *Echoes of Silence: The Untold Stories of the Nisei Soldiers Who Served in World War II.*
61. Diary, Dahlquist papers.

CHAPTER 8:
GO FOR BROKE

1. Marshall, *Men Against Fire*, p. 184.
2. My interview with Sadaichi Kubota.
3. My trip to the Vosges, October 2001; G-2 periodic reports, Archives II, RG 407.
4. Letter to Mrs. Telesforo Casanova (Wells Lewis's mother), Dahlquist papers.
5. *FM 100-5: Operations*, pp. 111–117.
6. 1st Battalion journal, Marty Higgins's personal files. Hereafter, 1st Battalion journal.
7. My interview with Higgins.
8. 36th Division unit history.
9. My interview with Guy.
10. Medal citation, Marty Higgins's personal files.
11. 1st Battalion journal.
12. 1st Battalion journal.
13. 1st Battalion journal.
14. Narrative of events, October 29, 1944.
15. Medal citation, affidavits, and supporting documentation for George Sakato, from my FOIA request (hereafter, Sakato, medal citation), my interview with Sakato, his unpublished autobiographical notes.
16. Sakato, medal citation.
17. Sakato, medal citation.
18. Sakato, unpublished autobiographical notes.

19. Narrative of events, October 29, 1944; Sakato, medal citation.
20. Sakato, unpublished autobiographical notes. For this action, the 2d Battalion would earn a Distinguished Unit Citation, War Department General Orders 83, August 6, 1946.
21. Doi, oral history in *And Justice for All*; my interview with Doi.
22. Takashi Senzaki, *Hanashi* oral history; my interview with Senzaki.
23. 100th Battalion journal, October 29, 1944.
24. 100th Battalion journal, October 29, 1944.
25. Letter to Casanova, Dahlquist papers.
26. Letter to Sinclair Lewis, Dahlquist papers.
27. Distinguished Unit Citation, 100th Battalion, War Department General Orders 78, September 12, 1945, Center of Military History.
28. Keith E. Bonn, *When the Odds Were Even: The Vosges Mountains Campaign, October 1944–January 1945*, p. 26.
29. Doi, oral history in *And Justice for All*, pp. 161–162.
30. Doi, oral history in *And Justice for All*, p. 165.
31. My interview with Jim Yamashita.
32. Hajiro, medal citation.
33. Kubota, oral history in *And Then There Were Eight*, pp. 108–109; my interview with Kubota.
34. Marshall, *Men Against Fire*, p. 60.
35. Kubota, oral history in *And Then There Were Eight*, p. 109; my interview with Kubota.
36. My interview with Hajiro.
37. Kubota, oral history in *And Then There Were Eight*, p. 109.
38. Joe Shimamura, JANM oral history.
39. Silver Star Citation for Yuki Minaga, General Orders 9, February 16, 1945, reproduced in *Charlie Battery: A Legend*, unpaginated. Also, my interview with Minaga.
40. Okubo, medal citation.
41. Hajiro, medal citation.
42. Hajiro, *Hanashi* oral history; my interview with Hajiro.
43. Distinguished Unit Citation, 3d Battalion, War Department General Orders 68, August 14, 1945, Center of Military History.
44. Narrative of events, October 29, 1944.
45. Ichigi Kashiwagi, *Hanashi* oral history.
46. 100th Battalion journal, October 29, 1944.
47. Distinguished Unit Citation, 3d Battalion, War Department General Orders 68, August 14, 1945, Center of Military History.
48. Marshall, *Men Against Fire*, pp. 208–209.
49. Keegan, *Hanashi* oral history.
50. Hajiro, medal citation.
51. Hajiro, *Hanashi* oral history.
52. Dahlquist papers.

53. Distinguished Unit Citation, 3d Battalion, War Department General Orders 68, August 14, 1945, Center of Military History.
54. My interview with Guy.
55. Although the record indicates otherwise.
56. 100th Battalion journal, October 29, 1944.
57. Higgins, speech at the Punchbowl; my interview with Higgins.

CHAPTER 9:
CASUALTIES

1. Marshall, *Men Against Fire*, pp. 208, 211.
2. My interviews with Guy and Wilson.
3. Ito, *Fire for Effect*, p. 87.
4. Ichigi Kashiwagi, *Hanashi* oral history.
5. Hiroo Endo, JANM Military Experience Database.
6. Ito, *Fire for Effect*, p. 87.
7. 100th Battalion journal, October 30, 1944; 442d narrative, October 30, 1944.
8. My interview with Guy.
9. Doi, oral history in *And Justice for All*, p. 166.
10. Narrative of events, November 2 and 7, 1944.
11. Dahlquist papers.
12. Okubo, medal citation.
13. Dahlquist papers.
14. Joe Shimamura, JANM oral history.
15. Narrative of events, November 8, 1944.
16. Medal citation, affidavits, and supporting documentation for Joe Nishimoto, from my FOIA request. Hereafter, Nishimoto, medal citation.
17. Nishimoto, medal citation.
18. Nishimoto, medal citation.
19. 100th Battalion journal, November 10, 1944.
20. Narrative of events, November 9, 1944.
21. U.S. Army Signal Corps photo SC-196716, RG 111-SC, National Archives.
22. Hajiro, *Hanashi* oral history.
23. Okubo, medal citation.
24. Distinguished Unit Citation, 100th Battalion, War Department General Orders 78, September 12, 1945, Center of Military History.
25. Distinguished Unit Citation, Companies F and L of the 2d Battalion, General Orders 14, March 4, 1945, Center of Military History.
26. Distinguished Unit Citation, 2d Battalion, General Orders 83, August 6, 1946, Center of Military History.
27. Distinguished Unit Citation, 3d Battalion, General Orders 68, August 14, 1945, Center of Military History.
28. Distinguished Unit Citation, 232d Engineer Combat Company, General Orders 56, June 17, 1946, Center of Military History.

29. VI Corps journal, conclusion, Archives II, RG 407.

30. November 17, 1944, Dahlquist papers.

31. VI Corps history, Archives II, RG 338.

32. Narrative of events, November 18, 1944.

33. B. H. Liddell Hart, *Strategy*, pp. 71–73.

34. Jacob L. Devers papers, York Heritage Trust.

35. Quoted in Clarke and Smith, *Riviera to the Rhine*, p. 440, in a chapter titled "Lost Opportunities."

36. Eisenhower to George C. Marshall, November 27, 1944, *The Papers of Dwight David Eisenhower: The War Years IV*, p. 2320.

37. Keith E. Bonn, *When the Odds Were Even: The Vosges Mountains Campaign, October 1944–January 1945*, Presidio, 1994, p. 228.

38. Higgins, unpublished autobiographical notes.

39. DeWitt, *Final Report*, p. 9.

40. Devers, letter to Merrow E. Sorley, August 7, 1961. Jacob L. Devers papers, York Heritage Trust, box 104.

41. Clarke and Smith, *Riviera to the Rhine*, p. 444.

42. Eisenhower, cable to Gen. Thomas Troy Handy, *The Papers of Dwight David Eisenhower: The War Years IV*, pp. 2346–47.

43. Gen. George C. Marshall, *Biennial Reports of the Chief of Staff of the United States Army to the Secretary of War, 1 July 1939–30 June 1945*, p. 121.

44. See *The Army Almanac*, revised and updated edition. See also Trevor N. Dupuy, David L. Bongard, and Richard C. Anderson, *Hitler's Last Gamble*.

45. Clark, quoted in Daniels, *Concentration Camps USA: Japanese Americans and World War II*, pp. 66–67.

46. Eisenhower, cables to Gen. Thomas Troy Handy, *The Papers of Dwight David Eisenhower: The War Years IV*, pp. 2347–48, 2360–61. See also Maurice Matloff, "The 90-Division Gamble," in Kent Roberts Greenfield, *Command Decisions*, pp. 365–381.

47. *Lend Me Your Ears: Great Speeches in History*, p. 704.

48. See Peter Irons, *Justice at War*, p. 345.

49. All Justices' quotes from U.S. Supreme Court, *Toyosaburo Korematsu v. United States*, 323 U.S. 214 (1944), No. 22, argued October 11, 12, 1944, decided December 18, 1944.

50. By Eugene V. Rostow of Yale University's law school, in "The Japanese American Cases—A Disaster," *Yale Law Journal*, 54 (1945), p. 489.

51. Peter Irons, *Justice at War*, p. 100. Irons uses the term "internment."

52. U.S. Supreme Court, *Ex parte Mitsuye Endo*, 323 U.S. 283 (1944), No. 70, argued October 12, 1944, decided December 18, 1944.

53. Memo from Henry L. Stimson to John J. McCloy, November 10, 1944, Archives II, RG 107, Entry 99.

54. Stimson, memo to McCloy.

55. Frederick Douglass, *Life and Times of Frederick Douglass: His Early Life as a Slave, His Escape from Bondage, and His Complete History to the Present Time*, p. 354.

CHAPTER 10:
HOMECOMING

1. Mauldin, *Back Home*, pp. 162, 168.
2. Memorandum from Maj. Gen. C. H. Bonesteel to Chief of Staff, War Department, September 19, 1944, Archives II, RG 499.
3. Portland *Oregonian*, December 15, 1944, Archives II, RG 499.
4. *People in Motion: The Postwar Adjustment of the Evacuated Japanese Americans*, p. 69.
5. Stimson, press conference, December 14, 1944, Archives II, RG 319.
6. Resolution of January 9, 1945, Archives II, RG 499.
7. *The Relocation Program*, p. 65.
8. *People in Motion: The Postwar Adjustment of the Evacuated Japanese Americans*, p. 58.
9. *People in Motion: The Postwar Adjustment of the Evacuated Japanese Americans*, p. 60.
10. *The Relocation Program*, p. 65.
11. My interview with Hajiro.
12. The arm patch of the 92d featured a buffalo, although direct lineage to the "buffalo soldiers" had ended with the 10th Cavalry, Marty Higgins's former unit.
13. Mark Clark, "Statement to the Commission on Wartime Relocation and Internment of Civilians," July 14, 1981, The Citadel Archives & Museum, Mark W. Clark papers, box 3, folder 2.
14. Mark Clark diary, volume 9, The Citadel Archives & Museum, Mark W. Clark papers, box 65.
15. Caption to U.S. Army Signal Corps photo SC-340934, RG 111-SC, Archives II.
16. Truscott, Jr., *Command Missions*, p. 477.
17. Doi, oral history in *And Justice for All*, p. 163; my interview with Doi.
18. *442d Combat Team*, p. 35.
19. Truscott, Jr., *Command Missions*, p. 485.
20. Inouye, *Journey to Washington*, p. 147.
21. Clark, *Calculated Risk*, p. 432.
22. All quotes in this section are from Inouye, *Journey to Washington*, pp. 148–152.
23. Inouye, *Journey to Washington*, p. 152. Also see Medal of Honor Citation, Center of Military History.
24. Hirasaki, *A Taste for Strawberries*, p. 78.
25. *Central Europe*, Center of Military History Publication 72–36, p. 21.
26. George Oiye, oral history in *Fire for Effect*, p. 169.
27. United States Holocaust Memorial Museum, *Holocaust Encyclopedia*, http://www.ushmm.org/wlc/en/.
28. Quoted in "Sushi & Bagel Reunion," *The New Yorker*, November 11, 1991, p. 33.
29. Quoted in Thelma Chang, *I Can Never Forget*, p. 168.
30. Intelligence report by Richard E. Rudisill to Commanding General, Ninth Service Command, Fort Douglas, Utah (May 18, 1945), Archives II, RG 499.

31. Shiro Kashino, oral history, Sons and Daughters of the 442, March 27, 1995.
32. Hajiro, *Hanashi* oral history; my interview with Hajiro.
33. Sakato, *Hanashi* oral history and unpublished autobiographical notes; my interview with Sakato.
34. Inouye, *Journey to Washington*, Chapter VI.
35. Inouye, *Journey to Washington*, pp. 189–191.
36. Lawrence Fuchs, *Hawaii Pono*, p. 306.
37. Inouye, *Journey to Washington*, p. 208.
38. Memo from Major James L. Sloan "for the officer in Charge," December 20, 1944, Archives II, RG 499.
39. Wakamatsu, *Silent Warriors*, p. 254.
40. *WRA: A Story of Human Conservation*, p. 120.
41. Doi, oral history in *And Justice for All*, pp. 157–158.
42. Headquarters, Western Defense Command, "Japanese-American Situation Summary No. 34," January 20, 1945, Archives II, RG 165.
43. Doi, oral history in *And Justice for All*, pp. 158–159; my interview with Doi.
44. Headquarters, Western Defense Command, "Japanese-American Situation Summary No. 46," February 1, 1945, Archives II, RG 165.
45. Doi, oral history in *And Justice for All*, p. 162. Also, my interview with Doi.
46. Mickey Akiyama, oral history in *And Then There Were Eight*, pp. 117–119; my interview with Akiyama.
47. *People in Motion: The Postwar Adjustment of Evacuated Japanese Americans*, p. 17.
48. Wilson Makabe, oral history in *And Justice for All*, p. 259.
49. *The New York Times*, July 3, 1946, p. 7.
50. My correspondence with "Bones" and Shiz Fujimoto.
51. Signed June 26, 1946, effective June 30, 1946. What was left of the WRA became the War Agency Liquidation Unit of the Department of the Interior. It was not until February 19, 1976, that President Gerald Ford formally rescinded Executive Order 9066.
52. Photo from National Archives, RG 79-AR, number 79AR647, Archives II.
53. *People in Motion: The Postwar Adjustment of the Evacuated Japanese Americans*, p. 19.
54. *The Washington Post*, June 5, 1948, p. B1.
55. Remarks at funeral ceremonies for Japanese Americans, Arlington National Cemetery, June 4, 1948. Jacob L. Devers papers, York County Heritage Trust Library & Archives.

AFTERWORD:
"HERE WE ADMIT A WRONG"

1. Ronald Reagan, "Remarks on Signing the Bill Providing Restitution for the Wartime Internment of Japanese-American Civilians," August 10, 1988. The Ronald Reagan Presidential Library, the Public Papers of the President, 1981–1989: Statements, speeches and papers released by the Office of the Press Secretary.

2. "Hunk of America," *The Washington Post*, October 16, 1945. See also *WRA: A Story of Human Conservation*, p. 123.

3. *Los Angeles Times*, December 9, 1945. See also *WRA: A Story of Human Conservation*, p. 123; *The New York Times*, December 8, 1945; *The Washington Post*, December 8, 1945; *The Santa Ana Register*, December 10, 1945.

4. Reagan, "Remarks on Signing the Bill Providing Restitution for the Wartime Internment of Japanese-American Civilians." Reagan was separated from active duty on the day after the rally.

5. Hajiro, *Hanashi* oral history; my interview with Hajiro.

6. Gregg K. Kakesako, "Debts of Honor," *Honolulu Star-Bulletin*, May 12, 2000.

7. Inouye, *Hanashi* oral history. The Big Five—the interlocking conglomerates that controlled sugarcane and pineapple production and shipping in the islands and, through the Republican Party, dominated local politics—opposed statehood. Within a decade, as the local economy shifted from agriculture to tourism, the power of the Big Five rapidly dwindled.

8. Letter from Maj. Gen. Walter B. Huffman, Judge Advocate General, U.S. Army, to Louise Kashino, December 9, 1997. Personal files of Louise Kashino.

9. Kim, *Hanashi* oral history.

10. Act of March 18, 1959, Pub L 86-3, 73 Stat 4, which was subject to referendum by the citizens of Hawaii.

11. *The Detroit News*, April 19, 1959.

12. Marshall, *Bringing Up the Rear*, p. 264.

13. H.R. 442, approved August 10, was assigned Public Law No. 100–383.

EPILOGUE:
HILL OF SACRIFICE

1. "Honolulu Memorial, National Memorial Cemetery of the Pacific, Honolulu, Hawaii," American Battle Monuments Commission, http://www.abmc.gov/hn_base.pdf.

2. This account is based on my interviews and correspondence with Marty Higgins and Sus Ito. See also Gregg K. Kakesako, "Race, Heroism & the Lost Battalion," *Honolulu Star-Bulletin*, March 25, 2000, and "Lost Battalion Reunites with 442d RCT," *Hawaii Pacific Press*, May 1, 2000.

3. Higgins's quotes are from the copy of his speech in his personal files. Reprinted in *And Then There Were Eight*, pp. 92–94.

4. Thomas Kuwahara testimony before Jefferson County commissioners, July 19, 2004, Houston JACL archive.

5. Daniel K. Inouye, letter to Jefferson County commissioners, July 16, 2004, Houston JACL archive.

6. George Sakato, letter to Kuwahara, November 23, 2003, Houston JACL archive.

7. Jack Wilson, letter to Jefferson County commissioners, July 7, 2004, copy courtesy of Marty Higgins.

8. Martin Higgins, letter to Jefferson County commissioners, April 26, 2004, Houston JACL archive; my interview with Higgins.

9. Gene Airheart, letter to Jefferson County commissioners, July 7, 2004, copy courtesy of Marty Higgins.

10. Marilyn Tennissen, "Jap Road Issue May Go to Voters," *The Port Arthur News*, July 14, 2004.

11. Thom Marshall, "Times Have Changed: Jap Road Finally Comes to End," *The Houston Chronicle*, July 20, 2004.

12. My interview with Sandra Tanamachi.

13. Marilyn Tennissen, "Jap Road Name to Change," *The Port Arthur News*, July 19, 2004; my interview with Sandra Tanamachi.

14. Micki Kawakami, testimony before Jefferson County commissioners, July 19, 2004, Houston JACL archive.

15. Pam Easton, "Texas County Votes to Change 'Jap Road,'" Associated Press, July 20, 2004; my interview with Sandra Tanamachi.

16. Kelly Kuwayama, testimony before Jefferson County commissioners, July 19, 2004, Houston JACL archive.

17. Sandra Tanamachi, testimony before Jefferson County commissioners, July 19, 2004; my interview with Tanamachi.

18. Marilyn Tennissen, "Jap Road Name to Change," *The Port Arthur News*, July 19, 2004.

19. My interview with Sandra Tanamachi.

20. Beth Gallaspy, "What Will It Be?" *The Beaumont Enterprise*, July 21, 2004.

21. Richard Stewart, "Wrong Ways? Officials Urged to Change Names of 'Jap' Roadways," *The Houston Chronicle*, January 31, 1993; my interview with Sandra Tanamachi.

22. Shiro Kashino, oral history, Sons and Daughters of the 442, March 27, 1995.

23. Eric Hanson, "2nd Jap Road May Be Renamed," *The Houston Chronicle*, August 4, 2004.

APPENDIX:
PEARL HARBOR AND 9/11

1. Francis Biddle, *In Brief Authority*, pp. 226.

2. Eric L. Muller, "An Arab American Internment?" See also Muller, "Inference or Impact? Racial Profiling and the Internment's True Legacy."

3. Joyce Purnick, "Metro Matters," *The New York Times*, September 15, 2001. See also Clyde Haberman, "NYC, Diallo, Terrorism and Safety vs. Liberty," *The New York Times*, September 13, 2001.

4. Damien Cave, "Where Are the War Heroes?" *The New York Times*, August 7, 2005.

5. For nearly six decades, there has also been considerable scholarly literature on the "evacuation" and "relocation." See particularly Morton Grodzins, *Americans Betrayed: Politics and the Japanese Evacuation*, Roger Daniels, *The Decision to Relocate the Japanese Americans*, and Peter Irons, *Justice at War*. For a damning indictment of Roosevelt's personal motives, see Greg Robinson, *By Order of the President: FDR and the Internment of Japanese Americans*.

6. William Petersen, *Japanese Americans*, pp. 72–73.

7. Peter Irons, *Justice at War: The Story of the Japanese American Internment Cases*, p. ix.

8. Norman Thomas, "Dark Day for Liberty," *Christian Century*, 59 (1942), quoted in William Petersen, *Japanese Americans*, p. 75.

9. The Justices' quotes are from U.S. Supreme Court, *Toyosaburo Korematsu v. United States*, 323 U.S. 214 (1944), No. 22, argued October 11, 12, 1944, decided December 18, 1944.

10. Under the Act of April 16, 1918, Chapter 55, 40 Stat. 531 as explained by Maj. Gen. Allen W. Gullion, provost marshal general, in a memo to Senator Elmer Thomas, on June 10, 1943, Archives II, RG 389.

11. William E. Rehnquist, *All the Laws but One: Civil Liberties in Wartime*, pp. 206–207.

12. In addition to Malkin, revisionists include David D. Lowman, author of *Magic: The Untold Story of U.S. Intelligence and the Evacuation of Japanese Residents from the West Coast during WW II*, Athena Press, 2001, and Keith Robar, *Intelligence, Internment & Relocation: Roosevelt's Executive Order 9066: How Top Secret "MAGIC" Intelligence Led to Evacuation*, Seattle: Kikar Publications, 2000. The grandmother of the revisionists was Lillian Baker, author of *American and Japanese Relocation in World War II*; [sic] *Fact, Fiction & Fallacy*, Medford, OR: Webb Research Group Publishers, 1996 ("Lillian Baker Memorial Edition"; the original edition appeared in 1990). Baker wrote several books on the topic, with titles such as *Dishonoring America: The Collective Guilt of Japanese-Americans* (1988) and *The japanning* [sic] *of America: Redress & Reparations Demands by Japanese-Americans* (1991).

13. Malkin, *In Defense of Internment: The Case for "Racial Profiling" in World War II and the War on Terror*, Washington, D.C.: Regnery, 1994, p. 41.

14. Marshall, interview with John P. Sutherland. This interview took place in the 1950s, long before most of the MAGIC material was declassified.

15. According to John J. McCloy. Phone call by McCloy to Lt. Col. Karl Bendetsen, February 11, 1942, Archives II, RG 107.

16. Rehnquist, *All the Laws but One: Civil Liberties in Wartime*, p. 309.

17. Malkin, *In Defense of Internment: The Case for "Racial Profiling" in World War II and the War on Terror*, p. xxx.

18. *Pensées* 223, from *The Essential Pascal*, selected and edited, with introduction and commentary, by Robert W. Gleason, S.J.; translated by G. F. Pullen. New York: New American Library, 1966.

19. Daniels, *Concentration Camps USA: Japanese Americans and World War II*, pp. 128–129. This book was published in 1971, just after the peak of the antiwar and civil rights movements.

20. In "To Resist or to Comply: A Human Dilemma," *Nichi Bei Times*, May 2, 2002.

21. As Peter Novick points out in *The Holocaust in American Life*, p. 32. See also Peter Skerry, *Mexican Americans: The Ambivalent Minority*.

22. Marshall, *Men Against Fire*, pp. 208–09, 211.

INDEX

Page numbers followed by "n" indicate notes.